ARIZONA

GUIDE

BE A TRAVELER - NOT A TOURIST!

OPEN ROAD TRAVEL GUIDES SHOW YOU HOW TO BE A TRAVELER – NOT A TOURIST!

*Whether you're going abroad or planning a trip in the United States, take Open Road along on your journey. Our books have been praised by **Travel & Leisure**, **The Los Angeles Times**, **Newsday**, **Booklist**, **US News & World Report**, **Endless Vacation**, **American Bookseller**, **Coast to Coast**, and many other magazines and newspapers!*

Don't just see the world – experience it with Open Road!

ABOUT THE AUTHOR

Larry H. Ludmer is a professional travel writer whose Open Road travel guides include *Arizona Guide, New Mexico Guide, Colorado Guide,* and *Utah Guide.* He is currently at work on *Washington Guide,* due out in Fall 2000. His other books include *Arizona, Colorado & Utah; The Northern Rockies; The Great American Wilderness: Touring America's National Parks;* and *Cruising Alaska.*

BE A TRAVELER, NOT A TOURIST – WITH OPEN ROAD TRAVEL GUIDES!

Open Road Publishing has guide books to exciting, fun destinations on four continents. As veteran travelers, our goal is to bring you the best travel guides available anywhere!

No small task, but here's what we offer:

•All Open Road travel guides are written by authors with a distinct, opinionated point of view – not some sterile committee or team of writers. Our authors are experts in the areas covered and are polished writers.

•Our guides are geared to people who want to make their own travel choices. We'll show you how to discover the real destination – not just see some place from a tour bus window.

•We're strong on the basics, but we also provide terrific choices for those looking to get off the beaten path and experience the country or city – not just see it or pass through it.

•We give you the best, but we also tell you about the worst and what to avoid. Nobody should waste their time and money on their hard-earned vacation because of bad or inadequate travel advice.

•Our guides assume nothing. We tell you everything you need to know to have the trip of a lifetime – presented in a fun, literate, no-nonsense style.

•And, above all, we welcome your input, ideas, and suggestions to help us put out the best travel guides possible.

ARIZONA GUIDE

BE A TRAVELER - NOT A TOURIST!

Larry Ludmer

OPEN ROAD PUBLISHING

2nd Edition

TABLE OF CONTENTS

1. INTRODUCTION   11

2. OVERVIEW   12

3. SUGGESTED ITINERARIES   19

4. LAND & PEOPLE   34

5. A SHORT HISTORY   39

6. PLANNING YOUR TRIP   43
Before You Go   43
  When to Visit   43
  What to Pack   44
  Arizona Tourism Information   46
  Booking Your Vacation   48
  Do You Need a Travel Agent?   49
  Individual Travel vs. Organized Tours   49
  Tour Operators   50
  Getting the Best Airfare   51
  Flying to Arizona   52
Getting Around Arizona   54
  By Air   54
  By Bus   54
  By Car   54
  By Train   59
Accommodations   61
  Major Hotel Chains   64
  Camping & Recreational Vehicles   65

7. BASIC INFORMATION   67

8. SPORTS & RECREATION   80

9. MAJOR EVENTS   88

10. FOOD & DRINK   91

11. ARIZONA'S BEST PLACES TO STAY   97

12. PHOENIX   110
Arrivals & Departures   112
Orientation   113
Getting Around Phoenix   114
Where To Stay   116
   Camping & RV Sites   140
Where To Eat   141
Seeing the Sights   152
Nightlife & Entertainment   167
Sports & Recreation   170
Shopping   173
Excursions & Day Trips   176
   The Apache Trail   176
   Casa Grande   179
   To the West   180
Practical Information   181

13. TUCSON   182
Arrivals & Departures   183
Orientation   184
Getting Around Tucson   185
Where To Stay   186
   Camping & RV Sites   195
Where To Eat   195
Seeing the Sights   204
Nightlife & Entertainment   214
Sports & Recreation   215
Shopping   217
Excursions & Day Trips   219
   To Nogales & Back   219
   Oracle   221
   Kitt Peak Observatory   222
Practical Information   223

14. FLAGSTAFF & SEDONA   224

Arrivals & Departures   224
Orientation   226
Getting Around Flagstaff & Sedona   227
Where To Stay   227
    Camping & RV Sites   238
Where To Eat   238
Seeing the Sights   244
    Flagstaff   244
    Monument Loop   246
    Sedona & Oak Creek Canyon   248
    Around the Region   252
Nightlife & Entertainment   257
Sports & Recreation   258
Shopping   259
Practical Information   259

15. GRAND CANYON NATIONAL PARK   261

Arrivals & Departures   262
Orientation   264
Where To Stay   265
    Camping & RV Sites   271
Where To Eat   271
Seeing the Sights   273
    The South Rim   273
    The Overland Route to the North Rim   281
    The North Rim   282
    Page & Lake Powell   286
    On the Fringes   288
Nightlife & Entertainment   289
Sports & Recreation   290
Practical Information   291

16. THE NORTHEAST - INDIAN RESERVATIONS & MORE   292

Arrivals & Departures   292
Orientation   293
Where To Stay   293
    Camping & RV Sites   299
Where To Eat   299
Seeing the Sights   302
    The Navajo Reservation & Monument Valley   302

Canyon de Chelly and the Reservation   304
Petrified Forest National Park   308
Arizona's White Mountains   309
The Mogollon Rim to Payson   312
On the Way Back   313
Nightlife & Entertainment   314
Sports & Recreation   315
Practical Information   316

17. THE SOUTHEAST - UNEXPECTED DISCOVERIES   317
Arrivals & Departures   318
Orientation   318
Where To Stay   318
    Camping & RV Sites   322
Where to Eat   323
Seeing the Sights   326
    Sierra Vista & Tombstone   326
    More Mining Towns & The Chiricahua National Monument   332
    Near the I-10 Corridor   336
Nightlife & Entertainment   340
Sports & Recreation   340
Shopping   340
Practical Information   341

18. THE WEST - WATER PLAYGROUND IN THE DESERT   342
Wickenburg   343
Kingman   348
Lake Havasu City   358
Yuma   364
Gila Bend & Ajo   371

19. ARIZONA FOR COWBOYS & COWGIRLS   376
Guest Ranches   378

INDEX   385

MAPS

Arizona 13
Arizona Touring Regions 21
Phoenix & Vicinity 111
Downtown Phoenix 115
Downtown Scottsdale 161
Tucson & Vicinity 183

Downtown Tucson 207
Sedona/Oak Creek Canyon 225
Grand Canyon National Park 263
Grand Canyon Village 277
Grand Canyon North Rim 283

SIDEBARS

Arizona Profile: Facts at a Glance 15
The Best of Arizona 18
Seeing Arizona from a "Home" Base 33
Two Arizona Geography Lessons 36
Indian Reservations in Arizona 37
A Sensitive Issue 38
Arizona During the Mining Era 41
Average Temperature & Precipitation 44
A Few Tips For Foreign Visitors 46
Arizona Tourism on the Net 47
Desert Driving: Dust Storms & Other Matters 55
Arizona's Driving Distances 58
Major Car Rental Phone Numbers 59
Price Range For Each Lodging Category 63
Native Pottery 77
Another Type of Park Passport 83
National Park Service Passports Are Great 85
Arizona State Holidays 93
Restaurant Price Guidelines 95
The Best of Arizona Dining 96
Hotels to Change Your Outlook on Life 109
The Valley of the Sun's Sky-High Hotel Prices 119
Points of Pride 153
"DASH"-ing About Downtown 156
A Night Out in the Old West 169
The Stately Saguaro 213
A Short Stay in Mexico – Visiting Nogales 221
Real City Slickers 228
Ski Arizona! 245

SIDEBARS

Sedona on the Wilder Side   251

The Geology of the Grand Canyon   262

Humans and the Grand Canyon   274

The Grand Canyon By Air   276

The World Famous Mule Train   278

South Rim Changes Are Coming   280

Preservation vs. Utilization: Where Do You Stand?   285

Houseboating on Lake Powell   287

Visiting the Indian Reservations   303

Do You Know What Time It Is?   304

A Visit to the Hopi Reservation   307

The Town Too Tough to Die   329

Legendary Indians: Cochise & Geronimo   334

The Coronado Trail   339

Touring Western Arizona   343

Historic Route 66   350

Games Across the Colorado   356

Arizona's West Coast   357

Cover All of Western Arizona   375

So You Wanna Be A Cowboy...   377

Rodeo Arizona   383

1. INTRODUCTION

The Grand Canyon, Arizona's greatest attraction, makes any visit to this wonderful state a memorable experience. But Arizona is far more diverse than simply being the home of the Grand Canyon. Every part of the state is filled with literally dozens of other amazing natural wonders. From the beautiful Sonoran desert to towering mountain peaks; from the strange and fiery red rocks of Oak Creek Canyon to the vivid array of colors found only in the incomparable Painted Desert; and from the fifty foot high Saguaro cactus to a huge high desert depression created by the impact of a meteorite – Arizona is truly a delightful place for anyone who revels in what nature offers to us.

Big city sophisticates won't be disappointed either. Fast growing Phoenix and Tucson combine all of the cosmopolitan offerings of any major American city with the state's own brand of Southwestern flavor. Throughout the state you'll find an incredible variety of places to stay. Whether it's an inexpensive highway motel, a classic bed and breakfast, a big city high-rise or one of the world's greatest full service luxury resorts, Arizona has it all. The warm winters that prevail through most of Arizona make it one of the nation's most popular destinations for weary Northern snowbirds.

The great outdoors of Arizona feature just about every leisure activity you could dream up. Hiking, mountain or canyon climbing, fishing, boating, swimming and white water rafting (yes, Arizona isn't all desert by any means) are all available. Add to that golf, tennis, and much, much more, and you're in for a great vacation!

This book contains all of the information you'll need to plan a short weekend jaunt or a lengthy trip through the entire state. Hotels, restaurants, recreation, nightlife and entertainment are all covered, as are dozens of practical tips. Extensive sightseeing information will acquaint you with the well known attractions as well as countless lesser known places of interest. With a little planning, you'll be set for exploring Arizona on your own. I'm sure you'll enjoy the ride!

2. OVERVIEW

Even though the number of Arizona residents has grown dramatically during the past several decades it remains, on a population per square mile basis, one of the most sparsely inhabited regions of the United States. I know you'll be cursing me for that statement while trying to negotiate traffic in Phoenix, but it's true. Once you get away from the two major metropolitan areas there are hundreds of square miles of wilderness to explore. Whether you're searching for that great view – and the state has an endless series of them – or looking to participate in outdoor recreation in one of Arizona's many federal or state parks, it's all here.

But the abundance of natural beauty, recreation, historical sites and entertainment venues are only part of the story. Arizona has a unique atmosphere that results from a mosaic of cultural influences. Both the Hispanic (in the form of Spanish and Mexican traditions) and Native American influences are strong. In fact, there are more Native Americans living in Arizona than in any other state except Oklahoma and almost the entire northwestern quarter of the state is occupied by Indian reservations, especially those of the Navajo and Hopi.

The "Old West" influence also still survives in Arizona's populace, despite the influx of people from all over the country that has accompanied the state's growth and attraction as a place to retire. It seems that in many little things, from politics to such mundane issues as Daylight Savings Time, Arizonians seem to march to the tune of a different drummer. All of this combines to make the state a great place to visit.

To make planning your trip a little easier, this book has been divided into seven different touring regions – one each for Phoenix and Tucson, and five geographic regions. Refer to the accompanying regional touring map to get a better picture of how these all fit together. The remainder of this chapter will briefly describe each of the regions.

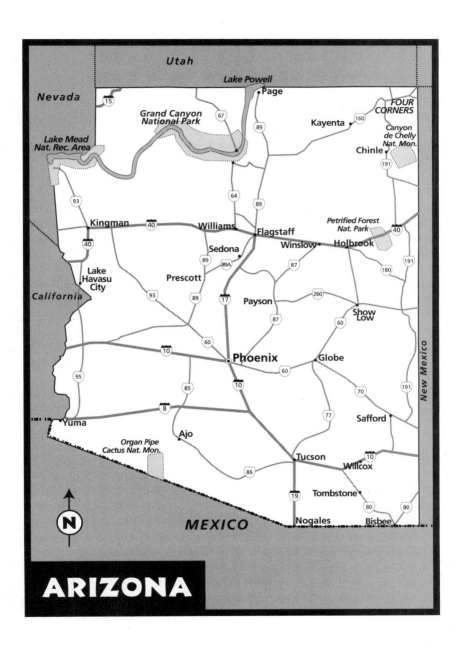

PHOENIX

The state's capital and largest city, **Phoenix** is also Arizona's economic, cultural and recreational heart. Centrally located (just a little south of the middle of the state), it is a good spot for reaching out into almost every other part of the state as well as the logical arrival point for visitors arriving by air. The city and it's sprawling suburbs comprise one of the nation's largest metropolitan areas. More than a dozen world class luxury resorts can be found in neighboring Scottsdale and other communities as well as within Phoenix's city limits.

A modern city with fine museums and numerous cultural attractions, Phoenix also has an interesting historic area although it's nothing like what can be found in Santa Fe and several other communities in New Mexico. Progressive and vibrant, Phoenix has something for everyone and is within easy reach of many nearby scenic attractions such as **The Apache Trail**. Even if you are only planning on using Phoenix as a gateway to the state's many other attractions, I think you'll find enough worthwhile things to see and do to stay around for at least several days.

TUCSON

Smaller than Phoenix but still more than large enough to have all of the things you look for in a major city, **Tucson** retains a greater Hispanic and Native American presence than it's more cosmopolitan bigger sister to the north. That influence, along with many fine museums and the University of Arizona combine to give Tucson a rich cultural life. The Sonoran desert, which reaches the very edge of the city, is also an important factor in any visit – you'll want to be sure to see the outstanding **Arizona-Sonora Desert Museum** as well as the **Saguaro National Park** where towering cacti soar to almost ten times the height of a human being.

As is the case in Phoenix, Tucson also has its share of luxury resorts where you can enjoy yourself while doing absolutely nothing. Guest ranches are also popular. It's also near a lot of fascinating scenery and interesting historic sites. The **Mission of San Xavier del Bac** is one of the most beautiful in the country. Day trips to **Nogales, Mexico** and other nearby sights are a popular diversion for many of Tucson's visitors.

FLAGSTAFF & SEDONA

The city of **Flagstaff** is known primarily as a gateway to the Grand Canyon. It's also located close to several fascinating national monuments. **Wupatki**, **Sunset Crater**, and **Walnut Canyon National Monuments** feature unusual geologic phenomena and remains of ancient civilizations. Flagstaff is also a winter resort destination as the **San Francisco Mountains** to the northwest of town has the best skiing in the state. To the

ARIZONA PROFILE: FACTS AT A GLANCE

You could certainly plan a great vacation in Arizona without knowing what the state's population is or where the highest elevation is. On the other hand, this list of facts gives a quick look at Arizona's remarkable diversity. Another reason for studying this section is that there will be a short quiz at the end of the chapter.

Entered the Union: *February 14, 1912, becoming the 48th state*

Area: *114,006 square miles, ranks 6th*

Number of Counties: *15. The largest county, Coconino, would alone be the nation's 43rd biggest state and three Arizona counties are larger than at least Rhode Island and Delaware.*

Number of State Parks: *28*

Number of areas administered by National Park Service: *21*

Population: *4,668,631 (Official 1998 Census Bureau estimate), ranks 21st*

Population Growth (1990-1998): *27.4%*

Population Density: *41 people per square mile (US average is 73)*

Largest localities: *Phoenix, 2,122,100; Tucson, 804,200; Mesa*, 360,000; Glendale*, 185,000; Scottsdale*, 174,490; Tempe*, 159,000; Chandler*, 137,000; Yuma, 68,160; Flagstaff, 58,145; Peoria*, 53,000. Communities with the asterisk are all part of the greater Phoenix metropolitan area. Figures are approximates for 1998.*

Nickname: *The Grand Canyon State*

Motto: *Ditat Deus (God enriches)*

State Flower: *Blossom of the Saguaro Cactus*

State Bird: *Cactus Wren*

State Tree: *Paloverde*

State Song: *Arizona*

Highest Point: *Humphreys Peak, 12,643 feet*

Lowest Point: *Along the Colorado River, 70 feet*

Tourism Industry: *$12 billion annually*

Major agricultural products: *Cotton, vegetables, citrus fruits, wheat*

Major natural resources: *Copper, molybdenum, silver*

Major manufactured products: *Electronics, printing and publishing, aircraft*

south, toward the picturesque artist's community of **Sedona**, are the famous red rocks of **Oak Creek Canyon**. Made famous in countless western movies, it is one of the most beautiful regions in all of Arizona. Numerous other scenic and historic attractions are within a short radius, including a train ride through an area of rugged mountains that isn't accessible by car.

This region is almost entirely within a series of National Forests, making it one of the best areas in the state for outdoor recreation, including fishing. Accommodations range from the simple to the elegant. Although the population of this region isn't great, Sedona has a sophistication and varied great dining that is usually associated with much larger urban areas.

GRAND CANYON NATIONAL PARK

You could easily take a long vacation and visit only the **Grand Canyon**. There's so much to see and do within the confines of the National Park and the surrounding area. Take the easy way and see the canyon only from the rim; or be more adventurous and hike or take a mule ride down into the canyon. Or maybe you want to see the canyon from the air or from a raft on the **Colorado River**. The possibilities are endless. And the best thing is, no matter how much time you have to devote to the Grand Canyon or in what manner you see it, the experience will be a most rewarding one.

The **South** and **North Rims** are geographically separated by only a few miles but are not directly connected by road. Each is equally fantastic and you should try to see both. For all their similarities, they are distinct – two different worlds. The ride from one rim to another includes its own share of interesting scenery and with a short detour you can reach beautiful **Lake Powell** and its national recreation area. Learn why the scenic area to the north of the Grand Canyon is known as the Arizona Strip. Back on the south side of the Colorado, the western portion of this region contains more remote sections of the Grand Canyon National Park and **Lake Mead National Recreation Area**.

THE NORTHEAST:
INDIAN RESERVATIONS & MORE

The **Navajo Indian Reservation** is the largest in the United States. It completely surrounds the smaller **Hopi Reservation**. Together they take up almost the entire northeastern portion of the state and are larger than some eastern states. Many areas in these reservations are open to the public and you can learn much about the Navajo and Hopi cultures. Scenery and history also abound in this region. The **Painted Desert** and the **Petrified Forest National Park** are certainly two highlights, as is famous **Monument Valley** on the Utah border. The Valley, home to huge monolithic rock formations, is frequently seen in movies and in television commercials.

Canyon de Chelly National Monument combines colorful canyon scenery with the remains of Anasazi Indian communities and, with your Navajo guide, makes for an unusual sight seeing journey.

To the south of the reservations along the edge of this region's "border" is the scenic **Mogollon Rim** and Arizona's beautiful **White Mountains**. Off the beaten track from the route of most visitors to Arizona, this area is well worth a detour.

THE SOUTHEAST: UNEXPECTED DISCOVERIES

Beginning not far from metropolitan Tucson, the Southeast has only a few attractions that rank in the well-known category. But that helps make it even better because the solitude in many parts of this region make it all the more wonderful. Typical of that is the virtually unknown **Chiricahua National Monument**, an area of eerie rock formations and beautiful mountains.

The region is best known for the remains of mining towns that boomed during the latter part of the 19th century. The best is **Tombstone** which today looks much as it did during the days of the gunfight at the **OK Corral**. Living history is the name of the game as you stroll down the dusty streets. The entire town is a National Historic Site! Other mining attractions, both historic and modern, can be found in **Bisbee** and nearby towns not far from the Mexican border.

THE WEST: STILL THE FRONTIER

Geographically, this is the largest of the seven touring regions and, overall, is the least developed both in terms of population and tourist facilities. However, there are exceptions to that, especially on the western border of the state (the Colorado River) where recreation and resorts abound. Among the attractions are the popular **Hoover Dam**, **Bullhead City**, which is located just across the river from the gambling town of Laughlin, Nevada; and **Lake Havasu City**, where the original London Bridge has been rebuilt brick by brick.

Recreational facilities are available not only in major towns, but in several state parks along the river. There are also quite a few national wildlife refuges. **Yuma**, near the extreme southwestern corner of the state, is the largest community in the region and has a number of interesting historic attractions.

Further east are vast stretches of desert and mountains. The **Organ Pipe Cactus National Monument** is a large tract that is not heavily visited, but should be. If you're looking for a wilderness experience, you'll likely find it in this section of Arizona.

THE BEST OF ARIZONA

When I get back from a trip I have a habit of listing all the things I've seen and done and rating them. I've combined all those things for Arizona and come up with this list. And you know what – I'll be the first to admit that it's highly subjective. However, if you asked the majority of visitors to Arizona to list the "must sees" within the state, you would find most of the following included on virtually every list. The real purpose of including the "best" list is to suggest that, given a limited amount of vacation time, you should try and do as many of these as possible. After you've been to Arizona try comparing your list with mine. The list is not in any particular order.

*• **Grand Canyon National Park**: Visiting either rim would be great, doing both is even better. Likewise, looking down into the canyon from the rim is surpassed only by entering it.*

*• **The Sonoran Desert**: other than the Grand Canyon no other geological feature is more representative of the state. At a minimum you should visit the Arizona-Sonora Desert Museum and the Saguaro National Park.*

*• **A boat ride on Lake Powell**: Relaxing and simply beautiful.*

*• **Tombstone**: Even though it's somewhat commercialized, a visit is loads of fun.*

*• **Petrified Forest National Park**: Marvelous scenery.*

*• **Visiting an Indian reservation**: What would a trip to Arizona be without discovering the color and tradition of its native population?*

*• **Monument Valley**: The awesome power of nature at its best.*

*• **Canyon de Chelly National Monument**: Still more scenery, but with the addition of ancient ruins. Eerie and beautiful. At it's best if you enter the canyon with a Navajo guide.*

*• **Oak Creek Canyon**: Inspiring sights. See for yourself why the surrounding area is becoming such a popular place to live.*

*• Basking in the brilliant sunshine of a luxury resort in **Scottsdale**: It speaks for itself!*

3. SUGGESTED ITINERARIES

You could literally spend months traveling through Arizona seeing its countless sights and enjoying its many varied recreational opportunities. Unfortunately, most of us don't have that much time to devote to our vacation or not enough expendable cash to stay away from home for so long. Therefore, the itineraries that follow range from a few days to as long as two weeks. Some should match the planned length of your trip or will do so with just a few minor adjustments one way or the other. The itineraries don't have attraction-by-attraction detail; instead, you'll find a broad outline for each day that allows you flexibility. You can add another museum or two or take some time to relax.

The itineraries are grouped according to the type of trip. The first seven correspond to each of the touring regions that provide the framework for this guide. Three additional trips are highlight tours – they cover the entire state, in varying lengths, and feature the best that Arizona has to offer. The final two tours are longer, allowing for seeing the highlights as well as further exploration. All of these itineraries (except for the Phoenix and Tucson tours) involve overnight stops in more than one place. If you would like to stay put and make a series of day trips, then look at the sidebar later in this chapter. Any of the trips can be extended for a number of days if you want to stay at a resort to hang around the pool, or play golf or tennis. No significant amount of time for that is built into the itineraries as they appear here.

You can manage all or most of the first two itineraries using public transportation. Although there is bus service throughout most parts of Arizona, it's certainly not the ideal way to get around. The state's size requires the flexibility of a car, either your own or a rental. Finally, as a matter of practicality, all of the itineraries are based on the likely assumption that you will be arriving in Phoenix and starting around mid-day. And remember that these are only suggestions. Toy around with them, combine parts of several different trips. Who knows what you might come up with?

ITINERARY 1: GREATER PHOENIX

(*5 days/4 nights*)

If you're primarily interested in Arizona's biggest city, or have a very limited amount of time, this itinerary will suit your needs.

Day 1

There will be time to see the main sights of the city's historic and government areas as well as a couple of its better museums before checking in.

Day 2

More cultural attractions as well as visits to some of Phoenix's several outstanding scenic parks and desert botanical gardens.

Day 3

Take an all day trip through the scenic Superstition Mountains along the famous Apache Trail. Ancient Indian ruins, old ghost towns, deep canyons containing mighty dams with man-made lakes and an outstanding desert botanical garden are all on the route.

Day 4

Today you'll have a chance to explore the sights of some of the many large communities that are adjacent to Phoenix. These include Mesa, Tempe and Scottsdale. The latter is the site of many spectacular resort hotels. They're worth seeing even if you don't stay at one of them. You can also take a short ride to the south to visit the outstanding ruins located at the Casa Grande National Monument.

Day 5

Time to relax or catch a few last sights before heading home.

ITINERARY 2: TUCSON & VICINITY

(*5 days/4 nights*)

Tucson is quite different than Phoenix. Although it's also a modern city, Tucson has more of a historic flavor and still shows a greater Hispanic and Native American influence. If that's your cup of tea, then this itinerary will be just right for you.

Day 1

Take a few hours to hit some of the highlights in Phoenix itself before embarking on the drive south to Tucson on Interstate 10. It's only a two hour trip, all on a fast and easy to drive interstate highway.

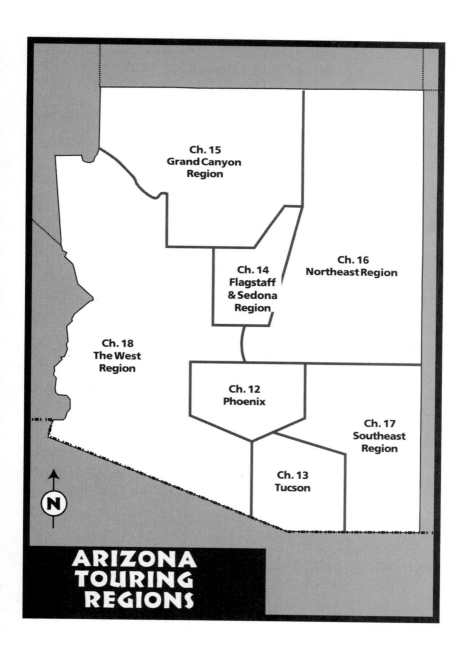

Day 2

A full day can be spent exploring Tucson's historic quarter as well as many fine museums throughout the downtown and on the campus of the University of Arizona. The Arizona State Museum is one of the finest in the nation and could take up several hours all by itself.

Day 3

Explore the ecosystem of the Sonoran desert. Take a drive through the western portion of the Saguaro National Park before visiting the outstanding Arizona-Sonora Desert Museum. The latter is located in a huge municipal park preserve known as Tucson Mountain Park. There's nice scenery and lots of fun for all ages if you stop in at the Old Tucson Studios.

Day 4

Head east from Tucson to see the Rincon Mountain section of Saguaro National Park. The largest specimens of this stately cactus are located here. Then push on to nearby Colossal Cave. Swinging around to the south of Tucson you'll encounter the beautiful San Xavier del Bac Mission. You can also visit the interesting Titan Missile Museum in suburban Green Valley.

Day 5

Your final day in the Tucson area. If you have a late afternoon departure scheduled you can spend the morning visiting Nogales in Mexico or go north to the town of Oracle where you can tour the Biosphere 2 ecosystem test site.

ITINERARY 3: FLAGSTAFF & SEDONA

(*6 days/5 nights*)

Some of Arizona's most beautiful scenery as well as a number of historic sites are all contained within this itinerary. It's a good way to get into the natural beauty of the state without driving too much, a plus for those of you who don't like spending a lot of time behind the wheel.

Day 1

Heading north from Phoenix on Interstate 17, stop at the Montezuma Castle National Monument to see the well preserved cliff dwelling. Then continue on to Flagstaff, your home for the next two nights. Flagstaff has a few interesting museums and you can also see the stars at the Lowell Observatory.

Day 2

A short loop tour today will bring you to three very interesting National Monuments. They are Wupatki, Sunset Crater, and Walnut Canyon. One is the remnant of extensive volcanic action while the other two feature ruins of various ancient Indian tribes. The areas in which the ruins are located also encompass some lovely scenery.

Day 3

It would be a shame to be so close to the Grand Canyon and not see it. So today you'll take a quick run up to the South Rim and have several hours to explore the West Rim Drive. If you don't want to drive the approximately 170-mile round trip, then consider taking a half hour ride to the town of Williams. From there you can travel to and from the canyon by railroad and still have 3-1/2 hours of sight seeing time along the rim.

Day 4

Today you'll travel south from Flagstaff through magnificent Oak Creek Canyon. Take your time exploring the brilliant red rock country. In Sedona itself, you'll find an attractive resort and artist community as well as the Chapel of the Holy Cross, a modern structure set amidst the glory of nature. Close by is the historic Tuzigoot National Monument. If you don't mind driving a bit further you can take the scenic route all the way to Prescott and back. Spend tonight and tomorrow either in Sedona or nearby Cottonwood.

Day 5

From the tiny town of Clarkdale take a four-hour train excursion through the Verde River Canyon. The scenery is fantastic and this is the only way to get to see it – there aren't any roads through the canyon. In Camp Verde the state's frontier days come alive at the Fort Verde State Historic Park. Or you might want to just relax, fish or swim in the many recreational facilities of Sedona and the Oak Creek Canyon area.

Day 6

An early morning return to Phoenix. On the way back you can stop at the futuristic city under construction at Arcosanti, or head directly to Phoenix to allow more time to catch some additional sights.

ITINERARY 4: THE GRAND CANYON
(6 days/5 nights)

Who could blame you if you come to Arizona just to see the Grand Canyon? Well, I'll throw in a few other worthwhile attractions that are located along or near the route.

Day 1

It's a 4-1/2 hour drive from Phoenix to the South Rim of the Grand Canyon National Park. So, unless you head out from Phoenix quite early there won't be much time to see anything beforehand. However, your first glimpse of the canyon will be something you never forget and there's almost always a brilliant canyon sunset to top off the day. You'll spend two nights on the South Rim.

Day 2

Today will be devoted to exploring West Rim Drive of the South Rim, the most famous and heavily visited portion of the park. It's also the area where you'll find the most visitor activities. These include museums and films about the canyon. With plenty of time available you should consider descending into the canyon itself, even if you only go a short way. Or use the entire day to go on the famous mule train trip.

Day 3

This morning you'll travel along East Rim Drive, stopping at many overlooks that have the most outstanding canyon views anywhere on the South Rim. Leaving the park at Painted Desert View you'll ride alongside the gorge of the Little Colorado River and then head north towards the North Rim. Stop at Marble Canyon and walk across the bridge that spans the Colorado River. The scenery is wonderful. Then traverse more desert and then forests before reaching the North Rim late in the day.

Day 4

The North Rim provides vistas that are as dramatic (or maybe more so) as the South Rim. What's really different here is the atmosphere. There are far less people and fewer activities. While many more people now visit than in years past, it still will provide more of a wilderness experience. Then head toward Page, where you'll spend the night.

Day 5

Page is situated on beautiful Lake Powell at the Glen Canyon National Recreation Area. The setting is magnificent but to truly appreciate it all take a half day boat ride on Lake Powell. There will be a stop at Rainbow Bridge National Monument (which is actually in Utah) before returning to the Wahweap Marina. From there it's on to Flagstaff for the night.

Day 6

Return to Phoenix this morning. You can use any available time you might have to stop at Montezuma Castle National Monument or do some exploring within Phoenix.

ITINERARY 5: THE NORTHEAST
(6 days/5 nights)

This itinerary covers an extensive portion of the state that is the tribal land of both the Navajo and Hopi Indians. It also will bring you face to face with some of the most dramatic scenery in the nation.

Day 1

From Phoenix you'll head into the mountains to the east, traveling along the scenic Mogollon Rim and then toward Holbrook, your first overnight stay of the trip.

Day 2

Drive east to Benson and then a little south to the fascinating underground world of Kartchner Caverns State Park, just opened to the public in November 1999. After this, you can explore some of the historic sites around Sierra Vista before visiting Tombstone, an entire town that's a National Historic Site. The day ends at Bisbee where some of the major mining operations are open to the public.

Day 3

The historic ruins and scenery of the Canyon de Chelly National Monument are the day's main event. Take a Navajo guided tour into the bottom of the canyon for a close up look at the cliff dwellings. In the afternoon continue your journey through the Navajo Reservation to the next overnight stopping place – Kayenta.

Day 4

Monument Valley's impressive rock spires and other strange formations can be seen via a loop road either in your own vehicle or by guided tour. Either way the sights are stunning. Minor attractions for the day are several widely dispersed units of the Navajo National Monument. You'll reach Flagstaff in late afternoon and check in for the next two nights.

Day 5

A loop tour covering Wupatki, Sunset Crater and Walnut Canyon National Monuments will take up the better part of the day. You can also make a short side trip to the Meteor Crater and see the huge depression made there millions of years ago.

Day 6

This morning you head back to Phoenix. Depending upon your scheduled departure for home you may have some time to take in a few of the city's sights.

ITINERARY 6: THE SOUTHEAST

(5 days/4 nights)

This trip covers a relatively small area but includes some very interesting sights, both man-made and natural. It can also be easily combined with the Tucson itinerary (# 2) if you have at least seven days and want to concentrate on this portion of the state.

Day 1

After driving from Phoenix to Tucson, you should have a couple of hours to take in some of the downtown sights before checking in.

Day 2

Travel through the historic area around Sierra Vista before reaching Tombstone. The entire town is a National Historic Site and is sure to be a highlight of your southeast Arizona trip. Then it's on to Bisbee, where a couple of major mining operations are open to the public.

Day 3

From Bisbee you'll drive to the fascinating and beautiful Chiricahua National Monument, located almost in the extreme southeastern corner of the state. Then head back to Tucson for the final two nights of your trip.

Day 4

Today you have a choice of seeing the man-made sights of Tucson or exploring the Sonoran Desert in the Saguaro National Park and Tucson Mountain Park. Or, take in a little of each.

Day 5

Stop at Casa Grande National Monument to see the excellent ruins before arriving back in Phoenix at the end of your trip.

ITINERARY 7: THE WEST

(6 days/5 nights)

If vast expanses of very sparsely inhabited desert are your thing, then Arizona's western frontier is the place to go. Despite the general barren nature of the region, the waters of the Colorado River also provide abundant opportunity for recreation as well as serving as a haven for wildlife.

Day 1

It's a long ride from Phoenix to Lake Havasu City so you won't have much time for sight seeing today. However, you'll probably be able to take a dip in the pool after checking in.

Day 2

Take a ride north along the river to Bullhead City. From there you can either drive across the river or take a water taxi to the many casinos of Laughlin, Nevada. Although not as flamboyant as their counterparts to the north in Las Vegas, you can lose your money just as easily. Then return to Lake Havasu City for another night. See the original London Bridge and browse the shops in the attractive community that has been developed around the bridge.

Day 3

Today will once again bring you alongside the Colorado River, but this time heading in a southerly direction. Several wildlife refuges are along the route and welcome visitors. Tonight will be spent in Yuma, which has a number of interesting historical attractions.

Day 4

Some more time in the Yuma area to either relax or take in some more sights before venturing back through the real Sonoran desert to the east and the small town of Ajo where you'll spend the night. It's the only town of any significance for miles around.

Day 5

Not too far from Ajo is the Organ Pipe Cactus National Monument, one of the most remotely located units of the National Park System. After exploring that area head for Tucson, stopping along the way at the Kitt Peak Observatory. A fascinating tour will acquaint you with the work of this renowned facility.

Day 6

The morning is free to hit a few of Tucson's highlights before returning to Phoenix for the return trip home.

ITINERARY 8: THE SHORT HIGHLIGHT TOUR

(*5 days/4 nights*)

It really takes at least a week to do any justice to the many great attractions of Arizona. But, alas, many people simply don't have the time. So, this short highlight tour makes the best use of the time available and allows you to return home with memories that won't soon be forgotten.

Day 1

From Phoenix you'll travel to the South Rim of Grand Canyon National Park. Depending upon your arrival time you may be able to take in some of the views and activities around the Village area.

Day 2

Use the morning and part of the early afternoon to take in as much of the South Rim as possible. Your overnight accommodations will be in Holbrook.

Day 3

The first stop today is Petrified Forest National Park, which certainly will rank close to the Grand Canyon on your list of favorites even though it's completely different. Then it's back on the fast Interstate to Flagstaff where you'll head through gorgeous Oak Creek Canyon and arrive at Sedona for the evening.

Day 4

Except for rest stops and a bite to eat it's non-stop highway today until you reach Tucson in the early afternoon. Tucson has so many sights that you can't possibly hope to do them in a half day so I suggest concentrating on those attractions relating to the Sonoran Desert.

Day 5

Back to Phoenix. Take in a couple of sights before completing your journey.

ITINERARY 9: ARIZONA SAMPLER

(7 days/6 nights)

A slightly extended version of Trip 8, this allows you to add on a couple of very worthwhile attractions that there wasn't time for in the shorter highlight trip.

Days 1 through 3

The itinerary follows the same route as in Itinerary #8.

Day 4

Travel from Sedona to Phoenix, but don't plan on any activities in the capital city for now. Instead, head east through the Superstition Mountains along the beautiful Apache Trail. Globe is the ending point of the Trail and your overnight stopping place.

Day 5

Heading south from Globe you'll be reaching Tucson by no later than the early afternoon. This will allow time to see the Arizona-Sonora Desert Museum and at least a portion of the Saguaro National Park. Tonight and tomorrow night will both be spent in Tucson.

Day 6

From Tucson you'll travel to Tombstone to visit the many attractions of that historic town. Then head back to Tucson. You should have time to stop at the beautiful San Xavier del Bac Mission south of Tucson.

Day 7

An early start from Tucson will get you back to Phoenix in time to at least take in a few sights before the end of your trip. Perhaps the State Capitol and Museum, or the Desert Botanical Garden.

ITINERARY 10: ARIZONA HIGHLIGHTS

(*9 days/8 nights*)

The final "highlight" trio covers what most people would consider to be all of the major attractions in Arizona. Just about the only area not visited (other than the North Rim of the Grand Canyon) is the western edge of the state, but most experts would agree that there's less of great significance there than in the other regions.

Day 1

Depart from Phoenix and arrive by late afternoon at the South Rim of Grand Canyon National Park. You should have enough time to acquaint yourself with the park at the Visitor Center and some of the other points of interest in the Village area.

Day 2

Almost the entire day can be devoted to touring the South Rim. Later in the afternoon you'll depart the park's east entrance gate and travel through the Little Colorado River Gorge before heading north to the town of Page, located on the edge of Lake Powell. Time permitting you can tour the Glen Canyon Dam.

Day 3

The beauty of Lake Powell and the Glen Canyon National Recreation Area is best seen by boat. Half day tours are appropriate for the time you have available on this trip. Then, in the afternoon travel to Monument Valley before continuing through the Navajo Indian Reservation to Chinle.

Day 4

Two wonderfully scenic attractions are on tap today. First you'll make a brief visit to Canyon de Chelly National Monument this morning (touring the rims only) before heading south to the Petrified Forest National Monument. Overnight is in Holbrook.

Day 5

Your route will take you eastbound this morning, stopping at Meteor Crater en route to Sedona and the fantastic Oak Creek Canyon area. Later in the day you'll head for Phoenix for the first of two nights in Arizona's capital city.

Day 6

Today you won't be seeing Phoenix for long. Heading east through the Superstition Mountains, the adventures of the beautiful Apache Trail await you. The loop returns to Phoenix by late in the afternoon, allowing some time to relax before dinner.

Day 7

Several hours can be devoted to seeing some of the attractions in Phoenix before you journey south, past Tucson to Tombstone. After you finish with the town's historic attractions double back to Tucson for the first of two nights here.

Day 8

The entire day will be devoted to seeing the Tucson area. I strongly suggest that you allow at least half of the day to learn about the Sonoran Desert at the Arizona-Sonora Desert Museum, Saguaro National Park and Tucson Mountain Park. Any other time available can be spent on "city" type attractions.

Day 9

The final day can begin with some more sight seeing in Tucson depending upon what time you have to be back in Phoenix for your departure.

ITINERARY 11: ARIZONA ADVENTURE

(11 days/10 nights)

This is the first of two more extended trips for those of you who have a bit more time to spend on your vacation. The extra days are useful for adding some of the lesser known attractions that can be so rewarding.

Day 1

From Phoenix you'll head north towards the historic town of Prescott, which also has some unusual geologic formations known as the Granite Dells. A scenic mountain road then takes you into the Sedona area, your home for the night. However, stop at the interesting ruins of the Tuzigoot National Monument before reaching Sedona.

Day 2

This morning will be devoted to the red rocks and other attractions of the Oak Creek Canyon area. In the afternoon visit another ancient Indian ruin amid pretty scenery at the Walnut Canyon National Monument. Nearby are the remains of volcanic activity at Sunset Crater National Monument. You'll arrive at the South Rim of Grand Canyon National Park in the late afternoon.

Day 3

You can spend about five or six hours exploring the South Rim before taking the scenic drive through the Little Colorado River Gorge, the Navajo Reservation, and Marble Canyon before arriving at the Grand Canyon's North Rim.

Day 4

We'll follow the same procedure as on the South Rim, spending the better part of the day touring before heading on to tonight's overnight stopping place – Page, on Lake Powell.

Day 5

Take the half-day boat ride through the colorful mountains and deep blue waters of Glen Canyon National Recreation Area's Lake Powell. Be sure to allow some time on your return to take the interesting tour of Glen Canyon Dam. Then it's on to Monument Valley for some more outstanding scenery. You'll spend the night nearby on the Navajo Reservation in the town of Kayenta.

Day 6

Travel to Chinle and see Canyon de Chelly National Monument. This longer tour allows sufficient time to visit both rims of the canyon as well as take a Navajo guided tour into the canyon for a close up look at the ancient ruins. Overnight is in Chinle.

Day 7

The major items on the agenda today are the unusually colored petrified rocks and visually stunning Painted Desert, both of which are found at the Petrified Forest National Park. Then, heading south through the Apache-Sitgreaves National Forest, you'll come to Show Low and a portion of the Mogollon Rim. Continuing on through the Fort Apache and San Carlos Indian Reservations you'll come to Globe, stopping place for tonight. Time permitting, take a short detour to the west on Scenic US 60 through Queen Creek Tunnel to Superior and the Boyce Thompson Southwest Arboretum.

Day 8
A two hour drive this morning will bring you into the Tucson area. The remainder of the day can be used to see the Arizona-Sonora Desert Museum, a portion of the Saguaro National Park and Tucson Mountain Park, including fun-filled Old Tucson.

Day 9
After the Tombstone National Historic Site, head for your overnight stop at Willcox – but on your way, south of Benson, be sure to visit the Kartchner Caverns State Park.

Day 10
This morning is devoted to visiting the wonderful scenery at the Chiricahua National Monument. Then it's back to Phoenix. You'll return to Globe via US 70 and then proceed on to Phoenix once again, this time via the fascinating Apache Trail, arriving very late in the day.

Day 11
Some time to spend sight seeing in Phoenix should be available to most visitors before you have to head home.

ITINERARY 12: ARIZONA IN DEPTH
(*14 days/13 nights*)
On this most ambitious itinerary you'll really have enough time to give Arizona its proper due. Much of it is similar to the previous itinerary but this one adds on quite a few other sights.

Day 1
Heading northwest from Phoenix through a portion of the Mojave Desert, your destination for the evening is Kingman.

Day 2
A little over an hour's drive north from Kingman on the border with Nevada is Hoover Dam, one of the great engineering marvels of the world and beautifully situated in narrow Boulder Canyon. Then backtrack to Kingman and head east on the old Route 66, stopping at cool Grand Canyon Caverns (not part of the National Park.) Overnight is in Prescott.

Day 3
A four hour train ride through the rugged scenery of the largely inaccessible Verde Valley is on tap today. In the afternoon visit Montezuma Castle National Monument before arriving in Sedona for the evening.

Days 4 through 12

These days correspond to days two through ten of Itinerary 11.

Day 13

This trip allows a full day to explore the Phoenix metropolitan area. You should have enough time to see the major cultural attractions in Phoenix as well as sights in Scottsdale, Tempe and Mesa.

Day 14

Alas, all good things must come to an end. Before departing Phoenix you may have time to take in a few more sights or maybe you would prefer relaxing at the pool after all that travel!

SEEING ARIZONA FROM A "HOME" BASE

Some travelers don't mind living out of a suitcase, spending a night or two in one place and then moving on to the next destination. Certainly this allows you to see the most. But, for those of you who feel more comfortable being settled into a nice hotel and staying there, Arizona offers a number of possibilities for seeing a great deal through a series of day trips. The regional tour concept is especially well suited to this approach. The following chart should help you plan a trip using this concept.

You can also combine the home base method with the more traditional point to point method. After several days at one base, go on to another and perhaps more, depending upon the total length of your trip.

TOURING AREA BASE(S)

Phoenix: *Phoenix (or any number of suburban locations)*
Tucson: *Tucson*
Flagstaff and Sedona: *Flagstaff or Sedona. You can also do it from Phoenix but the daily mileage will be quite high.*
Grand Canyon: *Grand Canyon (South Rim or North Rim). You can't get to and from one rim to another in a single day. If you're only seeing the South Rim you can also make Flagstaff or Williams your base but the mileage will be much more.*
Northeast: *Holbrook or Chinle*
Southeast: *Benson, Willcox or Tucson*
West: *The west regional touring chapter is divided into a home base approach.*

4. LAND & PEOPLE

LAND

While many of us probably picture all of Arizona as an arid wasteland, in reality, nothing could be further from the truth. One of the most remarkable features of the state's landscape is its great diversity. And diversity should be expected from such a large place. Covering a little more than 114,000 square miles, Arizona is almost shaped like a square with the maximum north-south distance being 395 miles and 345 miles from east to west. It is bordered on the north by Utah, on the east by New Mexico, by California and Nevada to the west and Mexico to the south.

The western border is quite irregular and is formed mostly by the **Colorado River**. The **Mexican border** is straight but the major portion of it heads northwest at an angle from around Nogales to where it reaches the Colorado River. The extreme northeastern corner of Arizona is part of the famous **Four Corners**, the only place in the United States where the borders of four different states meet. At that point Colorado joins with Arizona, New Mexico and Utah. The altitude ranges from a low of 70 feet along portions of the lower Colorado River to well over 12,000 feet. The mean elevation is a high 4,100 feet.

Geologically speaking, Arizona can be divided into three principal sections. These are, running from north to south, the Colorado Plateau, the central or Mexican Highlands, and the Sonoran Desert.

The greatest concentration of natural wonders is located in the **Colorado Plateau** region. It covers all of northeastern and most of the north-central portions of the state, running into the Highlands at the Mogollon Rim, a narrow rock escarpment that extends for many miles. At the rim the elevations are mostly in the 6,000-foot range with the terrain becoming slowly higher as you head further north. The Plateau's dramatic scenery consists of a half dozen major mountains and several large and mostly level plateaus that are characterized by deep gorges and canyons of which the **Grand Canyon** is the largest and most famous. Many of the flat plateaus and smaller mesas feature buttes and other geological formations that rise suddenly from the surface, often in unusual or even grotesque shapes and beautiful colors. The especially colorful **Painted Desert** is also an important feature of the Arizona portion of the Colorado Plateau, which extends into and covers large portions of neighboring Utah and New Mexico.

The **Mexican Highlands** is even a larger area than the Colorado Plateau. Cutting a broad swath across the state from the southeast corner all the way to the northwest, this region consists of a series of major mountain ranges interrupted by valleys both large and small. The **Valley of the Sun** (in which Phoenix is located) extends from the lower portions of the Highlands into the Sonoran Desert. The Highlands contain some of the most extensively forested areas in Arizona although many significant forests are also found in the higher elevations of the Colorado Plateau, especially in the areas around Flagstaff and the Grand Canyon.

The greatest portion of the **Sonoran Desert** is located in northern Mexico but a huge chunk extends into Arizona and covers the southwestern portion of the state. It is a rocky rather than a sandy terrain and contains broad valleys that with irrigation have become very productive agricultural areas. This is because the desert soil is blessed with an abundance of minerals. When arid it appears to be lifeless save for cactus plants and rolling sagebrush. Properly watered it can supply a large population with food. Isolated mountains and narrow chains at the edges of the valleys are also a feature of the Sonoran Desert.

Speaking of water, rivers are not a major part of the Arizonan geography with one notable exception. The **Colorado River** enters northern Arizona from Utah and runs in a mostly westerly direction until the Lake Mead Recreation area where it turns almost due south. It continues into Mexico and empties into the Gulf of California. The manmade lakes that form part of the course of the Colorado River are an important feature of the state's recreational system. Most other rivers in Arizona are tributaries of the Colorado River. Many of them are dry except after periods of heavy rain when they can quickly become turbulent and flood surrounding areas because the water cannot be absorbed in the hard, dry ground.

There are few large natural lakes but dam impoundments have created Lakes Powell, Mead, Mohave and Havasu. These are the four largest in the state and all are located along National Park Service lands adjoining the Colorado River. All are shared with neighboring states.

TWO ARIZONA GEOGRAPHY LESSONS

The Hispanic heritage of Arizona is nowhere in greater evidence than in the large number of places with Spanish names. The list runs into the dozens but here a few of them with their English translation: Agua Caliente (warm water), Ajo (garlic), Casa Grande (big house), Dos Cabezas (two heads), Mesa (table or tabletop), Palo Verde (green tree), and Rio Rico (rich river).

The unique quality of Arizonians is just as clearly evident in the number of towns with unusual if not crazy names. Just see what I mean with this ridiculous little story –

*It was **Christmas** eve when **Happy Jack** set out from **Bedrock City** holding **Two Guns** at his side. He soon came upon a **Rough Rock** where a **Cyclopic**-looking **Bumble Bee** and a **Grasshopper** sat chatting. Amazingly, they were **Blue!** "Why, what have we here?," he asked. "**Nothing**," replied the bee. "Move on." So he did, stopping at a **Hermits Rest** before reaching his destination in **Chloride**.*

If you haven't guessed it by now, the bold words are all names of Arizona towns.

PEOPLE

The Census Bureau estimated that Arizona had more than 4-1/2 million people in 1998. This figure has been growing rapidly for some time and the state is expected to continue to be among the fastest growing for some time to come. Much of the population is urban. In fact, almost three-fourths of the state's people live either in the Phoenix or Tucson metropolitan areas. The former had more than 2-1/4 million residents (about 55% of the state total) while the latter numbered somewhat under three-quarters of a million (or 17%). Arizona is unusual for a western mountain state in that it has two large metropolitan areas.

The population displays a diversity that is on a par with its geographical variety. The Phoenix area especially has the racial and ethnic diversity of any major American city, perhaps even more so because of the larger number of Native Americans. People of Hispanic origin represent 19% of the total population, mostly Mexican and concentrated in the southern half of the state. Their influence is considerably greater than would be expected from their numbers, perhaps because of the important role played by Spaniards and Mexicans in the state's past. Visitors are perhaps most interested in the Native American population, which is well over 200,000 people, the overwhelming majority of which choose to live on reservations.

INDIAN RESERVATIONS IN ARIZONA

The first thing you should know about Arizona's Indian reservations is that they are quite different from those often found in neighboring New Mexico. That is, you won't find much in the way of old pueblo style architecture or many groups still adhering to a way of life that shuns modern conveniences. Often you can travel onto a reservation and not know it except for the fact that you passed a sign saying that you are on one. But this doesn't mean that the Native Americans in Arizona have forsaken their customs and traditions. Quite the contrary and the reservations are a major means of preserving those customs. Just about every tribal group is extremely proud of their heritage and there are many attractions throughout the state's reservations that encourage visitors to view and learn about those traditions. That makes them an interesting place to visit even if a lot of Arizona's best scenery wasn't also located on land owned by the Indians. Rules for visiting reservations often aren't as restrictive in Arizona as in some of the pueblos of New Mexico. However, you must always remember to respect private property and not photograph or take videos of people without their permission. Festivals are frequently open to the public but visitors are expected to show respect for Native rituals. Photography may be forbidden in many cases.

Here's a list of most of the major Indian reservations by area: **North:** *Navajo, Hopi, Havasupai, Hulapai, Fort Mohave, Camp Verde, and Yavapai;* **Central:** *Fort Apache, San Carlos, Fort McDowell, Gila Bend, Colorado River, Ak-Chin, and Salt River;* **South:** *Cocopah, San Xavier, and Tohono O'odham.*

Arizona's Native American population is second only to Oklahoma and no state has more tribal land than Arizona. The major Indian tribes are the Navajo and the Hopi. Other significant groups are the Apache, Paiute, Papago, Yavapai and Hualapi. They live on 23 different Indian reservations throughout the state. The sidebar has more information on these reservations.

On a couple of occasions I've hinted at the uniqueness of Arizona's residents. What is it that makes them different? That is hard to answer but the fortitude of the pioneer settlers and the often contrary nature of the rugged prospector all remain at least partially evident in the contemporary Arizonian. The political views of those in state government are often at odds with the federal view of things – that's common out west but even more so in Arizona. Many people just seem to march to the tune of a different drummer. Sadly, to some, with the influx of so many new people from all over the nation that individualism may be slowly changing. But there will always be a group of independent minded folks who shun urban society and contemporary viewpoints. You'll find them scattered about the rural areas of the state.

THE GREAT RETIREMENT COMMUNITY: RETIRING ARIZONA STYLE

One of Arizona's largest population groups isn't based on ethnicity or place of origin at all. The sunny and warm climate has made Arizona one of the nation's most popular places for retirees to settle in. While many easterners retire to Florida, a surprisingly large number come out to Arizona and they are joined by hordes of western retirees. The Phoenix and Tucson areas attract the most but you can find retirement communities throughout the state.

Many of the larger retirement communities, especially those in the Valley of the Sun, pioneered the concept of the so-called "master planned community." MPC's feature housing, shopping, recreational, and cultural facilities, all within a relatively small area. The minimum age to reside in a retirement community can vary but is usually a young 50 years. One of the most famous is Sun City built by the Del Webb organization. Covering almost 9,000 acres, Sun City was begun in 1960 and was supplemented by the newer Sun City West. Together, they have almost 75,000 happy residents.

A SENSITIVE ISSUE

There has recently been a movement under way by some Native American groups to eliminate the use of the word "squaw" including its banishment from place names. The reason for this is because in Indian languages the word squaw is meant as a demeaning term. What the outcome of this movement will be, or when, is not for me to predict. However, in this book I have used the geographic name that was currently in use at press time. It is conceivable that some of these place names might change by the time you read this book. Regardless of whether they do or don't, the use of squaw in this book is not meant to affront any individual or group.

5. A SHORT HISTORY

ANCIENT ARIZONA

We tend to think of Arizona as being relatively "new" to human history. In fact, however, large areas of what we now call Arizona were inhabited for thousands of years by a series of rather advanced civilizations. The name "Arizona" is believed to be derived from an Indian word, **arizonac**, which meant "place of the small spring." That's appropriate because it was in places where water was available that the ancient Native American communities first developed. Excavations of ancient ruins indicates that the early inhabitants, the **Hohokam** and then the **Anasazi**, built elaborate cities, irrigation canals and even defense works in many of the valleys and canyons of northern Arizona. These locales provided shelter from the elements, a fairly stable water supply and a natural barrier against intrusion by enemies.

A number of factors are believed to have led to the demise of these civilizations. Extended drought is one of the two most important reasons. The other was a series of incursions by more warlike nomadic tribes from the north, especially the Navajo and Apache beginning around the middle of the 15th century. These incursions were taking place at around the time when Europeans were first arriving in the region. Because of their other problems, the Anasazi were even less prepared to deal with a new threat.

EUROPEAN COLONIZATION

The first European to set foot in what is now Arizona was a Franciscan missionary and explorer by the name of **Marcos de Niza**. His expedition in 1539 traveled all the way from Mexico City and returned with reports of great mineral wealth, especially gold. That led to a much larger expedition two years later by **Francisco Coronado**. He actually crossed the Colorado River and "discovered" the Grand Canyon. Coronado apparently wasn't impressed by its beauty – he saw it only as a barrier preventing further exploration.

But more exploration did take place. Settlement, however, was to remain slow because of intense Indian resistance. Despite these setbacks the area was made a part of New Spain in 1598. The next century saw the widespread establishment of Jesuit missions throughout the territory. Continued fear of Apache and Navajo raids was responsible for keeping the number of settlers at a low level. The Jesuits showed less fear and pressed forward with attempts to convert the natives to Christianity.

Development really began to take hold with the establishment of a **presidio** in Tucson in the year 1776. However, a major Indian revolt beginning in 1802 coupled with widespread rebellion in Mexico was too much for the Spaniards and even the Jesuits. Most of the missions were abandoned during the next 25 years.

HERE COME THE AMERICANS

Over a period of time the number of settlers gradually increased despite all of the hardships. Included in this sturdy group of pioneers were large numbers of Americans. During the Mexican War of 1846 through 1848, American troops seized the area. The **Treaty of Guadalupe Hidalgo** ceded all of current Arizona to the United States except for a small area south of the Gila River. This was added on in 1853 as a result of the **Gadsden Purchase**. At the time of the cession Arizona was part of the vast New Mexico Territory.

Arizona was officially separated from New Mexico in 1863. During the Civil War a number of Indian uprisings began (some with Confederate support and assistance). They didn't end with the cessation of hostilities between North and South but actually intensified into the Indian Wars that would not come to a close until nearly the end of the 19th century. It was during this period that such legendary Indian leaders as **Cochise** and **Geronimo** were active. They made their home bases in the many canyons of Arizona.

STATEHOOD

Arizona made its first application for statehood in 1891 but it was rejected by the United States Congress. During the period from 1904 through 1906 the sentiment in Congress was to admit both Arizona and New Mexico into the union, but as a single entity. This wasn't popular with the people of Arizona who flatly rejected admittance on such terms.

It was after Arizona finally adopted a state constitution in February of 1911 that Congress decided to confer statehood. However, their admittance as the **48th state** would be deferred for an entire year because President Howard Taft objected to a provision in the state constitution that allowed for judicial recall. In order to gain admission the provision

ARIZONA DURING THE MINING ERA

The days of the silver and gold mines during the second half of the nineteenth century and the boomtowns that developed around them is probably the most colorful era in the history of Arizona in the minds of most Americans. It was certainly among the most dangerous times. Americans' fascination with that era has long been evident in motion pictures, television and even in the popularity among today's tourists of such places as Tombstone. So it seems worth taking a closer look at.

Unlike many other areas of the west, Arizona's mining boom was not the result of an accidental discovery of ore. The competition for overworked resources resulting from California's gold rush led some prospectors to deliberately move to other areas in search of wealth. Gold was first discovered in Arizona in 1857 although the true glory years for Arizona mining were from around 1890 to 1917. It is interesting that the value of copper ore mined would eventually bypass both gold and silver. In all, over 400,000 mining claims were filed and about 4,000 companies existed at one time or another. Only a handful produced ore in excess of a million dollars, however, the Rich Hill mine in Wickenburg is reputed to have produced a half million dollars in gold from a single acre.

Many mining communities went from tent cities to boom towns of 10,000 people in a matter of months. Today many of them are ghost towns or small artist communities. Some, like Tombstone (1877), have been turned into historic sights while others still continue to have some mining activity. Colorful names and places like Goldfield (1898), Silver King (1875), Total Wreck (1879), King of Arizona (1896), Crown King (1890), and Vulture (1863), are now part of Arizona's legacy. So, too, are the "lost" mines like the Dutchman, Six Shooter, Frenchman's Gold, and Treasure of Del Bac. Historians continue to argue whether some or all of these actually existed or are just products of the vivid imaginations of some interesting frontier folks.

was dropped. Statehood was achieved and the people of Arizona had the last laugh on Taft – they restored the recall provision before the year was out! It was one of the first examples of Arizona's independent political streaks – something that continues in the present era.

MODERN ARIZONA

It was the extensive mineral finds of the second half of the 19th century that spurred the development of Arizona and led to statehood. Despite the rise and fall of mining boom towns, it wasn't until the major irrigation projects of the 20th century that real growth could take off.

Irrigation made the desert soil productive. Construction of dams insured adequate water for a growing population. All of this resulted in rapid growth in the early years of statehood. But that growth wasn't anything compared to what would take place after the Second World War. The importance of air conditioning can't be ignored in helping to explain Arizona's explosive growth.

The past several decades have seen Arizona at or near the top of population growth with the trend expected to continue with the new millennium. Diversification of the economy has occurred at the same time, putting Arizona among the most prosperous of states. Tourism continues to play a major role in that prosperity.

6. PLANNING YOUR TRIP

BEFORE YOU GO

WHEN TO VISIT

I know that many people have the impression that Arizona is hot and dry all the time from one corner of the state to another. But, like everything else you'll encounter with Arizona, variation is the name of the game. Yes, many parts of the state have blistering arid summers and mild dry winters. However, winter is a very literal term for northern Arizona where heavy snow provides great skiing near Flagstaff and closes roads to the North Rim of the Grand Canyon for several months of the year. Therefore, the best time to visit Arizona depends upon what areas of the state you're going to be concentrating on and what outdoor activities you're planning. So let's take a closer look region by region.

The northern portion of the state, roughly corresponding to the Colorado Plateau region has mild to warm summers and cold winters. Precipitation comes mostly in the form of summertime thundershowers and some significant winter snowstorms. If you plan to spend all or most of your Arizona vacation in the north, the months from May through September are best. Even the middle of summer isn't very hot as you can see from some of the readings in the weather chart below. The South Rim of the Grand Canyon is open all year round. An exception to the summer recommendation is in order if you're only heading to the north to ski. Then you can combine the milder winters of the south with a ski sojourn to the north.

The remainder of the state is mostly dry and hot. Temperatures in the summer sizzle during the day, especially in the Phoenix area and along the western edge of the state around Yuma. Tucson is a few degrees cooler and even that small difference can make quite a difference in comfort levels. In all cases the high temperatures are made a great deal more tolerable by the low humidity and the fact that the evenings are generally quite comfortable. The southern part of the state is even drier than the north. Again, a majority of the rainfall comes during late afternoon thunderstorms. For a sight seeing oriented vacation the fall through winter is a better time to visit than the middle of summer is. However, if you're coming to Arizona mainly to stay at a resort and sit by the pool, keep in mind that desert winters aren't like those in Florida – the heart of winter is often a little too cool to fully enjoy those types of activities – early spring or fall would be more appropriate.

A vacation that cuts across all parts of the state is also well suited to the less extreme weather conditions present in the fall or spring. However, it's probably much wiser to contend with the summer heat than risk not being able to get somewhere in the winter because of a heavy snow. I'll have some more to say about traveling in Arizona at different times of the year later on when we get to the matter of hotel costs. If you are going to be vacationing during the summer and it will include a lot of outdoor activity in the hotter parts of Arizona be sure to thoroughly read and understand the precautions which are described in the Health section of Chapter 7, *Basic Information*.

AVERAGE TEMPERATURE & PRECIPITATION
Highs/Lows, & Precipitation

	January	April	July	October	Annual Precip.
Flagstaff	41/14	57/27	81/50	63/31	19.8"
Grand Canyon	41/17	59/30	83/52	64/34	13.1"
Kingman	57/31	75/42	97/67	79/47	10.7"
Page	45/23	67/38	94/63	71/42	10.2"
Phoenix	65/38	84/52	105/77	88/57	7.0"
Prescott	51/23	69/38	91/61	74/42	15.4"
Tucson	63/38	81/50	98/74	84/56	11.0"
Yuma	68/43	86/57	106/81	90/62	3.2"

Grand Canyon data is for the South Rim. The North Rim is generally a few degrees cooler. Page temperatures include Lake Powell area.

WHAT TO PACK

The key to proper packing on any vacation is to take only what you are going to need and use. Excess baggage only weighs you down and makes packing and unpacking more of a chore. This is even more important if you're moving from one location to another every night or almost every night. An even more important consideration is to pack appropriate to the climate you can expect to encounter and appropriate for the types of activities you're going to be participating in.

The western mountain states are generally very informal and casual clothing is the rule, especially during the hotter months. However, the finer restaurants in larger cities may impose a dress code so if you plan on that type of dining you will want to bring along some fancier dinner attire. Dressing up for dinner or evening events is also normal in the more luxurious resorts in the Phoenix/Scottsdale area but less so in most other parts of the state.

For the hot summer weather you should dress in lightweight clothing that breathes, such as cotton. Lighter colors are best. Although its normal to think that the less you're covered the cooler you're going to be, this isn't necessarily the case. Exposed skin just soaks up the sun. I'm not saying that you shouldn't wear shorts or sleeveless tops for sight seeing activities. However, intensive outdoor activity is better done covered and that definitely includes wearing a hat all the time. The evenings don't generally require any sweater or jacket except in the north. However, it pays to bring one along even in warmer areas because you never know how much the temperature may drop at night.

In the mountains the temperature will be much cooler than in surrounding valley areas. Thus, you can be less than an hour from Phoenix, for example, and find that the temperature is 20 or more degrees lower. The best way to prepare for such changes (as well as winter weather) is to dress in layers. Have a sweater and an outer jacket with you for when it's colder and peel off one layer at a time as it warms up – or vice versa.

For those of you who are going to engage in more strenuous outdoor activity, dressing properly becomes even more important. Heavy boots or at least shoes with excellent traction are essential as is clothing that is sturdy enough to deal with rocks or sharp vegetation that you might unexpectedly encounter. Waterproof outer clothing is a must if you're going rafting or fishing and a light raincoat can come in handy at all times just in case of a sudden shower.

Finally, sunglasses are almost a must at any time of the year in every part of the state. In the summer you should use an effective sunscreen, especially if you're fair skinned. The sun is very relentless and you don't want a nasty burn to spoil your vacation.

It's very important to make sure that you not only bring a sufficient supply of any prescription medication that you're taking, but to have a copy of the prescription as well. An extra pair of glasses (or, again, a copy of your prescription) also makes sense. At the risk of overstating the obvious, make sure you that before you leave that your tickets and any other documents are in your possession and that you have plenty of film and tape for your cameras or video recorders. I have always found that the best way to make sure that you have everything you need is to make a packing list in advance of your trip and check things off as you pack them. Getaway day is always hectic and even confusing so it's easy to forget something if it isn't written down.

A FEW TIPS FOR FOREIGN VISITORS

Arizona is a very popular destination for visitors from all over the world, primarily because of the pulling power of the Grand Canyon.

American customs regulations and formalities are generally quick and easy. The American embassy or consulate in your home country can familiarize you with the exact requirements, which vary from one country of origin to another. Passports are always required except for visitors from Canada or Mexico; visas are only needed in a small number of cases. Also find out what the limitations are on what you can bring in or take out of the United States. If you plan to rent a car be sure to have a valid International Drivers License since the only foreign licenses recognized here are those from Canada or Mexico.

A common annoyance to overseas visitors is the fact that America doesn't use the metric system that almost the entire world has adopted. Formulas for conversions vary so much from one type of measurement to another that you shouldn't count on memory. It's best to have quick reference conversion charts for such things as temperature, distances, weights and clothing sizes if you plan to shop. One important item that you should commit to memory is the relationship of kilometers to miles – that will help you avoid a speeding ticket. One kilometer is equivalent to about 6/10 of a mile. So, those 55 and 65 mile per hour speed limits aren't as slow as you might think. Remember that 100 kilometers per hour is equal to 60 miles per hour.

ARIZONA TOURISM INFORMATION

I'm confident that all of the information you need to plan any trip to Arizona can be found between the covers of this book. However, I've never limited my own trip planning to a single source so I certainly wouldn't find fault if you wanted to look elsewhere too. One good source is to go straight to the source – in this case the Arizona Office of Tourism. They can supply you with a general state visitors' guide as well as numerous other brochures, special publications and maps. You can call their toll-free telephone information line at *Tel. 800/842-8257 or 602/542-8687.* Or you can write to them at *1100 W. Washington Street, Phoenix, AZ*

85007. More specific information on cities and regions is available from local chambers of commerce or visitor bureaus. Information on where to contact these offices is given in the Practical Information section of each regional touring chapter.

ARIZONA TOURISM ON THE NET

There are hundreds of internet sites devoted either exclusively or partially to Arizona and traveling in the state. Some of the more important statewide sites are listed here. Many localities have their own site as well. You can check on their addresses in the Practical Information sections of the destination chapters, or link to them from several of the sites listed here.

As any first-day cyber traveler knows, all of the addresses are preceded by "http://".

www.arizonaguide.com*: Extensive statewide information and many links to other sources.*

www.recreation.gov*: Areas managed by eight federal agencies with links to all of them.*

www.state.az.us*: Official state site has information on all aspects of Arizona, including tourism. Many links. Lodging reservations.*

www.aztourist.com*: More commercial version of arizonaguide.com but still useful.*

Other web sites of use (such as for airlines and hotels) will be shown in the appropriate section of this and other chapters.

If you've surfed the net for anything from almonds to zircons you know that some of the stuff out there is great, but much of it is trash, plain and simple. The same applies to using the internet to garner travel information. Be careful where you get your information. Although official sites of cities, regions, states and so forth are, of course, somewhat prejudiced in their outlook, the information will generally be accurate. Such is not always the case when using other sites.

Good maps are an essential ingredient for any driving trip. While the city maps in this guide are sufficient to get you to the major sights, a statewide road map showing all highways is beyond the scope of what can be included here. Therefore, make sure you procure one before you begin your trip (or at least no later than your arrival in the state). Members of the AAA can get an excellent Arizona map from their local office; other good maps are published by a number of companies and can be found in the travel section of your favorite bookstore. The map put out by the Office of Tourism is also an acceptable source. If you do wait until your arrival in Arizona you can purchase road maps at the Phoenix and Tucson airports. However, if you're driving into the state then you should stop at the first welcome center to get the state-issued map. These offices are located within a few miles of the state border on each of the Interstate highways entering Arizona.

BOOKING YOUR VACATION

There are two basic ways of approaching any trip. Pick a destination, get there and then decide what you want to do and where you should stay. The other is to plan in great detail and know exactly where you'll be each night and have room reservations in hand. Of course, there's a wide range in between if you want to combine methods. While there's definitely something positive to be said for the flexibility and spontaneity of the day-to-day or "ad hoc" approach, there are potential serious pitfalls. You can't always count on rooms being available when you show up. NO VACANCY signs are all too common in Arizona during the peak season at resorts and during the summer months in and near the state's greatest scenic attractions. Not having a place to stay can really be a bummer. So unless you have a great deal of time and are willing to risk the consequences of not having reservations I strongly suggest at least some degree of advance planning for any Arizona trip.

Planning can be a lot of fun and the whole family can get involved. Reading about what you're going to do and see creates a greater sense of anticipation, at least it always does for me. More importantly, for most people it makes it possible to ensure the best use of the time you have available for your vacation. Advance reservations is also often a good way to save money on travel and hotels, although I won't deny that when there is space available at the last minute it, too, can be had at a substantial discount.

In this section I'll offer advice on what to book in advance and how to go about doing it, first in a general sense and then on items specific to Arizona. After you've come up with an itinerary that you like you should be prepared to make advance reservations for (1) air transportation (or other form of common carrier) to and from Arizona, probably Phoenix but maybe Tucson; (2) lodging, and (3) car rental, unless you're driving your own car to Arizona. In that case hotel reservations are the only thing you generally have to worry about.

If your itinerary does include any guided tours or unusual activities such as rafting, historic train trips and so forth, be sure to ascertain whether or not advance reservations are required for these things. I'll mention them in the Seeing the Sights sections where appropriate. If reservations are "suggested" read that as being "required" – you might save yourself some big disappointments.

DO YOU NEED A TRAVEL AGENT?

Once you're ready to book your trip, the first question that you have to address is whether to use a professional travel agent or do it on your own. Securing and reading airline schedules isn't at all difficult nor is getting information about hotels, car rentals and other things. That adds up to my own preference of self-booking. (I can feel the glare from all those irate travel agents right now.) However, many people simply feel very uncomfortable about doing that – they figure why not let a travel agent do the work – they're professionals, know the travel world better and do it for no cost to the consumer. I can't argue with that. It's a matter of your level of confidence.

Don't always assume that your travel agent knows so much more than you do about the places you want to go. When using a travel agent make sure that they're reliable. Go on references from friends and relatives who were happy with the services of a particular agent. A good indication of their reliability is if the travel agency is a member of the American Society of Travel Agents (ASTA). Membership in that group or other industry organizations should be considered as a minimum requirement when selecting a travel agent.

Regardless of which travel agent you choose, their services should be free of any charge to you. They get paid commission by the airlines and hotels. The only time you should have to pay is for special individual planning which is commonly referred to as F.I.T. Although travel agents have on-line access to the best rates I have always found that it's a good idea to check the rates on your own first. You may find that it's better than what the agent tells you. If so, advise him or her of what rate you got and from where. They should easily be able to get the same rate or lower.

It is sometimes difficult if not impossible to, as an individual, book a reservation on organized tours. These are often exclusively handled through travel agents. If this is the type of trip you're planning to take then you are probably best off going immediately to a travel agent. Organized tours usually include discounted air options.

INDIVIDUAL TRAVEL VS. ORGANIZED TOURS

I almost always opt for travel on my own instead of being herded into a group. Many tourists do like the group situation for its "people interaction" and the expertise of the guides. However, there are a lot of shortcomings. The first one is that you are on a schedule that someone else sets. And that schedule has a lot of built in down-time to accommodate what will be the slowest person in the group. Organized tours generally dictate where and when you will eat, which is not always to everyone's liking. Careful reading of an organized tour itinerary will show that you do not always spend a lot of time seeing what you want to see. In fact, finding an itinerary that suits your own interests can be the single biggest problem with an organized tour.

While you may feel uncomfortable about being on your own in some exotic foreign destination where the food is strange and people may not speak English, you won't have any such problem while in Arizona. In short, organized tours in Arizona aren't necessary or even advisable for most people, especially those who take the time to read a book like this and get all the information they need to do things on their own. The primary exceptions are for people who do not drive and individual travelers. Having a group tour is certainly far better than not being able to see anything because you can't drive. It's also better than trying to get around the vast expanse of Arizona with a limited public transportation system. Likewise, while some people don't mind traveling alone I think almost everyone would agree that it's better to share your experiences with someone else, even if that person sitting next to you on the bus was previously a stranger.

Many airlines offer individual travel packages that include, besides airfare, hotel and car rental. Sometimes these plans can save money but often you can do even better still by arranging everything separately. You see, package "deals" are coordinated by a wholesale tour package company and that middleman has to make a profit too. So the savings that are gotten by bulk purchase of airline seats and hotel rooms aren't always passed on to you like they say in the travel brochures. Also, you should be careful about how restrictive "fly-drive" type packages are. Some are quite flexible but others have a lot of rules regarding which cities you can stay in or minimum number of nights required. If they fit into your plans, fine; if not, simply build the pieces of your trip block by block.

TOUR OPERATORS

Having said all of that I will give those readers who are going to opt for organized tours a few suggestions on who to contact. Travel agents, of course, will be able to provide you with brochures on lots of itineraries covering Arizona. The absolute best bus tour operators in North America are Tauck Tours and Maupintours. Tauck's basic Arizona trip is for eight days and seven nights. It departs from Tucson and ends in Phoenix. Among the highlights besides those two metropolitan areas are Sedona and Oak Creek Canyon, Flagstaff, and the Grand Canyon.

Another tour of the same length available from Tauck begins in Phoenix and spends about half of the time in Arizona. It does Sedona and Oak Creek Canyon, the Grand Canyon, Glen Canyon and the Lake Powell area before going onto some of southern Utah's national parks and ending in Las Vegas. Maupintour offers an eight day and a ten day Arizona tour from April through October. Both begin and end in Phoenix and visit the Grand Canyon, Lake Powell, Sedona and Oak Creek Canyon, and Monument Valley. They also both enter Utah to visit Zion and Bryce Canyon National Parks. The eight day trip goes to the Petrified Forest and Canyon de Chelly while the ten day trip covers more of central Arizona including Flagstaff, Montezuma Castle, and Jerome. Maupintour also offers an 11 day Four Corners itinerary that only skirts Arizona, doing Monument Valley and Canyon de Chelly.

If you are seeking a custom designed F.I.T. vacation in Arizona you should consider one of the following reputable organizations:

• **Arizona Western Tours International**, *Tel. 602/837-2630*. Specializing in individual and small group tours from one to 14 days. Customized service available.

• **Design Destinations, Inc.**, *Tel. 602/991-7022*. Statewide customized itineraries featuring both general and special interest tours.

• **JDR Tours**, *Tel. 800/759-8747*. This firm specializes in planning and booking fully individual fly/drive packages including air, hotel, car rental, attractions and recreation. Also handles California should you wish to take in parts of two states during your Arizona trip.

In addition to the above operators, visitors can see many attractions through Gray Line Tours, *Tel. 800/732-0327* or *Tel. 602/495-9100* in Arizona. Gray Line has one and multi-day trips departing from Phoenix, Tucson and other locations. Among the places you can see by this method are the Grand Canyon, Lake Powell, Sedona and Oak Creek Canyon, and Nogales as well as city tours throughout the Phoenix/Valley of the Sun area and Tucson.

GETTING THE BEST AIRFARE

Even travel agents have trouble pinning down what the best airfare is on a given flight on a given day. It's like trying to hit a moving object. If you call one airline ten times and ask what it will cost to fly from New York to Phoenix on the morning of July 10th and return on the afternoon of July 20th you'll probably get several different answers. I wouldn't even rule out the possibility of ten different responses. Unfortunately, such is the state of the airline fare game. There are, however, a couple of things to keep in mind about getting a good rate.

Midweek travel (Tuesday through Thursday for sure, but may include Monday afternoon and Friday morning depending upon the route and airline) is lower priced than weekend travel. Holiday periods are, of course, higher. Fares to places like Phoenix could well be higher during the entire peak travel season of December through March. Night flights are considerably less expensive than daytime travel if you don't mind arriving on the "red-eye" special.

Advance confirmed reservations that are paid for prior to your flight are almost always the cheapest way to go. The restrictions on these low fares vary considerably. In general you must book and pay for your tickets at least seven to 30 days in advance. In most cases they require that you stay over a Saturday night. They usually are non-refundable or require payment of a large penalty to either cancel or even make a change in the flight itinerary. So be sure when and where you want to go before reserving.

You can sometimes find big bargains by doing the opposite strategy – waiting for the last minute. If the airline has empty seats on the flight you select they're often willing to fill it up for a ridiculously low price – after all, they figure that some money in their pocket is better than none at all. The problem with this is that you don't know if there will be an available seat at the time you want to go. If you have definite reservations for everything else during your trip this can be a very dangerous game to play. If you do get a ticket at the last minute it can also wind up being at a very high price.

In this era of deregulation, airfares from one airline to another can sometimes be radically different, although carriers flying the same routes will often adjust their fares to the competition more often than not. Some of the low-cost carriers are as good as the major airlines. Since you're going to Arizona one airline that you should definitely familiarize yourself with is **Southwest Airlines**. They're a low cost operator that has an excellent safety and performance record and has developed a loyal following. I'll tell you more about the various carriers serving Phoenix and Tucson a bit later.

One thing you should always be on the lookout for regardless of who you plan to fly with are promotional fares. Scan the newspapers or just call the airlines. It's always best to phrase your inquiry something like "What's the lowest available fare between x and y on date z?"

Finally, I know that those accustomed to first class air are going to squirm in their seats at this but the cost of first class is simply not worth it – you're only going to be on the plane for a few hours. This isn't a week long cruise where you want to be pampered every minute. Go coach, bring along a good book and enjoy the flight.

FLYING TO ARIZONA

Arizona's busiest airport and the one with the greatest choice of airlines and flights is Phoenix's **Sky Harbor International Airport**. However, if you're going to be concentrating on the southern part of the state the airport in Tucson is a good secondary choice.

Two major airlines have important hubs in Phoenix. These are **America West** (which is headquartered there) and discount maverick **Southwest Airlines**. Both of them have more non-stop destinations from Phoenix than any other airline.

Here's a more detailed look at all of the carriers serving Phoenix:

- **American**, *Tel. 800/433-7300, www.aa.com*: Non-stops to Chicago and Dallas/Fort Worth with connections at either location to their entire route system.
- **America West**, *Tel. 800/235-9292, www.americawest.com*: Non-stop flights to more than 30 cities throughout the nation, but concentrated in the western United States. They also serve Mexico City and Vancouver with non-stop flights.
- **Continental**, *Tel. 800/523-3273, www.flycontinental.com*: Non-stops to Cleveland, Houston and New York. Good connections to their extensive nationwide system.
- **Southwest Airlines**, *Tel. 800/435-9792, www.southwest.com*: Non-stops to 17 different locations and easy connections to their entire route system. Known for low prices and efficient operation.
- **United Airlines**, *Tel. 800/241-6522, www.ual.com*: Non-stop service to Chicago, Denver, Los Angeles, San Francisco, and Washington, D.C.

Among some of the other nearly 20 airlines that provide service to Sky Harbor are **Air Canada**, *Tel. 800/776-3000*; **Delta**, *Tel. 800/221-1212*; **Frontier Airlines**, *Tel. 800/4321-FLY*; **Northwest**, *Tel. 800/225-2525*; **TWA**, *Tel. 800/221-2000* and **US Airways**, *Tel. 800/428-4322*.

Tucson International Airport is much smaller and handles far fewer flights, although a number of the same airlines that serve Phoenix can also take you to Tucson.

Here's the rundown:

- **American**: Non-stop flights to Chicago and Dallas/Fort Worth.
- **America West**: All flights to and from Tucson originate in Phoenix where you can connect with their entire system.
- **Continental**: They fly non-stop to Houston which is their hub, hence, you can make decent connections to most parts of the country.
- **Skywest**, *Tel. 800/453-9417*. Non-stop service to Salt Lake City with connections to their entire route system throughout the western United States.
- **Southwest**: Non-stop service to Las Vegas, Los Angeles, Oakland and San Diego with one-stop or change of plane service to all of their routes.
- **United**: Non-stop service to Denver and Los Angeles.

Most intra-state air travel within Arizona is done by **Mesa Airlines** or **Skywest**. See the section on public transportation.

GETTING AROUND ARIZONA

BY AIR

Inter-city air travel within Arizona is primarily handled by **Mesa Airlines**, *Tel. 800/MESA-AIR*, a major regional carrier throughout the southwest. Besides serving Phoenix and Tucson, Mesa flies to Bullhead City, Flagstaff, Sierra Vista (near Tucson), Kingman, Lake Havasu City, Prescott, and Yuma. Mesa operates within Arizona under the name **America West Express** and reservations can be made through America West's reservation service. **Scenic Airlines**, *Tel. 800/634-6801*, isn't so much a carrier as it is a tour operator. They have flights from several locations to such places as the Grand Canyon.

Depending upon the flight combinations you need, schedules often are reasonably convenient. Although the fares aren't that low it will almost always be a lot quicker than traveling by bus, even when you add on the time to and from the airport, check-in time and other built in delays associated with flying.

BY BUS

Bus service is provided by **Greyhound**, *Tel. 800/231-2222* (for route information and reservations). Within the large Navajo Indian Reservation there is regularly scheduled bus service along several different routes. This service is provided by the **Navajo Transit System**, *Tel. 520/729-5449* (for schedules and routes).

BY CAR

I've already indicated that a car, whether it's your own or a rental, is definitely the best way to get around in Arizona. Besides being the most time and cost effective method, it also offers the traveler a degree of flexibility that cannot be matched by any form of public transportation. That's true almost everywhere you travel in this country (except if your trip is confined to one or more major cities with a good transit system) but is even more so in the western United States in general and Arizona specifically.

Driving in Arizona will not, for the most part, present any significant problem for the majority of visitors. Although you'll often encounter heavy traffic in the Phoenix and Tucson areas and during peak times at

DESERT DRIVING:
DUST STORMS & OTHER MATTERS

Driving in the desert calls for a few special precautions and rules year-round, but even more so during the blazing summer sun. If you're renting a car in Arizona it is probably well suited to the climate. If you are using your own car be sure that the radiator has sufficient coolant and that all hoses are in good condition. Tires can be inflated a couple of pounds below where you normally keep them because the heat will build up tire pressure. However, don't seriously under inflate because that can cause a blowout. Properly functioning air conditioning is also very important. Tinted windows are useful although I certainly wouldn't advise going through the expense of having that done if it isn't needed where you live.

Although the desert can be quite beautiful it is also somewhat monotone in color in many places. This, in combination with the bright sunshine, can cause a driver to become sleepy or lose attention faster than normal. Avoid that problem by taking frequent rest stops. The strain on your eyes can be reduced by always wearing sunglasses when driving during the day. Using your headlights will make it easier for oncoming motorists to see you. This is more important on the many two lane non-divided roads which prevail in rural Arizona.

If you have a pet with you I must emphasize what should already be a well-known precaution. Do not leave your pet in the car alone. It's dangerous in warm weather in any part of the country. In the Arizona sun it can be quickly lethal.

And now about those Dust Storms. Although they're relatively infrequent (at least in more built up areas such as Phoenix and Tucson), it is always a possibility that you will encounter one. They can come up quite suddenly and often are severe enough to reduce visibility to zero. Be on the alert and try to take preventive action before it gets so bad that you can't see a thing. In minor storms you can probably get by with having your lights on and traveling at a greatly reduced speed. However, if it's more serious you should slowly and carefully pull well off the road. Turn the engine off and wait it out. I stress well-off the road because other drivers may be foolish enough to continue on. They won't really be able to see the road and may wander off of it. If you are parked too near the road it is possible that another car will smack into your vehicle.

More than likely you won't encounter any unusual problems. However, it is best to be informed about potential dangers and to know what to do in case one arises. These few simple precautions should help you avoid an unfortunate incident.

some National Park facilities, the road network in Arizona is usually free and clear. In fact, in many parts of the state you'll wonder where all the cars are – it isn't all that unusual not to see another car for several miles of travel in some areas. Parking facilities at major attractions are generally adequate or better. While big city on-street parking may be scarce or non-existent, there are plenty of garages. Details on these matters will be forthcoming in the regional touring chapters.

Interstate highways in Arizona are excellent. These and most other major roads (either state or federally designated) are kept in good driving condition and don't present any unusual hazards. However, Arizona has many mountainous areas where the roads may be very narrow and twisting along with steep grades and often an absence of comforting guardrails. Fortunately, most of the more important attractions of scenic Arizona don't require negotiating any road that's overly difficult.

But there are a lot of places mentioned in this book that will take you along such routes. If you are a novice when it comes to mountain driving and don't feel comfortable with the prospect of doing so, then just avoid them. I'll always let you know if the driving conditions are going to be difficult. As long as the roads are paved there usually won't be cause for great concern. When your route will take you onto unpaved roads you must exercise greater caution. Slow up to avoid kicking up dust that can block your view or send gravel pellets flying toward your windshield. And never attempt to travel on these roads during or after a heavy rain. In fact, if you're going to be going for a long distance on unimproved roads it's an excellent idea to check locally about the road conditions. If a place is only accessible with four-wheel drive or a high clearance vehicle, I'll also let you know about it. Finally, it's a good rule of thumb to take a 15 minute break for every two hours of driving. Long stretches of open road can be especially hypnotizing for a driver and cause drowsiness.

Two numbers that you can call for **road condition information** are, for the Phoenix area, *Tel. 602/861-9400*; and for the Flagstaff area, *Tel. 520/779-2711*. The former is mainly for getting information on construction delay information as the weather doesn't often affect Phoenix traffic.

This book will use several prefixes to designate various roads. The letter "I" before a number indicates an Interstate highway. "US" will precede a United States highway while Arizona state road numbers are indicated by "AZ". Some of the major Indian reservations have their own roads. These "Indian Routes" will contain the prefix "IR."

When it comes to familiarizing yourself with Arizona's road system there's simply no substitute for carefully studying a good road map. However, you should know a few major routes and that I can do for you here. It's even better if you read this section with a map in front of you. I-40 crosses the northern portion of Arizona from west to east, covering

358 miles. For most people coming from the east (as well as the Los Angeles area) it is the primary means of access into the state. Near the middle of the state I-40 intersects with I-17, which runs from that point south to Phoenix. In Phoenix, it ends at the junction of I-10, another east-west route that crosses the entire state, this time in the south. If you're coming from the San Diego area, I-8 cuts across southern Arizona from Yuma until it reaches I-10 between Phoenix and Tucson. The only other Interstate highway is I-19, which runs from Tucson south to the Mexican border at Nogales.

Several important US highways supplement the Interstate system. US 93 provides access from Las Vegas to I-40 at Kingman and on to the junction of US 60. The latter continues into Phoenix and beyond to the border with New Mexico.

Renting a Car

If you thought that trying to get a straight answer on airfares was difficult you'll be disappointed to learn that things won't be much easier when it comes to renting a car. Here, too, there are a jumble of rates depending upon a host of factors. However, a few basic rules apply at most rental companies that will put things into sharper focus. First of all it is almost always less expensive to rent a car if you return it to the same location. In other words, a loop trip is more economical than renting in one place and returning the car somewhere else. There are exceptions to this rule. In many cases the major companies will allow you to return the car at a different location with no extra "drop-off" charge so long as it is within the same state. As a result you may be able to do a Phoenix/Tucson rental without having to pay anything extra.

The second thing to look for in a rental is whether there's a mileage charge in addition to the basic rate. If there is, avoid it unless you plan to only use the car minimally. Arizona is a big state and the miles will add up quickly. When you tack on what you're paying per mile to the rate that you were quoted it won't be the great buy you thought it was. You should also inquire about weekly rentals because these are often less expensive than if you take a simple daily plan. Often you can wind up getting one or two days per week for free when you go weekly.

Other things to keep in mind are having the proper insurance. Every rental company will try to sell you coverage at significantly inflated prices. Check with your insurance agent at home if you can't determine whether or not your auto insurance covers a rental car. If it doesn't, then you have to decide whether or not to take a chance and waive the rental insurance coverage. Turning to another area, if more than one person is going to drive tell that to the renting agent because that has to be put on the agreement. Some companies do charge a small fee for this although I can't

ARIZONA DRIVING DISTANCES

	Flagstaff	Grand Canyon*	Phoenix	Show Low	Tucson	Yuma
Chinle	204	236	345	174	362	511
Flagstaff	– –	84	141	139	257	307
Gila Bend	208	292	70	251	126	116
Grand Canyon	84	– –	223	225	335	364
Kayenta	152	155	296	291	411	459
Kingman	145	174	182	283	297	222
Lake Havasu	63	237	198	376	313	153
Page	136	140	277	275	392	475
Payson	96	180	95	100	203	295
Phoenix	141	223	– –	181	115	200
Prescott	86	130	93	206	208	221
Safford	178	262	106	171	128	306
Show Low	139	225	181	– –	197	380
Tombstone	323	401	181	263	66	303
Tucson	257	335	115	197	– –	237
Winslow	60	144	201	79	276	367
Yuma	307	364	200	380	237	– –

*All mileages for the Grand Canyon are to the South Rim.

figure out what their justification is other than trying to make a few extra bucks.

Most companies won't allow rental cars to be taken out of the country (i.e., into Mexico). If you plan to drive into Mexico see the sidebar in Chapter 13, *Tucson*. Finally, ask about what discounts the car rental company offers. Members of AAA, AARP, some car insurance companies, as well as many major employers and other organizations that you may belong to have agreements with some of the biggest car rental firms.

Renting a car in either Phoenix or Tucson is no problem. All of the major companies are represented. The following list covers reservation numbers for the largest rental companies.

MAJOR CAR RENTAL PHONE NUMBERS

	Nationwide Toll-Free	Phoenix Airport	Tucson Airport
Avis	800/831-2847	602/273-3222	520/294-1494
Budget	800/227-3678	602/267-1717	520/889-8800
Dollar	800/800-4000	602/392-0695	520/573-1100
Hertz	800/654-3131	602/267-8822	520/294-7616
National	800/227-7368	602/275-4771	520/573-8050

You can often beat the rates offered by the major companies by dealing with a local or regional firm. These almost always require that you return the car to the same location but some regional renters may allow Phoenix to Tucson or vice-versa. Several possibilities within Arizona are smaller national operators such as **Alamo**, *Tel. 800/327-9633*; **Enterprise**, *Tel. 800/325-8007*; and **Thrifty**, *Tel. 800/367-2277*, who often have lower rates than the majors.

Some strictly local operations are **Diamond Rent-A-Car**, *Tel. 602/225-2002*; **Payless Car Rental**, *Tel. 602/231-9226*; **Value Rent A Car**, *Tel. 800/327-2501*; and **U-SAVE**, *Tel. 602/267-9505* in Phoenix, and *Tel. 520/889-5761* in Tucson.

BY TRAIN

Assuming that you aren't taking a guided tour of Arizona, I can't enthusiastically recommend seeing Arizona without a car. The distances can be great but, even more important, the public transportation system isn't very well developed. Like most of the western and mountain states, Arizona caters to the car driver. This doesn't mean, however, that you must have a car. For those willing to put up with the inconvenience of public transportation, here's some guidance on getting around from one city to another by train.

Amtrak, *Tel. 800/USA-RAIL*, serves a number of Arizona communities. The daily Southwest Chief (Chicago to Los Angeles) traverses the north-central portion of the state from east to west and has stops at Winslow, Flagstaff, and Kingman. Connecting bus service from Flagstaff is available to both the Grand Canyon and Phoenix. In the south two separate trains serve Benson, Tucson, Maricopa, and Yuma. Each of these trains, the Sunset Limited (Florida to Los Angeles) and the Texas Eagle (Chicago to Los Angeles), runs three times a week. From Tucson there is connecting bus service to Phoenix.

Amtrak also offers a number of package tours that combine train travel with bus tours or rail/drive options. Because of the limited number of places served and the infrequent schedules, traveling by train does have its drawbacks. Arizona does have a few positive things when it comes to using trains for sight seeing purposes.

Arizona's Four Historic Train Trips

If you are traveling without a car, then these delightful rail excursions need to be done in conjunction with bus service. Detailed information on schedules and prices is located in the appropriate destination chapter.

The Grand Canyon Railway: This is the best known of the four "tourist" trains now operating in Arizona. Passengers ride in carefully restored coaches that recreate the atmosphere of 1901 when service to the Grand Canyon was inaugurated. Vintage locomotives add to the authenticity of the 2-1/4 hour trip from Williams to the South Rim. You'll arrive at a depot that was built in 1910 and is the only log railroad station still in use in the nation. Visitors have about 3-1/2 hours of sight seeing time along the South Rim before the train returns to Williams, which is accessible from Phoenix via bus.

San Pedro and Southwestern Railway: Leaving from Benson (about 45 miles east of Tucson), the Sand Pedro and Southwestern rides through an historic section of southern Arizona. The four hour excursions pass through old mining and ghost towns and includes a western barbecue lunch during a stop in Tombstone. Benson is served by bus from Tucson.

Verde Canyon Railway: Public transportation aficionados will be joined in great numbers here by car riders since the Verde Canyon Railway travels through a scenic portion of the Verde Canyon and Sycamore Wilderness that cannot be reached by road. The trip departs from Clarkdale which is only a few miles from Sedona. The four hour journey offers thrilling trestles that span deep canyons as well as views of ancient Indian ruins. Bus service is available to Sedona. You need a car or taxi to get to Clarkdale.

Yuma Valley Railway: This shorter (two hour) trip travels along the Colorado River and goes into neighboring California as well as the Mexican states of Sonora and Baja California. Passenger coaches date from the 1920s while the locomotives are from the '40s or '50s. Yuma is served by bus and Amtrak.

ACCOMMODATIONS

Once you've decided where you're going in Arizona and come up with an itinerary, the next biggest decision for most people is where to stay. An unpleasant hotel or motel experience can be a big downer while an unusually nice place will become part of your fond vacation memories. Giving advice on where to stay is difficult because different travelers are looking for very different things when it comes to lodging.

The cost of lodging is only one factor. Some people just want a clean and comfortable room to plop themselves down for the night while many others want to be pampered in luxurious surroundings and take advantage of many of the amenities of either a first class hotel or resort. I have selected more than 125 hotels that run the gamut from simple budget motels to the some of the most luxurious resorts in the world. There is an emphasis on the higher end of the scale for several reasons. There's a lot more that needs to be said about them than a small roadside motel. But another important reason is one of simple logistics – there are a lot of expensive lodging establishments in Arizona.

This section will point out several things that should be kept in mind about lodging. Some are generic to travel anywhere but others are especially significant in Arizona. Most places in the west, including Arizona, have a casual and informal atmosphere. However, the more expensive resorts in the Phoenix/Scottsdale area are often host to the rich and famous. If you don't feel comfortable keeping up with the "Joneses" then you may find that these places are not suited to your style. This is even more so during the peak winter season. Tucson area resorts tend to be far less formal.

Regardless of what type of lodging you choose, it is very important to have advance reservations in all popular resort and tourist areas. Even those places that are more off the beaten track often fill up fast during the summer months. Finding a room in or near the important national parks is especially difficult. I strongly urge you to have advance reservations before arriving in Arizona.

Most chain properties do not require that you pay in advance so long as you arrive before 6:00pm. However, it's a good idea to guarantee a late arrival with your credit card. Many times the reservations agent will ask you for this information. Smaller, independent establishments and many resort properties require that you do pay in advance, at least for the first nights' stay. Be sure you understand and comply with payment regulations and cancellation rules at the time you make your booking.

Reservations can be made in a number of ways. All major chains and many independent hotels accept reservations made through travel agents. You can make reservations on your own by contacting the hotel directly or via a chain's central reservation system. It is also becoming increasingly common for independent establishments to belong to associations which handle reservations through a toll-free number.

Reservations for many hotels throughout Arizona can also be made free of charge by contacting:
- **Experience Arizona Central Reservations**, *Tel. 888-249-8470*
- **Flagstaff Central Reservations**, *Tel. 800/527-8388* (all of northern Arizona including the Grand Canyon)
- **Outwest Reservations**, *Tel. 800/688-9378*
- **Phoenix-Scottsdale Hotel Reservations**, *Tel. 800/718-3227* (for the Valley of the Sun).

Most of the preceding will also arrange package tours. Specialty reservation services include: **Advance Reservations Inn Arizona and Old Pueblo Homestays**, *Tel. 800/333-9776*, for stays in individual homes and guest ranches; and **Arizona Trails Bed and Breakfast Reservation Service**, *Tel. 888-799-4284*. Another central source for B&B stays is **Mi Casa Su Casa Bed and Breakfast**, *Tel. 800/456-0682*. The name of the service translates as My House is Your House. Finally, if you wish to stay in a condominium, casita (small house) or suite accommodations, then try **Condo Vacations of Arizona**, *Tel. 800/266-3680*.

Hotel prices for the same room can vary tremendously depending upon the time of the year, the day of the week, and whether or not you can qualify for any discounted rates. Don't be bashful when making reservations. Balk at what you believe to be a high price and they may well do better by miraculously finding that they have one more room left at a special price!

The recommended lodging listings in this book are arranged by location. They are further broken down in each touring chapter alphabetically by city. In larger cities they're divided by the area of the city as well. Then they'll be broken down one last time by price category during the peak season. The rates shown are known as the rack rate. That means what the normal rate for the room is. In Arizona that rate is often different in summer and winter. While Phoenix, for example, is more expensive in winter, the Grand Canyon is cheaper at that time. When only one rate is given it means that the rate is the same (or varies only slightly) all year. When the difference is significant I'll give the highest and lowest rates along with the approximate effective dates for each rate.

Furthermore, the quoted price will always refer to the room (not the per person) rate but are based on double occupancy. Single rates are often the same or only slightly less than the room rate. Hotel policies concerning additional charges, if any, for children in the same room vary considerably. If you plan to have your children stay in the same room with you inquire with the individual hotel as to the charge.

All prices listed in this book are for the room only (no meals) unless otherwise indicated. The majority of hotels (with the exception of some resorts) charge on this basis, which is often known as the European Plan. When another plan is involved it will be indicated. A Continental Plan includes a small breakfast consisting primarily of pastry and beverage. Depending upon the hotel and your appetite this may or may not be sufficient to satisfy your morning hunger pangs. A Breakfast Plan includes a full breakfast. The Modified American Plan (MAP) includes a full breakfast and dinner and is rarely found these days outside of resort facilities. Some hotels do offer plans where you can add on meals.

On-premise restaurants will be indicated and also mentioned if there is a separate listing for it in the "Where to Eat" section. All hotels listed have private baths in every room so no mention will be made of this in the individual listings except for a couple of establishments in isolated areas that have shared baths.

Quoted prices are for what can be termed "regular" guest rooms. More elaborate facilities, especially in luxury hotels and resorts, are almost always available at even higher prices (sometimes running into as much as four figures for a single night!). Because many facilities have a wide variety of accommodations, price ranges can often overlap two or even three categories. If these prices seem high keep in mind that Arizona hotel prices are higher than in many other parts of the country, especially during the peak season. Rates reflect what the hotel considers to be a standard room. Although hotel prices have been going up fast in recent years, it's usually still relative to their category. The prices were accurate

PRICE RANGE FOR EACH LODGING CATEGORY
Very Expensive Over $175
Expensive $126-175
Moderate $76-125
Inexpensive $75 or less

at press time but may be higher when you are ready to make your reservations.

MAJOR HOTEL CHAINS

In each destination chapter you will find many suggested places to stay, a sizable proportion of which are independent establishments. Many people, however, like the convenience of making reservations with nationwide hotel companies and the "no surprises" rooms and facilities of these chains. I myself often use them. Thus, this list will help supplement the destination chapter listings. The upscale chains (such as Doubletree, Hilton, Hyatt, Radisson and Sheraton) aren't included here because many of their properties in Arizona can be found in the suggested hotels in the chapters that follow. Other chain properties are generally only listed if they are among the best choices in a given location. The following are major nationwide chains that have a strong presence throughout Arizona:

BEST WESTERN, *Tel. 800/528-1234; Web site: www.bestwestern.com.* Properties in Benson, Bullhead City, Camp Verde, Chambers, Chandler, Chinle, Cottonwood, Eagar, Ehrenburg, Flagstaff, Gila Bend, Glendale, Goodyear, Grand Canyon (Tusayan), Green Valley, Heber, Holbrook, Kayenta, Kingman, Lake Havasu City, Mesa, Miami, Nogales, Page, Parker, Payson, Phoenix, Pinetop, Prescott, Safford, San Carlos, Scottsdale, Sedona, Show Low, Sierra Vista, Sun City, Tempe, Tombstone, Tucson, Wickenburg, Willcox, Williams, Winslow and Yuma.

CHOICE HOTELS, **Quality Inn**, *Tel. 800/228-5151; Web site: www.qualityinn.com.* Cottonwood, Flagstaff, Grand Canyon (Tusayan), Kingman, Mesa, Phoenix, Scottsdale, Sedona, Surprise, Tuba City and Williams. **Comfort Inn**, *Tel. 800/228-5150; Web site: www.comfortinn.com.* Camp Verde, Flagstaff, Fountain Hills, Globe, Holbrook, Page, Phoenix, Pinetop-Lakeside, Prescott, Safford, Scottsdale, Sedona, Tempe, Tucson, Williams, Winslow and Yuma. **Econolodge**, *Tel. 800/553-2666; Web site: www.econolodge.com.* Flagstaff, Holbrook, Page, Phoenix, Pinetop-Lakeside, Tempe, Tolleson, Tucson, Williams and Winslow. Other Choice brands with more limited Arizona locations are **Clarion, Sleep Inn** and **Rodeway**.

DAYS INN, *Tel. 800/329-7466; Web site: www.daysinn.com.* Properties in Benson, Buckeye, Bullhead City, Casa Grande, Chandler, Flagstaff, Globe, Grand Canyon (Tusayan), Holbrook, Kingman, Lake Havasu City, Mesa, Nogales, Page, Payson, Phoenix, Prescott Valley, St. Johns, St. Michaels, Scottsdale, Sedona, Show Low, Tempe, Tucson, Willcox, Williams, Winslow and Yuma.

EMBASSY SUITES, *Tel. 800/EMBASSY; Web site: www.embassy-suites.com.* Properties in Flagstaff, Paradise Valley, Phoenix, Scottsdale and Tucson.

HOLIDAY INN, *Tel. 800/HOLIDAY (Including Crowne Plaza & Holiday Inn Express); Web site: www.basshotels.com/holiday-inn*. Benson, Casa Grande, Chinle, Flagstaff, Glendale, Globe, Goodyear, Grand Canyon (Tusayan), Green Valley, Holbrook, Kayenta, Kingman, Lake Havasu City, Page, Payson, Phoenix, Pinetop-Lakeside, Prescott, Scottsdale, Sedona, Show Low, Tempe, Tucson, Williams and Yuma.

LA QUINTA INNS, *Tel. 800/NU-ROOMS; Web site: www.laquinta.com*. Properties in Chandler, Flagstaff, Mesa, Phoenix, Scottsdale, Tempe and Tucson.

MARRIOTT, **Courtyard by Marriot**, *Tel. 800/321-2211; Web site www.courtyard.com*. Mesa, Page, Phoenix, Scottsdale, Tempe and Tucson.. **Fairfield Inn**, *Tel. 800/228-2800; Web site: www.fairfieldinn.com*. Chandler, Flagstaff, Glendale, Mesa, Phoenix, Scottsdale, Tempe, Tucson and Williams. **Residence Inn**, *Tel. 800/331-3131; Web site: www.residenceinn.com*. Flagstaff, Phoenix, Scottsdale, Tempe and Tucson. (Marriott Hotels themselves can be found in the destination chapter listings.)

MOTEL 6, *Tel. 800/466-8356; Web site: www.motel6.com*. Properties in Benson, Casa Grande, Douglas, Flagstaff, Holbrook, Kingman, Lake Havasu City, Mesa, Nogales, Phoenix, Prescott, Scottsdale, Show Low, Sierra Vista, Tempe, Tucson, Willcox, Williams, Winslow, Youngstown (Sun City), and Yuma.

SUPER 8, *Tel. 800/800-8000; Web site: www.super8.com*. Properties in Apache Junction, Benson, Bullhead City, Camp Verde, Casa Grande, Chandler, Cottonwood, Eloy, Flagstaff, Gila Bend, Goodyear, Holbrook, Kingman, Lake Havasu City, Marana, Mesa, Nogales, Page, Phoenix, Pinetop, Prescott, St. Johns, Sedona, Show Low, Sierra Vista, Springerville, Tempe, Tucson, Wickenburg, Willcox, Williams, Winslow and Yuma.

CAMPING & RECREATIONAL VEHICLES

Camping sites or places to hook up an RV are in as much demand these days as hotel rooms. So, once again, early advance planning is an absolute must. Reservations are not always accepted for camping on public lands. Inquire as to whether or not they operate on a first come, first served or reservation basis. Campsites and RV facilities range from back to nature "roughing it" to, in some commercially run establishments, facilities that have almost as many amenities as an average motel. Most campgrounds in the northern portion of Arizona are only open between May and September while those in the south are available all year.

Aside from commercial RV parks that are often located near natural areas you'll find both camping sites and RV facilities in almost all national parks. Campsites are a part of most Arizona state parks except for "day use" type facilities that are generally near larger cities. Most also have RV hookups. Many sites are also located in the national forests of Arizona. Only a small fee is charged in these places. However, while you can just show up at sites within national forests, a permit is required for camping in national parks. The permits are free and can be obtained at the visitor center of the park you are visiting.

Some important contacts and general information on Arizona camping are:

• **Bureau of Land Management**: Camping is generally on a walk-in basis. You can call the BLM's Arizona office, *Tel. 602/417-9200* or the individual BLM site to inquire about reservation policies. The nightly rate is generally between $4 and $10 and there is a 14-day limit.

• **National Park Service areas**: Camping sites in the national parks are in greater demand than at any other location so advance planning is especially important. Policies regarding reservations vary from one location to another. See the listing for each park in the regional destination chapters for specific information and telephone numbers. The only location in Arizona that accepts advance reservations through the **National Park Reservation Service**, *Tel. 800/365-2267; Web site: www.reservations.nps.gov*, is Grand Canyon and that does not apply to all campgrounds within the park. In instances where advance reservations are not accepted, be sure to arrive to claim your space as early in the day as possible.

• **U.S. Forest Service**: The centralized reservation number for camping in all national forests is *Tel. 800/280-2267*. For specific information it is best to contact the appropriate Forest Service Supervisor's office (numbers given in destination chapters) or the Southwest Region Office, *Tel. 505/842-3292*.

• **Arizona State Parks**: Camping in all state parks is on a first-come, first-served basis. So, as in the case of many national parks, arrive early. Information can be obtained by calling the specific park office or the Arizona State Parks office, *Tel. 602/542-4174*.

For a sampling of commercially operated sites at major localities throughout the state, see the listings in each regional chapter. Major chain operators of campgrounds, such as KOA, offer nationwide directories and reservation services.

7. BASIC INFORMATION

ADVENTURE TRAVEL

Adventure travel has also become an important force in the travel industry in recent years. Its growth has been fueled by the large number of tour operators specializing in out of the ordinary experiences as well as by the popularity of four wheel and off road vehicles. A lot of people simply aren't satisfied with keeping their feet planted solidly on the ground and walking or riding by car from one sight seeing attraction to another. If you like to get involved in the action and aren't frightened by vigorous activity and sometimes highly unusual modes of transportation, then you're ready for adventure travel. And Arizona is one of the best places in the country to experience it.

Adventure travel includes a diverse number of activities, such as rock or mountain climbing, river running, mountain biking, horseback trips, overnight camping (and not in a comfortable RV), and much more, all of which is readily available in Arizona. Also included in this category is the fast growing dude ranch concept where guests actually get involved in the operations of a working ranch. The *City Slickers* motion pictures helped to popularize this genre. Actually, ranch vacations in Arizona, especially in the Tucson area, have been around for quite some time.

General information on the most popular types of adventure travel in Arizona can be found in the next chapter on Sports & Recreation. In addition, reputable operators can be found under specific categories in the various destination chapters. However, the following are some good examples of general adventure tour operators:

• **Ascend Adventures**, *Tel. 800/227-2363*. All sorts of outdoor adventure.
• **Canyon Calling Tours**, *Tel. 520/282-3586*. "Soft" adventure (for those not necessarily in the best shape or with little adventure travel experience). These trips are for women only, so this organization could also be under the alternative travel category.
• **Outdoor Adventures Unlimited**, *Tel. 602/253-2789*. Any and all types of outdoor activity, from mild to extremely strenuous.

All regions of Arizona have their fair share of adventure travel opportunities, although they are somewhat limited along the extreme western fringe of the state.

If you plan to build an Arizona vacation by doing a series of forays into the wilderness and back country you might want to consider studying back issues of Arizona Highways magazine. The magazine's format includes a monthly feature on hikes as well as back road trips for four-wheel and off-road vehicles. Many of these places are unusual to say the least.

ALTERNATIVE TRAVEL

Over the past few years a new industry has grown up within the overall travel industry. Going under various different names, I refer to it as alternative travel. It covers an enormously large range of possibilities – everything from special trips for gays, seniors, children traveling with grandparents, or any other of a number of groups to people interested in specific aspects of travel such as the environment, social history of various ethnic or national groups, and so forth.

I don't pretend to be an expert in the needs and interests of all these special groups and, frankly, in most cases don't even see a great need for "alternative travel." A broad-based vacation experience provides more than enough opportunity for intellectual improvement. However, at least a part of the traveling public is asking for this type of information and like the focus these types of vacations can bring to a trip, so I want to direct you towards a few organizations that may help bring out some of the special nature of Arizona:

- **Arizona Ed-Venture Tours**, *Tel. 888/249-1788*. Prescott-based outfit concentrates on eco-tourism as well as trips focusing on ethnic, cultural or historical perspectives.
- **Baja's Frontier Tours**, *Tel. 800/726-7231*. Professional naturalists lead personalized eco-tours that highlight the unique nature of the southwest as well as its history.
- **Friends of Arizona Highways**, *Tel. 602/254-4505*. Photo "safaris" with professional photographers on the staff of the Arizona Highways magazine. They have more than 20 scheduled trips to choose from.
- **Southwest Ed-Ventures**, *Tel. 800/525-4456*. Features tours that inform participants about the unique cultural traditions of the region.
- **Trails of Cochise**, *Tel. 520/298-9429*. This organization arranges custom escorted tours that concentrate on the "old West," you know – cowboys and Indians stuff.

CHILDREN

While some of the major attractions in Arizona aren't particularly well suited to children, especially very small ones, there is much that will appeal to youngsters. A child may appreciate the wonders of the Grand Canyon in a different way than adults, but appreciate it nevertheless. If you are in the habit of taking your children with you on vacation, I don't see any reason why you should change that for a visit to Arizona. There are three situations that have to be addressed when traveling with children. The first is what to do with the little tykes when you and your spouse (or whoever) decide that it's time for a night out on the town by yourselves. The second is what to do to keep the kids busy during long drives (also known as avoiding the "are we there yet?" syndrome). And, last but certainly not least, finding attractions and activities that the children will really enjoy. Hopefully, they'll be enjoyable for the grown-ups as well.

Getting back to the first situation now, how do you go about finding a good baby-sitter in a place you've never been before? The single best source of information is from the staff at the hotel where you are staying. They have experience having made recommendations in the past and getting feedback from their guests. This is especially true in the better hotels. Many of the major resorts, of course, provide first class care facilities for children.

Road activities don't have to be elaborate and shouldn't present a major hurdle. You know best what will occupy your children while riding in the car. It may be a coloring book, a small hand-held computer game, a favorite doll or toy or even something that doesn't involve having something with you, such as a sing-along or word games. It's easy to get children involved in simple little games that make the time go faster. For example, keeping track of license plates from various states can be both fun and an education in geography.

The list of places to see in Arizona and things to do that both children and adults will enjoy is a long one. Some of the very best are given here and each of the regional touring chapters will make special mention of what should appeal most to children. I haven't even included here one of the most obvious diversions for children which is amusement parks. They can be found listed under the Sports and Recreation category in both Phoenix and Tucson.

My selections of the best activities for children are:
• Arizona Museum for Youth
• Tucson Children's Museum.
• The Phoenix Zoo is the biggest and best of the state's zoological parks.
• For learning about the desert environment the Arizona-Sonora Desert
    Museum is the most child friendly as well as the most comprehensive.

- The Arizona Doll and Toy Museum is especially good for little girls while boys will be enthralled with the Champlin Fighter Museum.
- Old Tucson Studios can provide hours of fun but for learning about the ol' west nothing can beat a visit to Tombstone.
- The Flandreau Science Center and Planetarium will appeal to the curiosity of most school age children.
- Any of Arizona's several historic train rides makes an ideal outing for kids.
- Learning about the ancient native cultures of the southwest should be part of any child's trip to Arizona. There are many excellent sites that children can enjoy including Montezuma Castle, Casa Grande Ruins, and sites on the Navajo Reservation to name just a few. Indian reservations are in themselves worthwhile destinations for children.
- Finally, don't overlook the possibilities presented by Arizona's natural scenery. Yes, even children can appreciate the beauty and awesome grandeur of the Grand Canyon, Monument Valley, Oak Creek Canyon, and many other places.

CREDIT CARDS

Each hotel and restaurant listed in the regional destination chapters indicates whether credit cards are accepted. Where four or less cards are accepted the names of the valid cards are listed. If five cards are taken then the listing will indicate "most major credit cards accepted." When "major credit cards accepted" is shown it means that the establishment takes a minimum of six different cards.

Because of the high price of many admissions to visitor attractions more and more of these businesses are accepting credit cards for payment. However, acceptance of cards at these locations will only be mentioned if the admission price is greater than $15. If so, the listing will state "credit cards."

HEALTH

A trip to Arizona won't involve any unusual health risks for the overwhelming majority of visitors. With a few simple precautions and situations to be aware of, it shouldn't present a threat to anyone. The availability and quality of health care in the more populated portions of the state is a good as anywhere else in the United States. Care in sparsely inhabited regions is also good but sometimes may take time to reach in the case of an emergency. Always dial 911 for any medical or other emergency throughout Arizona.

If you are taking prescription medication be sure that you have an adequate supply for your entire trip with you. It's also a good idea to have a copy of the prescription. If you're going to be staying in one hotel for more than a day then leave your medicine in the room, only taking with you what you have to use during the course of the day. Otherwise, do what you can to keep all prescriptions out of excessive heat. Don't leave them in a closed car for any length of time; it's better to carry them with you even if it's extremely hot outside.

Most potential health problems are related either to the altitude, heat, outdoor activity or a combination of these factors. Let's take a brief look at each one. If you live in low country, a sudden increase to great heights can sometimes cause serious consequences. Few people experience problems below about 5,000 feet. **Acute Mountain Sickness** can occur at altitudes of 8,000 feet and above, an altitude reached in many portions of Arizona. Symptoms include difficulty in breathing, dizziness and disorientation. It can be avoided by increasing altitude slowly, over a period of a couple of days. Sometimes your schedule can't conform to that. In such instances it's a good idea to eat lightly and avoid alcoholic beverages for the first day or so that is spent at or above 8,000 feet. If you should start experiencing the symptoms of AMS then descend immediately – that will effect a quick cure.

The summer sun in most of Arizona can cause problems in two ways. First is **sunburn**. Even in areas that aren't as hot, such as the northern part of the state, the ultra-violet levels can be extremely high and result in a quick burn. Limit your exposure to the sun as much as possible for the first few days and always keep skin and your head covered as much as possible. If you are going to be spending a lot of time outdoors, either at the pool or hiking in the countryside, you should use a good sunscreen product. Because of the dry air, **dehydration** is always a constant threat if you don't drink enough fluids. Have drinks, especially during the warmer months, often. Don't wait until you're thirsty.

Water, fruit juices and so-called "sports" drinks are the best. Carbonated beverages are all right but aren't as useful. Alcoholic beverages don't count toward your liquid requirements nor do coffee and tea. **Heat exhaustion** or more serious **heat stroke** are also possible threats to those spending too much time in the sun, especially if engaged in strenuous activity. Both of these are medical emergencies. Call for help immediately.

As a rule of thumb you should drink four quarts of water per day if taking part in outdoor activity. Carry water with you on trails and in areas where towns are scattered. Don't wait until you reach a hotel or restaurant – by that time substantial harm can be done. Drink small amounts frequently throughout the day rather than large amounts at meal times. It is also important to keep your head covered. While shorts and sleeveless tops seem like a good way to keep cool, they aren't. It is better to keep as much of your skin covered from the direct rays of the sun. Light colors are also helpful.

Visitors who will be spending time in the back country hiking or camping are exposed to special hazards. The first is possible **water contamination**. Even the cleanest looking mountain stream can contain dangerous micro organisms. Be sure to boil all water or use filtration or purification equipment. Also, dress properly to prevent **hypothermia** which can be caused by wearing wet clothing or by sudden drops in temperature which can occur in the mountains. Clothing should also provide protection against insect bites and stings. Avoid contact with animals in the wild, even if they appear to be tame.

When hiking in remote areas it is always advisable to go with someone else. Hiking alone is often asking for trouble. Besides being with a partner you should **tell someone else about your hiking plans** – where you plan to go and when you expect to be back. In national and state park facilities you can leave this information with park rangers or officials. At other times you may want to tell someone at the hotel front desk. It may seem silly but an ounce of prevention can help to ensure that you won't have any problems. At a minimum it will make certain that someone else is aware of the fact that you may be in trouble when you don't return on time.

There have been sporadic cases of **bubonic plague** and **hantavirus** reported among backcountry enthusiasts in some of the more remote portions of the Four Corners region. These are rare and shouldn't cause any undue concern. However, if you are going to be camping or hiking in the backcountry, you should take special precautions to avoid coming into contact with wild animals and animal wastes. Familiarize yourself with symptoms of these illnesses and seek medical attention at their first sign.

INDIAN GAMING

There's hardly a state in the nation these days that has Indian reservations that doesn't have casino gambling to go with it and Arizona isn't an exception. There has been quite a lot of opposition to the expansion of Indian gaming in Arizona and that is reflected in the fact that the number of casino locations is considerably less than in neighboring New Mexico. Currently you can gamble on reservations in 14 different locations. These are Maricopa, Fountain Hills, Chandler, Tucson (two casinos), Yuma (two locations), Parker, Camp Verde, Prescott, San Carlos, McNary (Pinetop-Lakeside), and Payson.

As in many states, Indian gaming is in a state of flux due to disagreements between the states and the tribes over interpretation of gaming compacts. Thus, if gambling is going to be an important part of your Arizona journey, it is best to verify the status of the casinos you plan to patronize. Addresses and telephone numbers of all casinos are listed in the appropriate regional destination chapters in the Nightlife & Entertainment section.

Slot machines and most table games are available to those over 21 years of age. These casinos are strictly for those who want to gamble. By that I mean don't expect to find the many other amenities and attractions associated with Las Vegas casinos. If you are looking for more than a place to play while in Arizona you should consider a side trip to Las Vegas or at least across the river from Bullhead City in Laughlin, Nevada. The latter doesn't come close to Vegas either but is more glamorous than the casinos on Indian reservations.

NEWSPAPERS & MAGAZINES

Since both newspapers and magazines are published frequently they offer the most up-to-the-minute information on special events and what's going on in a particular area. Popular magazines geared towards visitors are distributed in most hotels and motels. Among the best are the monthly *Where* (Phoenix/Scottsdale) and *Key* (Phoenix and Tucson) guides. The *Arizona Quick Guide* is a quarterly publication concentrating on the Valley of the Sun and Sedona areas but with some information on the entire state. *New Times* is another weekly "what's going on" publication in Phoenix and its counterpart in Tucson is the *Tucson Weekly*. All are distributed free of charge.

Arizona Highways is a monthly magazine available at news stands within Arizona or nationwide by annual subscription that has feature articles on various destinations throughout the state, often off of the beaten track. Although it's a well-written publication with high quality photographs, it's geared more toward the experienced Arizona traveler. First time or general visitors will not glean that much from it so I don't recommend subscribing. But if you wish to do so their toll free telephone number is *Tel. 800/543-5432*. Also see the information on this publication in the section on adventure travel.

In smaller cities and towns it usually isn't necessary to read the paper in order to get information on what's going on. However, they come in handy in both Phoenix and Tucson.

Phoenix has recently joined the ranks of major cities with only one daily newspaper, in this case the nationally respected morning *Arizona Republic*. Tucson's daily papers are the morning *Arizona Daily Star* and the *Tucson Citizen* which comes out in the afternoon.

NIGHTLIFE & ENTERTAINMENT

There isn't any type of entertainment that isn't available in the Phoenix metropolitan area and the variety in Tucson is almost as great. What you will see will, of course, depend on your own personal taste but I would recommend entertainment that features things somewhat unique to Arizona. These would include Native American and Mexican entertainment. Detailed information on what to do at night is contained in each of the destination chapters. However, don't expect a wide choice in sparsely populated portions of the state, especially if they're away from the main tourist routes.

SAFETY

Safety from crime should always be on your mind when traveling. The typical tourist, always occupied, sometimes appearing perplexed and usually carrying more than a little cash, is often a target for thieves. This is true whether you're in a big city such as Phoenix, in a national park, or even in a small town in the proverbial middle of nowhere. Minimize such situations by always having a firm plan as to what you're doing next. Plan your route in advance whether it's by foot or by car. Don't carry much cash. Use credit cards or travelers checks whenever possible. Record credit card and travelers check numbers and keep them in a separate place. Don't leave valuables lying around exposed in your car, even for a short time. Cars with trunks that hide luggage completely are better than hatchbacks where you can see into the storage compartment.

Hotel security is also important. Keep your door locked and don't open it unless you are absolutely sure about the identity of the person seeking entry. Use the deadbolt where provided. Also be sure to familiarize yourself with the location of fire exits. If you must have expensive jewelry with you inquire as to the availability of safe deposit boxes in the hotel. While hotel safety is important in any location, it is especially true in metropolitan areas such as Phoenix and Tucson. Avoid narrow and deserted locations, especially at night. Don't hesitate to ask hotel personnel about how safe a certain area is if you plan to walk around.

In any emergency situation you should dial 911 for coordinated assistance. All of Arizona is on this system and your call will be automatically routed to the nearest emergency service.

SHOPPING

Shopping for unusual items while on vacation is a major activity for many travelers. If you're one of them then you'll be glad to know that few states offer greater opportunities for shopping than Arizona. From the fancy boutiques, galleries and malls of the large metropolitan areas to the roadside stands located in small towns on or near Indian reservations, you are likely to be able to find exactly what you're looking for – even if you don't yet know what "it" is.

Arizona shopping, at least in the sense that makes it different from most other places in the United States, falls into three major categories. These are fine arts and collectibles, native crafts, and western wear. This section will give you some general information on all of these but you should refer to some of the regional touring chapters for specific details. Of course, if you're looking for the more mundane you'll easily find that as well.

The Phoenix and Tucson areas are filled with huge suburban shopping malls containing all of the major national chains as well as regional and local operators. Outlet malls are also very popular in both locations. I can't see the point of spending time shopping at these types of facilities while on vacation since they are so similar to what is available at home. However, since many visitors will want to go to them anyway, I won't ignore them. Smaller towns sometimes have interesting shops but don't have large malls. Tourist locations do, however, so you'll find plenty of places to shop in such locations as Lake Havasu City.

Fine Arts & Collectibles

Included in this category are paintings, sculpture, and antiques. While all genres are available the majority of shoppers will probably be looking for western or Native American themes. These are found in great abundance throughout the state's many art galleries. The Phoenix metropolitan area (and especially more upscale Scottsdale) is the single largest art market in Arizona. Prices at galleries tend to be sky high. The range can be from about a hundred dollars to almost unlimited. If you are knowledgeable about art then you know how to deal with the price tags. The uneducated art consumer, however, should be hesitant to make purchases of this kind. Although the better galleries will be happy to tell you about individual works and their artists, you are still unlikely to know if it would make a good investment for the price. On the other hand, if you are simply looking to purchase something that appeals to your visual senses and the price is affordable, you don't have to worry about that aspect.

Other areas of Arizona with a sizable number of art galleries are Sedona and Jerome. Antiques are more commonly found in Prescott.

Native Crafts

This is a big category which can be subdivided into two sections, namely Native American crafts and Mexican crafts. The Native American crafts are especially prized by visitors and include, among other things, fine jewelry (silver and turquoise are featured), blankets and rugs with intricate geometric patterns, woven baskets, and pottery in all shapes, sizes and colors.

A few guidelines on some popular craft items:

Navajo and Zuni **jewelry** is of the highest quality. Navajo work features extensive use of silver while Zuni jewelry combines various stones and other items with the silver. Antique Navajo jewelry, the most prized type, is known as **pawn**. The price range for pawns starts at around $200 and can run as high as $10,000. Other Indian jewelry sells for anywhere as low as a few dollars to as high as $15,000, so there's something for every budget. The traditional **Navajo rug**, hand woven and produced with vegetable dyes is made by a painstaking process, which helps to explain the high prices. The designs feature intricate patterns and symbols and have rich color. Be sure that the weave is tight before purchasing. Contemporary rugs are priced between about $150 and $3,000 but historic pieces found in galleries can cost as much as $20,000. See the sidebar for information on Indian pottery.

Indian **Kachina dolls** are also in great demand. Kachinas, which are representations of spiritual beings, are Hopi crafts made of cottonwood roots and can range from an inch in height to a few feet. The quality of a doll is good if the anatomy is realistic looking and everything is in the proper proportions, especially the hands and feet. Prices depend upon the size, with miniatures going for around $30. Full size dolls, except for a few made by the most famous of Kachina artists, sell for about $250 up to $1,500.

Although less known to most people, Arizona's Indians are also important producers of **paintings and bronze works of art**. Native American crafts are sold both in fancy stores in Phoenix, Tucson and other cities but I think you are more likely to have more fun shopping for these items either on Indian reservations or small market towns near reservations where the Indians come to sell their wares. Often, these establishments will call themselves "trading posts." You'll find them all over the state. Here you are assured of authentic Native American products, although you can be reasonably certain of authenticity if purchasing at a reputable large city dealer.

At **native markets** you can often negotiate the price and at least tell yourself that you got a good buy! I do want to mention that throughout the Southwest the Navajo are among the most respected artisans, especially for fine **pottery**. Among the reservation towns where you'll find the largest selections are Chinle, Kayenta, Tuba City and Ganado.

Mexican crafts run the gamut from clothing to toys and from jewelry to rugs. There are many similarities to Native American crafts. These items are found in markets in Phoenix and vicinity, throughout the

NATIVE POTTERY

Native Americans have been making beautiful and functional pottery for about 2,000 years. The ancient Hohokam, Mogollon and Anasazi were all expert potters. The nature and quality of the pottery is determined first by the type of clay used. Most of the clay still comes from land on Indian reservations and has proven to be especially well suited to making pottery. The Indians believe that the finished product possesses special qualities because the clay holds the spirit of the earth and the power of the fire used to create the finished product. In fact, today's Hopi still say a prayer when collecting the clay, asking the earth for permission. It is common to leave an offering of cornmeal at the place where the clay is taken. The size and shape of the finished product can be as varied as the many colors and infinite geometric patterns that adorn it.

Again, the Navajo are considered to be the greatest artisans in this field, although Hopi work is also of excellent quality. Prices usually begin around $25 for smaller pieces and can range up to several hundred for larger works.

Tucson area and many other towns in the southern portion of the state. They are far less common in the north. At Nogales you can go across the border into Mexico and find even a greater variety of goods, often at lower prices.

Western Wear & Other Items

Everybody these days, it seems, likes to look like a cowboy or cowgirl. Well, in Arizona it's a way of life – you'll frequently see people on their way to work dressed in fancy western wear. The term basically includes jeans, shirts and blouses, belts (and the all important belt buckle), boots, and hats. However, skirts and dresses, suits and sport jackets, and outer jackets can all also be found in western styles. While most of these items can be purchased just about anywhere in the country, Arizona and the Southwest offer a far greater selection. Most are made locally and often aren't distributed to stores in the remainder of the nation. The quality is generally excellent and the prices are usually high. Almost every clothing store has at least some western wear but your best bet is to shop at locations that have the words "western wear" either in their name or listed after it. Again, some specific suggestions will be given in the destination chapters.

Western items are by no means limited to clothing and fashion accessories. Just about everything for the home can be found in a western style. This includes major pieces of furniture, lamps, wall decorations, and statues, to name just a few. Outdoor decorations for your lawn also often feature western themes.

I haven't yet mentioned the typical tacky gift shops that so many people find convenient to purchase a little gift for the neighbors. They're everywhere, from the big cities to the smallest trading post. You can find the key chains, coffee mugs, and the like. For something a bit more unusual, however, I will suggest taking a look at the gift shops in the more heavily visited national parks such as the Grand Canyon and Petrified Forest. There, in addition to the usual items, you'll often see more attractive items. Prices can range from low to high so there is something for everyone.

TAXES

The statewide sales tax rate is 5%, but most localities impose an additional levy on both goods and services. This is especially true for lodging where many Arizona communities, like just about everywhere else, help balance their budgets by getting every penny they can out of tourists. The amount can vary greatly in a short distance since, for example, Mesa has a different rate than Tempe. In general, hotel room taxes range from about seven to ten percent although there are several places where it can be in excess of 11.5%!

TELEPHONES

Arizona now has four area codes, three of which are in the metropolitan Phoenix area. The entire state, except for greater Phoenix, is in the 520 area code. The city of Phoenix uses the 602 area code. All communities in the West Valley (such as Glendale, Peoria, and Sun City) are in the 623 area code, while the East Valley (e.g., Mesa, Paradise Valley, Scottsdale, and Tempe) lie within area code 480. Calls from one metro Phoenix area to another are not considered toll calls and you do not have to dial "1" before the area code.

Calling into one of those three areas from the 520 area or to the 520 from any Phoenix area does require the "1" prefix and will be billed as a toll call. Many calls from a 520 exchange to another are also considered toll calls. Remember that all toll-free extensions (800, 877, and 888) are also preceded by "1".

TIME OF DAY

Although all of Arizona is on **Mountain Time** (two hours later than the east coast and one hour earlier than the west coast), things get complicated for two reasons. First of all, Arizona is one of the few places in the country that's always on Standard Time. As a result, when most places are observing Daylight Savings Time, Arizona isn't, making it one hour earlier than the rest of Mountain Time. One way to look at it is that if you're traveling in Arizona during the summer, then it's like being on Pacific Time!

The second issue is the Navajo Indian Reservation. They do observe Daylight Savings Time so the time is different on the reservation from the rest of the state during a large portion of the year. This part is especially confusing so if you plan to be on the reservations of the northeastern portion of Arizona you should consult the sidebar in the Northeast destination chapter.

TIPPING

The general "rules" of tipping, if there is such a thing, are the same in Arizona as anywhere else in the United States. Tipping is strictly a personal decision and, while I don't feel that it's appropriate to tell folks how to tip, for those of you looking for some generally accepted guidelines, it's standard to tip 15% on the total bill for meals (before tax), 10% for taxis, and $1-2 a day for maid service. And of course, if people provide exceptionally good service or go out of their way for you, a more generous tip is often given.

Keep in mind that most people who are employed in the tourist industry, specifically hotels and restaurants, don't get great salaries. They count on tips for a significant part of their income.

TRAVELERS WITH PHYSICAL DISABILITIES

If you are physically challenged you'll be glad to hear that most facilities in Arizona have your ease of access in mind. Of course, a lot of the outdoor activity for which the state is so popular can present problems. You must first realize your own limitations. I've tried to give some indication of the degree of physical abilities needed where appropriate in the destination chapters. Information and assistance for travelers with disabilities is available from the **Information Center For Individuals With Disabilities**, *Tel. 800/462-5015*, or the **Society for the Advancement of Travel for the Handicapped**, *Tel. 212/447-7284*.

If you have any doubt as to whether you are capable of visiting a particular area it is best to speak with someone at the attraction or area in advance to find out what restrictions may apply. Likewise, when making hotel reservations you should make inquiry concerning the availability of handicapped rooms and other special facilities, both of which are increasingly common.

8. SPORTS & RECREATION

Whether you participate in only an occasional recreational pursuit while on vacation or base your entire trip on them, Arizona is the ideal year-round place. From the most common of sports to the most unusual forms of outdoor recreation, you'll find it in the Grand Canyon state. General information on many of these activities is outlined in this chapter while specific listings can be found in the Sports & Recreation section of each destination chapter.

BALLOONING

If you just like watching balloons in action (that is, you're kind of a coward like me), then you should contact the various chambers of commerce where you'll be traveling to see what's happening in the way of balloon festivals. I mention some of the bigger events in Chapter 9, *Major Events*, as well as in the destination chapters. That's also true for those interested in riding in balloons. The best areas for doing so are in the Phoenix vicinity and around Sedona.

BICYCLING

Biking through Arizona's highways and back roads is a popular means of getting around during most of the year. Be aware of your level of riding experience since once you get away from the major metropolitan areas the terrain can be challenging, to say the least. Further information is available from the **Arizona Bicycle Club**, *Tel. 602/254-9572* and the **Governor's Arizona Bicycle Task Force**, *Tel. 520/627-5313*. If you are bringing your own bicycle into Arizona by air be sure to check with the airline for packaging requirements and possible restrictions.

BOATING

Arizona doesn't have a lot of natural lakes that are large enough for pleasure boating. The ones that do exist are primarily located in the White Mountains region. Man-made lakes from dam projects on the Colorado

River provide most of the boating opportunities in Arizona. **Lake Powell** in the Glen Canyon National Recreation Area and **Lake Mead** in the Lake Mead National Recreation area are two of the state's most popular and scenic boating venues. There's also dozens of marinas on the lower Colorado all the way from Bullhead City and Lake Havasu City in the north to Yuma in the south. Further information is listed in the appropriate chapters for those locations.

FISHING

In just about all instances the locations mentioned for boating are also the places that Arizonians go to fish. The most frequently found fish are trout (Native Apache, Rainbow, Brown, and brook varieties), catfish, bass, and walleye. An occasional Arctic grayling can also be found. Keep in mind that an Arizona fishing licenses is required on all state and federal lands. Licenses can be obtained in many sporting goods and other stores in areas where fishing is popular.

Further information on how to get a license and regulations concerning size and quantity limits is available from the **Arizona Game and Fish Department**, *Tel. 602/942-3000.* An exception to the fishing license requirement is Indian reservations. Although they may not require that you have a license it is still mandatory that you secure tribal permission before fishing on their lands. The larger reservations frequently have their own fish and game departments.

GOLF

Long before Arizona became one of the most popular places in the United States to visit, many avid golfers were coming here to spend some time out on the links. The climate allows year-round golfing in almost every part of the state and outstanding courses, including many designed by the greatest names in golfing, are all over the place.

In fact, Arizona may well be the golfing heart of America. Many major resort hotels have the word "golf" in their names and even those that don't often have their own course or are affiliated with one. Golfing vacation packages are commonplace. Trouble is, if one member of your party is a golf freak the rest of you may have difficulty in tearing him or her away from Arizona's beautiful courses, many of which are set against dramatic desert or mountain backdrops. A selective list of courses is contained in each destination chapter.

If you are planning on a golf vacation you might want to contact **American Golf Reservations**, *Tel. 800/GO-TRY-18.* They can make hotel package reservations at a number of the finest resorts throughout Arizona and can even confirm your tee time up to 60 days in advance. Another source of information for golf-aholics is the **Arizona Golf Association**, *Tel. 800/458-8484.*

HORSEBACK RIDING/DUDE RANCHES

Getting into the back country of Arizona is an increasingly popular method of travel. There are many stables located throughout the state and some of them are listed in the destination chapters. Less experienced riders might want to consider taking their rides on a guest ranch where the terrain is often easier.

Arizona is one of the western states with the biggest number of dude ranches, more commonly referred to these days as guest ranches. The final chapter of this book has more detailed information on many of the better ranches.

HUNTING

The single largest area for hunting game in Arizona is in the White Mountains, although other forested areas of the state do provide some opportunities as well. Among the game to be found are bears, deer, elk, Big Horn sheep and turkeys. Ducks and geese can be hunted in some of the wildlife refuges during season. Licensing requirements are as they were indicated for fishing, including the separate regulations on Indian reservations.

Contact the **Arizona Game and Fish Department**, *Tel. 602/942-3000*, for information. Also, if flying into the state be sure you fully comply with airline regulations for the transportation of firearms.

OFF-ROAD & FOUR-WHEEL DRIVE VEHICLES

The possibilities for exploring the back country of Arizona are virtually unlimited if you have the proper equipment for doing so. Recent years have seen tremendous growth in this type of recreation. Dirt roads and no road areas range from easy to the most challenging. National forest areas are among the most popular for four-wheel drive enthusiasts. Each area's Forest Supervisor can provide you with maps showing the roads and other areas that can be traveled on. Jeep rentals and jeep tours are especially popular in the Sedona area and some Indian reservations in the north offer them.

PUBLIC RECREATION LANDS

Arizona has an unusually large number of natural and historic areas that are protected and administered by either the federal or state government. These include both well-known and off-the-beaten track localities. In addition to the diverse recreational pursuits available at the majority of these locations, they include much of the best scenery in the Grand Canyon State. The majority of the areas in this list are described in greater detail in the appropriate regional destination chapter. Even if they aren't "recreation" related in the true sense, this section can serve as a convenient checklist of places that you might want to see or as a means of categorizing what you want to do. The touring region for each site is given after the name.

National Park Service (NPS) Facilities
- **Canyon de Chelly National Monument**. Northeast. Scenic and historic. Limited recreation other than hiking.
- **Casa Grande Ruins National Monument**. Phoenix. Historic. No recreation.
- **Coronado National Monument**. Southeast. Scenic and historic. Limited recreation.
- **Fort Bowie National Historic Site**. Southeast. Historic. No recreation.
- **Glen Canyon National Recreation Area**. Northeast. Scenic; diverse land and water based recreation.
- **Grand Canyon National Park**. Grand Canyon Region. Scenic.
- **Hubbell Trading Post National Historic Site**. Northeast. Historic. No recreation.
- **Navajo National Monument**. Northeast. Historic and scenic. Little recreation other than hiking.
- **Organ Pipe Cactus National Monument**. West. Scenic. Limited recreation.
- **Petrified Forest National Park**. Northeast. Scenic. Only recreation is hiking.

ANOTHER TYPE OF PARK PASSPORT

Visitors who plan on seeing lots of park service areas in Arizona as well as other states may wish to "collect" passport stamps as proof of their visit. Each National Park Service facility (at the Visitor Center) provides a place where you can stamp your passport upon entry in a manner similar to going into a foreign country. The stamp contains the name of the facility as well as the date of your visit. You can collect the stamp on any paper or book of your choosing but most people like to use the official park service passport booklet that is sold for this purpose. It looks almost like a real passport and makes a good record of your travels as well as an interesting conversation piece.

- **Pipe Spring National Monument**. Grand Canyon Region. Historic. No recreation.
- **Saguaro National Park**. Tucson. Scenic. Recreation limited to hiking and horseback riding.
- **Sunset Crater Volcanic National Monument**. Flagstaff/Sedona. Scenic. Limited recreation.
- **Tonto National Monument**. Phoenix. Historic. Only recreation is hiking.
- **Tumacacori National Historic Park**. Tucson. Historic. No recreation.
- **Tuzigoot National Monument**. Flagstaff/Sedona. Historic. No recreation.
- **Walnut Canyon National Monument**. Flagstaff/Sedona. Historic and scenic. Recreation limited to hiking.
- **Wupatki National Monument**. Flagstaff/Sedona. Historic and scenic. Limited recreation.

National Forests (US Department of Agriculture)
All national forests have extensive recreational facilities.
- **Apache-Sitgreaves National Forest**. Northeast.
- **Coconino National Forest**. Flagstaff/Sedona.
- **Coronado National Forest**. Southeast with some portions in Tucson region.
- **Kaibab National Forest**. Grand Canyon region.
- **Prescott National Forest**. Flagstaff/Sedona.
- **Tonto National Forest**. Primarily Northeast. Some portions in Phoenix region.

Bureau of Land Management (BLM) Facilities
Most BLM sites are far less developed than those administered by the National Park Service. However, among these are many beautiful areas where the sights and recreation are unencumbered by hoards of visitors. Recreational pursuits are mainly hiking and other vigorous outdoor activities. This list does not include all Arizona BLM sites.
- **Aravaipa Canyon Wilderness**. Southeast.
- **Route 66 Historic Back Country Byway**. Throughout northern Arizona.
- **San Pedro Riparian National Conservation Area**. Southeast.
- **Virgin River Canyon Recreation Management Area**. Grand Canyon region.

Among the many other federally administered areas are numerous national wildlife refuges under the jurisdiction of the Fish and Wildlife Service (mostly in the West region along or near the Colorado River), and several dams run by the Bureau of Reclamation.

NATIONAL PARK SERVICE PASSPORTS ARE GREAT

While high admission prices at many tourist attractions have always been a source of annoyance to me, I've never felt overcharged at any National Park when you consider what you get for the price. However, they have been rising dramatically in the past few years and a good way to save some money by taking advantage of one of the three National Park Service "passport" programs.

*The first is the **Golden Age Passport**, available to any United States resident age 62 or over. There is a one-time cost of $10. For that small fee you and anyone traveling with you is entitled to free admission to any area administered by the NPS as well as several other agencies. Individuals who are deemed to be permanently disabled are entitled to a free **Golden Access Passport** which has the same privileges as the Golden Age.*

*The third type of passport is available to anyone for $50 and it is good for one year from the date of issue. This **Golden Eagle Passport** also enables the holder and everyone he or she is traveling with to get into any federal fee area without additional cost. The Golden Eagle Passport can be purchased at any fee area as well as at regional offices of the Park Service or US Forest Service. The other passports are available at most fee areas.*

Passports do not cover anything other than admission. Many special activities like cave tours or facilities within the parks that are operated by private concessionaires (such as food, lodging and recreational activities) are not part of the passport program. However, passport holders (especially Golden Age/Access) may be entitled to significant discounts on tours and other activities. Be sure to inquire when at the park. Note also that "user fees" are not covered by the passports. These seem to be cropping up at many national recreation areas.

State Parks & Monuments

Arizona maintains a large system of parks throughout every corner of the state that run the gamut from historic to scenery, and they compare well with the biggest national parks. Numerous state parks are day-use areas primarily designed for resident recreation. The list that follows includes those state areas that will be of most interest to visitors. Day use entrance fees vary between $2 and $7 while camping fees run from $8-15 per night. No advance reservations are accepted for camping.

• **Alamo Lake**. West. Primarily recreational.
• **Boyce Thompson Arboretum**. Phoenix region. Educational/scenic. No recreation.
• **Catalina**. Tucson region. Primarily recreational in scenic setting.

- **Dead Horse Ranch**. Flagstaff/Sedona region. Limited recreation.
- **Lost Dutchman**. Phoenix region. Historic and scenic.
- **Fort Verde State Historic Park**. Flagstaff/Sedona region. Historic. No recreation.
- **Lake Havasu**. West. Recreational, primarily water sports.
- **Homolovi Ruins**. West. Historic/scenic. Limited recreation other than hiking.
- **Jerome State Historic Park**. Flagstaff/Sedona region. Historic. No recreation.
- **Kartchner Caverns**. Southeast. Scenic. Limited recreational facilities.
- **Lyman Lake**. Northeast. Water and other recreational pursuits.
- **Red Rock**. Flagstaff/Sedona region. Primarily scenic. Hiking and limited recreation.
- **Riordan Mansion State Historic Park**. Flagstaff/Sedona region. Historic. No recreation.
- **Slide Rock**. Flagstaff/Sedona region. Primarily recreational within a scenic area.
- **Tombstone Courthouse State Historic Park**. Southeast. Historic. No recreation.
- **Tonto Natural Bridge**. Northeast. Scenic. Recreation largely limited to hiking.
- **Tubac Presidio State Historic Park**. Tucson region. Historic. No recreation.
- **Yuma Crossing State Historic Park**. West. Historic. Limited recreation.
- **Yuma Territorial Prison State Historic Park**. West. Historic. No recreation.

RAFTING

River rafting is mainly confined to two areas in Arizona, both on the **Colorado River**. The first is in the vicinity of the Grand Canyon and the second is on the lower Colorado south of Hoover Dam to past Lake Havasu City. A selected list of operators will be found in those chapters. Any operator which I mention has met all requirements and safety protocols as established by the National Park Service. If you select another company be sure that you verify their credentials. Accidents can always happen, but rafting is considered safe when in the hands of experienced and capable guides.

It is standard operating procedure in this industry for the price to include all protective gear and transportation to and from either their office or local hotels to the raft launch site. Trips can range from an hour or two to several days. Full-day and longer trips usually include appropriate meals. Most rafting trips are of the whitewater variety. If you're hesitant about being able to handle it, here are a few things to keep in mind. Whitewater is officially designated by "class," or the degree of whitewater. Class I is the most gentle, with it becoming progressively wilder through Class V.

Some operators also offer "float" trips. These involve tame stretches of river and sometimes throw in a short segment of near-Class I level rapids. Float trips tend to be for an hour or two although some longer ones exist. When planning you're rafting adventure don't be afraid to ask the operator as many questions as you need to determine if it's the right one for you.

SKIING

While there is skiing available in Arizona it isn't found in the volume encountered in all other western states. However, winter vacationers will find good downhill skiing in the **Flagstaff** and **White Mountain** areas. The former is the best known of Arizona's ski resorts but the lesser traveled White Mountains is also a good choice. The chapters on Flagstaff and the northeast have more information. Cross-country skiing is also available.

SWIMMING

There's hardly a hotel or motel in the state of Arizona that doesn't have a pool. And if, by some chance, you happen to be in one that doesn't, there's likely to be a municipal swimming pool located nearby. Swimming in lakes is popular in the same locations that I previously described under boating.

TENNIS

Another popular diversion that's played year round in almost all places throughout Arizona, tennis courts are usually standard in the major resort properties. Non-guests are sometimes allowed to play for an additional fee. However, if you want to get in a game at more reasonable rates, then try one of the many public courts located in all major communities and even many smaller ones. There are simply too many to list. A good place to find them is in the local yellow pages. Another great source of information is the **Southwest Tennis Association**, *Tel. 602/947-9293.*

9. MAJOR EVENTS

Whether you're in a small town or a major city, the calendar of special events in Arizona is filled from January to December. It would, of course, be impossible to list all of the events here so I'll concentrate on those that have the broadest appeal. Many of these are important enough that travelers time their visits to coincide with the event. Good sources of additional event listings are magazines and newspapers in the areas you are visiting as well as local chambers of commerce.

As these are annual events, the dates will vary from year-to-year. It is best to contact the local chamber of commerce for the exact dates, times, and a complete listing of events.

JANUARY

Alpine, in the White Mountains, hosts its **Annual Sled Dog Races** early in the month. It's one of the few places outside of Alaska to hold such an event and is sure a different twist to what you would expect in Arizona.

The **Cloud's Jamboree** in Quartzsite is a well attended event featuring arts and crafts as well as displays and sales of jewelry, rocks and gems. Held the second half of the month and into early February.

The **West Valley Native American Invitational Fine Arts Festival** is held in mid-month in the Phoenix suburb of Litchfield Park. Almost 200 Native American artisans and performers take part.

FEBRUARY

The **Fountain Hills Great Fair** (Fountain Hills, east of Scottsdale during mid-February) holds a colorful fair that includes hundreds of artisans from throughout the nation, but especially the Southwest, along with a hot-air balloon race.

Flagstaff holds it's annual **Winterfest** the entire month. Dozens of events take place including skiing competitions, sleigh and snowmobile rides and skating. There's theater and art on the cultural side, snow sculpture and even special star gazing programs at the observatory.

The **O'odham Tash** in Casa Grande is a large Native American event held for three days in mid-month. Rodeo, arts and crafts, parades, and the crowning of a beauty queen are among the many events at this Pow Wow.

Gold Rush Days fill the streets of Wickenburg during mid-month as visitors enjoy rodeo, carnival events, barbecues, and gold panning, all to celebrate the town's origins in the 19th century.

Tucson's **Rodeo Parade**, a tradition for more than 70 years, is billed as the world's longest parade of it's type. A colorful event that appeals to all age groups and even those who don't care for rodeo.

MARCH

For something unusual, how about an ostrich race? Well, the **Chandler Ostrich Festival** (early in the month) attracts more than 200,000 people to see these ungainly creatures compete. There's also an arts and crafts fair, parade and carnival fun.

"Spring training" for major league baseball takes place throughout the Valley of the Sun during the entire month. The so-called **Cactus League** features the San Francisco Giants, Oakland A's, California Angels, Chicago Cubs, Colorado Rockies, San Diego Padres, Seattle Mariners, and Milwaukee Brewers.

Easter celebrations are held in several places. The best is probably in Mesa where the **Jesus the Christ Easter Pageant** is held in the Mormon Temple gardens. It's a big event that features plays and music as well as religious events. Phoenix's **Easter Pageant** is even bigger and has various events throughout the city. The Tucson area usually also offers several events. (These events may take place in April, depending upon the calendar.)

The beginning of March sees the celebration of **Territorial Days** in Tombstone. Races of old time wagons of some sort and unusual parades are among the highlights of this event.

APRIL

The **Maricopa County Fair** is held in Phoenix and features cooking contests, carnival rides, big-name entertainment and agricultural exhibits and competition.

During the middle of the month the town of Wickenburg holds its annual **Desert Caballeros Ride**, a tradition dating back more than 50 years.

Kingman hosts the **Route 66 Fun Run Weekend**, an event which celebrates the history and mystery of this legendary American road. The entire town gets involved in the fun and games.

MAY

The state's Hispanic heritage is celebrated during the **Cinco de Mayo Festival**. Events cover the better part of the state and feature Mexican style music and dancing as well as a host of food vendors. Two of the better celebrations are in Tucson and Florence.

A unique presentation of a classic Broadway show is held in Lake Havasu City with the **Showboat Musical**. The setting beneath the London Bridge couldn't be a more perfect place to watch.

It's Tombstone's chance once again to capture your imagination and take you back to the good ol' days – in this case, **Wyatt Earp Days** on the Memorial Day weekend. Besides the usual gunfights that take place in town, the streets come alive with hangings (hmm, perhaps I should rephrase that), cooking contests, 19th century fashion shows, and dancing saloon girls.

JUNE

The **Prescott Frontier Days and World's Oldest Rodeo and Parade** (whew – that's a mouthful) in early June is great for those who enjoy rodeo. I won't try to sell it to those who think it's cruel to animals. Those of you in that category can settle for the parade and other forms of entertainment that make up Frontier Days.

The town of Holbrook has an **Old West Celebration** highlighted by a marathon and bike race called the Bucket of Blood races (named after a famous saloon in town).

If you like colorful boats sailing down a beautiful blue river framed by mountains then you'll love the several **boat regattas** that are held in Lake Havasu City this month. They are among the biggest in the state.

JULY

There's hardly an Arizona town that doesn't have an old fashioned **Fourth of July** celebration including fireworks. Generally speaking the bigger the city, the bigger the event. However, it may be even more interesting to see how the celebrations are handled in some of the smaller towns, especially those on Indian reservations.

For something different try the **Gathering of Eagles** in Holbrook. This is one of the state's largest Indian art shows and can be enjoyed whether you're just looking or intend to buy.

AUGUST

The annual **Coconino County Fair** in Flagstaff starts late in the month and goes through Labor Day. It includes a demolition derby, livestock auction, ski jump show, and plenty of entertainment.

Learn something about Arizona's Hispanic heritage by taking part in the music, dancing, and abundant food fair associated with the **Fiesta de San Agustin**, patron saint of Tucson. Usually held on the 25th of the month.

SEPTEMBER

The town of Payson holds its annual **State Championship Old Time Fiddler's Contest** at the end of the month. Besides attracting the top fiddlers from all over the country, such events as clogging and buck dancing add to the fun. Not for everyone, but a good time if this type of entertainment is your cup of tea.

The **Navajo Nation Fair** in Window Rock is one of the largest Native American fairs in the nation. It features arts and crafts, concerts, racing, parades, rodeo and an authentic Pow Wow.

A fun event is held in the small lower Colorado River town of Oatman. The **Gold Camp Days and Burro Biscuit Tossing Contest** features, besides the biscuit toss, several gunfights and other reenactments. Both residents and visitors can be "arrested" for not having a beard.

The **Yavapai County Fair** in Prescott is one of the state's largest with many exhibits, a big carnival and plenty of entertainment and food booths. A highlight is the pig race.

Late in the month sees Cottonwood's **Verde River Days**, which celebrates the town's heritage in an unusual number of ways. Events can be as diverse as sand castle building, rubber duck races, archaeological tours, or who knows what else. One thing is for sure – you're going to have a real good time!

OCTOBER

The **Annual Cowboy Artists of America Exhibition** rolls into the Phoenix Art Museum. You don't have to be a connoisseur of fine art to appreciate the talents of the men and women who display their realistic western works.

Another Phoenix event this month is the **Arizona State Fair**. It combines industry oriented events such as livestock shows with entertainment for the masses in the form of concerts by nationally recognized performers, carnival rides and games and plenty of food to be sampled.

The resort town of Page holds it's annual **Air Affaire** early in the month. Besides plenty of colorful hot air balloons there are air shows featuring famous military air teams from the United States and Canada as well as displays of aircraft.

The **Butterfield Overland Stage Days** in Benson is a reenactment of the famous stage route and also features rides on old stage coaches, entertainment and dancing, a rodeo and a chili cook-off, among other events.

Even more popular are **Helldorado Days** in Tombstone, held around the middle of the month. Besides the usual gunfights, visitors are treated to a big parade, Indian entertainment, and other surprises, possibly even an 1880s fashion show.

Chile lovers will not want to miss Tucson's **La Fiesta de los Chiles**. You'll see chile prepared in more ways than you ever thought imaginable. In addition there is entertainment, musical performances and a big collection of arts and crafts booths. A hot one!

The Mexican heritage of Arizona receives attention in Phoenix during the one-day **Dia de los Muertos Festival**. Held on a traditional Mexican holiday, the festival features arts and crafts, a Mexican market, music and dance, and ceremonies honoring one's ancestors.

NOVEMBER

The holiday season gets off to an early start with the **Fiesta of Lights** at the end of the month in downtown Phoenix. It extends into December and culminates with the spectacular Electric Light Parade.

Phoenix also hosts the **Thunderbird Balloon Classic**, a very colorful event featuring participants from all around the world. A race highlights the events.

The **Native American Month Social Pow Wow** in Tucson is one of the largest gatherings of Native Americans in the nation and the public is welcome to many of the events. Among the best are shows featuring hundreds of dancers and many craft booths.

DECEMBER

Starting late in the month are a number of events connected with the **Fiesta Bowl**. Various sporting and cultural events as well as a huge parade precede the playing of the Fiesta Bowl college football game at Sun Devil Stadium in Tempe. The game itself, held on New Year's Day, matches two of the top teams in the nation, sometimes featuring the battle for the national championship.

Christmas time is a dazzling display of light throughout the Phoenix area. In Mesa, the **Christmas Lighting** features more than a half-million lights in a garden setting along with musical performances. The event covers the entire month. Tempe's **Fantasy of Lights** illuminates downtown's Mill Avenue, also for the entire month. An electric light parade, tree lighting ceremony, and fireworks add to the magic.

Another Christmas season event is Bullhead City's **Christmas Parade of Lights** held in mid-month on Lake Mojave. Hundreds of boats bedecked with ornamental lights pass by the marina area.

On the more esoteric side is the annual **Cowboy Christmas Poets Gathering** in Wickenburg. C'mon, now, a little culture won't hurt you!

Not all of December's events are Christmas related. The middle of the month sees the **Fourth Avenue Street Fair** in Tucson. Hundreds of vendors display their arts and crafts or sell all types of delicious goodies to eat. There's also entertainment provided by local musicians as well as performers from around the country.

ARIZONA STATE HOLIDAYS

In the various sight seeing sections you'll frequently read that attractions are closed on state holidays. Rather than keep repeating the list of holidays every time that's the case, I'll list them all here.

New Year's Day

Martin Luther King Jr.'s Birthday (second Monday of January)

Lincoln's Birthday (2nd Monday of February)

Washington's Birthday (3rd Monday of February)

Memorial Day (last Monday in May)

July 4th

Labor Day (1st Monday in September)

Columbus Day (2nd Monday of October)

Veterans Day (November 11th)

Thanksgiving

Christmas

10. FOOD & DRINK

ARIZONA CUISINE

I know there are a lot of readers out there who consider sampling the local cuisine to be one of the biggest attractions in traveling. I hate to disappoint you but there isn't anything that can truly be called "Arizona cuisine." The state, especially the larger cities and resort areas, has become so cosmopolitan that there isn't one type of dining that dominates. For many people that's a big advantage. You can take advantage of that diversity to pick from any type of cuisine found anywhere in the world and in a variety of budgets.

This is not to say that there aren't certain types of food that are more common in Arizona than others and seem to be the "staple" for the locals. The Southwestern influence is quite strong and so is Mexican cooking. Both are widespread throughout the state, although not to the extent found in neighboring New Mexico, for example. While New Mexico has refined both Southwestern and Mexican cuisine into a regional fare referred to as either New Mexican or Santa Fe style, Arizona does not have its own unique equivalent.

The Southwestern influence can be seen in the great number of steakhouses and barbecue restaurants that seem to be just about everywhere. Mexican is popular all over, too, but especially in the south around the Tucson area. A large percentage of Arizona's Mexican restaurants feature Sonoran style food, which is deliciously full of flavor but not particularly spicy. Again, this is a change from some other places in the southwest, notably New Mexico, where hot chile is king. Native American dishes can be found in some restaurants in Phoenix and Tucson but is primarily limited to smaller communities on Indian reservations. This style of cooking has also been influenced by Southwestern, Mexican and other tastes.

The destination chapters contain descriptions of almost 130 different restaurants. The descriptions are geared towards dinner but if a place is especially suitable for lunch I will certainly say so. The inexpensive category usually encompasses what is termed "family" dining, but also is generally good for lunch. I have tried to provide a sampling of as many different cuisines as possible to reflect the great diversity of the state's eateries. That cross section also applies to price so you'll find that the restaurants, besides being divided up by area, are classified according to the price for a dinner entree exclusive of alcoholic beverages, tip and taxes.

Fast food chains aren't mentioned but you can almost always find one for lunch in all big towns and along the major interstate highways. Likewise, nationwide restaurant chains aren't generally listed but can be found throughout Arizona, especially in the Phoenix area. I will sometimes include them in the listings if they are the best (or sometimes the only) choice in a given location. I don't pretend to be familiar with every restaurant in the state.

So when traveling, especially in smaller towns, don't hesitate to try a place simply because it may not look like what you expect a good restaurant to look like from the outside. More often than not you'll be pleasantly surprised. Then you can write and tell me about it so I can include it in the next edition. Asking hotel employees about good places to eat is almost always an excellent way to find out about unusual dining establishments.

RESTAURANT PRICE GUIDELINES

Very Expensive $31 or more
Expensive $21-30
Moderate $11-20
Inexpensive $10 or less

Prices are for the entree (but include a full course dinner where specified) and are exclusive of tax, tip and beverages.

HAVE SOME TAPAS...AND A MARGARITA

No doubt during your travels to Arizona (or just in reading about it) you'll encounter something called a tapas bar. Tapas is of Spanish origin and was transported to Mexico and on into the American southwest, including Arizona. While a literal translation is difficult it simply means finger foods in one of several forms. It can be something like chicken tenders or a mini sandwich of almost any ingredient. It's common for them to be served at a bar. In Spain they're usually consumed standing up at the bar although in Arizona you're just as likely to be seated. While you can have any alcoholic or non-alcoholic beverage with your tapas, beer or a Margarita seem to be the most popular choices.

The now nationally popular Margarita is, of course, even more favored in the Southwestern states and Arizona is no exception. The origins of the drink are clouded by dozens of conflicting tales but it seems, despite objections from Texans, that the Margarita was first concocted in Mexico. This is at least partly because the main ingredient is the Mexican "national" spirit – tequila. How it was named Margarita is also subject to conflicting stories. However, they all have something in common. It seems that there was a beautiful senorita name Margarita who was always unlucky in the game of love. And a sympathetic bartender named the drink not only for her, but for all the other men and women whose love affairs ended badly.

The authentic Margarita combines tequila, which is an extract of the desert agave plant, with either lemon or lime juice and flavored liquor, usually orange. A moistened glass is used so that salt will adhere to the inside rim. However, many Margarita lovers prefer their drink without the salt. Tequila is the name of a small town in the Mexican state of Jalisco where the agave plant is commonly found.

THE BEST OF ARIZONA DINING

Of all the selections that appear in the destination chapters, I have chosen the following ten restaurants as representative of the best in Arizona. They're listed in alphabetical order as I would have too much trouble differentiating first from second, and so on. The location and style cuisine is shown for each.

Cafe Poca Cosa *(Tucson): Mexican/Southwestern*
Capriccio's *(Tucson): Italian*
Different Point of View *(Phoenix): American and Continental*
Janos *(Tucson): Continental*
La Hacienda *(Scottsdale): Mexican*
L'Auberge de Sedona Restaurant *(Sedona): French*
Marquesa *(Scottsdale): Catalan*
Porterhouse Restaurant *(Prescott): American*
Versailles Ristorante *(Lake Havasu City): French and Italian*
Zinzibar *(Scottsdale): Mediterranean*

11. ARIZONA'S BEST PLACES TO STAY

With some of the most luxurious hotels in the world within its borders, picking out a few places as the "best" of Arizona lodging is no easy task. I've also tried to diversify the list to include a few delightful bed and breakfasts since not everyone will opt to stay at a resort and many smaller towns don't have this type of accommodation.

So, rather than rank them from one to ten, which is almost impossible to do in any case, I've simply listed them in alphabetical order and tried to include at least a few that almost everyone will be able to afford. Any list of this type is necessarily subjective, although some of the hotels in this chapter have been acknowledged by "experts" in such things to be among the very best. About half of those listed were easy choices for me; however, there are quite a few other hotels throughout Arizona that could also have been included. But a line has to be drawn somewhere in the sand, so here goes – my ten best places to stay.

ENCHANTMENT RESORT, *525 Boynton Canyon Road, Sedona. Tel. 520/282-2900, Fax 520/282-9249. Toll free reservations Tel. 800/826-4180. 162 Rooms. Rates: High season (late August to early July): $265; Low season (early July to late August): $235. American Express, Discover, MasterCard, and VISA accepted. Located about eight miles north of Sedona via AZ 89A, Dry Creek Road, and then Forest Route 152C.*

Sedona has a number of famous luxury resorts and perhaps the best known is the L'Auberge de Sedona Resort. However, while the L'Auberge is fabulous, I find this place to be more like its name – enchanting. It's located far enough from the town of Sedona for you to avoid having to battle the crowds but close enough if you want to take advantage of the town's many shopping and dining opportunities. But more important is the Enchantment Resort's spectacular setting in secluded Boynton Canyon. The exquisite natural beauty of the red rocks that have made Sedona world famous completely envelop this lovely hotel. From a distance it's hardly visible because the color of the southwestern style adobe structures blend in so well with the natural surroundings. Rather than trying to improve on mother nature at her very best, the architect has simply cooperated – guests at Enchantment do more than visit the red rock country, they live it!

The resort consists of dozens of buildings spread out over many beautifully landscaped acres. In fact, all of the guest rooms, be they one room, or one to two-bedroom suites are individual adobe casitas (literally, little houses). Within the casitas are a variety of special features including efficiencies or full kitchen units and some rooms with microwaves or refrigerators. All units have honor bars and coffee makers and a private patio where you can admire the wonderful scenery day or night. The casita interiors are beautifully furnished in colorful southwestern style and have plenty of room for you to spread out.

There are two good restaurants at the Enchantment Resort and a full service cocktail lounge. Recreational facilities are extensive. Guests can spend their leisure time in one of five beautiful heated swimming pools (a separate pool for each grouping of about 30 to 35 casitas), on the putting green or pitch and putt golf course, testing skills on one of the dozen tennis courts, or even playing croquet. There is also a large health and fitness center, sauna, and whirlpool facilities. Tennis instruction is available. You can also explore the surrounding countryside on one of the resort's rental bicycles or by partaking in a nature program conducted by local experts. The Enchantment provides a fully supervised children's activity program. Service is a hallmark of Enchantment. It's big enough to offer the amenities and services of a large resort but small enough to be personal and caring. The combination, along with the surroundings, just can't be beat.

GRAND CANYON LODGE, *Grand Canyon National Park (North Rim). Tel. 303/297-2757 for reservations, Fax 520/638-9247, direct dial Tel. 520/638-2611. 201 Rooms. Rates: $89 for cabins; $55 for motel style units. Closed from mid-October through mid-May. Most major credit cards accepted. Because of limited availability of rooms on the North Rim it is essential that you make your reservations as early as possible. Located at the end of the park road.*

This is the only lodging facility within the park on the North Rim but you won't just be settling for the "only place in town." The Grand Canyon Lodge is an excellent hotel sitting in what is perhaps the most glorious location for a hotel in the entire world. What more could you possibly ask for. I was debating whether to list the El Tovar Hotel on the South Rim since that area is more frequently visited. But it is precisely that which made me include the Grand Canyon Lodge instead. Not only do I prefer the majestic scenery afforded from the North Rim to that of the South, but it is so much less crowded on this side of the canyon. That enables you to enjoy the Grand Canyon experience even more.

Now about the hotel itself. The Lodge was constructed of limestone and massive timber beams in the 1920's and was designed by Stanley Underwood. He is known for his great work in many national parks. Among the fabulous structures that bear his signature are the unique Ahwahnee Hotel in Yosemite National Park. The Grand Canyon Lodge looks small and rather undramatic as you approach the main building. Once you step inside it gets a lot bigger because it has several sunken levels that hug the very rim of the canyon. A gigantic lounge with equally large windows offers dramatic views of the canyon. Even better is to go outside on either side of the lounge onto one of the two stone verandas. Pull up a lounge chair, soak in the sun and crisp air and feast your eyes on nature's handiwork. It simply doesn't get any better than this. The Lodge is listed on the national register of historic places and is by itself almost worth the trip to the North Rim.

Guest room accommodations come in two classes, only one of which is worth considering if you're coming here. The preferable way to go is in the higher priced cabins that spread out to the left of the main building in a thickly forested area along the canyon rim. The cabins are clustered together in groups of four and those rooms facing the rim have partial canyon views because trees usually block at least part of the sight lines. No problem, just go outside and walk a few steps if you want to see better. The cabins are spacious and charming. Each has a fireplace and high timbered ceiling. The appearance and furnishings are rustic but comfortable. There isn't any television set to spoil your evening back to nature experience. More modern but smaller motel style accommodations are in a forested area further away from the rim. While these rooms are more than satisfactory I wouldn't have included the Grand Canyon Lodge in the best list if they were the only type of accommodation available.

The Grand Canyon Lodge has a beautiful dining room with good food and service (see the listing in the Where to Eat section). Other facilities include a grocery shop, gift shop, snack bar, post office, cocktail lounge, and so forth, all within a short walk of the lodge's main building in a most delightful small village setting.

HYATT REGENCY SCOTTSDALE AT GAINEY RANCH, *7500 East Doubletree Ranch Road, Scottsdale. Tel. 480/991-3388, Fax 480/483-5550. Toll free reservations Tel. 800/233-1234. 493 Rooms. Rates: High season (mid-January to late May): $395-495; Low season (mid-June to early September): $175-225. Major credit cards accepted. Located in the Gainey Ranch development on the north side of Doubletree Ranch Road, which is off of Scottsdale Road between McCormick Parkway and Shea Boulevard.*

Here's a gorgeous resort that would make the rich and famous feel right at home. Hyatt has many world class properties in important resort destinations all over the globe and this one definitely ranks right up there with the best of them. Approached by a secluded palm-tree and cactus lined driveway, the low-rise facade of the main building with its glass fountain out front barely prepares you for what happens when you walk inside. The multi-level atrium lobby (extending one floor above and below the main level) is a gleaming dark marble accented with brass. The hotel's outstanding collection of paintings, statues, and other works of art blend perfectly with the elegant architecture. These works are mostly western or Native American themed. The back wall of the building is entirely glass, allowing a clear vista of a portion of the Hyatt's magnificent grounds. Step out the back and walk through a garden of cactus and palms along tiled paths into what is one of the most beautiful pool areas you could ever imagine.

The "water playground," as Hyatt calls it, covers 2-1/2 acres and consists of ten interconnected swimming pools, an artificial white sand beach, water slides, glass and marble water cascades and plenty of shaded lounging areas with colorful hanging flowers. The style is loosely southwestern but in some ways the whole area looks like the villa of a Roman emperor. Much of the pool area is surrounded by small, almost classic style colonnaded structures. Behind this delightful picture is a large lagoon which separates the main hotel from the immaculately landscaped golf courses. The resort covers an area of 27 acres but with the golf courses totals 560.

Guest room facilities are also first rate. Besides "regular" rooms there are 25 suites and 7 casitas to choose from. Most rooms have a patio or balcony and face the landscaped grounds or water playground. Room facilities are varied but many have honor bars, coffee makers, and refrigerators. The decor is modern southwestern – bright and cheerful colors with some desert accents, such as large cactus plants. Three excellent restaurants are on the premises. These are the elegant Golden Swan, featured in the upcoming Where to Eat section and which serves American cuisine in an open air environment (the area known as the Regency Court is sunken beneath a fountain pool); the Italian Sandolo Ristorante (complete with authentic gondola ride); and the more casual southwestern fare of the Squash Blossom. Light snacks are available poolside at the Water Garden Grill. The lobby bar has nightly live entertainment.

Fitness and recreation facilities include, besides the endless swimming pools and water slides, the Regency Spa, eight tennis courts, 27 holes of championship golf, and trails for jogging or bicycling. The outstanding concierge desk will be glad to arrange for horseback riding and other outdoor adventures in the nearby desert and mountains. Camp Hyatt is an outstanding facility for children ages three to 12 where a variety of recreational and educational programs can keep the little ones busy and happy while you're elsewhere. Finally, the hotel has a Hopi Learning Center to promote appreciation of Native American culture.

MARICOPA MANOR, *15 West Pasadena Avenue, Phoenix. Tel. 602/ 274-6302, Fax 602/266-3904. Toll free reservations Tel. 800/292-6403. 5 Rooms. Rates: High season (September 1st to May 31st): $129-229; Low season (June 1st to August 31st): $89-129, both including Continental breakfast. American Express, Diners Club, MasterCard, and VISA accepted. Located immediately to the west of Central Avenue, one block north of Camelback Road. Use either Exit 203 of I-17 or take Central Avenue north from downtown.*

Here's an intimate and exclusive bed and breakfast located in the upscale "uptown" area near the Biltmore and the famous "Camelback Corridor" of shopping and luxury resorts. Getting those things in Phoenix isn't that unusual but at the prices charged by the Maricopa it is almost unheard of. For relative bargains this takes the prize. Constructed during the late 1920's as a large Spanish mission style residence for an obviously wealthy family, the Maricopa has been completely refurbished. The two story building is surrounded by delightfully landscaped grounds that feature a variety of fruit bearing citrus trees and even some pecan trees. Your hosts might even be willing to let you pick a few samples if you ask. A pretty gazebo sits amid the tranquil scene and puts the finishing touch on what is a mini-oasis in the big city.

The luxurious and private accommodations are one-bedroom suites that are tastefully furnished with the same old-world charm that the building itself seems to project upon visitors. All rooms have coffee makers. There are also some microwaves and refrigerators for those who plan to do a little in-room snacking. While you usually don't associate a bed and breakfast inn with a lot of recreational facilities, the Maricopa Manor does boast its own heated swimming pool and a spa with whirlpool. And, with only five guest rooms, the Maricopa can and does provide a level of personalized service that even the most luxurious and expensive Valley of the Sun resorts cannot hope to match. The continental breakfast is more than ample – light eaters of the morning repast might even term it a full breakfast. For other meals you'll find that the surrounding area is loaded with restaurants of every type.

MOUNT VERNON INN, *204 North Mount Vernon Avenue, Prescott. Tel. 520/778-0886, Fax 520/778-7301. 7 Rooms. Rates: $115-125, all year including full breakfast. Discover, MasterCard, and VISA accepted. Located to the east of downtown and south of AZ 89 off of Sheldon and Montezuma Streets.*

This small inn was built at the turn of the century and consists of a main house and a few separate cottages. (The latter do not include breakfast but have full cooking facilities. Prices are within the same range.) One of the most charming bed and breakfasts you'll find anywhere, the Mount Vernon Inn is located on a pretty tree shaded block in an historic area that is brimming with fine examples of Victorian style architecture. The Inn has many distinctive features that make it visually memorable. Starting at the top is the unusual candle snuffer shaped turret with its stained glass windows that are beautifully illuminated during the evening. Below that are many interesting gables and a picturesque front porch with imposing Greek Revival style columns. The main house has a large parlor and sitting room where guests gather in the evening to read a book, watch a movie, or just talk with other guests or the friendly proprietors, Michele and Jerry Neumann. Breakfasts are a delicious affair served in a bright sunny dining room and made extra special with Mount Vernon's own coffee blend. Afternoon refreshments are also served to main house guests.

Each of the seven rooms is distinctively furnished. The Avalon, Arcana, Arcadia, and Aerie rooms are all in the main house. They feature large bay windows overlooking either historic Mount Vernon Avenue or the well known Thumb Butte rock formation. The Arcadia room may be the most beautiful of all with its delicate shades of mauve, rose, and cranberry while the Aerie is the largest and most private. It's reached by a separate stairway. All rooms have comfortable queen sized beds. The Carriage House cottage has two bedrooms, one upstairs in the loft, as well as a spacious living room. The smallest cottage is called the Doll House and it is an especially good place for a romantic getaway. Finally, the Studio House has an upstairs bedroom while the downstairs living room has a sofa that can be converted into a queen sleeper. It has two full bathrooms. The kitchens are stocked with coffee, tea, and condiments. All cottage rooms have televisions while those in the main house do not.

The Inn is close enough to the historic downtown area of Prescott that you can walk to some restaurants and shopping. The selection of both is much larger, however, if you expand the radius by taking a short ride.

PEPPERTREES BED & BREAKFAST INN, *724 East University Boulevard, Tucson. Tel. 520/622-7167, Fax 520/622-7167. Toll free reservations, Tel. 800/348-5673. 7 Rooms. Rates: High season (mid-December to mid-March): $108; Low season (June 1st to early September): $78-98; all rates include full breakfast. Discover, MasterCard, and VISA accepted. Located by the University of Arizona, west of Park Avenue.*

Situated on a quiet street that's close to everything, the Peppertrees is a stately Victorian style mansion that dates from way back in 1905. It is fronted by steps that lead up to a handsome white-fenced patio and is shaded by mature trees. The common areas as well as all of the guest rooms are furnished with family owned antiques that are perfectly suited to this style of building. The first class accommodations are either in the form of large and comfortable bedrooms (five units) or two larger and separate southwestern style guest houses ($110-150) that have separate living and sleeping areas and can easily handle four adults. The latter are located to the rear of the property and afford an even greater measure of privacy. While they are a little more expensive they can actually be the biggest bargain of all if two couples are traveling together.

A stay at Peppertrees is a wonderfully charming experience that includes a large and hearty gourmet breakfast that is personally prepared by the owner from her own cookbook of culinary delights. While you have many modern amenities (some rooms have refrigerators though not all have a telephone), this bed and breakfast is more suited to those travelers looking for a glimpse of how Tucson's earliest tourists experienced the city. Careful restoration work has made it one of the most authentic of the many turn-of-the-century homes that dot the University area. The warm and personalized service is more like what you would expect staying in the home of a friend than at a commercial establishment.

THE PHOENICIAN, *6000 East Camelback Road, Scottsdale. Tel. 480/ 941-8200, Fax 480/947-4311. Toll free reservations, Tel. 800/888-8234. 640 Rooms. Rates: High season (January 1st to mid-June): $450-3,500; Low season (mid-June to September 1st): $185-3,000. Major credit cards accepted. Located on the north side of Camelback Road and 64th Street on the Scottsdale/Phoenix border and about a half mile east of the Scottsdale Fashion Square at Scottsdale Road.*

I have to admit right up front that this is my favorite luxury resort in the Valley of the Sun. Combining truly spectacular architecture with the natural beauty of its desert and mountain surroundings, The Phoenician is a lush green oasis in the desert and the epitome of elegance. Others agree with that assessment since it is a distinguished member of the prestigious Leading Hotels of the World. If seen from overhead, The Phoenician, nestled at the base of a mountain, would appear as a small self-contained city. And that it is, covering 130 acres (250 if you count the golf courses). Some of the buildings are so spread out that guests often call the bell staff to come and pick them up by golf cart at their room to go to other parts of the resort.

The main structures are two long and gracefully curving arcs, one behind the other. A series of casitas out front arcs the opposite way and between them are breathtaking grounds and pools. It is a sight that can't be adequately described but has to be seen to be appreciated. The dazzling lobby is done in subdued earth tones, an exquisite mix of marble, glass, and metal, highlighted by rich chandeliers, big potted plants, what seem like countless fountains, and many works of art, especially statues. The theme, if there is only one, is European elegance with a distinctively southwestern flavor. The grounds, besides having greenery criss-crossed by shaded pathways, is dominated by water – seven tiered swimming pools, one of which is tiled in mother-of-pearl, and a tropical lagoon. But with all this beauty surrounding its guests, The Phoenician's hallmark is service. That's provided by more than 1,600 employees, giving the hotel a better ratio of employees to guests than many of the finest cruise ships afloat.

Most guest rooms are located in the main building but there are several separate buildings and the aforementioned casitas. Notable is the fact that even the smallest guest room features a generous 600 square feet of space, private balcony, bar, Italian marble bathroom with separate tub and shower, and use of a terry cloth robe during the winter. The decor is light shades and modern furnishings with a hint of southwestern influence. Standard rooms are more impressive for their size and range of amenities than for their beauty – not that there's anything wrong with the way they look! Rates depend upon (besides type of room) the view. These are classified as pool view, golf view, garden view, mountain view, and city view. The standard view overlooks a landscaped area by the main entrance.

Dining at The Phoenician is a big part of the experience of staying here. Southern French cuisine elegantly served in a sophisticated setting overlooking the mountains is yours at Mary Elaine's. See the Where to Eat section for more information on this fine restaurant. For Italian food with both indoor and outdoor sections (the latter overlooking the fabulous poolside gardens), there's the Terrace Dining Room. Music and dancing are available every night. What would a southwestern resort be without the famous cuisine of the region? The Phoenician's answer is Windows on the Green, delicious fare served in view of the manicured golf fairways. There's live music some evenings. Snacks, sandwiches, salads, and tropical drinks are featured at Oasis, located poolside. An outdoor misting system helps keep summer diners cooler. Other eateries include the Cafe & Ice Cream Parlor, a snack bar on the golf course, and the luxurious Lobby Tea Court where a traditional afternoon English tea with scones and pastries occurs every day. Piano music is available at the Thirsty Camel Lounge off the main lobby. For small groups (up to 16 people), the Praying Monk is a unique dining experience held in an intimate wine cellar.

Few resorts can match the Phoenician's wide array of recreation. The Tennis Garden has a dozen (mostly lit) courts as well as an automated practice court, tennis shop, private instruction, and spectator seating. Three miles of walking and jogging trails spread out over the property.

Mountain hiking and bicycling is also available. The less active might want to take a guided walking tour of the cactus garden. Golf enthusiasts can play to their hearts' content on 27 holes while others can seek out fitness through the incomparable Center for Well Being. Facilities include weight training, an aerobics and cardiovascular studio, massage and body therapy, mineral scrubs, a health food bar and fitness boutiques. You might need it after all that fine dining! Children can have their fun too through the Funician's Kids Club (ages 5 to 12) which features daily themed educational programs. Teens can volunteer to be counselors in the program. Finally, the Phoenician has several exclusive shops.

SCOTTSDALE PRINCESS, *7575 East Princess Drive, Scottsdale. Tel. 480/585-4848, Fax 480/585-0086. Toll free reservations, Tel. 800/223-1818. 651 Rooms. Rates: High season (January 1st to late May): $250-550; Low season (late May to mid-September): $155-440. Major credit cards accepted. Located in the northern part of Scottsdale about a half mile north of the intersection of Scottsdale and Bell Roads and then east about a half mile on Princess Drive.*

Few hotels in the United States have won as many awards as this top rated luxury resort situated on more than 450 acres in the northern part of Scottsdale, somewhat away from the busiest areas. Entry to the property is via a long and broad tree lined drive. The building is Mexican colonial style with graceful arches and long covered colonnades serving as walkways between sections of the hotel. It is reminiscent of an oversized hacienda. By the porte cochere of the main entrance are big fountains. The lobby, which isn't overly large, is rather simple in execution but manages to still be elegant. Many large paintings fill the walls.

The most spectacular portion of the Princess is the large area to the side of the main entrance and extending back to the main swimming pool. First is an open courtyard stepped downward to a deep pool (not for swimming). Water cascades from the top down all four sides, mesmerizing those who stop to watch for a while. Behind this on several levels are open arched walkways that look something like a Roman aqueduct. From them you can see the water garden on one side or the spectacular pool area behind it. Along the walks are several bridges that cross over artificial streams.

Over two-thirds of the Princess' rooms can be categorized as "regular," with the remaining being mostly private casitas and larger villas. The rooms are also classified according to their location (mountain view, courtyard, golf course, pool, etc.). Every room features separate sleeping and living areas, multiple telephones, honor bar, and safe. Some have refrigerators. The casitas and many suites feature fireplaces. Furnishings are southwestern style but at a level of luxury that exceeds most other Scottsdale resorts.

There are no less than seven places to dine at the Scottsdale Princess, each more wonderful than the next. Exquisite Catalan cuisine is served at the beautiful Marquesa restaurant while authentic Mexican fare highlights the menu at La Hacienda. The Grill is for the lover of steak, ribs, and seafood. All three of these outstanding dining spots are themselves award winners and each is described more in the Phoenix chapter on *Where to Eat*. Informal dining featuring southwestern dishes can be found at Las Ventanas which overlooks both the pool area and golf course. Another poolside restaurant is the Cabana Cafe and its accompanying bar. More entertainment is featured at Cazadores. This nightspot has a jazz pianist. While it's not a full service restaurant you can sample gourmet coffees, various appetizers and delicious desserts and pastries.

Finally, the unique Caballo Bayo Country Club has both indoor and patio seating, country music, a pool table and even shuffleboard. Basic "cowboy grub" is on the menu. While this isn't one of the Princess' gourmet eating establishments, it's a great place to go for a good time. Just seeing its odd assortment of old cowboy gear is worth the trip. It even has hitchin' posts just in case you arrive by horse!

The elaborate Spa and Fitness Center is smaller than the one at The Phoenician but still has everything you would expect and then some. Among the long list of facilities are massage, body wraps, trendy aroma therapy, whirlpool, sauna, Turkish steam bath, salon, complete workout equipment, racquetball, basketball, squash, and aerobics classes. The Stadium and Desert golf courses are each championship level. There are seven tennis courts including one surrounded by a 6,250 seat stadium used for major professional matches. There are three heated swimming pools and a one mile long fitness trail. Guests can also go hiking, desert bicycling, play croquet (how's that for class?), or even go fishing.

Parents of small children will appreciate the Baby Amenity Program which features, among other things a sand castle pail with shovel. Separate packages are available for children under two and a more "sophisticated" program for the mature age two to six group.

SHERATON EL CONQUISTADOR, *10000 North Oracle Road, Tucson. Tel. 520/544-5000, Fax 520/544-1222. Toll free reservations, Tel. 800/325-7832. 434 Rooms. Rates: High season (mid-January to April 30th): $85-160; Low season (June 1st to mid-September): $84. Major credit cards accepted. Located north of downtown via Oracle Road (AZ 77), about four miles north of the intersection of Ina Road.*

Perhaps Tucson's most famous "mega-resort," this spectacular 200-acre hotel sits in the foothills of the beautiful Santa Catalina mountains. Some of the best views of a desert sunset are available from the grounds and selected rooms of the El Conquistador. The low rise buildings are built in both Spanish and Native American styles of architecture in a manner that blends harmoniously with the spectacular natural surroundings. The designers have successfully managed not to interfere with nature but to actually enhance it. Spacious pool areas and landscaped grounds are also an integral part of the layout.

All of the guest rooms surround various swimming pools and courtyards in one of several larger buildings or in a more private area of luxury casitas. Minibars, private patio or balcony, coffee makers, and a safe are standard in every one of the hotel's substantially oversized rooms. Upgraded rooms and suites may have hair dryers, Jacuzzi, and a fireplace. The hotel also provides terry cloth robes to guests staying in suites. The style of the decor is what I can only term as "southwestern modern." It's not eye-catching or elegant but rather pleasing and comfortable.

An excellent variety of restaurants, possibly the best to be found at any Tucson area hotel, are located at the El Conquistador and have added to its well deserved reputation as a complete resort destination. Outstanding Mexican fare is yours at Dos Locos (see the separate listing under Where to Eat), while southwestern specialties are on order at the pretty and casual White Dove. The beef and steak lover will probably adore the Last Territory Steakhouse and Music Hall (western style entertainment is featured that is appropriate for the whole family), and continental dining comes with a view at the appropriately named La Vista. Breakfast and lunch can be taken either indoors or on the patio at the Sundance Cafe.

This resort city boasts four swimming pools, over 30 lighted tennis courts, nine racquetball courts, an excellent health and fitness center with full gym, sauna, whirlpool, aerobics and massage; and three different golf courses – a nine hole course right on the property and two 18-hole courses at the Sheraton's own country club (complimentary transportation is provided). You can also go horseback or bicycle riding. The El Conquistador has a supervised program of activities for young children. A beauty salon and classy southwestern gift shop are also located on the premises. With so much to do and see at the El Conquistador your only problem could be finding time to see the sights of Tucson!

THE WIGWAM RESORT, *300 Indian School Road, Litchfield Park. Tel. 623/935-3811, Fax 623/935-3737. Toll free reservations, Tel. 800/327-0396. 331 Rooms. Rates: High season (mid-January to late May): $330-475; Low season (late May to early September): $145-275. Major credit cards accepted. Located about 16 miles west of downtown Phoenix. Take I-10 west to Exit 128 (Litchfield Road) and proceed north about two miles.*

Here's proof that great resorts aren't confined to the Scottsdale side of the Valley of the Sun. An award winner by just about everyone's standards, the Wigwam Resort proudly proclaims itself to be "authentic

Arizona." And it is in many ways. Let's look at a bit of history first. The resort was built in 1918 for a small number of visiting executives of the Goodyear Rubber Company located in Litchfield Park. It was expanded slightly and opened to the public in 1929. Although it has grown more than a hundred-fold since then portions of the original structure are incorporated into the present resort. But it's often the little things that make this place so special – like the old fashioned swings in the garden.

The grounds are simply beautiful, without being overdone. The same holds true for indoor public areas which are elegant in a traditional sort of way. They reflect the appearance and atmosphere of a wealthy private home, something that extends to the guest rooms that are without equal in all of Arizona.

First of all they aren't just rooms...all are oversized territorial style casitas with rich wood furniture and decorated in the gentle tones of the surrounding desert. Many have gas lit fireplaces and all have in-room safes and honor bars. All have separate living and sleeping areas. The furniture, again, is like you would find in a rich residence. The mesquite woods used exclusively for fireplaces create a special aroma throughout the casitas. Native works of art adorn the walls and mantles. Whirlpools and refrigerators are standard in the upgraded units. Even the names of the classes of accommodation reflect the wonderful atmosphere of the resort – Garden Casita, Premier Casita, Courtyard Casita, Garden Suite, Fairway Suite, and Premier Suite (from lowest to highest price). To top all of this off the arrangement of the casitas is nothing short of wonderful – grouped like a small village around the gently fragrant gardens.

Dining is no less of an experience at The Wigwam with a choice of three different fine restaurants. The Arizona Kitchen which sports red brick floors, ceramic tile, and open kitchen which produces the finest in modern southwestern cuisine. The beautiful Terrace Dining Room has an elegant atmosphere and offers live entertainment and dancing every night. Continental cuisine is featured. Finally, The Grille on the Greens is a more casual restaurant serving lighter fare. For drinks and good times you can select from the Arizona Bar, Kachina Bar, or the Poolside Cabana which also serves light meals.

Recreational facilities are extensive. Three golf courses (two of which were designed by the illustrious Robert Trent Jones, Sr.) are respectively named the Gold, Blue, and Red courses. There are two swimming pools, one with water slide, water volleyball, Jacuzzi, basketball and sand volleyball courts, nine lighted tennis courts (with pro shop), and a full service health club with weight lifting equipment, sauna, and whirlpool. Other activities at The Wigwam that might interest you are skeet and trap shooting, horseback riding in the desert, croquet, ping pong, shuffleboard, or bicycling. A well organized children's program is also available.

Finally, there's an on-premise beauty salon. The Wigwam offers Modified and full American meal plans as well as numerous golf and other vacation packages.

And if there is anything you need while staying there, or any question needing an answer, just ask – the wonderful staff, many of whom are long-term employees, has helped to garner the well deserved reputation of The Wigwam.

HOTELS TO CHANGE YOUR OUTLOOK ON LIFE

Everyone knows that a stay at a great hotel can make you wake up in a better frame of mind – but completely change your outlook on life? I know you're wondering what kind of place can do that. Well, some Arizona resorts are dedicated to the view that a resort stay should result in better ways for you to manage stress, to learn how to properly relax, and even to discover your true inner self, whatever that means. This can be done at a small number of specialized resorts and at some of the more elaborate spas at the luxury resorts.

*Among the hotels that are included in my suggestions of where to stay that have programs of this type are the **Marriott Camelback Inn (The Spa)** and the **Phoenician's Center for Well Being**. The latter has a special place called the Meditation Atrium where guests can reflect in the soothing comfort of music and be inspired by the culture of Native Americans who believed in the importance of inner peace. Other hotels that you might want to consider if you're interested in this type of vacation are Tucson's **Mirval-Life in Balance**, Tel. 520/297-2271 or 800/528-4856, which is devoted solely to this premise, or the **Canyon Ranch Spa**, also in Tucson, Tel. 520/749-9000 or 800/742-9000. The latter also features more traditional physical therapy approaches to both body and mental health.*

12. PHOENIX

Now housing a population of around two million people, **Phoenix** is a big city by any standards. But unlike most large American cities, Phoenix continues to grow at a phenomenal pace that far exceeds the national growth rate. The same can be said for the local economy. The entire metropolitan area shares that growth. The contiguous suburban communities of Scottsdale, Mesa, and Tempe are all cities in their own right, and have many of their own attractions that make them of equal importance to Phoenix for the visitor.

The **Valley of the Sun**, known by locals simply as "The Valley," also includes several other communities in its 3 million population besides the big four previously mentioned. These are Avondale, Carefree, Chandler, El Mirage, Fountain Hills, Gilbert, Glendale, Goodyear, Litchfield Park, Peoria, Sun City and Sun City West, and Tolleson.

The present site of the city received its first American settlers in the late 1860s. They were mainly farmers who made use of a vast network of 500 year old Hohokam Indian irrigation ditches that provided water from the Salt River. The community received its name in 1870 from the mythical Phoenix bird that rose from its own ashes to new life. The remains of a long-dead civilization provided the rebirth in the case of this new settlement.

Over the next twenty years Phoenix became a major supply point for the Arizona Territory. Like many other boisterous frontier towns, Phoenix saw an era of lawlessness. It was made the Territorial Capital in 1889 and retained that status upon Arizona's statehood. The first major growth incentive was the completion of the Theodore Roosevelt Dam in 1911 because it assured an adequate water supply for the growing population. Further growth came on the heels of several other major water projects. The coming of the Southern Pacific Railroad in 1926 provided another important impetus. The widespread availability of air conditioning was, perhaps, just as important as the other developments in guaranteeing Phoenix's place in the sun.

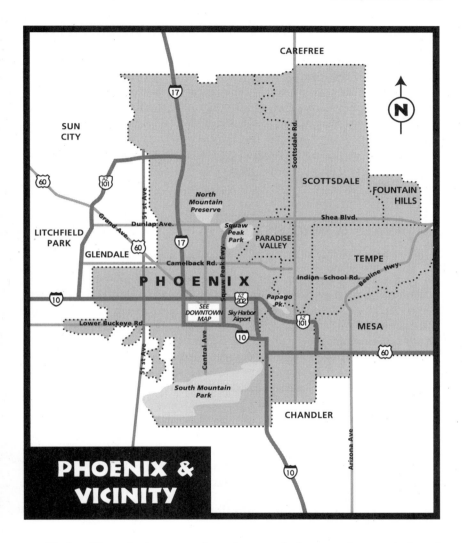

PHOENIX & VICINITY

Today Phoenix is more than the state's largest city, capital and cultural Mecca. It has a diverse industrial base (mainly electronics and other high-tech products), and is also a major agricultural shipping point. The towering skyscrapers of downtown Phoenix are an indication of its new status as the business and financial capital not only of Arizona but of the entire southwestern United States.

Geographically, Phoenix is in the Salt River Valley. The name Valley of the Sun has superseded that as its official and unofficial moniker. The city's elevation is 1,092 feet but rises to more than twice that height at

Dobbins Lookout in South Mountain Park. In fact, Phoenix is surrounded by mountains to the east and west, including the recreation filled Superstition Mountains. Other mountains provide a basis for a system of municipal and regional parks.

While the scenery around Phoenix is pleasant, it is the average of 300 sunny days per year that first made tourism a popular industry and still plays a major role. A Phoenix winter is not that much different from springtime in many parts of the country. It's no wonder, then, that Phoenix has become such a magnet for retirees from all over. But Phoenix is more than a nice climate and a big city. Retaining its mixed heritage of Native American, Hispanic and western frontier cultures, the area makes a wonderful place to vacation.

ARRIVALS & DEPARTURES

By Air

Sky Harbor International Airport has grown into a major travel destination and is an important hub for several carriers. The modern and efficient airport is also one of the most convenient to get to of any large American city – it's only about four miles from the heart of downtown Phoenix.

If you're renting a car at the airport here are some important things to know. The airport is large and has four separate terminals. While most of the major rental companies have counters in each terminal you will have to be taken to the lot by free shuttle buses provided by each company. Leave the airport via Sky Harbor Boulevard, which soon converges with I-10. Head west for downtown (use the Washington Street Exit, number 148). When you reach I-10 you're on the city's inner belt, so you have easy access to all points. See the Orientation section below for details.

Public transportation from the airport is available in a number of forms. These include, besides expensive taxis, **Courier Transportation**, *Tel. 602/232-2222*, and **SuperShuttle**, *Tel. 800/BLUE VAN*. If you want a limousine then try **Arizona Limousines, Inc.**, *Tel. 602/267-7097*. The city's bus system also has several routes going from the airport to parts of downtown but if you have a lot of luggage I wouldn't recommend this method.

By Bus

Intercity bus service is provided by **Greyhound**, which has two terminals in the Phoenix area. The first is located adjacent to Phoenix's Civic Plaza at 525 East Washington Street while the second is at 2647 West Glendale Avenue. The latter location is about five miles north of downtown and can be reached by municipal bus service or taxi.

By Car

Most visitors who come in by car will arrive by one of the two interstate highways that converge in central Phoenix. Interstate 17 provides access from the north and ends at Interstate 10 which traverses Phoenix and brings travelers from California and other points west as well as from the south and east. If coming from the east you may also find yourself arriving by US Highway 60 which is known within the Phoenix area as the Superstition Freeway. These highways, along with other controlled access routes designated as State Highways 143 and 217 all combine to form a loop around the central portion of Phoenix.

Where you should exit depends upon your destination. However, in general, Exits 194 through 198 of I-17 or Exits 144 and 145 of I-10 provide the most convenient access to downtown's major hotels and attractions.

By Train

Amtrak Thruway Buses provide connecting service from either Flagstaff or Tucson into downtown Phoenix. *Pick-up and drop-off point is 401 W. Harrison Street, about half-way between Civic Plaza and the state capitol.*

ORIENTATION

Phoenix lies mainly on the north bank of the Salt River. Both the airport and the downtown are close to the river, as is the city's historic area and most of its major cultural attractions. Several highways, including two interstates, merge in Phoenix and provide an easy means of arrival and getting around to more outlying areas.

A small highway belt system consisting of I-10 and I-17 surrounds the entire downtown area. An adjacent belt circles the airport and is comprised of I-10, AZ 143 (the Hohokam Expressway), and Loop AZ 202 (Red Mountain Freeway). I-17, also called the Black Mountain Highway, is the primary north-south artery and ends at I-10, which is the most important east-to-west route. I-10 goes by the name of Papago Freeway west of the airport and Maricopa Freeway to the east. Another important north-south artery is the Squaw Peak Parkway (AZ 51), running from the junction of I-10 and Loop 202 to the Phoenix Mountain Preserve. US 60 also heads to the east. On the west side of town, US 60 runs diagonally to the northwest and is known as Grand Avenue. The more important east-west city streets are, from south to north, Baseline Road, Van Buren Street, McDowell Road, Indian School Road, Camelback Road, Glendale Avenue and Bell Road.

Phoenix's streets are separated into quadrants which makes it easier to find any given location. Washington Street is the separation between north and south designations while Central Avenue is the border for east and west designations. Central Avenue is a major north-south street. Most north-south streets are numbered, starting from Central Avenue. Numbered Avenues are on the west side of Central while to the east the designations are 1st Street, 2nd Street, and so on. Streets running from east to west are named.

The city of Tempe lies directly to the south of Phoenix and Mesa is to the east of Tempe. Scottsdale and Paradise Valley are on Phoenix's eastern border. The methods used to designate streets within Phoenix continue into these suburbs. In most cases the borders are essentially transparent to the traveler. The visitor to Phoenix will almost certainly be going into those communities. While many interesting attractions are located within a relatively small downtown core, the Phoenix area is spread out. Public transportation is available and will be described in more detail later, but a car is almost a necessity for getting around outside of downtown.

GETTING AROUND PHOENIX

Since most of the Phoenix area is arranged in a neat grid pattern it isn't very difficult to find where you're going. But because the area is large I have arranged the sight seeing section into a number of more manageable pieces. Each will contain appropriate directions.

By Bus

Public transportation is provided by the **Valley Metro**. Their buses serve not only Phoenix itself, but Glendale, Mesa, Scottsdale and Tempe. All of the routes are clearly shown in the Bus Book which is available at any area library. Fares range from $1.25 to $1.75 depending upon whether the line is designated as local or express. Free transfers are available. Seniors ride for half a buck. Some important routes are "O" running along Central Avenue and the #3 which goes along Van Buren. Express routes to the suburbs are numbered in the 500 series.

A real bargain is the 30-cent **DASH** route serving downtown on weekdays from 6:30am to 6:00pm. It connects the Civic Plaza/Arizona Center area with the State Capitol and passes just about everything of importance in the downtown area. Also worth considering for tourists is the one day pass which offers unlimited riding privileges for only $3.00. Buses start running around 6:00am but, unfortunately, many routes cease operation as early as 6:30pm. Complete information on DASH and all bus routes is available by calling **Valley Metro**, *Tel. 602/253-5000.*

By Car

Driving in the Phoenix area is not all that bad considering the amount of people. The highway system is excellent and most streets are broad. However, you should try to avoid driving downtown (a box formed by I-

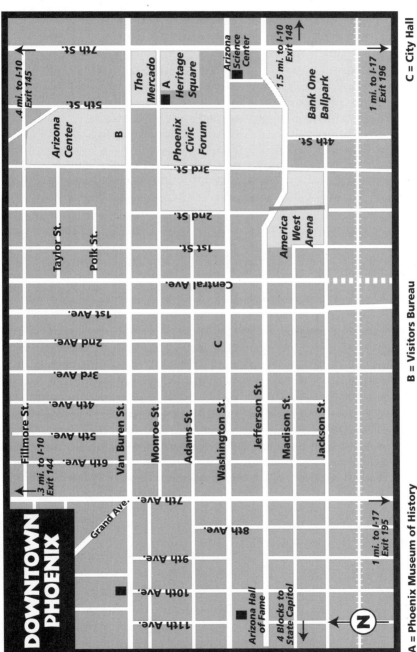

DOWNTOWN PHOENIX

A = Phoenix Museum of History   B = Visitors Bureau   C = City Hall

10 on the north and east, and I-17 on the south and west). It's also a good idea to avoid the entire freeway system during the rush hours which are between 7 and 9 in the morning and 4 to 6 in the evening.

Parking meters are used throughout Phoenix but the meters are restricted during some hours – you have to watch the signs carefully. There are many convenient parking garages throughout downtown Phoenix where you can leave your car. In the suburban communities most attractions have adequate parking facilities.

By Taxi

Many taxi companies operate throughout the Valley of the Sun but it's not an inexpensive way to get around. Some taxi companies are listed in the Practical Information section at the end of this chapter. More can be found in the Yellow Pages.

By Trolley

A fun way to get around the many resorts and shopping areas of Scottsdale is by taking **Ollie the Trollie**. The route covers 23 hotels and ten shopping centers on colorful buses made to look like an old-fashioned trolley. Call *Tel. 602/970-8130* for schedules and information.

WHERE TO STAY

The range of accommodations in the Phoenix area as to price, style and services can be mind boggling. The city has grown so much that the small "mom and pop" motels as well as simple bed and breakfast type lodging has become relatively scarce even though it can still be found. Larger high rise business hotels and sprawling luxury resorts are more numerous when compared to most comparable areas nationwide.

To make things a little easier I've divided the lodging listings into four sections – downtown Phoenix; other areas of Phoenix; suburban communities (including Scottsdale, Mesa, and Tempe); and outlying communities.

DOWNTOWN PHOENIX
Expensive

HYATT REGENCY PHOENIX, *122 North 2nd Street. Tel. 602/252-1234, Fax 602/254-9472. Toll free reservations Tel. 800/233-1234. 712 Rooms. Rates: High season (mid-September to mid-May) $179-305; Low season (mid-May to mid-September): $139-255. Major credit cards accepted. Located in the heart of downtown at the Civic Plaza.*

This imposing edifice is typical of the Hyatt chain's ultra-modern high-rise style in city centers. The huge atrium lobby is another Hyatt hallmark, with the upper floors reached by glass elevators and corridors overlooking the atrium. The exterior is a disappointingly drab color that is supposed to represent the desert. The building is dominated by a large circular portion that sits atop the middle of the building and contains a revolving restaurant. A better job is done with the softer interior colors and bright brass sculptures. Because the Hyatt is located right smack in the middle of downtown it is popular with businessmen on fancy expense accounts. That's reflected in the high price but it doesn't seem quite so high when you compare it to some of the luxury resorts. The convenience that business travelers like also applies to those on vacation.

The Hyatt's guest rooms are bright and spacious. Furnishings are modern and reflect desert hues that are soothing to the eyes. If you want to spend more you can try one of the two-level VIP suites. Depending on the room you may find a mini bar or refrigerator or coffee maker. Try to get a room on one of the upper floors since those provide the best views of the city and surrounding mountains. At night the lights of the city twinkling in the desert sky can be spectacular.

Facilities at the Hyatt are extensive and include an outdoor pool, whirlpool, and complete exercise facility. Arrangements can be made for nearby tennis and golf through the hotel's excellent concierge desk. Dining options are either an informal coffee shop or the lavish Compass, the gourmet restaurant where the view changes as Phoenix slowly circles around you (featured in the *Where to Eat* section). A full service lounge adjoins the restaurant. Another place for a friendly drink is in the atrium's Plaza Bar. You'll also find several upscale boutiques and shops.

CROWNE PLAZA PHOENIX, *100 North 1st Street. Tel. 602/257-1525, Fax 602/254-7926. Toll free reservations, Tel. 800/227-6963. 534 Rooms. Rates: High season (mid-September to mid-April) $119-179; Low season (late May to mid September) $59-109. Major credit cards accepted. Located in the heart of downtown at the corner of Adams Street near Civic Plaza and the Arizona Center.*

Another big downtown business hotel, the Crowne Plaza is a modern high-rise that lacks any real character. The lackluster appearance also extends to the public areas, which are spacious but don't do anything for me aesthetically. Nonetheless, the excellent location and better than average rooms make it worthy of being listed here. The rooms are large and airy with those on the upper floors of the 19-story building also providing some good views of the city.

Before or after a busy day you can dine in one of two restaurants or be entertained at the Crowne Plaza's lounge. There's also an outdoor swimming pool, jogging track, and exercise room where you can unwind.

Moderate

LOS OLIVOS EXECUTIVE HOTEL, *202 East McDowell Road. Tel. 602/528-9100, Fax 602/258-7259. Toll free reservations, Tel. 800/776-5560. 48 Rooms. Rates: High season (mid-January to mid-April) $79-129; Low season (mid-April to end of September) $59-79. Most major credit cards accepted. Located at Central Avenue and McDowell. Use either 7th Avenue exit of I-10 (if traveling eastbound) or 7th Street exit (westbound).*

This small property offers an unexpectedly large variety of accommodations at reasonable prices. The three story building features an attractively landscaped central courtyard which shields many of the guest rooms from the nearby center city traffic. About a third of the traditionally furnished units are one-bedroom suites complete with full kitchen for those who wish to save some more money by cooking in some meals. All rooms have coffee makers while some have microwaves or refrigerators. Other facilities include an on premise restaurant (closed on weekends since many guests at Los Olivos are business travelers), whirlpool, and two tennis courts.

PHOENIX, OUTSIDE DOWNTOWN
Very Expensive

ARIZONA BILTMORE AND VILLAS, *North 24th Street and Missouri Avenue. Tel. 602/955-6600, Fax 602/954-2548. Toll free reservations, Tel. 800/950-0086. 600 Rooms. Rates: High season (January 1st to mid-May): $330-395; Low season (mid-June to mid-September): $130-145. Major credit cards accepted. Located three blocks north of Camelback Road and the Biltmore Fashion Park shopping center. Use the Indian School Road exit of the Squaw Peak Freeway, go east to 24th Street and turn left.*

Designed by the famous architect Frank Lloyd Wright and built in the 1920s, the Arizona Biltmore was the first of the Phoenix area's modern luxury resorts. The Wright style, which creates a harmonious mixture of building and natural surroundings has been retained in the resort's recent renovations. The attractive main building looks like a large European manor house sitting amid a tranquil estate. You'll know it's something special as soon as you enter the dramatic two-story lobby with graceful marble columns flanking a comfortable seating area complete with piano.

Everywhere you'll find extensive use of stained glass and bright geometric designs to create a beautiful and serene atmosphere. The grounds are no less spectacular – beautiful gardens ablaze with color year round frame a mountain vista as guests sit on comfortable wicker lounge chairs. The pool area is another picture perfect spot with a 92-foot long water slide that comes down through two twin towers before splashing into the pool.

THE VALLEY OF THE SUN'S
SKY-HIGH HOTEL PRICES

There's no getting away from the fact that prices for lodging in the Phoenix and Scottsdale area are among the highest in the country. This is largely due to the market being dominated by the presence of so many luxury resorts. The quality is definitely world class but the downside is that, frankly, the prices are often out of reach for travelers on a more limited budget. High prices have filtered down to even the lesser quality accommodations. The result is that simple rooms in simple motels are also overpriced.

Since you're going to pay dearly for a room in the Phoenix area you might as well get something outstanding in return for your dollars. Consequently, my recommendations are heavily skewed towards the upscale side. I've tried hard to find at least a few relative bargains in the moderate and inexpensive categories. If that choice isn't sufficient then I suggest that you consider opting for one of the lower priced national chains. If you do follow this route then refer to the chain listings in Chapter 6, Planning Your Trip. You may find that even these are priced higher than you had expected. Also keep in mind that the price categories are based on the high season. Look at the rates during the low season and you'll find that even the most luxurious hotels become much more affordable. Finally, almost all of the resort properties have a variety of special package plans geared to a particular type of vacation, such as golfing, or a stay at the spa.

The Biltmore's rooms are another fine example of classic Frank Lloyd Wright style. They are large and filled with big, comfortable furniture that you can really live in. While you may be surrounded by history, every modern amenity is available to you. Besides the standard guest rooms there are 50 villa suites, one or two bedrooms with vaulted ceilings, gas fireplaces, and full kitchens. (Villa rates begin at $640 in the off season.) Special packages for golfing vacations are also available.

The aforementioned main swimming pool is only one of five on the property. Private cabanas are available. Other recreational opportunities include two 18-hole golf courses, the Biltmore Athletic club with full gymnasium and steam room, and tennis. Just walking around the 39 acres of landscaped grounds is another great way to pass the time. Several restaurants and lounges with entertainment are located within the Biltmore. Wright's is the gourmet restaurant and features Native American cuisine in an appropriate setting. There is free shuttle service to the neighboring Biltmore Fashion Park shopping center.

THE POINTE HILTON ON SOUTH MOUNTAIN, 7777 *South Pointe Parkway. Tel. 602/438-9000, Fax 602/431-6535. Toll free reservations, Tel. 800/876-4683. 638 Rooms. Rates: High season (January 1st to mid-May) $259-359; Low season (mid-May to mid-September) $119-169. Major credit cards accepted. Located to the east of the South Mountain Park near the confluence of Phoenix and Tempe. Use Exit 155 (Baseline Road) of I-10. The hotel is just west of the exit.*

This is one of three "Pointe Hiltons" located in Phoenix. All are of comparable quality and, as you will soon see, even have the same price structure. Each is a complete village in itself and comprises both hotel facilities, a residential community, and plenty of recreational facilities. The South Mountain property covers a huge 650 acres adjacent to the South Mountain Park. It's a beautiful natural setting yet is only minutes and a few short miles away from downtown. The expansive grounds are located high up enough on a hillside so as to overlook the downtown section of Phoenix.

Guest rooms are all large and furnished nicely in a modern southwestern motif. The rooms located on the upper floors of the five-story building offer the best views (if they face the city). There's also a luxury level with upgraded rooms. Every room has a coffee maker and refrigerator with honor bar. The hotel has four different restaurants ranging from coffee shop to gourmet. Another Pointe in Tyme and Rustler's Rooste are the two best, both featuring innovative American cuisine with the latter having an emphasis on western dishes.

The extensive recreational facilities include 18 holes of golf as well as a putting green, six heated swimming pools, sauna and whirlpool, ten lighted tennis courts and a racquetball facility, and a full service health and fitness center with professional massage. The South Mountain Preserve draws people who love outdoor activity, and bicycle and horseback riding in the Preserve can be arranged through the hotel. Complimentary transportation is provided to nearby areas including the Fiesta Mall.

All of the Pointe Hiltons schedule many events for their guests including cookouts and a daily manager's cocktail reception. The Pointe on South Mountain boasts an extensive program for children of all ages.

THE POINTE HILTON AT SQUAW PEAK, 7677 *North 16th Street. Tel. 602/997-2626, Fax 602/997-2391. Toll free reservations, Tel. 800/876-4693. 693 Rooms. Rates: High season (January 1st to mid-May) $229-349; Low season (mid-May to mid-September) $119-159. Major credit cards accepted. Located in Paradise Valley area about a half mile north of the intersection of Glendale Avenue and 16th Street. Use the Glendale Avenue exit of either I-17 (then head east) or Glendale Avenue exit of the Squaw Peak Parkway and go west to 16th Street.*

Consisting of many different low-rise structures, this modern resort destination manages to look "old" in a nice southwestern sort of way. The large main lobby is filled with six tall palm trees and gorgeous murals of the southwest. All of this is set amidst a background of low mountains and desert flora. Yet, despite the desert setting it is water that is at the heart of this Pointe Hilton's allure. Six swimming pools, graceful man-made waterfalls, and numerous fountains delight the senses of sight and sound. A nine acre recreation area called the Hole-in-the-Wall River Ranch is a series of interconnected pools and water slides that you can float along on a lazy day.

Guest rooms are all in the form of suites or larger casitas (little houses). They are arranged in small groups around a pool or courtyard so that it doesn't seem as if you're staying at such a large hotel. Comfortable earth-tone furnishings combine modern design with southwestern patterns. All rooms have coffee makers and refrigerators; some have microwave ovens.

The beautiful pool areas aren't the only forms of recreation available at Squaw Peak. There's golf and tennis as well as a complete spa and fitness center called Tocasierra. You can exercise on your own or take part in regularly scheduled fitness classes. Massages and facials are provided by an expert staff. Three exquisite restaurants provide a wide variety of dining options. There's the southwestern cuisine of Beside the Pointe, western and barbeque favorites at Hole-in-the-Wall, and colorful Mexican at Aunt Chilada's. If you have children you can leave them for an hour or the whole day at the hotel's professionally supervised kid's activity center. On premise shopping is available at the Rodeo Drive Retail Store and Cactus Rock General Store.

THE POINTE HILTON AT TAPATIO CLIFFS, *11111 North 7th Street. Tel. 602/866-7500, Fax 602/993-0276. Toll free reservations, Tel. 800/876-4683. 585 Rooms. Rates: High season (January 1st to mid-May) $222-259; Low season (mid-May to mid-September) $119-179. Major credit cards accepted. Located at the North Mountain Preserve. Proceed to intersection of Dunlap Avenue and 7th Street (take 7th from downtown or use Exit 207 of I-17 and head east) and then north on 7th for about two miles. Follow signs to hotel.*

Not far from the Pointe at Squaw Mountain, the Tapatio Cliffs version of this trio is similarly laid out on spacious grounds at the very foot of the mountains. Built in the style of a Spanish Mediterranean cliff side village, the atmosphere is elegant without being overdone. In fact, relaxation and enjoyment are the key words. The beautiful grounds fit in nicely with the natural surroundings with fountains, pools, and courtyards everywhere. The most elaborate outdoor area is "The Falls," a large oasis of patios and pools highlighted by a 40-foot high two-tiered waterfall and a pool that is designed to look like a grotto.

Guest accommodations are all luxurious. Each is a beautifully furnished two-room suite that offers an unusually large living space. All suites contain a wet bar and refrigerator. If you're on the lazy side, the hotel even offers a free shuttle service that goes to the restaurants and other public facilities. On the other hand, they can come in handy even if you aren't lazy because the grounds are so extensive.

Dining on French cuisine is an experience at the Different Pointe of View (nightly entertainment available in the adjacent Terrace Lounge) or at the American Pointe in Tyme Restaurant which also has a lounge. Both of these establishments are described in greater detail in the Where to Eat section. More casual dining can be found at the Waterin' Hole, a chuckwagon and western saloon style facility, and there is also the La Cabana bar and grill. On the recreational side there's golf, hiking on the mountain trails (maps available at the concierge desk), game room, and a workout center. There's also the Tocaloma Spa and Salon for massage, facial or body treatment. Horseback riding is the main event at Tapatio Cliff's Blackhawk Ranch. Finally, there's a large gift shop and sporting apparel store.

THE RITZ-CARLTON, *2401 East Camelback Road. Tel. 602/468-0700, Fax 602/468-9883. Toll free reservations, Tel. 800/241-3333. 281 Rooms. Rates: High season (mid-September to end of January) from $295; Low season (mid-June to mid-September) $155. Suites to $1500. Major credit cards accepted. Located in the fashionable Biltmore area at the intersection of Camelback Road and 24th Street.*

While many Phoenix and Scottsdale resorts will dazzle you with their lavish extravagance, the Ritz-Carlton chain is known for understated elegance. Their Phoenix property is no different. The 11-story building, which is located in an upscale development called The Esplanade, is simple but attractive. The public areas feature traditional European styling and furnishings. Beautiful chandeliers and large paintings dominate the scene. Across the street is the elegant Biltmore Fashion Park. With only 281 rooms the Ritz-Carlton is able to provide a level of personalized service that is hard to match starting with their renowned concierge staff.

That service is especially recognizable for guests who stay on the hotel's exclusive Club Level. This level has its own separate concierge staff, complimentary food and beverage tasting several times a day, and guest rooms with an exquisite marble bath, wet bar, in-room safe, and twice-daily maid service. Oh, yes, there are three telephones in each of these oversized rooms. But even the regular rooms are delightful – large and comfortable, with delicately colored accessories and rich wood furniture. All rooms have a refrigerator and safe.

Guests have three restaurants to choose from: the gourmet beef and seafood selections at The Grill, contemporary cuisine at The Restaurant, or outdoor dining at The Pool Bar & Grill. The Ritz-Carlton's famous afternoon tea is a tradition, as are the appetizers and drinks available in the Lobby Lounge. The Ritz-Carlton also has a full service fitness center, tennis court, outdoor swimming pool, and sauna. Several golf courses are within a few minutes drive.

Expensive

SHERATON CRESCENT HOTEL, *2620 West Dunlap Avenue. Tel. 602/943-8200; Fax 602/371-2856. Toll free reservations 800/423-4126. 342 Rooms. Rates: High season (mid-September to late May): $169; Low season (late May to mid-September) $119. Most major credit cards accepted. Located just east of I-17's Exit 207 (Dunlap Avenue).*

In general you can count on the Sheraton chain to provide better than average lodging in pleasant surroundings. As soon as you drive up to the Sheraton Crescent you'll know that this place goes well beyond that level. The bright white hotel building is in a modified southwestern style, stepped to look something like a pyramid. The nicely landscaped grounds are home to a large number of stately palm trees. Outside the main entrance is a statue of an Indian smoking a peace pipe. Then you enter the gracious tiled lobby with its southwestern motif rug. More statues of Indians and horses fill the interior. The spacious grounds and pool area feature many aromatic trees which fill the air with a delicious fragrance.

Among the hotel's collection of almost 350 units are a dozen suites and the Club Level on the top two floors. These rooms have upgraded furnishings, Italian marble baths, in-room safe, and balconies, among many other amenities. There's also a private concierge service, a library, and complimentary breakfast and evening cocktails. Regular rooms all have wet bars, coffee makers, and safes. Rooms are large and nicely furnished.

Charlie's Restaurant is open all day and features southwestern cuisine. Their champagne brunch is popular with guests as well as locals. For recreation and relaxation there's the swimming pool, lighted tennis courts and courts for basketball, racquetball, and squash, and a spa that includes a large fitness center with steam rooms and sauna. Sheraton guests are offered preferred tee times at several nearby golf courses.

WYNDHAM METROCENTER HOTEL, *10220 N. Metro Parkway East. Tel. 602/997-5900; Fax 602/943-6156. Toll free reservations 800/ WYNDHAM. 284 Rooms. Rates: $80-170 on weekdays and $64-139 (including breakfast) on Friday and Saturday evenings. Major credit cards accepted. Located just east of I-17, Exit 208 to 28th Drive and then south on Metro Parkway.*

The fairly upscale Wyndham chain is strong in the Phoenix area, and this modern five-story structure is one of their nicest. The nicely furnished and well equipped guest rooms that surround the pretty landscaped courtyard are quieter and more desirable than outside facing units. There are also a number of one-bedroom suites available. A good, reasonably priced restaurant is on the premises. Facilities include a swimming pool, cocktail lounge, and tennis court.

Moderate

HOMEWOOD SUITES HOTEL, *2536 W. Beryl Avenue. Tel. 602/674-8900; Fax 602/674-1004. Toll free reservations 800/CALL-HOME. 126 Rooms. Rates: High season (January through April): $152; Low season (May through December): $79-109. All rates include Continental breakfast. Most major credit cards accepted. Located along the east side of I-17 at Exit 208 (Peoria Avenue).*

Almost all of the units are very spacious one-bedroom suites with separate living area, but there are some two bedroom units for large families. It's super-modern, spanking clean and still smells almost new (having opened in late 1998). The breakfast buffet is quite ample. For other meals there are literally dozens of restaurants within a five minute radius, including several in one of the region's biggest shopping centers. The pool is inviting. Many rooms, all of which have kitchen facilities, have nice mountain views. Area transportation is provided free of charge.

MARICOPA MANOR, *15 West Pasadena Avenue. Tel. 602/274-6302, Fax 602/266-3904. Toll free reservations, Tel. 800/292-6403. 5 Rooms. Rates: High season (September 1 to May 31st): $129-229; Low season (June 1st to August 31st): $89-129, both including Continental breakfast. American Express, Diners Club, MasterCard, and Visa accepted. Located immediately to the West of Central Avenue, one block north of Camelback Road. Use either Exit 203 of I-17 or take Central Avenue north from downtown.*

The Maricopa is an intimate B&B that's conveniently located near the famous "Camelback Corridor" of luxury shops and resorts. The Spanish style mission house was built in the 1920's and has been completely refurbished. Nicely landscaped grounds surround the two-story building. With its fruit bearing citrus trees and a charming gazebo, the Maricopa is a veritable mini-oasis in the middle of the city.

The accommodations are luxurious, especially for the price. The tastefully decorated one-bedroom suites have a lot of old world charm while offering quite a few modern amenities such as coffee makers, microwaves, or refrigerators. The Maricopa even has a small swimming pool and whirlpool. The personalized service is genuinely warm. Although they only have a continental breakfast it is quite ample. Many restaurants are located within a short distance.

Selected as one of my Best Places to Stay (see Chapter 11 for more details).

PHOENIX INN, *2310 East Highland Avenue. Tel. 602/956-5221, Fax 602/468-7220. Toll free reservations, Tel. 800/956-5221. 119 Rooms. Rates: High season (January 1st to mid-April): $149-159; Low season (mid-June to early September): $79-139, all rates include a continental breakfast buffet. Major credit cards accepted. Located 2 blocks southeast of the intersection of Camelback Road and 24th Street, near the Biltmore Fashion Park.*

One of the Phoenix area's newest hotels, this attractive four-story all mini-suite facility is ideally situated near the Biltmore shopping area, close to downtown and Scottsdale attractions. The comfortably furnished suites include a large bedroom and separate sitting area. All units feature a microwave oven, refrigerator, and coffee maker. Some rooms have whirlpools. On the premises are a heated swimming pool with whirlpool and a good exercise facility. Free airport transportation is provided upon request. The Phoenix Inn doesn't have a restaurant but there are ample choices available within a radius of a mile. If you're simply looking for a nice place to spend the night without the amenities of a luxury resort, this is a good choice and a relatively good value.

Inexpensive

PARK INN, *1624 N. Black Canyon Highway. Tel. 602/269-6281, Fax 602/278-3715. Toll free reservations, Tel. 800/437-7275. 95 Rooms. Rates: $42-80, including continental breakfast. Most major credit cards accepted. Located within a short drive of downtown on the west side service road of I-17 (Black Canyon Highway) just south of the McDowell Road exit.*

A fairly standard motel facility but one of the few close to the heart of things, the Park Inn offers true budget rates without resorting to the drab cookie-cutter rooms of some inexpensive chains. Guest rooms are a bit on the small side but comfortable and modern. No swimming pool or other recreational facilities are on the premises. Restaurants are plentiful nearby – you can choose from either downtown or along the 1-17 corridor to the north of the motel.

SCOTTSDALE & OTHER SUBURBS
Very Expensive
THE BOULDERS, *34631 North Tom Darlington Drive, Carefree. Tel. 480/488-9009, Fax 480/488-4118. 160 Rooms. Rates: High season (Christmas to early May): $425-545; Low season (late May through June and most of September): $175-255. Closed during July and August. Most major credit cards accepted. Located in Carefree, just north of Scottsdale. Take Scottsdale Road north to Carefree Highway and then just north to hotel entrance.*

The Boulders is one of the premier golf resorts in Arizona and in the nation. A big percentage of the guests who stay here probably spend a sizable portion of their time out on the links; however, I'll include it as a recommended place to stay because of its high general quality. Even if you don't play golf a stay at The Boulders can certainly be a relaxing experience either for its own sake or as a way to unwind after doing the sights.

It's located a bit out of the way from most of the action in the Valley of the Sun, but that can sometimes be as much as an advantage as a disadvantage. The name of the hotel comes from its natural setting amid massive boulders of granite strewn about by the dozens as if they were the playthings of a race of giants. It is also in the foothills of the surrounding mountains in a typically Sonoran desert environment. If it weren't a private resort the terrain would probably at least be a state park. The golf course which surrounds the resort's buildings is laid out around the boulders.

Guest rooms are located in many widely scattered small adobe style buildings. The rooms are spacious and all feature patios and fireplaces. There are also one and two-bedroom "vacation homes" available for rental on a daily or monthly basis (up to $750 per day).

The Boulders features several different restaurants as well as a cafeteria for those on the go (maybe it's for those who can't afford to eat any better after paying the room rate). A variety of cuisines are available. The Latilla Dining Room is The Boulders' most exclusive restaurant and features a health conscious menu. Golf is by no means the only source of recreation at The Boulders. There are two swimming pools, a health facility with steamroom, sauna, whirlpool, and exercise equipment. Six tennis courts are also on the premises. The golf courses encompass a total of 36 holes. Some unusual activities which are arranged for guests include balloon and bi-plane rides. If you're not that adventurous then try one of their guided hiking experiences. Located within a two minute drive from The Boulders (or accessible by walkway through the golf course) is El Pedregal, a unique outdoor marketplace with designer boutiques, restaurants, and entertainment.

THE BUTTES, *2000 Westcourt Way, Tempe. Tel. 480/225-9000, Fax 480/438-8622. 353 Rooms. Rates: High season (February 1st to late May): $245-265; Low season (late May to mid-September): $99. Major credit cards accepted. Located near the intersection of 48th Street and Broadway. Use I-10 Exit 153 (Broadway) if traveling westbound, or Exit 152 (48th Street) if going eastbound. The Hohokam Expressway also runs into 48th Street near the hotel.*

Billing itself as "Arizona's natural wonder," The Buttes is a beautiful and impressive mountaintop resort that covers 25 acres and provides a panoramic vista of Phoenix and the Valley of the Sun. The most striking feature of the modernistic architecture is how it conforms to the natural terrain of the mountain, almost as if it was carved out of it. Broad pathways and steps connect the terraced levels from the main building at the top to the exquisite pool and garden areas beneath it. Perhaps the best view is from behind the large windows of the gracefully curving rear of the main building. Desert landscaping reminds guests that you are, despite the water, in an arid climate. A mountain stream and waterfall tumble effortlessly into one of the mountainside swimming pools.

The Buttes' guest rooms are large, airy and modern. They have just undergone a thorough renovation even though it wasn't really needed. Keeping up with the Jones's is a passion in the pricier Valley establishments. All feature coffee makers and bars. For recreation there are two heated swimming pools, one with water slide, exercise facility, whirlpool and sauna, four lighted tennis courts and two for volleyball. Professional massage services are also available. For dining with a view try the delicious Top of the Rock Restaurant which features American cuisine and has nightly entertainment. There's also a more casual restaurant on the premises. Plenty of activities for children are offered in a well supervised program.

DOUBLETREE PARADISE VALLEY RESORT, *5401 North Scottsdale Road, Scottsdale. Tel. 480/947-5400, Fax 480/946-1524. Toll free reservations, Tel. 800/222-8733. 387 Rooms. Rates: High season (January 1st to mid-June): $145-255; Low season (mid-June to mid-September): $55-99. Major credit cards accepted. Located just north of Chapparal Road (about a half mile north of Camelback Road).*

The Doubletree Resort's nearly 400 guest rooms are all in two-story buildings so you can imagine that this place is quite spread out. As you approach the front entrance you'll be struck by the brilliant life size statue of three wild horses galloping triumphantly in a large fountain of splashing water. The impressive grounds of the Doubletree are a desert oasis of green lawns, abundant trees, and water gushing fountains, all done in a simple style. The result is an atmosphere of tranquillity. There's also a small garden with the vegetation of the Sonoran Desert. The only problem with this setup is that it can sometimes be confusing to find your way from the lobby to your room in the maze of buildings and walkways. I have a good sense of direction and sometimes found myself wandering around, momentarily lost.

The resort's guest rooms are large and cheerfully decorated, although they aren't anything special. All rooms have an honor bar and coffee maker. Some have refrigerators. Facilities include courts for tennis and racquetball, health spa with massage facility, two swimming pools, sauna, and whirlpool. There is a dining room and more casual coffee shop style facility and a full service bar. The main restaurant is a beautiful skylit room bedecked with flowers. And since this is a Doubletree property, don't you dare forget to try their world famous cookies!

HOSPITALITY SUITE RESORT, *409 N. Scottsdale Road, Scottsdale. Tel. 480/949-5115; Fax 480/941-8014. Toll free reservations 800/445-5115. 210 Rooms. Rates: High season (January through April): $199; Low season (May through December): $109-139. All rates include full breakfast. Major credit cards accepted. Located near the southern edge of Scottsdale between McDowell and Highway 99 (Scottsdale Road exit).*

This almost qualifies under the Expensive category, especially for Scottsdale. Maybe because it isn't in the *most* fashionable part of town. Nevertheless, the Hospitality Suite Resort is a good value. There are a wide variety of accommodations including studios, suites and two-bedroom units. All have plenty of space, full cooking facilities and lovely decor. The majority of rooms have a view of the pretty pool area. There's an on-premises restaurant. Recreational facilities include, in addition to the pool, shuffleboard and horseshoe area, ping-pong and pool tables, and an area for barbecue mavens to do their thing. Not a resort in the sense of the word usually associated with Scottsdale but more than good enough for those looking for a comfortable place to stay without having to take a loan out.

SOUTHWEST INN AT EAGLE MOUNTAIN, *9800 N. Summer Hill Boulevard, Fountain Hills. Tel. 480/816-3000; Fax 480/816-3090. Toll free reservations 800/992-8083. 42 Rooms. Rates: High season (mid-December through May): $295-445; Low season (June through mid-December): $100-345. All rates include Continental breakfast. American Express, Discover, MasterCard and VISA accepted. Located approximately 9 miles east of Scottsdale Road and then south via Eagle Mountain Parkway.*

This small and exclusive property is for the discriminating traveler who wants luxury and privacy yet still wants to be relatively close to the attractions and activities of the city. Each of the units is either a suite or oversized bedroom beautifully decorated with authentic southwestern flair. In the mountain foothills, every room either has a great mountain vista or almost as dramatic views of the exquisitely manicured fairways of the Golf Club at Eagle Mountain.

Among the in-room amenities are a warm fireplace, oversized whirlpool tub and private patio (all units) as well as a comfortable and attractive sitting area (most units). The property has a swimming pool, although the golf course will definitely attract some guests as will the hiking opportunities in the surrounding hills. The Continental breakfast almost qualifies as a full meal. The only complaint that I have with the Southwest Inn is the lack of an on-premise restaurant for dinner. Some are within a short drive but you have to go all the way into Scottsdale to have a wide selection.

HYATT REGENCY SCOTTSDALE AT GAINEY RANCH, *7500 East Doubletree Ranch Road, Scottsdale. Tel. 480/991-3388, Fax 480/483-5550. Toll free reservations, Tel. 800/233-1234. 493 Rooms. Rates: High season (mid-January to late May): $395-495; Low season (mid-June to early September): $175-225. Major credit cards accepted. Located in the Gainey Ranch development on the north side of Doubletree Ranch Road, which is off of Scottsdale Road between McCormick Parkway and Shea Boulevard.*

With so many glorious Hyatt properties all over the world I still can feel comfortable stating that this is one of the best. It most certainly is among the most beautiful. A long driveway with tall palm trees brings you up to the main entrance with its unusual fountains. Inside is a multi-level atrium in gleaming marble and brass and housing an outstanding collection of paintings, statues, and other works of art, mostly with western or Native American themes. Behind the lobby is another world – magnificent grounds of cactus and palms laced by tiled walkways and leading to a stunning area of pools that Hyatt refers to as the "water playground."

That 2-1/2 acre area has ten interconnected swimming pools, sand beach, cascading waters and shaded lounging areas with colorful hanging plants and flowers. A classic colonnade frames much of the area which is separated from the hotel's golf courses by a man-made lagoon. The thoughtfully decorated rooms mostly have a patio or balcony that overlooks the impressive grounds. The Hyatt has three excellent restaurants or you can just get a light snack poolside. There is live entertainment at the lobby bar. Other recreational pursuits besides swimming and golf include tennis, jogging and bicycling trails, and a complete health and fitness center. For the children, the hotel has a Camp Hyatt program of activities.

Selected as one of my Best Places to Stay (see Chapter 11 for more details).

MARRIOTT'S CAMELBACK INN RESORT, *5402 East Lincoln Drive, Paradise Valley. Tel. 480/948-1700, Fax 480/483-3424. Toll free reservations, Tel. 800/228-9290 (Marriott central reservations) or Tel. 800/ 242-2635 (direct to hotel). 423 Rooms. Rates: High season (January 1st to mid-June): $255-429; Low season (mid-June to mid-September): $109-305. Major credit cards accepted. Located just east of Scottsdale (about 3 miles west of Scottsdale Road) and to the immediate west of the intersection of Lincoln Drive and Tatum Boulevard. Directly behind Camelback Mountain.*

This is a famous Phoenix area classic resort, one of the first to follow the trend that was begun by the Arizona Biltmore. The Camelback Inn has been in the business of pampering and pleasing its guests for more than 60 years. Beautifully situated across the road from the base of famous Camelback Mountain on 125 landscaped acres (excluding the golf courses), the Camelback Inn is, in many ways, the essence of the comfortable southwestern style that attracts so many people.

The grounds combine both desert landscaping and flowers bursting with color, all interconnected by winding paths. The lobby of the main building is neither big nor brassy or architecturally inspiring – but simply warm and cozy. White brick walls, wagon-wheel chandeliers, a glowing fireplace, and comfortable furniture all provide a livable touch of home. Two things best exemplify what the Camelback is all about – the hotel's clock towers which proudly display their motto of "where time stands still," and the numerous citrus trees on the grounds which guests are allowed to pick fruit from.

All of Camelback's guest rooms are pueblo style adobe casitas that boast beautiful views, private landscaped entryway and patio or balcony, huge beds covered with spreads in Native American geometric patterns, and all the modern amenities. Beyond the standard casitas are various types of suites whose luxury level goes all the way up to having a private swimming pool!

The resort has several different places to eat. Chaparral serves continental cuisine in an elegant setting with refined service (featured in the *Where to Eat* section), Navajo cooks up regional Arizona dishes, and lighter fare can be found at Dromedary's. In addition, there is a grille located at the golf course for those who don't want to take the time to leave their favorite place, a poolside lounge, and the Kokopelli Cafe which is a gourmet coffee house.

The Camelback has long been known as a place for diverse recreational pursuits. The Padre and Indian Bend courses offer 36 holes of golf; in addition there is a putting green, pitch-and-putt course, and a fully equipped golf shop. There are eight tennis courts (five lit) with instruction available, volleyball and shuffleboard, bike trails, nature walks through the desert and mountain foothills, and three inviting swimming pools. For children there is a large playground and supervised activities. Finally, The Spa is a 27,000 square foot European style health spa that has, in addition to its own pool, Turkish steam baths, sauna, body wraps and facials, hydrotherapy, professional massage, and even your own personal trainer if you desire. The finishing touch on The Spa is its specialty restaurant that serves up only healthy dishes.

MARRIOTT'S MOUNTAIN SHADOWS RESORT, *5641 East Lincoln Drive, Paradise Valley. Tel. 480/948-711, Fax 480/951-5430. Toll free reservations, Tel. 800/228-9290. 338 Rooms. Rates: High season (January 1st to the end of April): $249-365; Low season (May 1st to mid-September): $89-105. Major credit cards accepted. Located immediately to the east of Marriott's Camelback Inn. See directions above.*

Named for the fact that it is located in the shadow of Camelback Mountain, the Mountain Shadows is a stone's throw from the Camelback Inn. While this is definitely the poorer cousin of the two, it is, nonetheless, a first rate establishment. In many ways its a downsized version of the former – fewer rooms, smaller grounds, and somewhat less extensive facilities. The beautiful grounds make use of the area's natural vegetation.

The low-rise buildings house spacious guest rooms with either patio or balcony. The decor is typically southwestern and some of the amenities are honor bars (all rooms), coffee makers, and refrigerators. Some rooms even have their own private whirlpools. Mountain Shadows has two restaurants and a coffee shop, all with cocktail service. For the golf nut there are 54 holes in addition to a driving range and putting green. Other facilities are the eight lighted tennis courts, three swimming pools, several whirlpools, a sauna, and fitness center. There's also a playground for your small children. Free transportation is provided within a two-mile radius which includes some of Scottsdale's best shopping.

THE PHOENICIAN, *6000 East Camelback Road, Scottsdale. Tel. 480/941-8200, Fax 480/947-4311. Toll free reservations, Tel. 800/888-8234. 640 Rooms. Rates: High season (January 1st to mid-June): $450-3,500; Low season (mid-June to September 1st): $185-3,000. Major credit cards accepted. Located on the north side of Camelback Road and 64th Street on the Scottsdale/Phoenix border and about a mile east of the Scottsdale Fashion Square at Scottsdale Road.*

The Phoenician is my favorite Valley of the Sun luxury resort and the reason is the dramatic and beautiful way that it combines imaginative architecture with the natural features of the surrounding desert landscape. It is a lush oasis in the desert and the epitome of elegance and has earned membership in the exclusive and prestigious Leading Hotels of the World. The 250-acre resort city has two large arc-shaped buildings forming one half of a near semi-circle, with the swimming pools, gardens, and casita style accommodations forming the other half. It is a dazzling sight.

Equally eye catching is the hotel lobby with its marble, glass, and metal accentuated by chandeliers, plants, fountains, and many statues and other works of art. It is European on the one hand and southwestern on the other. The combination is unique and inviting. Despite the brilliant architecture and beautiful grounds, the Phoenician is just as well known for its fine service. With more than 1,600 employees it has a better ratio of employees to guests than many of the finest cruise ships.

To say that the guest rooms are oversized is putting it mildly. The smallest measures a generous 600 square feet. All have a private balcony and a host of convenient amenities. Light earth tone shades dominate. The furnishings may not be as elegant as you might expect from such a place but perhaps the decorators wanted to make you feel more comfortable and that the rooms most certainly are.

Choices for both dining and recreation seem almost limitless. Five eating places run the gamut of tastes and luxury. One restaurant, Mary Elaine's, is featured in the Where to Eat section. The Phoenician has 12 tennis courts (as well as pro shop, automated practice court, and professional instruction), miles of walking and jogging trails, golf, and the amazing health and fitness facility known as the Center for Well Being. This is almost like a resort within a resort. The Funician's Kid Club has an excellent program for children ages five through 12.

Selected as one of my Best Places to Stay (see Chapter 11 for more details).

RADISSON RESORT, *7171 North Scottsdale Road, Scottsdale. Tel. 480/ 991-3800, Fax 480/948-9843. Toll free reservations, Tel. 800/333-3333. 318 Rooms. Rates: High season (mid-January to mid-May): $165-375; Low season (mid-May to mid-September): $79-295. Most major credit cards accepted. Located just north of the intersection of Indian Bend Road on the east side of Scottsdale Road.*

While this doesn't quite measure up to, say the Hyatt at Gainey, The Phoenician, or the soon to be described Scottsdale Princess, the Radisson is still a beautiful first class facility and I'd be proud to say that I stayed here. Covering several acres of lushly landscaped grounds, the Radisson has just about every facility and amenity that you could want or think of. Consisting of one and two-story buildings, the Radisson has an understated kind of elegance. The main lobby is surrounded by glass that looks out on the beautiful pool area and grounds. Rich light colored wood interspersed with off-white paint creates an eye catching combination that is reminiscent of an earlier era but without losing a contemporary look at the same time.

The Radisson's guest rooms (there are also suites and multi-level villas) are all beautifully appointed and spacious. Every room boasts oversized beds, large sitting area, honor bar, plenty of closet space, and a balcony or patio that overlooks the immaculately maintained grounds and its colorful gardens. For your dining pleasure try either Andre's, serving all three meals in a beautiful room overlooking one of the swimming pools; or the Oasis, a French patisserie located in the lobby and serving a tantalizing array of fresh baked-on-the-premises pastries and desserts along with a selection of gourmet coffees from around the world. Yum-yum, my mouth is watering!

The lobby lounge, called Markers, boasts a clubhouse decor and atmosphere where you can just relax and enjoy your beverage by the fireplace, shoot a game of pool, or try your hand at backgammon. Other facilities at the Radisson are 21 tennis courts (with professional instruction available); health center with exercise area, steamroom, sauna, and spa with massage; four swimming pools, and 36 holes of golf.

REGAL McCORMICK RANCH, *7401 North Scottsdale Road, Scottsdale. Tel. 480/948-5050, Fax 480/991-5572. Toll free reservations, Tel. 800/243-1332. 125 Rooms. Rates: High season (early January to end of April): $201-285; Low season (late June to mid-September): $135-215. Major credit cards accepted. Located about a mile north of the intersection of Indian Bend Road.*

One of Scottsdale's smaller and more intimate resorts, the Regal McCormick sits astride a beautiful lake in full view of the surrounding mountains. Combine that setting and the fewer guests with the spacious and beautiful landscaped grounds and you have what can almost seem to be your very own private resort. What could be a better way to relax then to rent a canoe, sailboat or paddleboat and take a spin out on the lake? Every one of the large and attractively furnished rooms features an honor bar and either a balcony or patio overlooking the lake or mountains.

When it comes time to eat you can choose from either Diamondback's Bar & Grill (entertainment during the high season) or the award-winning southwestern cuisine of the Piñon Grill. Recreation is yours at one of four swimming pools, whirlpool, shuffleboard, lighted tennis courts, and 36 holes of golf.

RENAISSANCE COTTONWOODS RESORT, *6160 North Scottsdale Road, Scottsdale. Tel. 480/991-1414, Fax 480/951-3350. Toll free reservations, Tel. 800/HOTELS-1. 171 Rooms. Rates: High season (mid-December to January 31st): $255-325; Low season (early June to mid-September): $119-179, both including Continental Breakfast. Major credit cards accepted. Located at the intersection of McDonald Drive.*

Located adjacent to the unique environment of the Borgata shopping center, this relatively small resort is set on an expansive and immaculately landscaped 25-acre site near the base of Camelback Mountain. There is a small "main" building containing the restaurant but the heart of the property is the grouping of guest accommodations in a village setting amid green lawns, towering palm trees, and succulent cactus plants.

Every guest room is wonderfully decorated in soft pastel tones reminiscent of the desert and features southwestern style wood-beamed ceilings. There's also an honor bar in each room. Over a hundred of the Cottonwood's 171 rooms are casita style and contain their own outdoor hot tub on the private patio. These casitas, referred to as either Tucson or Phoenix Suites, are authentic looking whitewashed houses with brown painted trim in Native American style.

Excellent southwestern cuisine is featured at the attractive Moriah Restaurant. There's also a small lounge in the lobby and an adjacent patio courtyard that have fabulous sunset views. There are two heated swimming pools, whirlpool, and water aerobic classes. Other recreational pursuits include shuffleboard, a putting green (plenty of golf courses are located within minutes), croquet, and ping pong. Two of the resort's four tennis courts are lighted. The best recreation at the Cottonwoods to my way of thinking is the par course, a jogging trail surrounded by desert cactus.

SCOTTSDALE PLAZA RESORT, *7200 North Scottsdale Road, Scottsdale. Tel. 480/948-5000, Fax 480/948-0513. Toll free reservations, Tel. 800/832-2025. 404 Rooms. Rates: High season (January 1st to end of April): $270-545; Low season (late May to mid-September): $135-350. Major credit cards accepted. Located at the intersection of Indian Bend Road.*

Covering 40 beautifully landscaped acres, the Spanish-Mediterranean style Scottsdale Plaza is like a refined residential community. A member of the prestigious Leading Hotels of the World, it's rich terra cotta Mission tile floors, stone fountains, and arched walkways, welcome you to a relaxed and peaceful environment. Restaurants, lounges, and conference facilities are in the main building while all guest rooms are located in a Mediterranean village-like setting around carefully groomed courtyards. A large section of the ceiling in the main building is painted to resemble the unparalleled beauty of the southwestern desert sky.

About half of the Plaza's rooms are referred to as "deluxe," while almost another quarter are villa suites. The remainder are much more pricey patio and bi-level suites as well as six Executive Lodge Suites (the latter starting at around $1,500 per night). So let's talk about the deluxe rooms and villa suites. Each has a full-service bar, many have coffee makers, microwaves, refrigerators, or whirlpool. Most have a gas-lit fireplace. All rooms have finely detailed decor that is in keeping with the Spanish style architectural theme. Patios or balconies provide views of the grounds or, in some locations, the nearby mountains.

Remington's restaurant features regional cuisine and there is nightly live jazz in the adjacent lounge. J.D.'s Lounge recreates the atmosphere of an English sports pub, while the Garden Court offers more traditional fare, including a bountiful breakfast buffet and Sunday brunch. There's also a poolside bar and another in the main lobby. Five imaginatively designed pools are interspersed throughout the guest room buildings area. There's a completely equipped health club or you can opt for one of three outdoor spas. Tennis courts and an excellent pro shop will delight racquet enthusiasts (the Plaza also has indoor racquetball). Golf is available nearby and the hotel's concierge will be glad to arrange a tee time or any other sort of outdoor activity for you.

SCOTTSDALE PRINCESS, *7575 East Princess Drive, Scottsdale. Tel. 480/585-4848, Fax 480/585-0086. Toll free reservations, Tel. 800/223-1818. 651 Rooms. Rates: High season (January 1st to late May): $250-550; Low season (late May to September): $155-440. Major credit cards accepted. Located in the northern part of Scottsdale about a half mile north of the intersection of Scottsdale and Bell Roads and then east about a half mile on Princess Drive.*

One of the most awarded hotel properties in the United States, the Scottsdale Princess is a 450 acre luxury resort in northern Scottsdale, away from the busiest areas. The graceful Mexican colonial structure is surrounded by immaculate grounds that feature large fountains and an amazing water cascade as well as bridges and arches that cross over river like waterways.

There are first class rooms as well as private casitas and even larger villas. Some have fantastic views of the surrounding mountain and desert while others look out on the grounds. Every room has a separate living and sleeping area, two or more telephones, and many other amenities. Casitas and suites feature fireplaces. The furnishings are southwestern but are more luxurious than is usually the case with this genre.

The Princess has seven different restaurants, many of them award winners and several of which are featured in the Where to Eat section. They range from home style western cooking to exquisite Catalan and the atmosphere ranges from the most elegant to cook-out casual. On the recreational side, the Scottsdale Princess can match any resort in the state with its elaborate Spa and Fitness Cener, golf courses, seven tennis courts (and stadium), three swimming pools, fitness and hiking trails, and much more.

Selected as one of my Best Places to Stay (see Chapter 11 for more details).

THE WIGWAM RESORT, *300 Indian School Road, Litchfield Park. Tel. 623/935-8111, Fax 623/935-3737. Toll free reservations, Tel. 800/327-0396. 331 Rooms. Rates: High season (mid-January to late May): $330-475; Low season (Late May to early September): $145-275. Major credit cards accepted. Located about 16 miles west of downtown Phoenix. Take I-10 west to Exit 128 (Litchfield Road) and proceed north about two miles.*

The "authentic Arizona" resort was founded in 1918 as a small lodge for executives of the Goodyear Rubber Company. It soon expanded and was opened to the general public in 1929. Since then it has gone through many expansions and remodelings although portions of the original structure are incorporated into the present resort. The combination of old and new and little touches make the Wigwam extra special.

The grounds and public areas reflect the atmosphere of a wealthy private home. No resort has guest rooms that are better than here. Each "room" is an oversized territorial style casita with rich furniture and wonderful desert tone decor. Many have gas fireplaces and all have in-room safes and honor bars. They all feature separate living and sleeping areas and have Native American works of arts adorning the walls and mantles. Upgraded units have whirlpools and refrigerators. The casitas are grouped in small numbers into cozy villages that surround a gently fragrant garden.

The Wigwam has three wonderful restaurants with Continental, southwestern, and casual American fare. The best of the eateries is the famous Arizona Kitchen. Details can be found in the *Where to Eat* section. There are several lounges and poolside bars. Recreation includes three golf courses, two swimming pools, water volleyball, jacuzzi, basketball, sand volleyball, and nine tennis courts. There is also a full service health club. Many activities are available at the Wigwam. You might want to try skeet and trap shooting, horseback riding in the desert, or bicycling. Outstanding service is another tradition of the Wigwam with many of their employees having devoted a lifetime to taking care of guests.

Selected as one of my Best Places to Stay (see Chapter 11 for more details).

Expensive

ARIZONA GOLF RESORT, *425 South Power Road, Mesa. Tel. 480/832-3202, Fax 480/981-0151. Toll free reservations, Tel. 800/528-8282. 186 Rooms. Rates: High season (mid-January to mid-May): $130-190; Low season (mid-May to October 31st): $79-130. Most major credit cards accepted. Located about 1-1/4 miles north of Exit 188 of the Superstition Freeway (US 60), the Power Road exit.*

No, you don't *have* to play golf to stay at the Arizona Golf Resort although its 18 hole course is considered among the tops in the Valley. There are plenty of other good reasons to stay here including its good location and lower rates than some of the more famous area resorts. The grounds are large and nicely landscaped although nothing so dramatic as is the case in many of the Phoenix/Scottsdale luxury hotels.

Guest rooms are a nice size and attractive. They're furnished in a bright, modern style and feature coffee makers, refrigerators, microwave ovens and safes in all rooms. The resort also has a number of two-bedroom suites with full kitchens (up to $390 during the high season).

About a third of the non-suite rooms are efficiencies with kitchenette. On the premises are a decent restaurant as well as a coffee shop and snack bar for those looking for more informality or who just want to eat less. Besides the golf course which gives the hotel its name there is a putting green, large heated swimming pool, whirlpools, four tennis courts, basketball and volleyball court, and fitness center.

One of the most popular recreational activities is to use one of the hotel's bicycles to take a ride in the nearby desert and mountain parks.

DOBSON RANCH INN RESORT, *1666 S. Dobson Road, Mesa. Tel. 480/831-7000; Fax 480/831-7000. Toll free reservations 800/528-1234. 213 Rooms. Rates: High season (January through May): $87-185; Low season (June through December): $75-160). All rates include full breakfast. Major credit cards accepted. Located just off of exit 177 of the Superstition Freeway (US 60).*

Excellent accommodations and an equally impressive value if you can snag a rate at the lower end of the scale. Some suites and units with whirlpools. Swimming pool. When it comes time to dining you can opt for either the family style cafe or go for the on-premise steakhouse called Monti's at the Ranch. Easy access to the entire Phoenix area via the adjacent freeway.

SCOTTSDALE PIMA INN, *7330 N. Pima Road, Scottsdale. Tel. 480/948-3800; Fax 480/443-3374. Toll free reservations 800/344-0262. 127 Rooms. Rates: High season (mid-December through May): $85-154; Low season (June through mid-December): $52-112. All rates include Continental breakfast. Major credit cards accepted. Located off of Scottsdale Road via Indian Bend Road east to Pima Road and then north to inn.*

Comfortable, clean and attractively furnished units located within a couple of minutes of the heart of Scottsdale. About half of the units have kitchen facilities. Amenities include a swimming pool, spa and sauna as well as a fitness center. There is a lounge on the premises, but no restaurant. A good choice of eating places is located within a short drive.

TWIN PALMS HOTEL, *225 E. Apache Boulevard, Tempe. Tel. 480/967-9431; Fax 480/968-1877. Toll free reservations 800/367-0835. 140 Rooms. Rates: High season (October through April): $89-169; Low season (May through September): $69-89. Major credit cards accepted. Located adjacent to Arizona State University just east of the intersection with Mill Avenue.*

A modern, seven-story high motor inn facility with better than average room size, decor and comfort. And that's probably as much as you could ask for at these prices. The only recreational facility is a swimming pool. The on-premise restaurant is open 24 hours and is a good place for breakfast. Dinners are very reasonably priced and will be adequate if you're tired and don't want to travel for a restaurant.

Moderate

FIESTA INN, *2100 S. Priest Drive, Tempe. Tel. 480/967-1441, Fax 480/ 967-0224. Toll free reservations, Tel. 800/528-6481. 270 Rooms. Rates: $77-155. Major credit cards accepted. Located south of the Priest Road and Broadway intersection. Use Exit 152 (eastbound) or 153 (westbound) of I-10 and take Broadway east to Priest Road.*

This large motor-inn style facility (but nicer than most of that genre) offers much better than average room accommodations with extensive resort-style facilities at a fraction of the cost of a luxury resort. So if you don't need the little extras and pampering that you can pay so dearly for, consider the Fiesta. The three-story building is attractive but especially pretty is the big pool area that is surrounded by colorful flowers and shady trees. The comfortable guest rooms are modern and large. Each features a coffee maker and mini-refrigerator. A decent restaurant is on the premises and it has a full service cocktail lounge. Besides the heated swimming pool guests can take advantage of the sauna and whirlpool, three lighted tennis courts and trails for both jogging and bicycles.

SCOTTSDALE'S FIFTH AVENUE INN, *6935 5th Avenue, Scottsdale. Tel. 480/994-9461, Fax 480/947-1695. Toll free reservations, Tel. 800/528-7396. 92 Rooms. Rates: High season (mid-January to April 30th): $82-87; Low season (May 1st to September 30th): $43-48, both including Continental breakfast. Major credit cards accepted. Located in central Scottsdale just east of the intersection of Scottsdale and Indian School Roads.*

Considering the prime location that the Fifth Avenue Inn has it's kind of surprising to see it priced so moderately. Most of that can be explained by the fact that this motel is a place to sleep rather than a full service resort. However, that doesn't seem to stop some lodging establishments from gouging the public. If you're going to make shopping an important component of your Scottsdale stay then this could be the ideal place to spend a few nights because it is right in the middle of one of Scottsdale's best shopping areas.

The three story building is of typical motor inn design and is nothing to rave about. However, the rooms are quite large and comfortably furnished. A few rooms have refrigerators. There's a heated swimming pool. The Fifth Avenue Inn serves a nice continental breakfast. Although there isn't any restaurant on the premises you'll find plenty of good places to eat within a short radius, including a few within walking distance.

TEMPE MISSION PALMS HOTEL, *600 East 5th Street, Tempe. Tel. 480/894-1400, Fax 480/968-7677. Toll free reservations, Tel. 800/894-1400. 303 Rooms. Rates: High season (January 1st to late May): $169; Low season (Late May through Labor Day): $69. Major credit cards accepted. Located in downtown Tempe just east of Mill Avenue and a little north of University Drive. From downtown Phoenix take Van Buren Street east into Mill Avenue or the*

Hohokam Expressway to the University Drive exit. Within a few blocks of Arizona State University.

Here's another decent value considering what you'll get. This attractive hotel doesn't quite make the luxury class that I've been describing in so many listings but I don't think most people would find anything to complain about. The location is right in the center of Tempe, putting it within walking distance of a wide variety of restaurants, night spots, and shopping as well as the University. The four-floor building is an attractive colonial mission style and contains a pretty central courtyard filled with tall palm trees and the hotel's outdoor recreation and dining areas.

The guest rooms are oversized and tastefully decorated in a colorful and cheerful southwestern motif. All rooms have coffee makers and some have refrigerators. When you get hungry the Arches Restaurant serves ample portions of excellent southwestern cuisine. Or, for just a snack try the great hors d'oeuvres featured at the Monster Bar. Recreational facilities include a beautiful large heated swimming pool, two lighted tennis courts, sauna and whirlpool, and an exercise facility. Several golf courses are located within a short drive.

OUTLYING COMMUNITIES

The places listed here are located further from Phoenix than any in the preceding section and require that you have a car to reach them. However, they do provide a possible alternative to the problem of high prices in and around Phoenix.

Moderate

WINDMILL INN AT SUN CITY WEST, *12545 West Bell Road, Surprise. Tel. 623/583-0133, Fax 623/583-8366. Toll free reservations, Tel 800/547-4747. 127 Rooms. Rates: High season (February 1st to mid-April): $107-155; Low season (June 1st to September 30th): $63-117. Most major credit cards accepted. Located northwest of Phoenix near Sun City retirement community. Take Bell Road exit of I-17 (Exit 15) and proceed west or, coming from downtown Phoenix, use Exit 11 of I-17 and take US 60 (Grand Avenue) to Bell Road and turn right.*

This new property offers excellent accommodations and personal service at a far lower price than you'll generally find in the resort communities on the east side of the Valley. Southwestern architecture, of course, is enhanced by an attractive tiled patio and courtyard area graced with trees and fountains. Another big fountain sits near the lake that fronts the grounds of the hotel. Every guest unit is a spacious and attractively decorated two-room suite that features a wet bar as well as a microwave oven. A swimming pool and whirlpool constitute the on-premise recreational facilities. However, something unusual that the

Windmill Inn offers its guests is complimentary use of a bicycle. With its location on the edge of the Valley of the Sun's built up areas, you should be able to find plenty of places to roam about. Another nice touch for a quiet evening is their lending library featuring best sellers.

The only significant drawback to the Windmill Inn is its lack of an on-premise restaurant. While that isn't a problem in many areas, it can be here since the number and variety of nearby establishments is more limited than in most parts of the Phoenix area. The nearest big concentration of restaurants is about five miles east on Bell Road.

Inexpensive

CLOUD NINE MOTEL, *1699 East Ash Street, Globe. Tel. 520/425-5741, Fax 520/425-5741. 80 Rooms. Rates: $55-89, all year. Major credit cards accepted. Located about 70 miles from the Phoenix metropolitan area via US 60. It is approximately a mile east of the center of Globe.*

This is a modest two story motor inn with some multiple bedroom units. All rooms have a refrigerator and some feature a Jacuzzi. On the premises are a heated swimming pool and whirlpool. Several restaurants are located close by. Because it is 87 miles to downtown Phoenix (about 1-1/2 hours driving time) this motel might not appeal to many readers who are looking to save a little money on lodging. However, since it is located at the end of the Apache Trail it can be a good choice if you are going to be taking that excursion from Phoenix. In that regard it may be able to at least save you one night of higher prices.

PHOENIX GOODYEAR INN (Member of Best Western), *1100 North Litchfield Road, Goodyear. Tel. 623/932-3210, Fax 623/932-3210. Toll free reservations, Tel. 800/528-1234. 85 Rooms. Rates: $69-89. Major credit cards accepted. Located about 15 miles from downtown Phoenix via I-10 westbound to Exit 128 and then south approximately one mile.*

This is a standard one and two-story motel property in modified southwestern style with in-room coffee makers. Some rooms have microwaves or refrigerators. Deluxe suites and efficiencies available at slightly higher rates. The motel has a heated swimming pool surrounded by nicely manicured wide open green spaces. There's also an on premise coffee shop serving decent food. It also has cocktail service.

For additional alternatives to Phoenix lodging refer to the listings under Wickenburg in Chapter 18. Wickenburg is a little more than 50 miles from Phoenix.

CAMPING & RV SITES
• **Desert Edge RV Park**, *22623 N. Black Canyon Highway. Tel. 602/869-7021*
• **Monte Vista Village**, *8865 East Baseline Road, Mesa. Tel. 480/833-2223*

• **North Phoenix RV Park**, *2550 W. Louise Drive. Tel. 602/581-6022*
• **Paradise RV Resort**, *10950 W. Union Hills Drive, Sun City. Tel. 623/977-0344*
• **Seven Springs**, *Farm Route 24, Carefree. Tel. 480/445-7253*

WHERE TO EAT
DOWNTOWN PHOENIX
Moderate

COMPASS RESTAURANT, *122 N. 2nd Street, in the Hyatt Regency Phoenix. Tel. 602/252-1234. Major credit cards accepted. Lunch and dinner served daily; Sunday brunch. Dress code. Reservations are suggested.*

Located in the circular 24th floor of the hotel and providing a panoramic view of Phoenix and the Valley of the Sun as it slowly revolves, the Compass breaks from my usual disappointment with the cuisine in high-altitude revolving restaurants – the food here is excellent and the service is equally high quality. The cuisine is American and the large menu contains a wide variety of entrees that is sure to have something to please your palate. Cocktail service and lounge. Many health-conscious menu items. Sophisticated atmosphere that is good for couples rather than families with small children. The Sunday brunch is superb.

EDDIE'S GRILL, *4747 North 7th Street, Tel. 602/241-1188. American Express, Diners Club, MasterCard and Visa accepted. Open for lunch Monday through Friday and every day for dinner.*

Eddie's has become one of the Valley's most popular eateries. Its success is based on the premise that people like good food in an inviting atmosphere. The place has both. Chef Eddie Matney is known for taking ordinary foods such as chicken or beef and bringing them into the category of unique taste by adding unusual ingredients and seasonings. The decor is modern and lively but the latter is not to the point of distraction sometimes found in contemporary restaurants. Eddie's brings new meaning to the term New American Cuisine. They also have an excellent collection in their wine cellar.

THE OYSTER GRILL, *455 North 3rd Street, in the Arizona Center, Tel. 602/252-6767. Most major credit cards accepted. Lunch and dinner served daily.*

You can select from a big variety of fish and seafood items expertly prepared in a very bright and cheerful atmosphere. Guests can chose between a traditional restaurant dining room or sit at the counter in the huge oyster bar. The latter is usually quicker and the highly informal atmosphere is quite conducive to enjoying the excellent cuisine. Alcoholic beverages are served.

Inexpensive
   THE DOWNTOWN DELI, *130 North Central Avenue, Tel. 602/258-3069. Most major credit cards accepted. Breakfast and lunch are served from Monday through Friday.*

Here's the ideal place for lunch while on your downtown Phoenix walking tour. This restaurant is in keeping with the best traditions of a "New York" style deli – something I can't quite define but which, if you're familiar with the genre, you'll immediately recognize. Featured are humongous sandwiches that you'll have trouble getting your mouth around. Or you can opt to nosh on a hot dog if you're not so hungry. It's also the kind of place where kids will enjoy themselves.

OTHER AREAS OF PHOENIX
Very Expensive
   CHRISTOPHER'S, *2398 East Camelback Road, Tel. 602/957-3214. Most major credit cards accepted. Lunch and dinner served daily; Sunday brunch. Dress code. Reservations are suggested.*

This is actually two restaurants in one – Christopher's and Christopher's Bistro. The Bistro is a more informal place and has continental as well as American cuisine. Christopher's concentrates on French cuisine. Either way the dining experience is outstanding as owner and chef Christopher Gross has built a national and even international reputation. The place has won many awards and has been selected as one of the 50 best restaurants by the sophisticated readers of *Conde Nast* magazine. The desserts are exceptional. The wine list is extensive and the staff will gladly help you select the one that is just right for your meal.
   DIFFERENT POINT OF VIEW, *11111 North 7th Street, in the Pointe Hilton at Tapatio Cliffs, Tel. 602/863-0912. Major credit cards accepted. Dinner and Sunday brunch only. Dress code. Reservations are required.*

For absolutely superb continental and American cuisine in a refined and elegant setting, you couldn't do much better than this unusually named restaurant. (Virtually all of the restaurants in the three Pointe Hiltons have names geared to the word "point" and most are rather whimsical which, given the formal nature of many of them, strikes some people as being kind of odd.) The dining room has an excellent view of the city from its hillside vantage point and impeccable service is a highlight of the evening. Choose from such imaginative appetizers as grilled Portabello mushroom or sauteed shrimp with escargot. Some of the mouth watering main courses are the unusual macadamia crusted ono or the grilled rack of lamb served with mushrooms in a delicate madeira wine sauce. Your waiter will be glad to help you select one of the many wines available from the large cellar. There's nightly entertainment in the adjacent Terrace Lounge.

MORTON'S OF CHICAGO, *2501 East Camelback Road, Tel. 602/955-9577. Most major credit cards accepted. Dinner served nightly. Reservations are suggested.*

Located at the upscale Shops at the Esplanade, Morton's is known for its excellent prime-aged steaks and fresh seafood including whole Maine lobster. The atmosphere is that of a luxurious and comfortable private club and the service is attentive and efficient. Morton's has an extensive wine list that has won awards from local experts.

Expensive

AVANTI, *2728 East Thomas Road, Tel. 602/956-0900. Most major credit cards accepted. Lunch and dinner served daily. Reservations are suggested.*

Another award winning restaurant, Avanti specializes in Italian cuisine but also has a good selection of continental dishes. Wonderful appetizers include calamari fritti and fresh mussels. Salads and pasta dishes are served in generous portions. Among the more notable main courses are delicious veal and paella. Traditional Italian desserts such as tiramisu and tartufo gelato round out the meal. The subdued atmosphere is very pleasant. Outdoor dining is available during most of the year. Avanti is quite popular with visiting celebrities as well as the Phoenix elite, yet it maintains a casual approach. There is dancing and a piano bar, a full service lounge, and a children's menu.

DURANT'S RESTAURANT, *2611 North Central Avenue, Tel. 602/264-5967. Most major credit cards accepted. Lunch and dinner served daily. Reservations are suggested.*

One of the better known steak houses in the Phoenix area, Durant's also has a wide selection of fresh seafood, including Florida Stone Crabs, but is probably best known for their now famous three pound "Porterhouse Club" steak. Mesquite style cooking dominates both the steak and fish menu. Prices are for a three course dinner (excluding dessert). Try the out of this world roasted garlic mashed potatoes for a delicious change from the ordinary. Full service lounge.

THE FISH MARKET RESTAURANT, *1720 East Camelback Road, Tel. 602/277-3474. Most major credit cards accepted. Lunch and dinner served daily. Reservations are suggested.*

One of the favorite places for fish and seafood amongst Phoenix area residents, the Fish Market features a wide selection of fresh items that can change from day to day based upon availability of the best catch. The menu is printed each day on that basis. The restaurant has two dining rooms. Downstairs is the more casual Fish Market while those who desire more formal surroundings can go upstairs to the Top of the Market. The name of the restaurant comes from their takeout fish department where many locals come to shop. Cocktails are served in both dining rooms and a children's menu is available.

LA FONTANELLA, *4231 East Indian School Road, Tel. 602/955-1213. Most major credit cards accepted. Lunch served Monday through Friday; dinner nightly.*

Great Northern Italian cuisine along with a few tempting Sicilian style delights have been attracting crowds at La Fontanella. The rack of lamb is probably the best in town but such dishes as seafood Diablo, Ossobuco and Calamari Romana are all excellent choices. The dining room is attractive. In the style of an Italian villa, it is elegant without being overbearing. There's a good selection of wines.

POINTE IN TYME RESTAURANT, *11111 North 7th Street, in the Pointe Hilton at Tapatio Cliffs, Tel. 602/866-6348. Major credit cards accepted. Breakfast, lunch, and dinner served daily. Reservations are suggested.*

A beautiful dining room decorated in turn-of-the-century motif makes for a warm and welcoming environment to enjoy delicious American cuisine featuring charbroiled steaks and a good selection of seafood. The bar is known for its extensive selection of quality ales. Full cocktail service is available and the adjoining lounge has live entertainment nightly. Although the atmosphere is grown-up children are given their own menu featuring less sophisticated dishes. For a similar dining experience you can also try **Another Point In Tyme Restaurant**. The latter is located in the Pointe Hilton on South Mountain.

STEAMED BLUES, *4843 North 8th Place, Tel. 602/966-2722. Major credit cards accepted. Lunch and dinner served daily.*

Fresh east-coast seafood doesn't have the widespread appeal out west that it does in other parts of the nation, but crab lovers can find the real McCoy at Steamed Blues – delicious blue crab and other Chesapeake Bay style seafood, expertly prepared and efficiently served in a casual but attractive setting. Cocktails and entertainment are both part of the fun.

T-BONE STEAKHOUSE, *10037 South 19th Avenue, Tel. 602/276-0945. Most major credit cards accepted. Lunch and dinner served daily.*

On a hillside overlooking the city (great views of the twinkling lights during the evening), the T-Bone is one of many fine steakhouses in the Phoenix area. This one has won awards over the past decade from local newspapers. The atmosphere is a rustic old west and casual enough for you to feel comfortable dressed in jeans. Even children will like the style although the clientele sees a large proportion of young adults. Cocktail service is available.

VINCENT GUERITHAULT, *3930 E. Camelback Road. Tel. 602/224-0225. American Express, Diners Club, MasterCard and VISA accepted. Lunch and dinner served daily (except for Sunday from Memorial Day weekend through October). Dress code. Reservations are suggested.*

Exquisite cuisine and service in a romantic atmosphere makes this a definite plus if you're looking for chic dining. The menu features many French entrees as well as southwestern. In fact, there's a definite hint of both in whatever you order – a most appealing and flavorful combination despite the seeming mismatch when you hear "southwestern French." Most entrees are mesquite grilled. Especially delicious is the rack of lamb or pheasant. Fresh lobster is also a culinary highlight at Vincent's place.

Moderate

BEEF EATERS RESTAURANT, *300 West Camelback Road, Tel. 602/264-3838. Major credit cards accepted. Lunch and dinner served daily; Sunday brunch.*

Charcoal broiling is the key to the delicious fare at Beef Eaters. The name says it all – this place is for the beef lover, although there are several fish and seafood items to chose from including sole, salmon and shrimp dishes. The prime New York steaks, filet mignon and barbecued ribs are the true stars, however. Specialties of the house (for two) are carved tableside and include Chateaubriand and roasted rack of lamb. The decor is that of an English Tudor style manor house and is highlighted by beamed ceiling and pewter chandeliers. Artwork adorns the walls. This contrasts with the greenery and extensive use of daylight to brighten the dining room. Full service lounge. Children's menu. Beef Eaters also has live entertainment.

BILL JOHNSON'S BIG APPLE, *3757 East Van Buren Street, Tel. 602/275-2107. Most major credit cards accepted. Breakfast, lunch, and dinner served daily. Other locations at 3101 West Indian School Road and 19810 North 19th Avenue.*

Beginning modestly nearly 40 years ago, Bill Johnson's has grown to become one of the most popular eateries in the Valley of the Sun. Big breakfast spreads and overstuffed sandwiches make it a good choice for either breakfast or lunch (without spending your dinner budget). In the evening the Big Apple has a good selection of entrees to choose from with the emphasis on barbecue prepared dishes. Children's menu. Cocktails.

GREEKFEST, *1940 East Camelback Road, Tel. 602/265-2990. Most major credit cards accepted. Breakfast, lunch, and dinner served daily.*

I try to balance my restaurant selections by listing my own favorites as well as establishments that have been recognized for their excellence. In the case of Greekfest I have to admit my own infatuation with Greek cuisine. While the Greeks are known for great dining you won't find too many Greek restaurants in Phoenix so this place is something special. A family operation that uses their own tried and true recipes, Greekfest is especially known for its unique appetizers (almost a meal in themselves). Main dishes are also generous. Traditional Greek desserts such as baklava are delicious. The warm and cozy surroundings are reminiscent of a sun drenched Greek isle. Enjoyable eating at a reasonable price.

HUNTER STEAKHOUSE, *2511 West Indian School Road, Tel. 602/ 266-2471. American Express, Diners Club, MasterCard, and Visa accepted. Lunch and dinner served daily. Reservations are suggested. Other locations at 10237 Metro Parkway and 3102 East Camelback Road.*

Practically an Arizona institution for more than 20 years, the Hunter Steakhouse offers casual dining in a warm and attractive setting. Their prime rib is award winning, the result of a day long slow roasting process. Deliciously tender steaks and a good selection of fish and poultry are also available. Combination dishes are a good choice. Hunter uses top of the line corn-fed Midwestern beef and serves it up lean. Tasty appetizers such as crab stuffed mushrooms or onion rings with zucchini are a great introduction to the entrees. Try the double sauced twin filets. If you like chicken then go for the citrus ginger chicken. Grilled swordfish or shrimp scampi are also excellent choices. Cocktails are served and there is a children's menu.

MACAYO'S, *4001 North Central Avenue and several other locations. Tel. 602/264-6141. Major credit cards accepted. Lunch and dinner served daily.*

It's been fifty years since the first Macayo's location opened its doors and they're still pleasing everyone with their big selection of colorful and tasty Sonoran dishes. The service is friendly and the atmosphere is sunny and pleasant. Although Mexican food tends to be high in the fat and cholesterol categories, Macayo does offer a number of lighter dishes. Full cocktail service is available but Macayo's is probably best known for its stupendous Margaritas.

MUELLER'S BLACK FOREST INN, *4441 North Buckboard Trail, Tel. 602/970-3504. Most major credit cards accepted. Lunch served Monday through Friday; dinner nightly except Sunday.*

Good German food is on the difficult side to find in Phoenix but an exception is this excellent restaurant decorated in the casual and comfortable style of a German country inn. Generous portions of delicious dishes such as braised pork shanks (schweinehaxen) and rabbit stew (hassenpfeffer) are available along with such traditional Teutonic favorites as sauerbratten and wienerschnitzel. Great strudels highlight the dessert menu. What would a German restaurant be without a huge selection of beer? Well, Mueller's has that in addition to an extensive list of wines and other drinks.

NOLA'S MEXICAN RESTAURANT, *2590 East Camelback Road, in the Biltmore Fashion Park, Tel. 602/957-8393. American Express, MasterCard, and Visa accepted. Lunch and dinner served daily.*

With its location in the Biltmore Fashion Park the first surprise for diners at Nola's is the relatively low prices. Second comes the big variety of entrees that represent several different regional styles of Mexican cooking served in the chef's own unique manner. For lunch why not give one of the several combinations of soup and sandwiches a try. Cocktails.

PASTA SERGIO'S, *1904 East Camelback Road, Tel. 602/277-2782. Most major credit cards accepted. Lunch and dinner served daily.*

Take it from "Dr. Pasta" (also known as co-owner Tony Caputo), home style pasta and other Italian dishes don't get much better than this. You won't find anything fancy here either in the atmosphere or in the presentation. But if you're simply looking for ample portions of great pasta served in a friendly and home-like environment, you will more than get your money's worth at Pasta Sergio's. Beer and wine are served. A good family restaurant if you're looking for a place to go with children.

PRONTO RISTORANTI, *3950 East Campbell Avenue, Tel. 602/956-4049. Major credit cards accepted. Lunch and dinner served daily except Sunday. Reservations are suggested.*

Fine European style service combines with an attractive atmosphere and authentic regional Italian cuisine to make for a most memorable dining experience. The antipasti (calamari fritti, for example), and the pasta are great for starters but you'll be thrilled with the entrees such as medallions of filet mignon, stuffed veal and sauteed pork loin. The bruschetta, which is grilled Italian bread topped with fresh tomatoes, basil and garlic, is out of this world and you'll keep asking for more. Entertainment. Beer and wine.

STOCKYARDS RESTAURANT, *5001 East Washington Street, Tel. 602/273-7378. Most major credit cards accepted. Lunch served Monday through Friday, dinner nightly.*

For steaks and prime ribs at moderate prices you'll be hard pressed to do any better than the Stockyards. Almost an Arizona legend, this restaurant goes back to the city's early days (in fact, it used to overlook a cattle feed lot) and the decor still reflects the heritage of the 1890's. The elegant interior features rich wood paneling, western pictures, and rich dark brown leather booths surrounding hard wood tables. Perhaps the most beautiful part of the decor is the original 1889 bar made of hand-carved cherry-stained mahogany. The food is equally satisfying – choice prime ribs of beef and aged on the premises as well as fish, chicken, and pork entrees. Children's menu available. There's also a separate cocktail lounge.

Inexpensive

ED DEBEVIC'S SHORT ORDERS DELUXE, *2102 East Highland Avenue, Tel. 602/956-2760. Most major credit cards accepted. Lunch and dinner served daily.*

When dinner time rolls around it's not easy to find a place where you can have a meal for under $10. But you can here, in the atmosphere of a 1950's roadside diner. The menu matches the theme with its emphasis on burgers, chili dishes, and sandwiches. But the portions are ample and the taste surprisingly good. Ed also serves cocktails and there's even entertainment on Friday and Saturday. Children's menu. A good place to go to when you want your meal to be fun!

THE EGGERY, *4326 East Cactus Road, Tel. 602/953-2342. American Express, MasterCard, and Visa accepted. Breakfast and Lunch served daily. Other locations at 5109 North 44th Street and 50 East Camelback Road.*

When you're looking for a real nice place to have breakfast or lunch, look no further than The Eggery. Great omelettes for breakfast or lunch are a staple but the menu goes well beyond that with a big selection of soups, salads, and sandwiches. In addition to the locations listed above, another similar chain called The Good Egg has two locations in Phoenix and another two in Scottsdale. They also serve only breakfast and lunch.

SCOTTSDALE & OTHER SUBURBS
Very Expensive

THE CHAPARRAL, *5402 E. Lincoln Drive, Scottsdale, in Marriott's Camelback Resort. Tel. 480/962-4652. Major credit cards accepted. Dinner served nightly. Dress code. Reservations are suggested.*

Casually elegant, like almost everything at the Camelback Resort, the staff at the Chaparral serve up delicious continental cuisine and serve it with attention to detail and flair. While I don't have any particular bone to pick with this place I do think that it is too pricey – it's one of the most expensive in the Valley, but the dining experience itself is a small notch below the top dining experiences. Tableside cocktail service and separate lounge.

GOLDEN SWAN, *7500 East Doubletree Road, Scottsdale, in the Hyatt Regency at Gainey Ranch, Tel. 480/991-3388. Major credit cards accepted. Dinner served nightly; also Sunday brunch. Reservations are suggested.*

The most elegant of the Hyatt Regency's several restaurants, Golden Swan still maintains a casual atmosphere. There is an indoor dining room along with a beautiful open air patio area with a view of the mountains and overlooking a pretty Japanese koi pond as well as the beautiful gardens. The cuisine is regional American with a definite southwestern influence as in such appetizers as smoked duck Taquito and crabs with piñon nutcakes. The same interesting combinations are evident in the main courses, for example, grilled lamb chops with Jalapeno honey or fajita marinated filet of beef. Cocktails; children's menu.

MARQUESA, *7575 East Princess Drive, Scottsdale, in the Scottsdale Princess, Tel. 480/585-4848. Most major credit cards accepted. Dinner served nightly; also Sunday brunch. Dress code. Reservations are suggested.*

One of the most beautiful restaurants in Scottsdale, Marquesa specializes in Spanish cuisine – or to be more exact, Catalan. Mediterranean influences such as Italian, French, and other types of Spanish cooking are all blended in and the result is a unique taste. Sitting in an elegant Spanish colonial setting you'll receive impeccable service from a knowledgeable staff. Head chef Chaz Frankenfield has created some marvelous dishes, turning ordinary meat, fish, and chicken into an art with careful use of delicate herbs, garlic, saffron, and olive all. Try the peppercorn crusted beef with dried cherries and mushrooms or fideva, a combination of lobster, mussels, clams, and fish mixed in a Catalan style pasta. Fabulous Paella Valenciana is also on the menu. Marquesa is famous for its outstanding Sunday brunch held on the patio and accompanied by live Spanish guitar music. This restaurant also has one of the world's greatest selection of Spanish wines along with many others from Europe and the United States. There is a separate cocktail lounge with entertainment and a tapas bar.

MARY ELAINE'S, *6000 East Camelback Road, Scottsdale, in The Phoenician, Tel. 480/423-2530. Major credit cards accepted. Dinner served nightly. Dress code. Reservations are required.*

First class service and delicious contemporary French cuisine with a touch of North African and Asian influences are the hallmarks of this noted restaurant. Elegant surroundings overlook the Valley of the Sun from atop the hotel. Little touches such as magnificent floral centerpieces on each table add even more style. Mary Elaine's has one of the Valley's most impressive wine lists – don't hesitate to ask what to order if you aren't an expert. The menu is imaginative as you'll see from this brief sampling: for appetizer, roasted quail risotto; main course, rack of lamb with garlic crust and stewed peppers; for dessert, chocolate decadence. If you're watching your weight then a good dessert alternative (in season) is wild berries served in natural syrup. Live entertainment in the form of soft jazz is available in the lounge.

Expensive

ARIZONA KITCHEN, *300 Wigwam Boulevard, Litchfield Park, in the Wigwam Resort. Tel. 623/948-1700. Major credit cards accepted. Dinner served nightly (except on Sunday from late June through mid-September). Dress code.*

For authentic southwestern regional cuisine you can't do much better than the Arizona Kitchen. The decor is reminiscent of the Arizona territorial period and is both elegant and relaxing. Service is deft without being overly stuffy. The display kitchen will have your mouth watering long before the food arrives. But when it does you won't be disappointed.

CHART HOUSE, *7255 McCormick Parkway, Scottsdale, Tel. 480/951-2550. Most major credit cards accepted. Dinner served nightly. Reservations are suggested.*

A tropical atmosphere pervades this upscale eatery that overlooks Camelback Lake. Patrons can dine indoors or out. Steaks, prime rib, and seafood are the menu staples but there are far more imaginative dishes available such as east and west prawns with garlic steak or coconut crunchy shrimp. The extensive salad bar is excellent. Cocktails are served in the dining room and there is also a separate lounge. Children's menu available.

LA HACIENDA, *7575 East Princess Drive, Scottsdale, in the Scottsdale Princess, Tel. 480/585-4848. Most major credit cards accepted. Dinner served nightly. Dress code. Reservations are suggested.*

This is one of several award-winning restaurants featured at the Scottsdale Princess. In this case it is an outstanding Mexican restaurant. Located in a turn-of-the-century Mexican ranch house in the middle of one of the hotel's huge courtyards, the setting alone is magnificent and worth seeing. Dining on the beautiful outdoor patio is also available. The specialty of the house is the now famous spit roasted suckling pig but there is also an excellent selection of grilled seafood, chicken, and beef entrees. Cocktails are served either tableside or in the adjacent lounge which has live entertainment. In the main dining area strolling mariachi musicians add a nice touch. Children's menu.

Moderate

THE AMERICAN GRILL, *1233 South Alma School Road, Mesa, Tel. 480/844-1918. Major credit cards accepted. Lunch is served daily except Sunday; dinner nightly. Reservations are accepted.*

The attractive decor in this popular Mesa restaurant is highlighted by a generous use of bright brass. The menu has a wide selection of seafood and steak dishes as well as numerous southwestern entrees. Both the food and the service are well above average and, at the price charged, it is one of the better values in the Phoenix area. The cocktail lounge has live entertainment. Children's menu.

LA LOCANDA, *10201 North Scottsdale Road, Scottsdale, Tel. 480/998-2822. Most major credit cards accepted. Dinner served daily. Reservations suggested.*

This intimate restaurant serves some of the best Northern Italian cuisine anywhere in the Valley of the Sun, and that's without the added high prices that often seems to come with the prefix "northern." The staff is efficient and attentive without being intrusive. Try the delicious antipasto featuring calamari in a delicate lemon sauce. For the main course you'll find generous use of risotto and pasta. Veal is a specialty of the house and is served in many forms. Two delicious veal dishes are the ossobuco alla milanese or veal chops grilled with roasted peppers, garlic, and mushrooms. La Locanda has a full service bar.

THE LANDMARK RESTAURANT, *809 W. Main Street, Mesa. Tel. 480/962-4652. Major credit cards accepted. Lunch and dinner served daily.*

One of the more interesting restaurants around and, given the reasonable prices, an excellent choice. The restaurant is located in a former church building and the decor reflects the best of the Victorian era. Historic photographs of Mesa line the walls. The menu offers a wide choice of well-prepared American cuisine including beef, seafood and poultry. I'm especially fond of the immense salad bar that contains no less than a hundred different items. You could make a meal of that alone and the quality is uniformly high. Casual and friendly, the Landmark is a wise choice for a quiet dinner for two or for the whole family.

RUTH'S CHRIS STEAKHOUSE, *7001 North Scottsdale Road, Scottsdale, Tel. 480/991-5988. American Express, MasterCard, Visa and Diners Club accepted. Dinner served nightly. Reservations are suggested. Other locations throughout the Phoenix area.*

The name says it all. Ruth's features the finest in corn fed US prime beef prepared in butter. Chicken and seafood dishes are also on the menu. The casual restaurant has an outdoor dining area and is well known among locals for its big portions. Meat and potato lovers will appreciate the huge tender slabs of beef and the option to choose from seven different types of potatoes. Cocktails are served.

ZINZIBAR, *3815 North Scottsdale Road, Scottsdale, Tel. 480/990-9256. Most major credit cards accepted. Dinner served nightly.*

This is an unusual restaurant and one of my favorites. The cuisine covers the gamut of Mediterranean nations, even extending to the sea's south shore by including several Moroccan dishes. A variety of fondues is a specialty. California chef Aaron Kirsch has combined modern cuisine with traditional recipes to create a most rewarding dining experience. Try the lobster ravioli or sea bass with lemon oil. Zinzibar is justly proud of its extensive wine list (with more than a hundred selections) as well as an inventory of 30 different beers, many on tap. The charming old world setting has rough brick dividing walls to create a feeling of privacy and the walls are decorated with tapestry like designs. The separate bar is a popular place and even serves fine cigars. Don't worry about smoke, though – Zinzibar uses the most modern smoke eating system in the bar.

SEEING THE SIGHTS

There's so much to be seen in a widespread area that you could easily get bogged down making a plan of attack. So I've done it for you by dividing the attractions into five different tours. Excursions that venture further afield are described in a separate section. As you'll soon see each tour can take quite a bit of time. Therefore, if you're in a situation where you can't possibly do all of them, you might want to take a few highlights from each of the tours.

Tour 1 is the downtown itinerary and is best done on foot, although a few of the longer walks can be avoided by using public transportation. All of the other tours are best done by car even though most of the attractions can be reached by one or more bus routes. The biggest problem using the bus for the other tours is that you spend a lot of time traveling and waiting instead of seeing and doing.

Tour 1: Downtown Phoenix

Approximate duration (by foot including sightseeing time) is a full day. Begin at the city's visitor center at the Arizona Center, East Van Buren and North 4th Streets.

The visitor center is a good place to start because in addition to being able to pick up a lot of useful brochures and ask questions, it's very centrally located. The **Arizona Center** itself is an attractive and modern complex of office buildings and shops. The shaded walkways are generously planted with trees and attractive gardens. Outdoor entertainment is often featured.

From there walk south for two blocks on North 5th Street to **Phoenix Civic Plaza**. Covering several square blocks the Plaza is home to, among other things, Symphony Hall and the huge Convention Center which spans Washington Street. Just to the east of Civic Plaza, between Monroe and Washington Streets is **Heritage Square**, the most historic part of Phoenix. This was the original site of the city and preserves eight structures from the latter portion of the 19th century. The three main buildings are the Rosson, Silver and Stevens Houses. The **Rosson House** is a Victorian style mansion that was owned by the mayor of Phoenix in 1895. It was especially elaborate for a frontier home, even for a rich family. *Guided tours every half hour on Wednesday through Saturday from 10:00am to 3:30pm and from noon on Sunday; admission is $3 for adults, $2 for seniors and $1 for ages 6-13; hours can vary during the summer so it is best to call for information; Tel. 602/262-5071.*

The **Stevens House** now contains the **Arizona Doll and Toy Museum**, which includes a large collection of antique dolls from all over the world. The **Lathe House Pavilion** is a modern structure that is the scene of various community events and festivals. It also contains a small botanical

POINTS OF PRIDE

Every city has something about which its residents are proud of. Well, the city of Phoenix went a step further a few years ago. They questioned 10,000 residents and came up with a list of 24 of their favorite places in the Valley of the Sun. In effect, this is what the locals say you should see on a visit. Heritage Square, the Arizona Center, Symphony Hall Plaza, the Phoenix Art Museum, Heard Museum, South Mountain Park and Mystery Castle, Encanto Park, Camelback Mountain, the Desert Botanical Garden, Papago Park, the Phoenix Zoo, and Pueblo Grande are all on the list and are described in one of the five area tours.

Other places on the list that you might be interested in taking at least a brief look at are St. Mary's Basilica, 3rd and Monroe Streets, the historic Orpheum Theatre, 203 W. Adams Street, the famous Arizona Biltmore hotel, 24th Street and Missouri Avenue, the Shemer Arts Center and Museum, 5005 E. Camelback Road, and Tovrea Castle, 5041 E. Van Buren Street, an unusual tiered house located at the top of a hill surrounded by towering cactus.

The remaining items on the Points of Pride list include some small plazas and parks.

garden. Each component of Heritage Square is operated independently of the others. Hours for other portions of Heritage Square vary but you can always walk around the area. *Open Tuesday through Saturday from 10:00am to 4:00pm and from noon on Sunday; admission is $2 for adults, 50¢ for children; Tel. 602/253-9337.*

From Heritage Square go south on 7th Street until Washington Street and then turn right. You'll immediately encounter the **Arizona Science Center**. Beginning its fourth year in this location in 1999, this large facility has more than 350 interactive exhibits. Here the inquisitive mind can learn about science in a fun atmosphere where visitors get involved in the exhibits ranging from biology to weather. It's best suited for school age children although adults will likely enjoy it too. *600 E. Washington Street, corner of 7th Street; open Monday through Saturday from 9:00am to 5:00pm and on Sunday from noon to 5:00pm; admission is $8 for adults, $6 for children; Tel. 602/716-2000.*

Near the Science Center and a part of the **Heritage and Science Park** (which encompasses both Heritage Square and several museums) is the **Phoenix Museum of History**, *105 N. 5th Street (at Monroe)*. The museum houses an extensive collection of exhibits and artifacts spanning more than 2,000 years of civilization in the Valley of the Sun. Many of the exhibits are interactive. *It is open Monday through Saturday from 10:00am to 5:00pm and on Sunday from noon to 5:00pm. Admission is $5 for adults, $4 for senior citizens, and $3 for children. Tel. 602/253-2734.*

Then make a right and return to Washington Street. Another right turn and a few short blocks will bring you to the respected **Arizona Mining and Mineral Museum**. It's one of the largest museums of its type in the world, containing more than 3,000 specimens. *1502 W. Washington Street. Open from Monday through Friday from 8:00am until 5:00pm and on Saturdays from 11:00am till 4:00pm; closed on state holidays; admission is free; Tel. 602/255-3791.*

Once you're done with the Heritage and Science Park area, continue south on N. 5th Street to the southeast corner of Civic Plaza at Jefferson Street. Phoenix's major sports venues are located in this vicinity. The massive **Bank One Ballpark** is home to the Arizona Diamondbacks baseball team. The retractable roof covers 5-1/2 acres and can be closed in under five minutes. Sports fans (and stadium architecture fans) will be interested in guided tours which cover, in addition to the usual playing field, clubhouse, and press box areas, the Sun Pool Party Pavilion! In a baseball stadium? Of course, this is Phoenix, land of the swimming pool. *Tel. 602/562-6543. Guided 1-1/4 hour tours daily except Saturday at 11:30, noon, 1:30 and 3:00. Subject to cancellation when daytime events are held. Adults, $6, seniors and ages 7-12 is $4 and children 4 to 6 pay $2. Ticket purchase 48 hours in advance is recommended.* (Note that time for stadium tours is not included in my time allocation for Tour 1.)

Two blocks west is the **America West Arena** which, among other things, is the home of the city's basketball and hockey teams. Go north one block back to Washington Street and make a left turn. Between 1st and 4th Avenues is the Phoenix government area. While there isn't anything of great note you can take a quick look at the City Hall, county courthouse, and several other municipal office buildings.

A few blocks further west is the **Arizona Hall of Fame**. Housed in the 1908 Carnegie Public Library Building, this unusual museum features exhibits on people who have contributed to the development of Arizona, even if that contribution wasn't always positive. The last few years have seen a shift in emphasis at the museum to the contributions of notable Arizona women. An especially interesting feature is the exhibit on Fred Harvey and the Harvey Girls. *1101 West Washington Street in Library Park between 10th and 11th Avenues. Open from Monday through Friday (except State holidays) from 8:00am until 5:00pm and is free of charge. Tel. 602/255-2110.*

Continuing on Washington after the Mining Museum, the street immediately runs into Adams Street and the large and nicely landscaped grounds of the **State Capitol** complex. Covering several blocks, the center of the area is dominated by the **Wesley Bolin Memorial Plaza**, where several statues commemorate important Arizonians. There are two capitol buildings, the old and the new. The current capitol was built in 1974 and houses the executive branch of government and has adjacent legislative galleries that are sometimes open to the public. One of the most beautiful features of the complex is the large white statue of "Winged Victory" that stands proudly on top of the capitol's dome.

Of more interest to visitors, however, is the **Arizona State Capitol Museum**, which was built in 1889 to serve the Territorial government and later became the state's first capitol. The legislative chambers, governor's office, and offices of several other state officials have been carefully restored to their Territorial days appearance. Also housed in the four-story structure are numerous exhibits and documents. *The Capitol museum is open Monday through Friday from 8:00am until 5:00pm except for state holidays; guided tours are offered at 10:00am and 2:00pm; there is no admission charge; Tel. 602/542-4675.*

Standing with your back to the Capitol complex you should head north (to the left) up 15th Avenue towards the next attraction. It's a good sized walk that covers over 1-1/2 miles, so if the weather is hot or your feet are already hurting you may want to hop on the bus that goes up 15th. **Encanto Park** is a tropical oasis in the middle of the big city, a great place to take a rest while you enjoy the beautiful surroundings that are highlighted by unusual trees and shrubbery. The lagoon and islands are a refuge for waterfowl. After you've relaxed and are ready to resume walking, why not try one of the park's nature trails? Boat rentals are available. Performances are frequently scheduled at the park's Music Shell. There is also a small amusement park with rides and a sandy playland called the Enchanted Island.

The next attraction for most visitors will be the famous Heard Museum. However, those interested in religious history might want to make a detour to the **Plotkin Judaica Museum,**. The history of the Jewish people is retold through artifacts and interesting exhibits. *3310 North 10th Avenue, at the intersection of Osborne Road, about one mile northeast of Encanto Park; open from 10:00am to 3:00pm Tuesday through Thursday and on Sunday from noon to 3:00pm; admission is free; Tel. 602/264-4428*

The **Heard Museum** is reached from Encanto Park via Monte Vista, or from the Plotkin Museum by taking Osborne to Central and then proceeding south to Monte Vista. The museum contains one of the world's most outstanding collections of Southwestern art and culture. Housed in an attractive Spanish Colonial Revival style building, the museum contains over 35,000 Native American objects in seven different galleries. The most popular exhibit is the Native Peoples of the Southwest which chronicles the cultures of 23 different tribes of the American southwest. You can get involved in native crafts and activities with the interactive Old Ways, New Ways exhibit. Besides the exhibits there are frequent demonstrations of crafts given by Indians and native artists' works are on display in the outdoor sculpture garden. The museum has an excellent shop and bookstore. *22 East Monte Vista Road, off of Central. Opens daily at 9:30am. Prices: $6 adults; $5 seniors; $3 children. Telephone: 602/252-8840; Tel. 602/252-8848.*

After leaving the Heard Museum walk back to the corner of Central Avenue and turn right. In a few blocks you'll reach the final stop on this tour, the **Phoenix Art Museum**. The museum features changing exhibits as well as a fine permanent collection. The latter is separated into 11 different galleries. Among the more noted ones are the Western American, American, European, Asian and Spanish Colonial galleries. There is also an outstanding collection of miniature rooms depicting historic American, English, French and Italian styles. Among other things to see and do in this large museum which has recently undergone considerable expansion are an orientation theater about the museum collection, a museum store and cafe. *1625 North Central Avenue, open from Tuesday through Saturday from 10:00am till 5:00pm and on Thursday and Friday until 9:00pm, Sunday hours are from noon to 5:00pm, closed on most state holidays; guided tours are available at 2:00pm and also at 6:00pm on Thursday and Friday; admission is $6 for adults, $4 for seniors and $2 for children ages 6 through 18 and admission is free to all on Wednesdays; Tel. 602/257-1222.*

"DASH"-ING ABOUT DOWNTOWN

*The downtown tour includes a lot of walking, which some readers might find enjoyable but others will see it as a burden, especially if the weather is bad (translation: hot). So now's a good time to remind you about the **DASH** bus service that serves the downtown corridor and reaches most of the attractions in Tour 1. It runs frequently (every 6 to 12 minutes) on weekdays and costs only 30 cents!*

DASH operates in a continuous loop. The routing (beginning from the northeast corner of Civic Plaza at Monroe and 5th Streets) is: north on 5th; west on Van Buren; south on 2nd Street; west on Monroe; south on 1st Avenue; west on Washington Street, around the state capitol via 18th Avenue; then returning east on Jefferson Street; north on Central Avenue; east on Adams Street; north on 2nd Street; and finally east on Monroe back to 5th Street.

You can easily return to the tour's starting point by continuing south on Central Avenue until you reach Washington Street. A left turn there and a few more blocks will bring you back to the Arizona Center. Along the way on Central you might want to stop for a break at Hance Park. The park sits above two tunnels that speed traffic along the Papago Freeway. Also in the park is the **Phoenix Public Library**.

Tour 2: The North & West

Approximate duration (including sight seeing) is about 6 hours. Begin at the Deer Valley Rock Art Center (take I-17 north from downtown).

This tour starts less than a half hour from downtown by car. Use Exit 215 (Deer Valley Road) and then travel west for about two miles to the **Deer Valley Rock Art Center**. Native Americans made paintings on rock beginning thousands of years ago. This type of painting is known as a **petroglyph**. In this area, located at the base of some large hills, are more than 1,500 petroglyphs. They are connected by an easy quarter-mile long trail. An indoor museum features a 45-minute film about petroglyphs as well as exhibits which interpret the petroglyphs, many of which are considered sacred by Native Americans and are used as a teaching tool to preserve their tribal heritage. A fascinating experience which is worth going out of the way for. *3711 W. Deer Valley Road. From September through May the center is open on Tuesday through Saturday from 9:00am until 2:00pm (till 5:00 on Saturday) and on Sunday from noon to 5:00pm. During the summer months the hours can vary and it is best to confirm them by calling the center at 602/582-8077. The admission fee is $3 for adults, $2 for senior citizens and students with identification and $1 for children ages 6-12.*

North Mountain Park is one of several large natural areas within the Phoenix urban zone that have been set aside in a relatively undeveloped state. To get there from the Rock Art Center take I-17 south to Exit 207 and then head east on Dunlap Avenue. Upon reaching 7th Street (don't get confused when you reach 7th Avenue – you still have a while to go), turn left to the park. Covering more than 7,000 acres, North Mountain isn't as well known among visitors as Phoenix' South Mountain Park, but it is just as worthwhile. Besides the usual features of a municipal park, North Mountain features extensive hiking trails in a mountainous desert terrain and good views of Phoenix.

Upon leaving North Mountain Park take 7th Street for about two miles to Northern Avenue. Then turn right and follow that street to the final stop on this tour – the **Wildlife World Zoo**, *16501 West Northern Avenue, located in the neighboring community of Litchfield Park.* One of three zoos in the Phoenix metropolitan area (all of which are quite different although you may want to study them and do only one), Wildlife World features the most exotic of animals from Asia and Africa, as well as the

Americas. There's even an aquarium. The Zoo has Wildlife Encounter Shows throughout the day and a walk-through bird aviary that is one of the largest of its type. *The zoo is open every day of the year from 9:00am to 5:00pm. Admission is $8 for adults and $5 for children ages 3 through 12. Tel. 602/935-9453.*

After making your way back to I-17, head north one more time to this tour's final attraction. The **Pioneer Arizona Living History Museum** is a re-creation of an Arizona settlement in the 1880's. The more than 20 buildings include both reconstructions as well as original structures. Costumed guides offer demonstrations of daily living. The Opera House is the scene for live entertainment at various times (not included in the time allowance for this tour). Once you get back on I-17 it is only about a half-hour drive back to downtown. *Pioneer Road immediately off of Exit 225. Open Wednesday through Sunday from 9:00am until 5:00pm from October through May and 7:00am until 3:00pm the remainder of the year. Closed on Christmas. Admission is $6 for adults and $4 for children ages 6 through 12. Tel. 602/465-1052.*

Tour 3: The South

Approximate duration (including sightseeing) is a minimum of 6 hours. Begin at the Desert Botanical Gardens (east of downtown via Van Buren Street).

Upon reaching the lush greenery of huge **Papago Park** (accessible by bus) or reached by car via Van Buren Street east to Galvin Parkway and then left. You'll begin your visit with the park's remarkable **Desert Botanical Garden**, *open daily from 7:00am till 10:00pm from May through September and daily from 8:00am to 8:00pm, closed only on Christmas Day; admission is $7 for adults, $5 for senior citizens, and $1 for children ages 5 through 12; Tel. 602/941-1225.* Spread out among some 145 acres, the garden has more than 20,000 plant specimens representing about 4,000 different species that are native to the world's most arid climates. Among the areas you'll see are the Cactus House, Succulent House, and the Arizona Native Plant Trail.

The most colorful time to visit is during the cactus blooming season which occurs from the early part of March through early May. The gardens are lovely at any time of the year but summer visitors are advised to come here in the morning before the sun starts to make things difficult for walking outdoors. Within the gardens are the three-acre Plants and People of the Sonoran Desert, which describes the life of the deserts earliest human inhabitants. The theme of how people have prospered in the desert is continued at the Center for Desert Living. If you live in an arid climate you'll especially enjoy the useful tips at the Desert House Information and Technical Center.

From the Botanic Garden you should return south on Galvin Parkway. Just south of the gardens (following signs) is a formation known as the **Hole In The Rock**. The hole has been created by the forces of erosion over tens of thousands of years. It is the most famous natural feature in the park. Also within Papago Park (a little bit further south and still on Galvin Parkway) is the **Phoenix Zoo**. The largest of Phoenix's zoos is also one of the finest in the nation, featuring more than 1,300 animals on 125 nicely landscaped acres. The animals can be seen in natural habitats along five different easily marked trails. The Phoenix Zoo is especially known for its programs to help endangered species. Trail's End Marketplace has an excellent gift shop as wall as a cafe. Visitors can opt to see the zoo by narrated safari tour trains. *Open daily from 7:00am until 4:00pm between May 1st and Labor Day and from 9:00 to 5:00 the remainder of the year. It is closed only on Christmas Day. The adult admission price is $9 while seniors pay $8. Children ages 4-12 are admitted for $4.25. Credit cards. There is an additional charge for the Safari train tour. Note the early opening times for both the zoo and the Desert Botanic Gardens during the summer months. That's a hint about avoiding the mid-day heat! Tel. 602/273-1341.*

Another attraction that's located just outside the borders of Papago Park is the **Hall of Flame Museum of Firefighting**, *6101 East Van Buren* (take Galvin back to Van Buren and turn left). Why is it that every place seems to bill itself as the world's largest this or that? Good advertising promotion, I guess, but in the case of this museum it appears to be true. The Hall of Flame, with more than a hundred pieces of fire fighting apparatus, is the world's most impressive collection of its kind. The equipment dates from as early as 1725 and goes all the way up to 1961. Uniforms, safety equipment and other memorabilia round out the collection. *The museum is open daily from 9:00 am until 5:00pm except Sunday when its hours are noon till 4:00pm. It is closed on New Years, Thanksgiving and Christmas. Guided tours are given daily at 2:00pm. Admission is $5 for adults, $4 for seniors and $3 for children ages 6-17. Tel. 602/275-3473.*

From the Hall of Flame go back on Van Buren to the intersection of Galvin Parkway. Turn right (on this side of the street the thoroughfare changes names to Priest Drive) and proceed for four blocks to Washington Street. A right turn and a drive of less than two miles will bring you to the next stop – the **Pueblo Grande Museum**. Located on the site of an ancient Hohokam Indian community that vanished more than 500 years ago, the museum documents this advanced civilization's culture through artifacts and exhibits. There is also a trail leading to the top of a burial mound that overlooks the remains of the settlement's dwellings. You can also see evidence of their extensive canal system, parts of which form the basis for today's irrigation projects. *4619 E. Washington Street. Open daily (except state holidays) from 9:00am until 4:45pm (from 1:00pm on Sundays) and* *the admission is $2 for adults, $1.50 for seniors, and only $1 for children; Tel. 602/ 495-0900.*

Just to the east of the museum complex is an entrance to the southbound Hohokam Expressway. Take that to the end where it runs into 46th Street and continue south until you reach Baseline Road. Turn right and follow Baseline until you reach Central Avenue. Another right and you'll see the imposing South Mountain directly ahead of you.

However, immediately before entering the park turn left on Mineral Road for a few blocks to **The Mystery Castle**. Construction on this large house began in 1930 and lasted for fifteen years. It was built by Luther Gulley for his daughter and is made out of native stone and just about any other material that Gulley could come up with. The house's 8,000 square feet are filled with interesting antiques as well as hundreds of authentic Native American artifacts. Southwestern arts and crafts are on display, some of which include those done by Mary Lou Gulley. *The castle is open from Thursday through Sunday from 11:00am until 4:00pm and is closed from July through September. The admission price is $4 for adults, $3 for senior citizens and $2 for children 5 through 14. Tel. 602/268-1581.*

South Mountain Park is a vast area that covers more than 17,000 acres. The terrain varies from mountain peaks to deep canyons and contains some very unusual rock formations. The flora represents a good cross-section of Arizona's trees and cactus plants. The area of South Mountain was explored by the Spaniards as early as 1539, a fact which is attested to in an inscription on a rock on the park's Pima Canyon Road. Besides the recreational activities associated with a city park, a highlight to South Mountain is to drive up to the summit of **Dobbins Peak**, from which there is, on clear days, a fantastic view of the entire Phoenix metropolitan area and the Valley of the Sun. The road to the summit is very narrow and winding.

The easiest way to complete this tour and return to the city center area is to head straight up on Central Avenue. It's about six miles from the park entrance to the heart of downtown.

Tour 4: Scottsdale & Fountain Hills

Approximate duration (including sightseeing) is approximately 5-1/2 hours. Begin at Scottsdale Civic Plaza.

Scottsdale, although it has a number of excellent attractions, is best known for its world class resorts. This itinerary doesn't specifically include any of them but if you are interested in seeing beautiful grounds that rival the best botanical gardens and buildings with stunning and varied architecture, then I strongly suggest that you find the time to tour at least some of the most outstanding examples of the luxury resort genre. These include, among others, The Phoenician, Scottsdale Princess, Hyatt

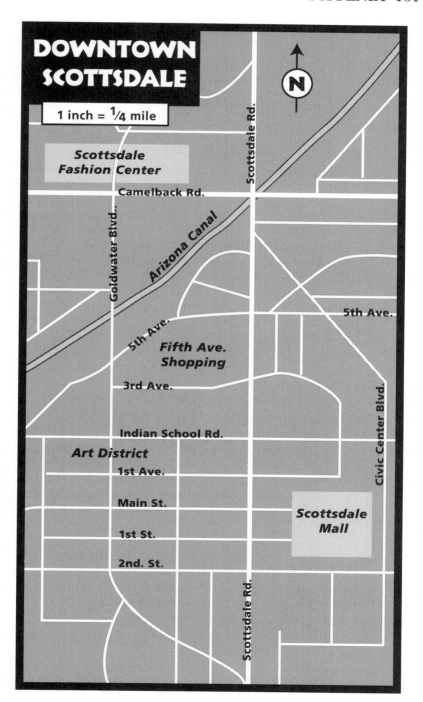

Regency at Gainey Ranch, and Marriott's Camelback Resort. In each case the grounds and public areas are sights worth seeing and no one will mind you standing around and gawking. Actually, hotel management likes it – that's one of the reasons they are so elaborate. You could spend anywhere from an hour to a full day resort hopping.

Another noted feature of the Scottsdale scene is its excellent shopping, mostly of an upscale nature. Shopping is described separately after the Phoenix area tours and, again, time for that is not included in the suggested time frame for this particular tour.

To get to **Scottsdale Civic Plaza** from central Phoenix take I-10 to Exit 147 and then east on the Red Mountain Freeway to the Scottsdale Road exit. Go north about four miles on the latter and you'll reach Scottsdale Civic Plaza on your right. Scottsdale is an affluent and mostly modern city and nowhere is it more evident than in its beautiful municipal complex. The architecture is modified Spanish and fits in nicely with both the natural surroundings and the small historic area of Scottsdale which lies on the other side of Scottsdale Road from Civic Plaza. Within the Plaza area are a park with paved walkways that lead through beautifully landscaped flower beds, by ponds and fountains and various sculptures. A highlight for visitors is the **Scottsdale Historical Museum**, housed in an old grammar school dating from 1909. *Open only from September through June; hours are Wednesday through Saturday from 10:00am until 5:00pm and on Sunday from noon till 4:00pm; no set admission charge but donations are requested; Tel. 480/945-4499.*

Also within the Civic Plaza area (on Civic Center Boulevard) is the **Imax Theater**. Special films, sometimes including double features, are presented on a screen that measures six stories high and 78 feet across. Films change regularly but are always of a visually stunning nature to take advantage of the huge screen. *The theater is open every day except Christmas from 11:00am with the last showing beginning at 9:00pm. Admission is $7 for a single feature and $6 for double features. Children under 12 and senior citizens pay $5, depending upon the number of features seen. Credit cards. Tel. 480/945-4629.*

When you're through with the Civic Plaza area drive north on Scottsdale Road until you reach Doubletree Ranch Road. Turn left and proceed about a mile to the **Cosanti Foundation**, *6433 Doubletree Ranch Road,* which is actually located in the neighboring community of Paradise Valley. Paolo Soleri is a world renowned Italian-born architect who has lived and worked in Arizona since 1956. He coined the term *arcology* to define a type of architecture that is integrated with the ecological workings of its surroundings.

At the Cosanti Foundation you can tour "earthformed" concrete structures amid a natural desert setting that includes cactus, palo verde, and olive trees. You can also watch the manufacture of so-called "cause bells," which are actually wind chimes in honor of various worthy causes around the world. The chimes are for sale. There is also information on Soleri's prize project – Arcosanti. Arcosanti itself is considerably north of Phoenix in the town of Cordes Junction and is described in Chapter 14, *Flagstaff & Sedona. The Foundation headquarters is open daily except for most major holidays from 9:00am until 5:00pm. There is no admission charge but donations are appreciated. Tel. 480/948-6145.*

Scottsdale is quite narrow from east to west but extends far in a north to south direction. You'll appreciate this on your way to the next destination. Return to Scottsdale Road and head north by making a left turn onto Scottsdale. When you reach Shea Boulevard turn right and take that street to Pima Road. Go north on Pima (to the left) until Bell Road, which is just beyond the Tournament Players Club golf course, and make another left. That will bring you to the **Fleischer Museum**. The collection includes two main galleries, one devoted to the California School of Impressionism from 1880 through about 1930. The other highlights Russian Impressionist art from the 1930's through the '70s. It's interesting to see the influence of the Cold War years on Russian art from that period. *Bell and Pima Roads. Tel. 480/585-3108. Open daily except for holidays, from 10am to 4pm; no admission.*

Now retrace your route back to Pima Road and go south as far as Cactus Road where you'll turn left onto that street. Follow Cactus to 114th Street and the impressive structure known as **Taliesin West**. This is the office and school of the **Frank Lloyd Wright Foundation**, named for one of the world's great architects. Tours of Mr. Wright's residence and architectural studio are given and provide insight into his genius. While architecture buffs will surely be delighted to be in this "holy place" of design, children will probably be bored. However, almost every adult will appreciate the beauty of the architecture set amid 600 acres of desert and mountain background The area is located near a sizable section of Sonoran desert. *Tours depart on the hour from 9:00am until 4:00pm from the middle of September through May. During the remainder of the year tours are given at 8, 9, 10 and 11am only. Adult admission begins at $10 except during the summer when it is $8. Senior citizens and students with ID cards pay $6 year-round. Tour options vary with the time of the year but usually include the Panorama Tour (1 hour); the 90-minute Insights Tour and Nature of the Site Desert Walk; and the three hour long Behind the Scenes Tour. Call 480/860-2700 for exact tour times and reservations.*

Now you can take Frank Lloyd Wright Boulevard south for a short distance to Shea Boulevard. If you don't go to Taliesin West simply remain on Pima all the way to Shea. In either case you'll have to make a left turn onto Shea. The large developed areas will give way to tracts of mountain and desert. Soon after passing from Scottsdale into Fountain Hills there will be a pull-out for the **Fish Point Scenic Lookout**. A brief stop here will provide an excellent view of the McDowell Mountains which separate Scottsdale from Fountain Hills.

Fountain Hills is another attractive community. After the Lookout watch for Palisades Boulevard on your left. This road skirts the mountains and then turns toward the heart of the town, taking you to beautiful **Fountain Park**, entered via Saguaro Boulevard. This municipal park surrounds a 28-acre lake whose focal point is known simply as The Fountain. Every 15 minutes a jet of water is shot 560 feet into the air, which reputedly makes it the highest such fountain in the world. The fountain may not operate if it's very windy.

After viewing the fountain follow the winding course of Saguaro Boulevard to the south until it rejoins Shea. Turn left and take it for a short distance to the Beeline Highway, which is also designated AZ 87. Another left onto Beeline will soon bring you to the **Out of Africa Wildlife Park**. This lovely park features two main sections. The first is the wild cats of the world, including several varieties of leopards, mountain lions and tigers, all in their natural settings. The Arizona section is another natural habitat that contains several types of animals found in the state. These include bears, wolves and cougars. Nine different shows are offered, the best of which is called the Tiger Splash. Not only tigers but other large cats frolic in the water with their human trainers.

This, as well as the other "shows," are largely spontaneous interaction of animal and trainer, so no one knows exactly what's going to happen – which makes the whole thing even more enjoyable. *The park is open daily except Monday between Labor Day and Memorial Day weekend from 9:30am to 5:00pm. It is closed Thanksgiving and Christmas Day. Hours during the remainder of the year are 9:30am to 3:00pm on Wednesday and Thursday, 9:30am to 9:30pm on Friday and Saturday and on Sunday from 9:30am to 5:00pm. Dinner shows are offered on Friday and Saturday nights as part of the Summer Nights and Summer Lights program. The admission fee is $14 for adults, $13 for seniors and $5 for children ages 4 through 12. Credit cards. Tel. 480/ 837-7779.*

There are many possible routes back into Phoenix and the best one for you depends upon where you're staying. However, if you're baffled about returning to downtown, you should return to Shea Boulevard and take that to the Squaw Peak Highway (AZ 51). Go south and the road links up with the highway loops in the city center area.

Tour 5: Mesa & Tempe
Approximate duration (including sight seeing) is about 5 to 6 hours. Begin at Arizona State University in Tempe.

You can make your way to **Tempe** from downtown Phoenix via a number of different highway routes, but the most direct way to go is to head east on Van Buren Street. After Papago Park it becomes Mill Avenue and will, at the intersection of University Drive, bring you right to the edge of **Arizona State University**. The large and modern ASU campus covers many blocks on either side of University Drive.

The two most important points of interest for visitors are the **Arizona State University Art Museum**, *Nelson Fine Arts Center, 10th Street and Mill Avenue, open Tuesday through Saturday from 10:00am until 5:00pm (until 10:00pm Tuesday evenings) and Sunday from 1:00-5:00pm; free of charge; Tel. 602/965-2787,* and the **Arizona State University Museum of Geology**, *Building F, University Drive and McAllister Street, open Monday to Friday from 9:00am until noon, closed on state holidays; free of charge; Tel. 602/965-7065.* Both museums are located on the south side of University Drive. The Art Museum features an excellent collection of American and European works spanning 600 years beginning with the 15th Century. The Geology museum has, among its collection of interesting items, the world's largest display of meteorites. As you walk around the campus you're sure to bump into huge Sun Devil Stadium, home of the college's fine football team and host to New Year's Fiesta Bowl.

The remainder of the attractions on this tour are in neighboring **Mesa**, which has roughly twice the population of Tempe. Continue east on University Drive into Mesa. Make a right on Robson Street (the second block after the major intersection of Country Club Drive) and go several blocks to the **Arizona Museum for Youth**. The museum is intended for children so if there are only adults in your party you can skip to the next attraction by going directly to the Mesa Southwest Museum which is only two blocks to the northeast at the intersection of North Macdonald Avenue and West 1st Street. *35 N. Robson Street. Open Sunday and Tuesday through Friday from 1:00 to 5:00pm and on Saturday from 10:00am, closed on major holidays; admission is $2; Tel. 480/644-2467.*

The **Mesa Southwest Museum** documents the history of the southwest, but especially of the Mesa area. There's an interesting exhibit on the Lost Dutchman Mine, displays of dinosaurs and a gallery about ancient Indian cultures. This has always been a good museum but was rather small. However, the completion in 2000 of a substantial expansion makes it even more worthwhile. *53 N. MacDonald Street. Open Tuesday through Saturday from 10:00am to 5:00pm and Sunday from 1:00pm to 5:00pm, except for major holidays. The admission price is $4 for adults, $3.50 for senior citizens* *and students with ID cards, and $2 for children ages 3 through 12. Tel. 480/644-2230.*

From either of the above museums drive south to Main Street and make a left turn. In just under a mile you'll come to the **Arizona Temple Visitor Center**. Located on the beautifully landscaped grounds of the Mormon Temple, the center has exhibits on the Mormon faith and outstanding works of religious art. Guided tours are available but unless you're interested in hearing a sermon from the guides, you're better off browsing on your own. The temple itself is closed to non-Mormons, as are all Latter Day Saint temples. However, like all Mormon temples, it is a work of architectural beauty. *525 East Main; open daily from 9:00am until 9:00pm; no admission charge; Tel. 480/964-7164.*

Now you should once again proceed east on Main Street to the intersection of Greenfield Road. A left turn here will soon bring you to alongside Falcon Field, a small airport which is the home to the **Confederate Air Force-Arizona Wing**. The museum has nothing to do with the Civil War or the Confederacy but is one of many such affiliated facilities with that name. The museum has a large collection of World War II aircraft and interesting artifacts that show what it was like to be a part of the Army Air Corps during that time. *Open daily from 10:00am until 4:00pm except Thanksgiving and Christmas; admission is $5 for adults and $2 for children ages 6 through 14; Tel. 480/924-1940*

Also located within Falcon Field just a short hop away is the **Champlin Fighter Museum**, which is run by the members of the American Fighter Aces Association. The more extensive collection here includes about 30 different aircraft covering the period from 1914 through 1970 and representing the air forces of the United States, Great Britain, France, Germany, and 11 other countries. There is also an extensive display of aircraft paintings and numerous types of automatic weapons. Most people seem to especially like the vintage World War I aircraft, including famous Fokker Triplanes, a Sopwith Camel and Spad XIII. Aircraft enthusiasts will probably also enjoy the many video presentations that are offered on subjects ranging from the aircraft themselves to the heroic wartime pilots. Unless you have a lot of time or are a real aviation buff, I recommend the Champlin Museum as the better of the two. *Operates daily from 8:30am till 3:30pm but is closed on Easter, Thanksgiving and Christmas; adult admission is $6.50 while children ages 5 to 14 pay $3; Tel. 480/830-4540.*

To return to Phoenix by the fastest route from either the Confederate Air Force or Champlin Museums, go to the Superstition Freeway via Greenfield Road and take the highway west where it meets up with Interstate 10.

NIGHTLIFE & ENTERTAINMENT

Out On The Town

In considering nightclubs it is always wise to keep in mind that "in spots" can change rapidly upon the whims of a fickle populace. While many of the establishments mentioned here have been around for quite a while there is no guarantee that things will be as I say when you arrive. Check local newspapers and entertainment guides for the latest. Addresses are in Phoenix unless stated otherwise.

MOON DOGGIE'S TOORIST TRAP, *455 N. 3rd Street, Tel. 602/253-5200*.

Despite the name, the majority of the Moon Doggie's here are locals as this is one of downtown's hottest spots. It might be in the middle of the desert but the atmosphere is decidedly beach-like, complete with electronic surfing lights, coconut trees and more. Hip crowd, great music.

DECADES/PHOENIX LIVE! AT ARIZONA CENTER, *455 North 3rd Street. Tel. 602/252-2502*.

A huge dance floor is the main feature of this popular night spot that plays music from the 70s through the latest sounds. Because of that it appeals to a fairly broad range of customers from those just old enough to drink to those already into middle age.

MR. LUCKY'S, *3660 Northwest Grand Avenue, Tel. 602/246-0686*.

Country and western music dominates one floor of this giant entertainment center while the sounds of the current top 40 hits reverberates on another floor. Live bull riding is also a hallmark of Mr. Lucky's.

THE ROCKIN' HORSE, *7316 East Stetson Drive, Scottsdale, Tel. 480/949-0992*.

One of the most popular of the many country western places (this is, after all, the west!), The Rockin' Horse has a mixture of local bands as well as touring acts from all over the country. A lively and attractive looking honky tonk, it's the place to go if you like dancing to the beat of country and western music.

THE TEMPE IMPROV, *930 East University Drive, Tempe, Tel. 480/921-9877*.

This place has frequently been voted the best nightclub of its kind in the Phoenix area. It's location near Arizona State University brings in mostly a college-aged crowd but you won't feel out of place if you're older. The Improv also has a full menu for those who want dinner. Diners also get priority seating. As for the entertainment, if you like stand-up comedy and audience interaction, then you should have a good time.

TOOLIES COUNTRY SALOON AND DANCE HALL, *4231 West Thomas Road, Tel. 602/272-3100*.

Here's an unusual place that's a bit more than just another country western club. For starters, it was selected as the best country nightclub in the nation by people who ought to be good judges – the Academy of Country Music, no less. The entertainment program varies between live dance music and concerts. Food service is available. And, oh yes, for those of you gals out there who don't get to go dancing as much as they like because your beau says he can't dance – well, Toolies offers free dancing lessons!

AZZ JAZZ CAFE, *1906 East Camelback Road, Tel. 602/263-8482.*
The Valley's most popular jazz and dinner club features live music every night. Reservations are suggested.

BUZZ FUNBAR, *10345 N. Scottsdale Road, Scottsdale, Tel. 480/991-3866.*
A huge dance floor covering 20,000 square feet so even the biggest clod shouldn't have to worry about crushing someone else's toes! There are three different theme bars as well as a nice rooftop patio. Music is the best of the 70's through 90's.

THE RAWHIDE SALOON, *23023 North Scottsdale Road, Scottsdale, Tel. 602/563-1880.*
The last of my recommendations for country and western music and dancing. This is part of an old west complex (see the sidebar below) and recreates an old west saloon and gambling parlor with appropriately dressed saloon girls and their cowboy customers. Even the card dealers are a page out of the old west – they are of questionable honesty. A lot of fun!

Finally, there are no doubt going to be some guys traveling out there who are looking for entertainment of a more risqué nature. Phoenix has more than its share of topless go-go bars but two places with a reputation for more "class" should be mentioned. In fact, you'll even see some couples there. These are **LE' GIRLS CABARET**, *5151 East Washington Street, Tel. 602/244-8000* and **TIFFANY'S CABARET**, *44 North 32nd Street, Tel. 602/275-3095.* Le' Girls is a modern and very attractive multi-million dollar facility featuring true "centerfold" models. Tiffany's boasts more than 150 "Las Vegas style show girls." They also offer full-service dining.

Casinos
- **Harrah's Ak-Chin Casino**, *15406 Maricopa Road, Maricopa. Tel. 800/427-7247*
- **Fort McDowell Gaming Facility**, *Fountain Hills. Tel. 800/843-3678*
- **White Horse Pass & Vee Quiva Casino**, *1205 South Nader, Chandler. Tel. 800/946-4452*
- **Casino Arizona**, *10005 East Osborn Road, Scottsdale. Tel. 480/850-7777*

A NIGHT OUT IN THE OLD WEST

Rawhide Western Town, 23023 North Scottsdale Road, Scottsdale, Tel. 602/563-1880, is a big complex that seeks to recreate the atmosphere of an 1880s western town. There's something for adults as well as children. In addition to the aforementioned saloon, you can wander along Main Street where you'll find more than 20 shops. Some, such as the blacksmith, are demonstrations of frontier life. The town has its share of gunfights and stagecoach robberies. Or you can pan for gold, or take a ride on an old fashioned train or burro. You can even ride a camel! Excellent food is available at the Rawhide Steakhouse.

The Rockin' R Ranch, 6136 East Baseline Road, Mesa, Tel. 602/ 832-1539, is a similar if less ambitious complex than the Rawhide Western Town. The highlight here is a chuckwagon supper served just like the cowboys had it out on the range. This is followed by western entertainment. Rockin' R can be enjoyed by all ages, even though it doesn't feature the nightclub style entertainment that is available at Rawhide.

Performing Arts

Here again it is important to either call the facilities listed or to consult current publications in order to find out exactly what is being offered on a given evening.

• **Arizona Opera**, *4600 North 12th Street, Tel. 602/226-7464.* Five different operas are performed each season at Symphony Hall, which generally runs from October through March, plus a special production in June.

• **Arizona Theater Company**, *808 North 1st Street, Tel. 602/252-8497.* Also performing from October to May, this excellent company stages six different plays in the Herberger Theater Center.

• **The Phoenix Symphony**, *3707 North 7th Street, Tel. 602/264-6363.* The season usually runs from the fall through the latter part of spring, mostly at Symphony Hall but sometimes at other venues. Performances include, besides the great classics, pop programs and chamber music.

• **Sundome Center for the Performing Arts**, *19403 Johnson Boulevard, Sun City West, Tel. 602/975-1900.* With over 7,000 seats, the Sundome is one of the largest facilities of its type in the nation. A part of Arizona State University, the year-round calendar features a wide variety of performing arts including appearances by major celebrities.

Other cultural venues that you might be interested in include Broadway style shows and other events at the **Grady Gammage Audito-**

rium, *Arizona State University, Tel. 602/965-3434;* the **Arizona Ballet,** which performs at Symphony Hall, *Tel. 602/381-1096;* and the **Phoenix Theater** (plays), *1625 North Central Avenue, Tel. 602/254-2151.*

Somewhere between the cultural attractions and the preceding section on nightclubs comes the **Red River Opry,** *Mill Avenue and Washington Street, Tempe, Tel. 602/829-6779.* A large award-winning cast performs two different but equally spectacular productions throughout the year in a beautiful thousand-seat theater. The shows often have country music themes or sometimes more broad-based tributes to a variety of American music forms. Finally, if you've seen and enjoyed such shows as Legends in Concert that are given in a number of cities, then you probably will also like the **Legendary Superstars,** *11518 East Apache Trail, Mesa, Tel. 602/380-0200.*

SPORTS & RECREATION
SPECTATOR SPORTS
Baseball

The so-called **Cactus League,** spring-training and exhibition games for major league baseball takes place from late February through March in Phoenix, Tempe, Mesa, Chandler, Peoria and Scottsdale. If you're in town at that time and are interested in attending a game, check the local newspapers for information or call the convention and visitors bureau. There is also an **Arizona Fall League** where the best major league prospects play. This takes place in October through December in Mesa, Tempe, Peoria, Sun City, Scottsdale and Phoenix, *Tel. 602/496-6700.*

With the completion of the new enclosed BankOne Stadium in downtown Phoenix, baseball of the major league variety has come to town with the expansion **Arizona Diamondbacks.** Although they hvae only been around a few years, the team isn't too bad at all. Ticket information is available by calling *Tel. 602/514-8400.*

Basketball

Both professional and college level action are available. The **Phoenix Suns** of the National Basketball Association occupy the America West Arena in downtown from October through March and well beyond if they make the playoffs. The phone number is *Tel. 602/379-7867.* Arizona State's team plays at the **McKale Memorial Center** on campus from late November through early March.

Football

Gridiron action takes the form of both professional and college teams. The National Football League's **Arizona Cardinals** currently play in Tempe at Sun Devil's Stadium. Call *Tel. 602/379-0101 or 800/999-1402* for ticket information. That stadium also houses fall action for the Arizona State University team in the **Pacific-10 Conference**. They're perennially one of the better college teams in the nation. The **Sports Information Center**, *Tel. 602/965-6592*, can provide information on all Arizona State intercollegiate athletics.

Hockey

The **Phoenix Coyotes** of the National Hockey League cool things off from early October through the end of March. They also play in the downtown America West Arena and the number to call for information and tickets is *Tel. 602/379-2800*.

Horse Racing

Thoroughbred racing is available at the *Turf Paradise Race Course, Bell Road and 19th Avenue, Tel. 602/942-1101*. Both live and simulcast racing are offered.

There's also a variety of other spectator sports available, from indoor or arena football to soccer, as well as boat racing, car racing, professional tennis matches, greyhound racing, and more. It's best to consult the local papers or magazines for complete information on these sports.

On the participant side the picture is equally diverse. I'll take a brief look at most of them and devote some extra time to golf.

PARTICIPANT SPORTS

Amusement Parks

- **Castles 'N Coasters**, *9445 Metro Center Parkway, Tel. 602/997-7576*.
- **Fiddlesticks Family Fun Park**, *8800 East Indian Bend Road, Scottsdale, Tel. 602/951-6060*; and *1155 West Elliot Road, Tempe, Tel. 602/961-0800*.

Biking

- **Desert Biking Adventure**, *7119 East Shea Boulevard, Scottsdale, Tel. 602/320-4602*. Mountain biking in the Sonoran Desert with trips for advanced riders as well as beginners.

Golf

In the chapter on sports and recreation I mentioned that Arizona can rightfully stake its claim to being the golfing capital of the United States. The Phoenix area is clearly the leading location in Arizona. With over a hundred courses in the Valley, it's simply golfing heaven. Again, keep in mind that many hotels offer golfing packages. A brief rundown on some of the Valley's better courses that allow visitors to play without being members follows.

However, the true golf enthusiast will do well to pick up a copy of the *Phoenix and Valley of the Sun Golf Guide*. It has detailed full page descriptions of almost 25 different courses and complete listings of every area course, including par/yardage figures and prices. It can be found at just about every major hotel and at many other locations throughout the Phoenix area.

- **Arizona Biltmore Country Club**, *24th Street and Missouri Avenue. Tel. 602/955-9655*. Two 18-hole PGA championship courses. Instruction available.
- **Arizona State University Karsten Golf Course**, *1125 E. Rio Salado Parkway, Tempe. Tel. 602/921-8070*. A popular course designed by world renowned Pete Dye in the Scottish style.
- **The Boulders Resort Golf Club**, *Carefree Highway, Carefree. Tel. 602/488-9028*. Located at the famous Boulders resort hotel and built amid large rock outcroppings. Non-hotel guests must arrange for play one day in advance.
- **Club West Golf Club**, *16400 S. 14th Avenue. Tel. 602/460-4400*. Championship 18-hole course. Great mountain vistas.
- **Fountain Hills Golf Club**, *10440 Indian Wells Drive, Fountain Hills. Tel. 602/837-1173*. Championship 18-hole course on a mountainside. At a higher elevation so it's a little cooler in summer, but not much.
- **Hillcrest Golf Club**, *20002 Star Ridge Road, Sun City West. Tel. 602/584-1500*. 18-hole championship course, reasonable rates. Its location means you'll probably be playing with a more mature crowd.
- **Kierland Golf Club**, *15636 Clubgate Drive, Scottsdale. Tel. 602/922-9283*. A gorgeous Scott Miller designed course with challenging elevation changes.
- **Las Sendes Golf Club**, *7555 E. Eagle Crest Drive, Mesa. Tel. 602/396-4000*. A friendly atmosphere amid nice views.
- **McCormick Ranch Golf Club**, *7505 E. McCormick Parkway, Scottsdale. Tel. 602/948-0260*. Two championship courses.
- **Scottsdale Country Club**, *7702 E. Shea Boulevard, Scottsdale. Tel. 602/948-6000*. One of the most famous in the Valley, this 27-hole course was designed by Arnold Palmer.
- **Superstition Springs Golf Club**, *6542 E. Baseline Road, Mesa. Tel. 602/962-GOLF*. Lots of water and bunkers to make it challenging. Instruction available.

Horseback Riding
• **All Western Stables**, *10220 S. Central Avenue, Tel. 602/276-5862.*
• **Ponderosa Stables**, *10215 S. Central Avenue, Tel. 602/268-1261.*

Hot Air Ballooning
• **A Aerozona Adventure**, *7418 E. Cortez Street, Scottsdale, Tel. 602/991-5624.* In business for 20 years.
• **Adventures Out West**, *4901 E. Bloomfield Road, Scottsdale, Tel. 800/860-6000.* Features dawn wildlife photography flights over the desert.
• **Get Carried Away Hot Air Balloon Company**, *Tel. 800/74-BALLOON.* Sunrise flights year round and sunset flights from November through March..
• **Hot Air Balloon Company Off-N-Flying Balloons**, *Tel. 800/843-5987.* The Arizona state balloon champions have been offering sunrise flights for 19 years. Seasonal sunset flights also available.

Swimming
The availability of swimming facilities is so widespread at Phoenix area hotels that I don't feel it's necessary to mention any other facilities. However, if you are staying at a place that doesn't have a pool you can check out the location of the nearest municipal pool in the yellow pages.

Tennis
In addition to the tennis facilities that are available at so many hotels, you might want to check out one of the following:
• **Gold Key Racket Club**, *12826 North 3rd Street, Tel. 602/993-1900*
• **Scottsdale Racquet Club**, *8201 E. Indian Bend Road, Scottsdale, Tel. 602/948-5990*
• **Waterin' Hole Racquet Club**, *901 E. Saguaro Drive, Tel. 602/997-7237*

SHOPPING
The first thing I'll do to help sort out your shopping excursions is to list some of the best shopping areas, markets and malls in the Phoenix area, separated by location. Then I'll go on to some specific store recommendations for particular items.

REGIONAL SHOPPING MALLS
Phoenix
• **Chris-Town Shopping Center**, *Bethany Home Road between 15th and 19th Avenues.* Over 150 stores plus four department stores.
• **Metrocenter**, *Metrocenter Parkway between Dunlap and Peoria Avenues.* Arizona's largest, with more than 200 stores.

- **Paradise Valley Mall**, *Cactus Road and Tatum Boulevard.* 150 plus stores and five department stores.

Scottsdale
- **Los Arcos Mall**, *Scottsdale and McDowell Roads.* 60 stores and a department store.
- **Scottsdale Fashion Square**, *Scottsdale and Camelback Roads.* One of the most luxurious malls in the country, with beautiful fountains, skylights and sculpture. Full concierge service. Over 165 stores plus three department stores.

Other Areas
- **Arrowhead Towne Center**, *75th Avenue and Bell Road, Glendale.* Over 130 stores and five department stores.
- **Fiesta Mall**, *Superstition Freeway and Alma School Road, Mesa.* 147 stores.
- **Superstition Springs Center**, *Superstition Freeway and Power Road, Mesa.* Unusually attractive with desert botanical garden and canyon walks. Over 130 stores and five department stores.

FACTORY OUTLETS
- **Arizona Factory Shops**, *I-17 and Desert Hills Road, Phoenix.* 60-plus stores.
- **Tanger Factory Outlet Center**, *Exit 198 off of I-10, south of Phoenix.* 50 stores.
- **Wigwam Outlet Stores**, *I-10 and Litchfield Road, Goodyear.* More than 50 stores.
- **Factory Stores of America**, *Baseline and Power Roads, Mesa.* Over 30 stores.

SPECIALTY SHOPPING
Phoenix
- **Arizona Center**, *Van Buren between 3rd and 5th Streets (downtown).* More than 50 stores.
- **Biltmore Fashion Park**, *East Camelback Road and 24th Street.* 60-plus stores and 14 restaurants. Upscale.
- **Town and Country Shopping Center**, *East Camelback Road and 20th Street.* Over 50 stores and 16 restaurants.

Scottsdale
- **Agua Caliente**, *69th Street and Shea Boulevard.* 25 stores in an attractive village style setting.
- **The Borgata**, *Scottsdale Road and Lincoln Drive.* 50 stores. One of the area's most unusual shopping centers. Narrow streets and courtyards

resemble an old-world Italian village. Worth seeing even if just to look around.

- **5th Avenue shopping district**, *both sides of Scottsdale Road on the south side of Camelback Road.* An area containing dozens of exclusive shops and galleries.
- **Papago Plaza**, *Scottsdale and McDowell Roads.* Another unique setting – 25 shops arranged in the style of an ancient Aztec village.
- **The Shops at Rawhide**, *Scottsdale Road about four miles north of Bell Road.* More than 20 shops in an old western town setting. A variety of stores but with the emphasis on western items.

Other Areas
- **El Pedregal Marketplace**, *Scottsdale Road and Carefree Highway, Carefree.* In a pretty natural setting of huge boulders. Emphasis on art galleries but there are several boutiques as well.

ART GALLERIES
Fine arts can be found throughout the Valley of the Sun but are concentrated in two areas, both of which are in Scottsdale. The first is along Marshall Way between 5th Avenue and Indian School Road. Called the **Marshall Way Arts District**, there are a half dozen very exclusive galleries for the most discerning clients. The service is known throughout the world. The bigger area is on **Main Street** east of the Scottsdale Civic Center, and contains over 50 galleries spread out over four blocks. There are also many antique dealers interspersed among the galleries.

Two final recommendations don't fit into any of the above categories. The **Mercado**, *7th Street and Van Buren, Phoenix*, is an outdoor village of cobblestoned walkways much like you would encounter in Mexico. There are a variety of shops but this is a good place to go if you want Hispanic handicrafts. The **Historic Old Town** *in the Scottsdale area east of Scottsdale Road and south of Indian School Road* has many stores with the emphasis on unique gifts and western wear. Now let's move on to some individual stores.

Native American Crafts
- **Grey Wolf**, *7239 East 1st Avenue, Scottsdale.* Indian artifacts, Hopi Kachinas and Navajo dolls, Pueblo pottery, jewelry.
- **Atkinson's Indian Trading Post**, *3957 N. Brown Avenue, Scottsdale.* Huge selection of Native American and southwestern gift items.
- **Al Zuni**, *Chris-Town Mall, Phoenix.* Specializing in Indian jewelry but also has Kachina dolls. Will custom design.
- **Gilbert Ortega Galleries of Indian Arts**, *122 N. 2nd Street, downtown Phoenix; 7237 E. Main Street, Scottsdale; and other locations.* The largest

purveyor of Native American jewelry and other items. Ortega's has been around a long time and has earned an excellent reputation.
• **Silver and Gold House Fine Indian Art**, *7158 East 5th Avenue, Scottsdale*. Indian jewelry of all types. They have a Navajo silversmith on the premises.

Western Wear & Arizona Items
• **The Cactus Hut**, *7249 E. 1st Avenue, Scottsdale*, has, in addition to the area's biggest selection of cactus plants (which they'll ship to anywhere), unique southwestern gifts, including food.
• **Az-Tex Hats**, *15044 N. Cave Creek Road, Phoenix*, and *3903 N. Scottsdale Road, Scottsdale*, features an outstanding selection of western hats, from the ordinary to the comical – even custom made to your specifications. Hats of fur, felt, and straw are available.
• **Frontier Boot Corral**, *7th Avenue and Van Buren in the Phoenix Mercado*, specializes in western cowboy and cowgirl boots but also has a complete line of western wear.
• **The Boot Barn and Denim World**, *7005 North 58th Avenue, Glendale*, and *Bell and Cave Creek Roads, Phoenix*, has one of the best selections of western wear for men and women when it comes to both boots and jeans. They also have hard to find very small and extra large sizes.

Antiques
• **The Antique Centre**, *2012 N. Scottsdale Road, Scottsdale*, has consistently been selected by numerous local information sources as the best place to look for antiques when in the Valley of the Sun. The Centre isn't a store; rather it is a collection of over 200 separate antique dealers under one roof. The prices here are a lot better than in fine galleries that also feature antiques.

EXCURSIONS & DAY TRIPS
You definitely need to have a car in order to reach the many interesting historic and scenic attractions that lie to the east and south of the metropolitan Phoenix area. These sights have been divided into two separate excursions. Each of them requires a full day but the second one can be shortened if you don't have a lot of time to spare. A third excursion to the west is shorter.

The Apache Trail
Our first excursion covers a loop of approximately 190 miles. Although it isn't all that much mileage a good portion of it is on slow roads so you do need a full day. In fact, I suggest starting out early especially if

you're doing it during the summer. An alternative is to make it an overnight trip staying in Globe. From Phoenix take I-10 east to Exit 154 and then east on US 60, which is the Superstition Freeway. Approximately 27 miles on that road will bring you to the junction of AZ 88 and the town of Apache Junction.

The Junction is the official starting point of the **Apache Trail**, which was built in 1905 to help transport supplies from Phoenix to the town of Globe during the construction of the **Roosevelt Dam**. The route was not new, however, since it more or less followed the same path taken by the Apache Indians as they traveled through the canyons of the **Salt River**. The route is a very scenic one, encompassing both mountains and desert. Immediately to the east of town are the **Superstition Mountains**, so called because of the many different legends that have been told about them. The most famous of these tales is the one about the **Lost Dutchman Gold Mine**, said to have been located amid the mountains. Whether or not it ever really existed depends upon who you talk to. Local historians are themselves divided.

About four miles into AZ 88 you will find the **Goldfield Ghost Town and Mine Tours**. You'll tour an authentic mine, be allowed to pan for gold, and take a narrow-gauge train ride through a very scenic portion of the Superstition Mountain. Gunfights and a variety of shops complete the picture at Goldfield. *The Ghost Town is open daily from 10:00am until 6:00pm. The town can be entered free of charge but there are separate admissions for the mine tour ($4 for adults and $2 for children ages 6 to 12) and the train ride ($3 for adults and $1 for children under 12). Tel. 602/983-0333.*

Only a mile away from Goldfield is the **Lost Dutchman State Park**, *admission is $3 per vehicle, Tel. 602/982-4485.* The park covers about 350 acres of scenic high desert terrain and has frequent historic programs (including visits by the Lost Dutchman himself). Hiking trails are a popular diversion. Once you get past the park the better scenery begins in earnest. The natural mountain terrain is enhanced by the lakes that have been created as a result of several dams. Beautiful **Canyon Lake** stretches for ten miles between **Mormon Flat** and **Horse Mesa Dams**.

Excellent views of the lake are available from the road which starts above the lake, comes down to the shore level and then rises once again. There are 90-minute boat tours on the lake aboard **Dolly's Steamboat**, *Tel. 602/827-9144.* The ride is a pleasant one, with very nice scenery. If you do take the ride there is the possibility you won't have enough time to complete the entire Apache Trail loop in a single day. Schedules vary according to the time of the year. It is best to call for information and reservations. Past **Tortilla Flat** a narrow 26-mile section of the Apache Trail that is unpaved begins. However, if you take it nice and slow the road isn't all that difficult. Just be prepared for frequent sharp turns. Among the sights along this stretch are a dizzying view of the 2,000-foot high multi-colored walls of **Fish Creek Canyon**.

The pavement returns where the road reaches the impressive **Roosevelt Dam**, largest along the Trail. Just beyond that in the cliffs to the right side of the road is the **Tonto National Monument**, *open every day except Christmas from 8:00am until 5:00pm (last admission to trail at 4:00pm); admission is $4 per vehicle for those who don't have a Park Service Passport; three hour guided tours of the 40 rooms in the dwelling are available by reservation only from November through April; call Tel. 520/467-2241 for information.* A well-preserved two-story cliff dwelling dating from the 14th century Salado Indian tribe is built into a natural cave in the side of the cliff about 350 feet above the visitor center. You can get there by a half-mile trail but as it rises very steadily it can be difficult, especially if the day is a hot one. If you don't make the climb you can get a good view of the dwelling from below.

The final 28 miles of the Apache Trail into **Globe** are a much easier drive although the scenery isn't nearly as good as during the first half of the trip. In Globe you'll have the opportunity to see a **Salado Indian pueblo** if you didn't take the trail in Tonto National Monument. The 300-room remains of a 13th century dwelling have been restored and furnished at the **Besh-Ba-Gowah Archaeological Park**. There's also an interesting museum that documents life during that period. *The park is open daily from 8:00am until 5:00pm. It is closed on New Year's, Thanksgiving and Christmas. Admission is $2. Tel. 520/425-0320.*

From Globe you'll start the return trip to Phoenix via US 60, which is a much faster route than the Apache Trail. However, it's also a scenic one. Almost immediately upon leaving town the road passes through the **Devil's Canyon**, an area characterized by very jagged and rocky ridges and unusual pointed formations. The road traverses the **Queens Creek Gorge** via a bridge and a tunnel. There are a number of pull-outs where you can safely park and get out of the car to take a closer look at the scenery. Portions of the drive through the **Salt River Canyon** go through areas where the rocky walls are as high as 2,000 feet.

Things begin to flatten out by the time you reach the town of **Superior**, still a rich mining area. Three miles west of town, still on US 60, is the outstanding **Boyce Thompson Southwestern Arboretum**. A staggering variety of desert vegetation has been gathered from all over the world and is beautifully planted on the Arboretum's 420 acres. Founded in 1924, the garden is Arizona's oldest. The easy paths that meander through the property cover desert terrain as well as areas with an unexpected amount of dense vegetation. These areas are home to numerous colorful birds. *The Arboretum is open every day except Christmas from 8:00am until 5:00pm. Admission is $4 for adults and $2 for children ages 5 through 12. Tel. 520/689-2811.*

Stay on US 60 and you'll return to the Phoenix area in about 45 minutes.

Casa Grande

This excursion is named for the route's highlight, the ancient ruins of Casa Grande National Monument. However, the 145-mile trip covers a number of interesting historic attractions and towns. Head south on I-10 and get off for Sacaton at Exit 175 (Casa Blanca Road).

The site of an ancient Indian settlement, **Sacaton** was first visited by Spanish explorers in the closing years of the 17th century. Still largely a Native American community, Sacaton is the focal point of the **Pima Indian Reservation**. Adjacent to the highway is the **Gila River Cultural Center**, *open every day except for major holidays from 8:00am to 5:00pm; no admission charge; Tel. 520/963-3981*, which contains an extensive recreation of several Indian villages that span about 20 centuries. Several of the cultures represented, such as the Akimel and Tohono O'odham, existed in a relatively small geographic area and are unknown to most visitors. Others, such as the Apache, are more recognizable. One village depicts life in a Hohokam community, an important group because they were the precursor to the Anasazi. There is also a museum and an area where native crafts are demonstrated located next to the park-like setting of the villages.

Return to the Interstate and continue south to Exit 185. Follow AZ 387 east until it runs into AZ 87, passing the Casa Grande Ruins by for now. Then take AZ 287 into the town of Florence. An important frontier town in the middle of the 19th century, **Florence** became the Pinal County seat. It retains an historic flavor with many of its buildings being more than a hundred years old. They claim to have more historic buildings than any other Arizona town and the center has been designated as an historic district. (On a percentage basis this may be true but the town of Prescott definitely has more.)

Two sights of historic merit are both located on Main Street. The first is the excellent **Pinal County Historical Museum**, *open from noon until 4:00pm on Wednesday through Sunday (extended from 11am and till 5:00pm in winter) and is closed on Easter, Thanksgiving and Christmas; admission is free; Tel. 520/868-4382*, which depicts area history both before and since the founding of Florence. I bet that you didn't know that there are more than a hundred different types of barbed wire – but you will after visiting this museum, which has all of them on display. Nearby **McFarland State Historic Park**, *open Thursday through Monday from 8:00am to 5:00pm, year-round except Christmas; admission charge is $2; Tel. 520/868-5216*, concentrates on more modern history. The central feature of the park is the 1878

Pinal County Courthouse. The building has also served as a hospital and an old-age home (we don't use that term anymore but they did when it served that purpose).

Leave Florence in the opposite direction from whence you came until you reach the **Casa Grande Ruins National Monument**. Meaning "the big house," Casa Grande was constructed around 1350 by the Hohokam Indians. The settlement was abandoned approximately a hundred years after it was built for reasons unknown. It consists of a large central structure, four stories high and built of layers of mud. It is surrounded by the remains of a walled village. Portions of the house and village are in ruins. There is a museum in the visitor center and you can take either self-guided or ranger conducted walks through the ruins. Casa Grande is of great historical importance because it represents the ultimate architectural achievement of Hohokam society. *The monument is open every day of the year from 7:00am until 6:00pm. Admission is either $2 per person or $4 per vehicle for those people who do not possess a park service passport. Tel. 520/723-3172.*

Return via AZ 87 and 387 to the Interstate. If you want you can continue south on the highway into the town of Casa Grande. However, there isn't that much there except for another regional museum which isn't any better than the one in Florence. For a different experience, go back north to Exit 175 and then west to the town of **Maricopa**. Located at the edge of the **Ak-chin Indian Reservation**, it is the home of (at least for the time being) of the nearest Indian casino to Phoenix. The casino is owned by the Indians and run for their benefit but it is operated by the well-known Harrah's gaming company.

From Maricopa you can get back to Phoenix by heading north on AZ 347, passing through the **Gila River Indian Reservation**, until you reach I-10 in the southern Phoenix suburb of Chandler. From there it's easy to get back to whatever part of the Phoenix area you're staying in.

To The West

The main attraction to Phoenix's west is **Wickenburg**. This town is included as a major destination in Chapter 19; however, you can make it a day trip from Phoenix. Just take US 60 (Grand Avenue) westbound. It's about a hundred miles round trip.

Another destination heading west is the **Palo Verde Nuclear Generating Station**. Take I-10 west to Exit 98 and follow Winersburg Road south for eight miles. The information center has interactive exhibits on different sources of energy available to mankind. More interesting are guided bus tours of the station. *The Center is open Monday through Friday from 9:00am to 4:30pm with bus tours at 9:00am and 1:00pm by reservation* *only. Admission is free. Tel. 602/393-5757.* Total round trip distance from downtown Phoenix is approximately 110 miles. It may be a more worthwhile destination if you're coming or going to Gila Bend from Phoenix. In that case it only adds a total of about 40 miles.

PRACTICAL INFORMATION

- **Airport:** *Tel. 602/273-3300 or 273-3455*
- **Airport Transportation:** *Tel. 602/232-2222*
- **Bus Depot:** *Tel. 602/271-7425*
- **Hospital:** *Downtown Phoenix, Tel. 602/230-2273; Scottsdale, Tel. 602/481-4000*
- **Hotel Hot Line:** *Tel. 800/666-1316*
- **Municipal Transit Information:** *Tel. 602/253-5000*
- **Police** (non-emergency): *Tel. 602/262-6151*
- **Taxi:** *Checker Cab, Tel. 602/257-1818; Statewide Cab, Tel. 602/994-1616; Yellow Cab, Tel. 602/252-5071*
- **Tourist Office/Visitors Bureau:** *Tel. 602/254-6800.* Automated information 24 hours a day is available by calling *Tel. 602/252-5588*
- **Train Station:** *Tel. 602/253-0121*

13. TUCSON

Founded in 1775, **Tucson** predates Phoenix by a wide margin and was for many year's the territory's and state's biggest city. It's still growing fast and is rapidly approaching a population of a half million people. Although it's not the capital and is smaller than Phoenix in both size and number of residents, Tucson has a rich cultural heritage and a spirit that doesn't recognize second place. It doesn't play second fiddle to its bigger northern neighbor as far as being a tourist destination either.

Located in a high desert valley (the city's altitude is officially listed as 2,389 feet) surrounded by mountains, the dry and somewhat cooler climate of the Tucson area has long made it a popular tourist destination, health resort and retirement community. There are a number of suburban communities in the area but Tucson is different from Phoenix in this respect as well. The city itself is, in large measure, the metropolitan area since the surrounding mountains and nearby desert make expansion opportunities somewhat more limited here.

The area was occupied by Indian civilizations as much as 12,000 years ago because the mountains afforded some protection and there was a source of water. The Spanish Jesuit priest Eusebio Kino explored the area in the 1690s and founded the mission San Xavier del Bac in 1700. It is still active today. The name Tucson is derived from a Papago Indian term roughly meaning "spring at the foot of the mountain." The spring refers to the Santa Cruz River. A *presidio*, or fortified post, was established in 1776 and a town started to grow within its walls. It remained through the turbulent period of conflict with the Indians during Spanish and then Mexican rule. The area came under United States jurisdiction as a result of the Gadsden Purchase in 1853 and Tucson was named Territorial capital in 1867. However, it held that status for only two years. Growth was spurred in 1880 with the coming of the railroad as Tucson was a rough and tumble stopping point on the southern route to California. However, it was not until the end of World War II that growth really took off.

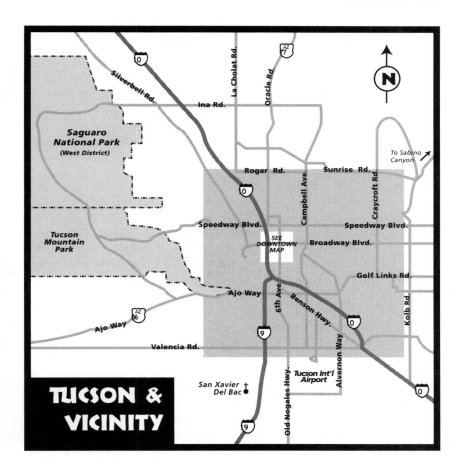

TUCSON & VICINITY

Today Tucson is, besides a major tourist destination, a diversified city where mining and electrical manufacturing are both significant. Native American and Mexican cultural influences are still very important as both groups comprise major segments of the population. Tucson is physically dominated by adobe buildings and the pueblo style. Unlike Phoenix, Tucson has more similarities to the cities of New Mexico. It is a most delightful place to visit.

ARRIVALS AND DEPARTURES

By Air

Tucson International Airport is less than ten miles from the heart of downtown. Taxis and buses can bring you to the city in well under a half hour. If you're renting a car at the airport, exit via Tucson Boulevard. At the intersection of Valencia Road turn left. You can then reach the city center either by taking Valencia to 6th Avenue and turning right or by turning right on Campbell Avenue and taking that to I-10. The time difference for one route versus the other is minimal. The largest airport transportation company is **Arizona Stagecoach**, *Tel. 520/889-1000.*

By Bus & Train

Tucson's train and bus stations are located within a very close proximity to one another on the eastern edge of downtown.
• **Amtrak Station**, *400 East Toole*
• **Bus Station**, *corner of Toole and East 4th Avenue*

By Car

Getting into Tucson couldn't be much easier. Although there are several state routes that come into different parts of Tucson, there's only one highway of note. If you're arriving by car the chances are that you'll be coming from Phoenix. It's just under a two hour drive from Phoenix via I-10. Actually, even if you're coming from the other direction it will almost still certainly be on I-10. Exits 251 through 270 all provide access to various parts of the Tucson area. The only exception to the I-10 routing is for those driving in from Mexico. They will arrive via I-19 but that road, too, will eventually lead into I-10.

Tucson's traffic is about what you would expect for a city of this size – not a breeze but not a nightmare, either. During rush hours pay careful attention to traffic signs. The center turn lanes of several major streets become reverse traffic flow routes during these periods. Parking on street is regulated by meters and is usually not that difficult to find except in the heart of downtown. Most attractions have adequate parking, especially if they're located away from the city center area.

ORIENTATION

The greater portion of Tucson lies on a triangular point of land formed by the Santa Cruz River on the west and the smaller Rillito River to the north and east. The mountains are close by in all directions. Interstate 10 is the primary arterial route coming from Phoenix and runs from the northern border of the city in a south to south-easterly direction. South of downtown, I-19 begins at the junction of I-10 and heads along the Santa Cruz River towards Nogales and the Mexican border.

The city is mostly arranged in a fairly neat grid pattern. South of Speedway Boulevard are numbered streets than run east to west. There are numbered avenues running north to south starting west of Euclid Avenue. Otherwise, streets are mainly named. All streets have a direction prefix (north, south, east, or west). Broadway is the dividing street between north and south designations while Stone Avenue is the divider for east and west. Major east/west streets are (beginning from the north) Speedway Boulevard, 6th Street, Broadway, 22nd Street and Ajo Way. All of these have exits along I-10.

The most important north/south streets are (heading east from the Santa Cruz River) Stone Avenue (which is one-way southbound), 6th Avenue (the northbound only equivalent of Stone), Euclid Avenue, Country Club Road, Craycroft Road and Kolb Road. Many of the Tucson area's most important attractions are located on the west side of the Santa Cruz River and are reached via Speedway Boulevard. Exit 257 on I-10 is Speedway Boulevard.

GETTING AROUND TUCSON

Tucson's attractions are spread out over a rather extensive area and, as usual, a car is most definitely the best way to get around. **Taxis** are plentiful but rates are not regulated so it is quite easy to be charged an exorbitant amount. The most reliable regular cab company is **Yellow Cab**, *Tel. 520/624-6611.* Several limousine companies also cater to tourists, including **Caddy Cab**, *Tel. 520/887-8744* and **Sir Lancelot Limos**, *Tel. 520/880-3030.*

Bus service throughout the metropolitan area is provided by Sun Tran, which operates many routes that cross the city in all directions. The basic fare is 75 cents. Many routes originate from the downtown Ronstadt Transit Center, Sixth Avenue and Congress Street. You can get personalized routing information at the Transit Center or by calling **Sun Tran**, *Tel. 520/792-9222.* Another public transit alternative is the **Old Pueblo Trolley**, *Tel. 520/792-1802.* They operate historic electric streetcars between the downtown business district on Fourth Avenue and the University of Arizona.

Tucson is much easier to digest if you divide it into several different pieces based on location. That's what I've done for you by suggesting three separate tours – one for downtown, another for attractions on the west side of the Santa Cruz River, and a final one covering the remainder of the city and nearby areas.

There are also three more extended excursions. Similarly, dining is divided into downtown and the remainder of the city.

WHERE TO STAY

DOWNTOWN, INCLUDING UNIVERSITY OF ARIZONA VICINITY
Moderate

ADOBE ROSE INN, *940 N. Olsen Avenue. Tel. 520/318-4644, Fax 520/ 325-0055. Toll free reservations Tel. 800/328-4122. 5 Rooms. Rates: High season (early September to May 31st): $95-125; Low season (June 1st to early September): $70-105; all rates include full breakfast. American Express, Discover, MasterCard and VISA accepted. Located two blocks from the University of Arizona, just south of Speedway Boulevard.*

The Adobe Rose is an authentic adobe style house built in 1933. Surrounding a small but lushly planted central patio are the spacious guest facilities which consist of three charmingly furnished rooms as well as two larger cottages. Two of the regular rooms feature wood-burning fireplaces and beautiful stained glass windows. The cottages have efficiency kitchens. All rooms have easy access to the private patio which has a small swimming pool.

EL PRESIDIO BED & BREAKFAST INN, *297 North Main Avenue. Tel. 520/623-6151. Toll free reservations Tel. 800/349-6151. 4 Rooms. Rates: High season (September 1st to mid-May): $95-125; Low season (mid-May to August 31st): $70-90; all rates include full breakfast. No credit cards accepted. Located in the heart of downtown's El Presidio Historic District just north of Congress Street.*

If the El Presidio wasn't an active inn it would certainly be visited as a component of the El Presidio Historic District. The 1880's adobe style mansion fits in perfectly with its surroundings. The inn is spacious and the grounds are simply gorgeous – a lush garden and courtyard featuring cobblestone walkways and a beautiful fountain. It's like taking a trip back in time to Old Mexico. Each of the large suites (two with kitchen) is attractively furnished in a manner appropriate to the building style, including many antiques. However, the inn doesn't sacrifice the modern amenities that guests appreciate. The breakfast is gourmet by any standards and in the evening your hosts invite you to have beverages and fresh fruit.

El Presidio doesn't have parking, however, you can obtain a permit to park your car curbside overnight, which would otherwise be prohibited. There are some restrictions on small children.

LA POSADA DEL VALLE, *1640 N. Campbell Avenue. Tel. 520/795-3840, Fax 520/795-3840. 5 Rooms. Rates: High season (September 1st to June 1st): $90-145; Low season (June 2nd to August 31st): $65-95, both including full breakfast. MasterCard and VISA accepted. Located walking distance from the University of Arizona, a half mile north of Speedway Boulevard.*

Another of the several excellent and charming bed and breakfast inns that can be found in the University area. Built in 1929 this southwestern adobe style residence is surrounded by orange trees and features a lovely, colorful garden highlighted by a large decorative fountain. Each room has a private entrance and is furnished with antiques dating from the period when La Posada was built. Modern amenities include a wetbar, microwave, and refrigerator. Some rooms do not, however, have telephones. A lavish breakfast is served in a pretty dining room that has a good view of the Catalina Mountains.

PEPPERTREES BED & BREAKFAST INN, *724 East University Boulevard. Tel. 520/622-7167, Fax 520/622-7167. Toll free reservations: Tel. 800/348-5763. 7 Rooms. Rates: High season (mid-December to mid-March): $108; Low season (June 1st to early September): $78; all rates include full breakfast. Discover, MasterCard, and VISA accepted. Located by the University of Arizona, west of Park Avenue.*

A pretty Victorian style residence built in 1905 and located on a quiet street close to everything, the Peppertrees has a fenced in patio and is shaded by many trees. The entire building, public areas, and guest rooms are filled with antiques dating back to turn-of-the-century Tucson. There are five large bedroom units and two larger southwestern style guest houses. Rooms have many modern amenities without sacrificing the careful restoration work that makes this one of the most authentic historic homes in the University area. Every guest receives a hearty gourmet breakfast personally prepared by the owner as well as warm and friendly service.

Selected as one of my Best Places to Stay (see Chapter 10 for more details).

PLAZA HOTEL, *1900 East Speedway Boulevard. Tel. 520/327-7341, Fax 520/327-0276. Toll free reservations Tel. 800/843-8052. 150 Rooms. Rates: High season (January 1st to end of May): $85-105; Low season (end of May to September 30th): $49-59. Most major credit cards accepted. Located about 3 miles east of I-10, Exit 257.*

A modern seven story hotel built in 1972 (thoroughly renovated in 1990), the Plaza represents a good value given its excellent location – the convenience of access to attractions offered by Speedway Boulevard and its proximity to the University and downtown. All of the rooms are spacious and well equipped; many offer an excellent view of either the city or the mountains.

The large and attractive sundeck contains a heated swimming pool and whirlpool and is graced by a pretty gazebo that makes a nice place to relax after a busy day. The Plaza Cafe is an adequate restaurant should you not want to venture out to eat and Zonies Bar provides a lively atmosphere to unwind in. Some rooms have refrigerators. Secure covered parking garage.

OTHER AREAS OF TUCSON
Very Expensive
ARIZONA INN, *2200 East Elm Street. Tel. 520/325-1541, Fax 520/881-5830. Toll free reservations Tel. 800/933-1093. 83 Rooms. Rates: High season (early January to late May): $184-245; Low season (late May to mid-September): $134-201; all rates include full breakfast. American Express, MasterCard, and VISA accepted. Located about a half mile north of the intersection of Speedway Boulevard and Campbell Avenue, not far from the University of Arizona.*

While the Arizona Inn does quality for the highest price category, it is still priced considerably less than other resorts of comparable or even lesser quality, so I would have to characterize it as a decent value. Arizona Inn is one of the state's oldest luxury resorts, having opened in 1930 and it is listed on the National Register of Historic Places. A major renovation was completed in 1994 to bring guest rooms up to snuff but the overall atmosphere of the old resort has been nicely retained. Covering about 14 acres close in to the city, the Inn provides a secluded and tranquil desert oasis that's only minutes away from all of the action. The small number of rooms allows for more personalized service. The Inn consists of several dark adobe style buildings and cottages that, along with the main building, enclose a beautifully landscaped courtyard with a rich, carpet like lawn dotted with flowers blazing with color.

All of the rooms and suites are each warmly decorated in a unique manner of understated elegance – no two rooms are alike. Many rooms have private patios or balconies and some have fireplaces. The accommodations are as varied as the decor with two-room suites, kitchens, and efficiencies all being available. Several large private cottages are priced at considerably higher rates.

Facilities are quite varied considering that this isn't a huge resort. These include two lighted tennis courts, a croquet court, and exercise equipment. You can even play table tennis. Of course there is a heated outdoor swimming pool. On the dining side the Arizona Inn boasts two restaurants. One, called the Main Dining Room at the Arizona Inn features outstanding service and fine continental cuisine. The other is more casual and offers outdoor poolside dining. The dignified Audubon Lounge is a quiet retreat for relaxing and conversation while having a drink. A pianist provides easy listening music. A final touch is the hotel's Library where guests can cozy up with a good book on Tucson or other topics.

THE LODGE AT VENTANA CANYON, *6200 N. Clubhouse Lane. Tel. 520/577-1400; Fax 520/299-0256. Toll free reservations 800/828-5701. 49 Rooms. Rates: High season (October through April): $495-695; Low season (May through September): $215-495. Major credit cards accepted. Located approxi-*

mately 8 miles east of intersection of Oracle and Ina Roads and then east via Ina to Skyline and then Sunrise Road to Clubhouse Lane.

Now that you've recovered (I hope) from absorbing the Scottsdale-like prices, let's explore why they can get away with charging so much. The epitome of luxurious living, the spacious (mostly two-bedroom and two-bedroom suite units) are done in an elegant southwestern motif that would be hard to improve on. Almost every unit overlooks the beautiful Catalina Mountains as the Lodge is picturesquely situated in the foothills.

Recreational opportunities are abundant. For starters there's 36 holes of golf and 12 tennis courts. A complete spa is also on the premises. You can rent bicycles to explore the Catalina Mountains and surrounding areas. Massage is also available. Because of the very small nature of the Lodge, service is definitely personalized and up to the highest standards. Somewhat disappointing is the on-premise restaurant, which is good but little more. The choice of restaurants in the area is also somewhat limited.

Despite these minor shortcomings I was almost going to put the Lodge at Ventana Canyon among Arizona's best places to stay. But with price/value consideration in mind, it just misses by the barest of margins.

LOEWS VENTANA CANYON RESORT, *7000 North Resort Drive. Tel. 520/299-2020, Fax 520/299-6832. Toll free reservations Tel. 800/234-5117. 398 Rooms. Rates: High season (January 1st to June 30th): $295-325; Low season (July 1st to mid-September): $130-165. Major credit cards accepted. Located off of Sunrise Drive in the foothills of the Santa Catalina mountains. Take Oracle Road (AZ 77) north to Orange Grove Road and then east via Skyline Drive into Sunrise Drive.*

This is a gorgeous resort, too, but far different than the Arizona Inn. For one thing, its style is much more modern, having been built in 1984. Spread out on almost 90 beautifully landscaped acres at the foot of the Catalina Mountains and providing magnificent views of both mountain and city, Loews Ventana Canyon is a full-service and self-contained resort. The grounds have been designed to take advantage of the natural flora of the area and cactus plants are abundant. The showcase of the property is an 80-foot high man-made waterfall that leads into a "river" that travels serenely throughout the grounds of the resort.

Guest rooms are large and attractive without being dazzling. They feature all of the amenities you could ever want (including refrigerator/mini-bar) and have a patio or balcony. Some suites have full kitchen facilities. For dining there are four different restaurants to choose from ranging from a casual coffee shop all the way up to the formal and elegant continental cuisine featured in the Ventana Room (featured in the *Where to Eat* section). There's also a nicely done afternoon tea and lounges with entertainment as well as a nightclub. One of the cocktail lounges is poolside.

Complete recreational facilities are available at Ventana Canyon Resort. These are two outdoor swimming pools, jacuzzi and whirlpool, fully equipped health club, ten lighted tennis courts and 18 holes of golf in a setting par excellence. You can also jog or walk to your heart's content on the jogging trail or separate three-mile long nature trail. Bicycle rentals are also available.

SHERATON EL CONQUISTADOR, *10000 North Oracle Road. Tel. 520/544-5000, Fax 520/544-1222. Toll free reservations Tel. 800/325-7832. 434 Rooms. Rates: High season (mid-January to April 30th): $175-280; Low season (June 1st to mid-September): $85-160. Major credit cards accepted. Located north of downtown via Oracle Road (AZ 77), about four miles north of the intersection of Ina Road.*

The 200-acre "mega-resort" has been a leader in Tucson from well before the days when that term was used to describe full service luxury hotels. Nestled in the foothills of the beautiful Santa Catalina Mountains, the El Conquistador has some great desert sunset views. The buildings are low rise and built in both Spanish and Native American architectural styles. Here, too, the man-made blends in well with the natural surroundings.

All guest rooms are located in groups of small casita style buildings and feature private balcony or patio, coffee maker, and safe. The rooms are spacious. Upgraded units and suites have even more amenities such as a jacuzzi or fireplace. The decor is an attractive "southwestern modern."

Of all the major Tucson hotels none has a better selection of restaurants than the El Conquistador. These range from Mexican (Dos Locos is featured in the Where to Eat section), to southwestern (White Dove), western steak and beef (Last Territory Steakhouse) and continental with a fabulous view at La Vista. The Sheraton El Conquistador has four swimming pools, full service health and fitness center, three golf courses, horseback and bicycle riding, and supervised children's program.

Selected as one of my Best Places to Stay (see Chapter 11 for more details).

OMNI TUCSON NATIONAL RESORT, *2727 W. Club Drive. Tel. 520/297-2271, Fax 520/297-7544. Toll free reservations Tel. 800/528-4856. 167 Rooms. Rates: High season (late December to May 31st): $240-350; Low season (June 1st to mid-September): $95-115. Most major credit cards accepted. Located about two miles west of I-10, Exit 248; then via Mona Lisa Road north to Magee Road west, and finally north on Shannon Road. An Omni International Hotel.*

A world class resort covering almost 650 acres (including the golf course, of course), this property caters mainly to those interested in golf and/or spa type vacations. However, the high level of service and beautiful surroundings definitely makes it appropriate for anyone willing to spend the bucks necessary for this level of luxury. The landscaped grounds are surrounded by low-rise buildings containing the very large guest rooms and suites. Even bigger and more luxurious villa suites are available at the upper end of the price scale. Many rooms and suites overlook the magnificently manicured fairways of the golf course. All rooms feature honor bars and coffee makers. There are two restaurants and cocktail lounges.

As the Tucson National Golf Resort bills itself as a place to play in the sun, let's take a look at the extensive facilities offered to guests. The 27 holes of golf are on courses that challenge the pros. Other sports include tennis (two lighted courts), volleyball, and two beautiful swimming pools, one with an adjacent bar. The first class health spa has exercise equipment, whirlpool, and professional massage services available.

WESTIN LA PALOMA, *3800 East Sunrise Drive. Tel. 520/742-6000, Fax 520/577-5886. Toll free reservations Tel. 800/876-3683. 487 Rooms. Rates: High season (January 1st to May 31st): $325-430; Low season (June 1st to early September): $119-215. Major credit cards accepted. Located northeast of downtown via Oracle Road (AZ 77) to Orange Grove Road and then east to Skyline Drive into Sunrise Drive.*

Westin resorts worldwide are known for their award winning service and luxurious appointments. The Tucson version won't disappoint you at all regarding either category. The modern (1986) resort is built in the beautiful Spanish Mission style at the foot of the Catalina Mountains, like the majority of Tucson resort hotels. The grounds are gorgeous and are highlighted by the huge pool area that has a magnificent waterfall with separate pond, Arizona's longest waterslide (so says the hotel), and even a bar and grill that you can swim up to. After all, why bother getting out of the water to eat or have a drink.

Guest rooms and suites at the Westin La Paloma are certainly among the best in Tucson. Spacious and beautifully decorated, all feature such amenities as a hair dryer, minibar and refrigerator, coffee maker, and safe to keep personal belongings. Balconies or patios are also standard with some offering spectacular vistas. There are four restaurants ranging from casual to gourmet and lounge facilities with entertainment nightly.

The recreational facilities are also first class. Besides the aforementioned main swimming pool, there are two other pools, saunas, whirlpools, and a health and fitness center with personalized service and therapy pools. The 27 holes of golf bear a Jack Nicklaus signature, so you know they're among the best, or you can play racquetball, tennis (12 courts of which ten are lighted), and try an aerobics workout. The extensive grounds are also laced with a network of nature trails so you can see the desert and mountains without ever leaving the resort.

WESTWARD LOOK RESORT, *245 East Ina Road. Tel. 520/297-1151, Fax 520/297-9023. Toll free reservations Tel. 800/722-2500. 244 Rooms. Rates: High season (February 1st to April 30th): $239-369; Low season (June 1st to mid-September): $89-159. Major credit cards accepted. Located north of downtown. Take Oracle Road (AZ 77) to Ina Road and turn right. If coming from the north, use Exit 248 of I-10 and proceed east on Ina Road.*

This desert oasis is a contemporary style resort nestled in the Catalina Mountain foothills. Covering almost 50 acres, the Westward Look features landscaping that is in harmony with the Sonoran Desert of which it is a part. Large Saguaro cactus dot the manicured grounds. Dramatic views of Tucson and the mountains come with most rooms and public areas. Several buildings house the guest rooms and are situated around courtyards and landscaped pool areas. The accommodations are modern and large. Amenities include mini-refrigerators with wet bar, coffee makers, and iron with ironing board. Every room also has either has a private patio or balcony so you can get a good look at those fantastic desert sunsets. Besides all of the beauty that surrounds you, guests at the Westward Look will appreciate the award-winning service of its attentive staff.

The Gold Room is the premier restaurant and is listed in the Where to Eat section that follows. Lighter fare and more casual dining is also available in the Bar and Grill. The latter features live entertainment on weekend evenings. When you're ready to relax try out one of the three swimming pools, each with its own hot spa or work out in the fully equipped fitness center. The health center staff conducts group and individualized wellness programs. Sports available at the Westward Look are tennis (eight courts/five lighted), basketball, volleyball, and jogging trails. The grounds also feature a picturesque nature trail for easier strolls. Horseback riding can be arranged through the activities desk.

Expensive

DOUBLETREE HOTEL AT REID PARK, *445 S. Alvernon Way. Tel. 520/881-4200; Fax 520/323-5225. Toll free reservations 800/222-TREE. 295 Rooms. Rates: High season (late September to mid-May): $94-149; Low season (mid-May to late September): $67-89. Major credit cards accepted. Located about five miles east of I-10, Exit 258 via Broadway to Alvernon and then just south.*

Attractive combination of motor inn and high-rise styles surrounding nicely landscaped grounds. High quality rooms especially given the prices. Heated swimming pool, tennis courts and complete fitness center on the premises. A golf course is across the street and the front desk personnel will help you arrange a tee time. Restaurant on the premises.

HACIENDA DEL SOL, *5601 N. Hacienda del Sol. Tel. 520/299-1501, Fax 520/299-5554. 31 Rooms. Rates: High season (mid-November to May 31st): $115-155; Low season (July and August): $75-80. American Express, MasterCard, and VISA accepted. Located in the foothills of the Catalinas. Take N. Oracle Road (AZ 77) to River Road; turn right and proceed about four miles to Hacienda del Sol. Turn left to hotel.*

The Hacienda del Sol is a cross between a luxury resort and a more casual guest ranch. In fact, I wasn't quite sure which category to include it in. This hotel exudes a warm old world charm throughout the historic hacienda style buildings and the expansive grounds which surround it. Also offering great views of the Catalina foothills and mountains, a stay at del Sol is almost like having your own private retreat. The 31 rooms, which makes it private enough, are located on a spacious 34 acres of meticulously cared for grounds. A major part of the property is surrounded by a white washed adobe wall with a dark wooden gate. In the courtyard created by this arrangement are lush green lawns, mature trees of several different varieties, paved walkways, and fountains. It is an oasis of tranquillity and beauty. You could spend many hours just letting the time float by as you casually walk around.

The accommodations are excellent. Oversized rooms are the rule and several even larger suites and casitas with separate living areas are available ($195-295 during high season and $125-175 low season). The decor is in keeping with the hacienda atmosphere. The hotel has on-premise dining, a swimming pool and spa with professional massage available. Sporting activities are tennis and horseback riding.

MARRIOTT UNIVERSITY PARK HOTEL, *880 East 2nd Street. Tel. 520/792-4100; Fax 520/882-4100. Toll free reservations 800/228-9290. 250 Rooms. Rates: High season (mid-September to mid-May): $114-214; Low season (mid-May to mid-September): $69-179. Major credit cards accepted. Located slightly to the east of downtown, south of Speedway Boulevard. From downtown, proceed north on 6th Avenue to 2nd Street and turn right.*

One of Tucson's newest luxury hotels, the Marriott was completed in 1996 and is just on the outside edge of the downtown area. The atrium lobby adds a nice modern touch, but at only nine stories it shouldn't make those concerned with heights too unsteady. The guest rooms are all attractively furnished and well equipped with the expected amenities. They're also a good size. The restaurant is decent. The only recreation is a swimming pool. Pay parking.

Moderate

THE LODGE ON THE DESERT, *306 North Alvernon Way. Tel. 520/325-3366, Fax 520/327-5834. Toll free reservations Tel. 800/456-5634. 40 Rooms. Rates: High season (November 1st-May 31st): $110-205; Low season*

(June 1st-October 31st): $69-125. Major credit cards accepted. Located about four miles northeast of downtown near the intersection of Speedway Boulevard.

An historic property dating back to 1936, the Lodge on the Desert is constructed in traditional Mexican adobe style. It was completely renovated in 1994. The 40 guest rooms are located in eight separate lodge buildings, attractively grouped around a garden-like courtyard. The courtyard is covered by precisely manicured lawns and has several attractive stone fountains as well as the hotel's heated swimming pool. The rooms are mostly average size although most have a working fireplace. Guests looking for a nice place to relax can wander into the Lodge's private library and reading room. Also on the premises are a restaurant and cocktail lounge.

SMUGGLER'S INN, *6350 East Speedway Boulevard. Tel. 520/296-3292, Fax 520/722-3713. Toll free reservations Tel. 800/525-8852. 150 Rooms. Rates: High season (February 1st to April 30th): $99-119; Low season (June 1st to September 30th): $56-63. Major credit cards accepted. Located at the intersection of Speedway and Wilmot Road, about seven miles east of downtown.*

This is another motor inn style hostelry, which is generally what you'll find in Tucson in the two lower priced categories. However, Smuggler's is a beautiful property that has a lot to offer. The guest rooms, each with a private patio or balcony, surround a large central courtyard that has a tropical motif. Colorful gardens and a picturesque small lagoon highlight the area. The lagoon is home to a population of ducks as well as many giant goldfish that seem to especially delight children (no fishing, please!). The rooms are larger than most motor inns and feature attractive furnishings. There's even an extra telephone in the bathroom. Coffee makers are standard. Upstairs units have vaulted ceilings. Some rooms have refrigerators. There are also 24 efficiency units that have kitchenette and separate living areas.

When you get hungry the Jamaica Bay Cafe has full service dining and drinks can be had at the Calypso Bar. Recreational pursuits are the heated swimming pool with spa and a putting green. Guests at the Smuggler's Inn receive privileges to play at nearby golf and tennis facilities.

WINDMILL INN AT ST. PHILIP'S PLAZA, *4250 N. Campbell Avenue. Tel. 520/577-0007; Fax 520/577-0045. Toll free reservations Tel. 800/547-4747. 122 Rooms. Rates: High season (January through mid-April): $135; Low season (June through mid-September): All rates include in-room Continental breakfast upon request. $65. Major credit cards accepted. Located just north of the Rillito River Bridge by River Road. Take Speedway east from city center to Campbell and then turn north.*

Very spacious two-room units with separate living and sleeping areas. All units also have fully equipped kitchen including wet bar and microwave oven. Nicely decorated. Some rooms have pretty mountain views.

Among the amenities provided to guests are free rental bicycles and a book lending library. Although the hotel itself doesn't have a restaurant it is located adjacent to an attractive commercial plaza that contains four different kinds of restaurants as well as quite a bit of shopping. A good value in a good location, especially for families or those who like a lot of room to spread out.

Inexpensive

WAYWARD WINDS LODGE, *707 W. Miracle Mile. Tel. 520/791-7526, Fax 520/791-9502. Toll free reservations Tel. 800/791-9503. 40 Rooms. Rates: High season (mid-December to mid-April): $99-149, including continental breakfast; Low season (June 1st to September 30th): $69-99. Most major credit cards accepted. Located approximately one mile east of I-10, Exit 255.*

A friendly family run operation that's been pleasing guests for over 35 years, the Wayward Winds is an attractive motel on a generous five acre site. All of the guest rooms overlook an attractively landscaped courtyard. The higher rates are for larger apartment and suite style units which contain either kitchens or refrigerators. However, even the standard rooms are bigger than in most motels, especially those with comparable prices. The courtyard grounds contain a heated swimming pool with slide and shuffleboard courts. There's also a barbecue area. Plenty of nearby restaurants in all price ranges make up for the lack of an on-premise dining room.

CAMPING & RV SITES
• **Butterfield RV Resort**, *2601 N. Campbell Avenue, Tel. 800/863-8160*
• **Cactus Country RV Resort**, *10195 S. Houghton Road, Tel. 520/574-3000*
• **Catalina State Park**, *9 miles north of Tucson on US 89, Tel. 602/628-5798*
• **Crazy Horse RV Park Campgrounds**, *6660 S. Craycroft Road, Tel. 800/279-6279*
• **Justin's RV Park**, *3551 San Joaquin, Tel. 520/883-8340*
• **Prince of Tucson RV Park**, *3501 N. Freeway, Tel. 800/955-3501*
• **Rincon Country West RV Resort**, *4555 S. Mission Road, Tel. 800/782-7275*
• **Western Way RV Resort**, *3100 S. Kinney Road, Tel. 800/292-8616*

WHERE TO EAT
DOWNTOWN
Moderate

CARUSO'S, *434 N. Fourth Avenue, Tel. 520/624-5765. Most major credit cards accepted. Dinner served nightly.*

The Zagona family has operated Caruso's at this location since 1938 and the place has become something of a local legend for expertly prepared Italian fare. The menu selections aren't fancy (featuring such favorite staples as ravioli, lasagna, manicotti, spaghetti and even pizza) but they are all are just about as good as you can make them and served in generous amounts. The decor is attractive but for the ultimate experience try dining on the beautiful patio with its casual furniture and pretty checkerboard tablecloths, all surrounded by a refreshing row of shade trees. A delightful experience. Beer and wine are served.

EL CHARRO MEXICAN CAFE, *311 N. Court Avenue, Tel. 520/622-1922. Most major credit cards accepted. Lunch and dinner served daily. Other locations are in the El Mercado shopping area (6310 E. Broadway) and near the airport at 7250 S. Tucson Boulevard.*

The original El Charro location on Court Avenue has been serving guests since 1922 and may well be the oldest existing restaurant in all of Tucson. This location is my favorite even though all three spots offer great food and excellent service. Perhaps knowing it is the first makes it feel more authentic, but it may also have to do with the fact that it has an excellent gift shop. The value here is outstanding, with some entrees being priced in the inexpensive category. The food tends to be on the hot side so let your server know if you would like the spice toned down a bit. El Charro features authentic Sonoran-style food, which is very hard to find in many parts of the US. The carne seca is excellent.

The nice decor features several small and cozy dining rooms or you can try the pleasant outdoor cantina called Bar Toma! Full service bar and cocktail service.

EL MARIACHI RESTAURANT, *106 W. Drachman, Tel. 520/791-7793. Most major credit cards accepted. Lunch and dinner served daily; entertainment Wednesday through Sunday evenings (reservations suggested).*

Just as a restaurant, El Mariachi makes the grade as one of the best places for Mexican food in Tucson. The mesquite broiled steaks and such specialties as Tequila Shrimp are outstanding. However, what makes a dinner at El Mariachi so special are the performances of the widely acclaimed group called International Mariachi America. Many places in the Tucson area have mariachi entertainers but none are better than these. Show times vary so it is best to call in advance. Cocktails are served.

GERONIMO'S RESTAURANT AND BAR, *University Boulevard and Euclid Avenue (in the Geronimo Hotel), Tel. 520/623-1711. American Express, MasterCard, and VISA accepted. Lunch and dinner served daily.*

The Geronimo Hotel is an historic Tucson landmark and the restaurant is no different – it's like stepping back a half century in time. The place has become increasingly popular with locals over the years and offers a nice variety of American and southwestern dishes in a comfortable and casual atmosphere. Geronimo's is especially popular with the late night set since the kitchen remains open into the wee hours. Of course, part of that popularity is due to the excellent bar that, among other things, features more than 50 different kinds of beer. The atmosphere and crowd at Geronimo's tends toward young adult and up – it's not the best place to bring kids.

CAFE POCA COSA, *88 E. Broadway and 20 S. Scott, Tel. 520/622-6400. Lunch and dinner, Monday through Saturday. MasterCard and VISA.*

This gets our vote for one of the very best restaurants in Tucson, and really the entire state. The location on South Scott is only open for breakfast and lunch on weekdays; the dinner location on East Broadway is attached to the Clarion Hotel. You'll be treated to extremely imaginative, elegantly prepared, wonderful Mexican specalties. The menu changes daily, but a typical menu consists of shredded chicken, beef, pork, and seafood dishes with various sauces and molés, cooked with a terrific South of the Border flair. There's a sampler platter where the chef picks out for you a sample of three of the night's entrees. Molés are incredibly good, and are not limited to the traditional chocolate: there's green, yellow, etc.

O'MALLEY'S ON FOURTH, *247 N. Fourth Avenue, Tel. 520/623-8600. Most major credit cards accepted. Lunch and dinner served daily.*

About the closest thing you can get to an Irish pub in Tucson, O'Malley's menu has several different types of cuisine but with an emphasis on southwestern. Popular with locals because of its casual atmosphere and the lively sports bar, O'Malley's is located in an historic warehouse that has been nicely renovated. An old trolley car is the centerpiece and is used for dining. Imported draft beers are a specialty. For entertainment there are pool tables and plenty of TV stations pulled in by the satellite dishes.

OTHER AREAS OF TUCSON
Very Expensive

DESERT GARDEN, *3800 East Sunrise Drive (in the Westin La Paloma Hotel), Tel. 520/742-6000. Major credit cards accepted. Breakfast, lunch, and dinner served daily; Sunday brunch. Reservations are suggested.*

A beautiful dining room that has fantastic views of the Catalina Mountains, this is one of the most elegant restaurants in Tucson. The service is first class and the food is expertly prepared. Menu staples are steak and fresh fish. Lighter fare includes imaginative salads. Be sure to find out what the special entree is because it's usually a worthwhile selection. The best part of dinner, in my opinion, is the southwestern-style tapas that is served with each entree. They're delicious and what differentiates Desert Garden from a lot of other similar restaurants. Even so, the prices are quite high. Cocktails and full service lounge.

JANOS RESTAURANT, *at the Westin La Paloma, 3800 East Sunrise Drive. Tel. 520/615-6100. Most major credit cards accepted. Dinner nightly; closed Sunday and Monday mid-May to mid-November. Reservations are required.*

An extraordinary dining experience awaits you in this historic adobe pueblo constructed in the 1850's, now designated as a national landmark. The furnishings and service are equally elegant. The inspired cuisine is southwestern with a French influence. I'm not sure what you call the result but the taste is simply delicious. The selection of wines isn't huge but has been carefully chosen to perfectly complement the menu. Cocktails are served and there is also a separate lounge.

THE TACK ROOM, *2800 N. Sabino Canyon Road, Tel. 520/722-2800. Major credit cards accepted. Dinner served nightly; closed first half of July, on Monday from mid-May to mid-January, and on Tuesday from mid-July to September 30th. Dress code. Reservations are suggested.*

This may be Tucson's highest priced restaurant but it most certainly ranks among the finest and is worth the steep payout if you appreciate elegance. Located in an old Spanish colonial-style hacienda, The Tack Room is one of the most beautiful dining rooms you're likely to encounter. The food preparation and service is highly sophisticated and formal. Delicious southwestern dishes are featured. The Tack Room has an extensive wine cellar.

THE VENTANA ROOM, *7000 N. Resort Drive, in Loew's Ventana Canyon Resort. Tel. 520/299-2020. Major credit cards accepted. Dinner served nightly. Dress code. Reservations are suggested.*

Definitely among the most sophisticated dining spots in the entire Tucson area, if not the state, the Ventana Room offers elegant surroundings and exquisite views of the city. After dark, especially, it is a superb setting for a delicious meal. And that you will get for sure. Continental cuisine is on tap and it will be beautifully prepared and presented. If anything, the service is a bit too formal. The staff, however, is exceedingly knowledgeable and will be able to fully explain what each dish is and how it is prepared.

Expensive

ANTHONY'S IN THE CATALINAS, *6440 N. Campbell Avenue, Tel. 520/299-1771. Most major credit cards accepted. Lunch served Monday through Saturday; dinner nightly. Dress code. Reservations are suggested.*

A good selection of continental entrees expertly prepared and served with great style and efficiency is the hallmark of Anthony's. The restaurant is beautiful as is the view of either the mountains or the city. The wine selection, from their own cellars, is outstanding. Although it might be a small notch down from The Tack Room I would have to say it represents a better value. Full cocktail service.

CAPRICCIO'S, *4825 N. First Avenue, Tel. 520/887-2333. Most major credit cards accepted. Dinner served nightly except Sunday. Reservations are suggested.*

For one of the best places for northern Italian cuisine in Tucson you simply have to come to Capriccio's. The atmosphere and surroundings are rich without being overwhelming. The same can be said of the service which is outstanding but in a friendly sort of way. The menu features a wide variety of dishes including beef, lamb, fresh seafood, and pasta, of course. A specialty of the house is the delicious roast duck served in a blend of Grand Marnier and green peppercorn sauce. Be sure to leave some room for Capriccio's excellent selection of super rich desserts. Live music. Full service bar and a good wine list.

DANIEL'S RESTAURANT, *4340 N. Campbell Avenue, Tel. 520/742-3200. Major credit cards accepted. Dinner served nightly. Reservations are suggested.*

If there's a northern Italian restaurant that can effectively match Capriccio's it is Daniel's. (How convenient that they come one after another alphabetically. This way you can compare without flipping pages.) The restaurant is nicely divided into several small and intimate rooms so you almost feel as if you're in a private dining room. My only complaint, and it's a little one, is that the art deco design, although pleasant, doesn't seem "Italian" to me. The service adds to the private atmosphere as your attentive waiter will tend to your every need. You can also dine outdoor on the patio which overlooks the attractive courtyard of St. Philip's Plaza. Veal, lamb, pasta, and fish are featured with the specials varying according to season and, in the case of fish, daily by availability. Desserts are also something special at Daniel's. The restaurant has one of the largest selections of wine in the city as well as providing full cocktail service.

DOS LOCOS CANTINA, *10000 N. Oracle Road (in the Sheraton El Conquistador), Tel. 520/544-1705. Major credit cards accepted. Lunch and dinner served nightly.*

An attractive and casual restaurant featuring authentic Mexican cuisine, Dos Locos overlooks the beautiful grounds of the El Conquistador resort. Weather permitting (which is most of the time) you can get even closer to those grounds by dining out on the pretty patio. The feel of old Mexico is enhanced by the live mariachi music during dinner. Dos Locos also offers dancing. Full cocktail service.

EL PARADOR RESTAURANT AND CANTINA, *2744 E. Broadway Boulevard, Tel. 520/881-2808. Major credit cards accepted. Lunch and dinner served daily; Sunday brunch.*

A popular eatery serving Tucson residents and visitors since the mid 1940's, El Parador has both southwestern and Sonoran cuisine along with a small selection of American dishes. Although many Tucson restaurants feature outdoor dining, this all-indoor room has the feel of the great outdoors with its beautiful tropical garden decor. Cocktails are served. (Sometimes listed as John Jacob's El Parador.)

ENCORE MED ON SWAN AND CAFE TRIANA, *2959 N. Swan Road, Tel. 520/881-6611. Most major credit cards accepted. Lunch and dinner served daily. Reservations are suggested.*

If you're not quite sure what kind of food to have then Encore Med might be the solution to your dilemma since they serve French, Spanish, and Italian cuisine. The dining room is beautifully decorated, the service is attentive and efficient, and the food is delicious. Although Encore Med is a fine restaurant it isn't overly formal. However, if you're looking for a very casual dining experience, you can eat in the adjoining Cafe Triana. The cafe also serves a good variety of excellent Mediterranean fare but is especially popular for their authentic Spanish tapas. Cocktail service.

THE GOLD ROOM, *245 East Ina Road (in the Westward Look Resort), Tel. 520/297-9023. Major credit cards accepted. Lunch and dinner served daily; Sunday brunch. Dress code. Reservations are suggested.*

Tucson doesn't have any revolving restaurants high above the city but the Gold Room is about as close to that as you can get. The view of the city from the higher elevation of northern Tucson is gorgeous, especially after dark. The restaurant features continental cuisine, beautifully prepared and elegantly served. The daily specials, however, are often the best price value. Cocktail service and separate lounge.

PENELOPE'S, *3071 N. Swan Road, Tel. 520/325-5080. Most major credit cards accepted. Lunch served Tuesday through Friday; dinner nightly except Monday. Reservations are suggested.*

This is one of the most attractive restaurants in town. Situated in an adobe ranch house and decorated in the style of an old country inn, Penelope's is beautiful without being fancy and has a genuinely warm atmosphere. Part of that warmth comes from the wood burning fireplaces and colorful stained glass. Dine either inside or on the attractive patio. The cuisine is provincial French and features such specialties as escargot, quail, and fresh fish. The authentic French onion soup is first rate. The staff is knowledgeable and friendly which adds immeasurably to the charming dining experience that awaits you at Penelope's.

RANCHER'S CLUB OF ARIZONA, *5151 East Grant Road (in the Hotel Park Tucson), Tel. 520/323-6262. Most major credit cards accepted.*

Lunch served Monday through Friday; dinner nightly except Sunday. Reservations are suggested.

For great steaks and seafood the Rancher's Club is a top Tucson priority, although there are some excellent chicken dishes as well. The food is grilled to perfection and flavor is added through the use of specially selected aromatic woods placed on the grill. The prime rib of beef is thick, juicy, and tender and the portions are generous. The luxurious decor (fine leathers and rich woods) is that of an old-time private ranchers club where cattle barons would come to spend some time with their industry colleagues and bring samples of their beef so that they could prove that theirs was the best. These people were used to being served in high style and you'll be treated that way too. The Ranchers Club has live entertainment. Cocktails are served tableside or in the separate lounge with its ornate bar.

Moderate

CITY GRILL, *6350 East Tanque Verde Road, Tel. 520/733-1111. Most major credit cards accepted. Lunch and dinner served daily.*

A new and deservedly popular eatery that's ideally suited for either a light or full meal for busy tourist wanting efficient service. The menu is extensive and features everything from gourmet pizzas to wonderfully prepared Angus steaks. Grilled fresh seafood, rotisserie chicken and several pasta dishes are also good choices. City Grill has a surprisingly large wine list along with a full service bar. Take-out service is available.

CAFE TERRA COTTA, *4310 N. Campbell Avenue. Tel. 520/577-8100. Major credit cards accepted. Lunch and dinner served daily. Reservations are suggested.*

The hallmark of Cafe Terra Cotta is modern southwestern cuisine that is well prepared using fresh (mostly local) ingredients. The dining room is comfortable and casual but most people seem to prefer the outdoor patio. Seems that southwestern cooking tastes even better under the stars. If you're not in the mood for a full meal try their wood-fired pizza. It may not be southwestern but it is delicious. The restaurant also has a takeout section that is popular with the local populace because you can have gourmet quality food right in your own home (or hotel room in this case). A few entrees edge into the Expensive category.

EL CORRAL RESTAURANT, *2201 East River Road, Tel. 520/299-6092. Most major credit cards accepted. Dinner served nightly.*

There are several entrees in the inexpensive category, although it generally borders on the moderate price range. Regardless of which side of the price line it falls into, El Corral serves fabulous steaks and prime rib at a price that will easily beat most of the competition. Some non-beef entrees are also on the menu. The restaurant is a beauty, too, occupying an historic adobe territorial style ranch house that dates back to the closing years of the 19th century. The interior decor is authentic Mexican and is highlighted by flagstone floors, wood beamed ceiling, and attractive fireplaces. The service is excellent – and more than what you would expect from such a reasonably priced place. If you like beef than you can't do much better than the El Corral.

FUEGO, *6958 E. Tanque Verde Road. Tel. 520/886-1745. American Express, MasterCard and VISA accepted. Dinner served nightly. Reservations are suggested.*

Another good entry in the southwestern cuisine department. After all, this is Tucson. While it isn't quite up to the level of quality or atmosphere as Cafe Terra Cotta, the check will set you back a few dollars less per person and that is an important consideration for many travelers. You won't go wrong dining at Fuego.

J-BAR, *at the Westin La Paloma, 3800 East Sunrise Drive. Tel. 520/615-6100. Dinner served nightly except Sunday. American Express, MasterCard and VISA.*

In the same building as Janos, its more expensive sister restaurant, at the Westin La Paloma hotel in the Catalina foothills, the J-Bar has a very pretty patio where you can watch the Tucson city lights twinkling below while consuming very tasty Mexican, Latin American, and Caribbean cuisine. Quesadillas, jerk chicken and beef, pork adabo are typical dishes. Most dishes are expertly grilled, the margaritas are powerful (and large), and your wallet won't complain as much as it would next door at Janos's other establishment.

LI'L ABNER'S STEAKHOUSE, *8500 North Silverbell Road. Tel. 520/744-2800. Major credit cards accepted. Dinner served daily.*

Featuring sumptuous mesquite grilled steaks, this is also a great place for chicken and ribs. Guests can select from either indoor or outdoor dining in this large and popular gathering spot. Friday and Saturday nights are especially busy, perhaps because of the live Western band and dancing on those evenings.

LOTUS GARDEN RESTAURANT, *5975 East Speedway Boulevard, Tel. 520/298-3351. Most major credit cards accepted. Lunch and dinner served daily.*

One of the most popular Chinese restaurants in Tucson (and there are several good ones), the Lotus Garden has been serving up delicious Cantonese and Szechuan style cuisine since 1968. The Wong family does the cooking and a lot of the serving as well. The latter is done in an efficient and businesslike manner but without a loss of friendliness. Lotus Garden features a full service bar.

THE OLIVE TREE RESTAURANT, *7000 E. Tanque Verde Road, Tel. 520/298-1845. MasterCard and VISA accepted. Lunch and dinner served Monday through Saturday; dinner only on Sunday. Reservations are suggested.*

My enthusiasm for Greek food may be showing once again but the Olive Tree has been recognized for several years running as one of the best in Tucson. They also feature a diverse selection of continental dishes, seafood, and pasta in addition to traditional Greek favorites like mousaka and numerous lamb based entrees. The indoor dining room is an attractive Mediterranean style decor and the courtyard patio is simply delightful. Olive Tree boasts an impressive list of European and domestic wines along with full cocktail service and a separate lounge. Children's menu.

PINNACLE PEAK STEAKHOUSE, *6541 E. Tanque Verde Road, Tel. 520/886-5012. Most major credit cards accepted. Dinner served nightly.*

This is a large restaurant that's almost always crowded with locals. And with good reason. The Pinnacle serves up thick and tender mesquite broiled steaks and chicken, fabulous barbecued ribs, and fresh fish in generous portions at a price that is much lower than you would expect to pay in a nice looking restaurant with good service. A few entrees are actually priced in the inexpensive category. While it may not be a gourmet dining experience, this is an excellent value choice if you're looking for tasty western style food. Cocktail service and bar.

SCORDATO'S, *4405 W. Speedway Boulevard, Tel. 792-3055. Major credit cards accepted. Dinner served nightly except Monday. Dress code. Reservations are suggested.*

Nearing its silver anniversary in Tucson, Scordato's is a beautiful restaurant serving excellent Italian cuisine along with a smaller selection of continental dishes. Veal, seafood, chicken, and pasta entrees are all good choices. Scordato's has a lengthy wine list and a full service bar. The service is professional and attentive. Children's menu.

YE OLDE LANTERN, *1800 N. Oracle Road, Tel. 520/622-6761. Most major credit cards accepted. Lunch and dinner served daily.*

Western and southwestern style foods are the mainstays of this popular eatery that has been pleasing folks for almost 75 years. The atmosphere is casual and the surroundings quite comfortable. The mesquite broiled steaks and prime ribs are fabulous. One of the things that makes Ye Olde Lantern such a popular spot is the salad bar which features several different types of seafood dishes. Cocktails are served.

Inexpensive

COCO'S BAKERY RESTAURANT, *2990 N. Campbell Avenue, Tel. 520/795-7494; 6095 East Broadway Boulevard, Tel. 520/745-6108; 345 W. Drachman, Tel. 520/622-8722; 7250 N. Oracle Road, Tel. 520/742-2840; and*

4565 N. Oracle Road, Tel. 520/884-4100. No credit cards. Breakfast, lunch, and dinner served daily.

The name of this local chain might lead you to think that they only have baked goods and the usual light things that sometimes are served in cafes. While Coco's does specialize in pies, muffins, and cookies that are baked fresh daily on the premises, they also have a full service family style dining room that is good for dinner as well as lunch. The menu is somewhat limited and features American fare. The bakery products are superb and worth having no matter what time of day you stop in.

SEEING THE SIGHTS

As I previously indicated, Tucson's sights can best be seen one area at a time. The downtown tour is best suited to walking. The second tour, covering the west bank of the Santa Cruz River contains what are probably the best of Tucson's sights, so I suggest that you do this one if short on time. This tour is easiest to do if you're driving but most of the attractions can be reached by bus if you don't mind a little inconvenience. The third tour cannot be done without a car.

Tour 1: Downtown

Approximate duration (by foot including sight seeing time) is from a half to a full day depending upon how much time you wish to devote to various museums. Begin at the center of the downtown area, Broadway and Stone Avenue.

Walk two blocks south on Stone to see the beautiful **St. Augustine Cathedral**. Construction began in 1896 on this sandstone structure modeled after the Cathedral of Queretaro in Mexico. A block further on is the headquarters of Tucson's police department. The lobby has a display of antique police equipment and artifacts taken at the capture of John Dillinger and his gang. *Police exhibit open weekdays during regular business hours. There is no admission charge.*

Now go back to the starting point and head west on Broadway (it converges with Congress Street) to the intersection of Granada Avenue. This is an unusual area because you can see the high rise offices of downtown, the modern Convention Center and the most historic section of Tucson all converging. The mix goes quite well. The historic is represented by the **Sosa-Carillo-Fremont House**.This Mexican adobe style dwelling has been carefully restored to its appearance in 1880 when **John Fremont** was the Territorial Governor. Besides this famous casa, there are many other historic buildings in the surrounding streets. You can walk around on your own or, if you have a lot of time and interest in this type of attraction, take a two-hour guided walking tour that leaves from the Sosa-Carillo-Fremont House. *151 South Granada Avenue (but actually on a small alley-way off of Granada). The house is open Wednesday* *through Saturday from 10:00am to 4:00pm except on holidays. The walking tours are given only once a day, at 10:00am from October to March and at 9:30 in April. Reservations are required and can be made by calling 520/622-0956. Admission to the house is $4.50 for adults, $2.25 for children.*

Walking back north on Granada you'll pass the imposing pink adobe **State Building** at the corner of Congress Street. It is best known for the colorful mosaic of inlaid tiles. A block further north is Alameda Street where you should go east (to the right) for one block to North Main Avenue. Turn left and you'll soon be at the **Tucson Museum of Art**, *140 North Main Avenue*. The museum is in what is known as the **El Presidio Park Historic District**, where Tucson first began, and is surrounded by five historic homes. Some have been converted to other uses, such as a museum school and a restaurant, while the **La Casa Cordova** is a museum of Mexican history. The emphasis is on Mexico's role in what is now Arizona. The house was built around 1850 and is one of the oldest in Tucson. Also of interest within the historic district is the **Goodman Pavilion** which houses a fine collection of western art.

Other structures are the 1868 **Romero House**, 1906 **Corbett House**, and the large **Fish House**, which contains a collection of western art. I didn't forget about the art museum, which houses a fine collection that spans the area's long history, from pre-Columbian all the way to Western American. *The art museum is open daily from 10:00am to 4:00pm except from noon on Sunday. It is closed on Monday from September through May and on major holidays. Admission is $2 for adults and $1 for students and senior citizens. Children under 12 are admitted free and everyone gets in for nothing on Tuesday. La Casa Cordova is always free; the hours are the same as for the art museum. Tel. 520/624-2333.*

Before leaving the museum area it's worth a couple of minutes of your time to go a block to the corner of Alameda and Church Avenue to see the **Pima County Courthouse**, *115 N. Church Avenue*. A combination of Spanish and southwestern architecture, the beautiful building features graceful columns and arches, a colorful tiled dome, and courtyard with a big stone fountain. Some people have compared the appearance of the Courthouse to Jerusalem's famous Dome of the Rock mosque. The contrast between the Courthouse's architecture and the surrounding modern glass towers of downtown are an amazing sight. Also at this location is the only remaining portion of **Tucson's original presidio wall**.

Return to Main, make a right and continue for a short time until you reach 6th Street. Turn right and go to 6th Avenue – that's right, you're at the intersection of 6th and 6th! Another right will soon bring you to the **Tucson Children's Museum**. The name should tell you something. If your party is adults only you might as well skip to the next attraction. Just continue on 6th Avenue to the corner of University Boulevard. The museum promotes understanding and interest in science, history and other subjects through a variety of interactive exhibits. *1200 South 6th Avenue. Hours from Memorial Day to Labor Day are Tuesday to Friday from 11:00am to 5:00pm, Saturday from 10:00am to 5:00, and Sunday from noon to 5:00pm. Winter hours are shorter; call for exact times. Admission is $5 for adults and $4 for seniors and $3 for children ages 3 through 16 . Tel. 520/792-9985.*

From the intersection of 6th Avenue and University Boulevard, go to the right on University. That street will bring you onto the attractive 320-acre campus of the **University of Arizona**. Besides taking some time to walk around or to relax under a shady tree, the campus contains no less than six attractions of note. These include several museums, a planetarium, and an interesting exhibit on photography. The tour will follow a clockwise route around the campus, returning you to the origination point.

The first stop is the **Arizona State Museum**, *Park Avenue & University Blvd.* Like most "state" museums, it is devoted to the cultural development of the state. While many such museums are excellent, this is one of the best of its type in the nation. Many scholars come here to do research in the museum's extensive archives, which are also open to the public. The collection of Hohokam and Mogollon culture artifacts are the largest in the world. Some of the relics date back more than 10,000 years. The exhibits are arranged in a chronological sequence and are well marked. A huge exhibit explains the cultures of many of Arizona's native groups including the Apache, Navajo, Hopi and the locally important Tohono O'odhams.

The next stop is the **Arizona Historical Society and Tucson Museum** located across the street from the campus, which also traces both state and local history. However, emphasis here is on developments after the arrival of Europeans and especially the American era. *949 East 2nd street at Park Avenue. Hours for the State Museum are daily from 10:00am until 5:00pm except on Sundays when it opens at noon. Tel. 520/621-6302. The Historical Society is open Monday through Saturday from 10:00am until 4:00pm and on Sunday from noon to 4:00pm. Tel. 520/628-5774. Both facilities are closed on state holidays. There is no set admission fee but donations are requested at each location.*

Continuing the loop around the campus you'll next come upon the **University of Arizona Museum of Art**. The most outstanding part of the museum is the Kress Collection, consisting of over 50 major European works from the Renaissance through the 17th century. There is also a very good 20th century collection of both paintings and sculpture by such notable artists as Picasso, Rodin and Henry Moore. *Park Avenue and Speedway Boulevard; open Monday through Friday from 9:00am to 5:00pm and Sunday from noon to 4:00, from September through May the closing time during*

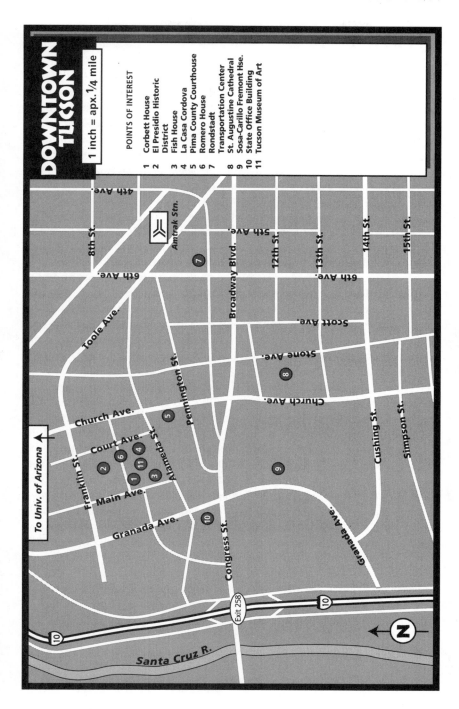

DOWNTOWN TUCSON

1 inch = apx. 1/4 mile

POINTS OF INTEREST

1 Corbett House
2 El Presidio Historic District
3 Fish House
4 La Casa Cordova
5 Pima County Courthouse
6 Romero House
7 Rondstadt
8 Transportation Center
8 St. Augustine Cathedral
9 Sosa-Carillo Fremont Hse.
10 State Office Building
11 Tucson Museum of Art

the week is 3:30pm, closed on state holidays throughout the year; admission is free; Tel. 520/621-7567.

Only a few steps away from the art museum is the noted **Center For Creative Photography**. Their collection includes more than 50,000 still pictures taken by photographers from all over the world, including many of the best known professionals. Most visitors will only see the main gallery which has hundreds of photos from the Center's own collection as well as many on loan. The entire collection is available to the public in special print viewing rooms but reservations to use these facilities are recommended. *Olive Road & 2nd Street. Open from Monday through Friday from 11am to 5:00pm and on Sunday from noon to 5:00pm; no admission charge; Tel. 520/621-7968.*

The last two stops at the campus and on this tour are both located on the eastern edge of the University. The **Flandreau Science Center and Planetarium**, *University Boulevard and Cherry Avenue*, has several large halls devoted to astronomy, the exploration of space, and the science of optics. Many of the exhibits encourage participation by visitors and both children and adults are likely to appreciate most of them. The Center has a 16-inch telescope where the public is invited to take a peak at night as long as the weather is clear. In the Center's Dome Theater is an hour-long planetarium and laser show using the most advanced projection and sound systems available. The shows, which change periodically, are only for those over three years of age.

Finally, the **Mineral Museum** is a separate facility that is housed on the lower level of the Science Center. On display are countless minerals, gems and fossils from all over the world. Copper, gold and silver mining, all of which are important in Arizona, receive special attention. Many fluorescent minerals can be viewed under special ultraviolet lighting. *The Science Center is open from Monday to Thursday from 8:00am to 5:00pm with extended hours on Wednesday and Thursday to 9:00pm. On Friday the hours are from 8:00 to 5:00 and again from 7:00pm to midnight. Saturday and Sunday hours are from 1:00 to 5:00pm with an 8:00 to midnight session on Saturday. For the schedule of planetarium shows call 520/621-STAR. All exhibits in the Science Center are free but the admission charge for the planetarium is $4.50, $4 for those over 55 and between 13 and 18, and $3 for children age 3 to 12. The laser show (given on Wednesday and Thursday only) is $5 for adults and $4 for ages 3-13 and over 55. The Mineral Museum is free of charge and is open daily from 9:00am to 5:00pm except on Saturday and Sunday when it opens at 1:00pm. The mineral museum is closed state holidays. Tel. 520/621-4227.*

To return to the tour starting point, go back to the west side of the campus and take either 6th Street or University Boulevard to Stone Avenue. Turn left and walk to the intersection of Broadway. Just before you get to that point you'll pass the **Bank One Building** (corner of

Congress Street). This was Tucson's first high rise office building and has several giant murals that show the development of Arizona from prehistoric times through the Territorial era.

Tour 2: The West Bank of the Santa Cruz River

Approximate duration (including sightseeing) is a full day. Begin at Speedway Boulevard on the west side of the river.

You can reach the starting point easily from anywhere in Tucson. Most major north/south streets intersect with Speedway, which you then take west across the bridge over the river, or you can take I-10 to Exit 257. Of all the wonderful things to see and do in Tucson, this tour contains the majority of my own favorites. From a fun time at a family amusement park to the outstanding mountain and desert scenery that surrounds the city, this tour has it all. Once you cross the river you're close to a very different world from that of downtown.

You have to make a decision whether to bypass the first suggested stop. **Sentinel Peak**, located in a park of the same name, offers an outstanding view of both the city and mountains. It is often referred to as "A" Mountain because of the large letter that is whitewashed onto it's side each year by freshmen at the University of Arizona. The view is particularly impressive at night when the city lights sparkle below. The view is great but the road to the 2,899-foot high summit is very narrow, steep and winding, and has no guide rails. However, if that doesn't bother you, then go for it. Use extreme caution on the short ride at all times but especially at night. The peak is reached by taking a left off of Speedway onto Grand Avenue. Turn right on Congress and then left again on Cuesta Street.

After descending "A" Mountain return to Speedway Boulevard and go west about five miles to the **International Wildlife Museum**. The building is easily recognizable because the exterior has been designed to resemble a Saharan fort of the French Foreign Legion. Also outside are larger than life statues of big game. Inside are very realistic dioramas of more than 300 animals from all over the world. The centerpiece of the museum is Sheep Mountain, an artificial mountain soaring two stories and filled with very alive-looking bighorn sheep. Another great exhibit is the trophy room, with mounted specimens of big game arranged by continent of origin. The museum also offers changing wildlife films in a hundred seat theater. *The museum is open daily from 9:00am to 5:00pm. The admission is $5 for adults, $3.75 for seniors and students with identification and $1.50 for children ages 6-12. Tel. 520/617-1439.*

Three miles west of the Wildlife Museum (Speedway changes names to the Gates Pass Road) is one of the outstanding municipal parks in the nation. **Tucson Mountain Park** covers more than 17,000 acres of rugged mountains and valleys as well as a large area of desert. There are extensive foot trails or you can go horseback riding. (Time for this isn't included in the full-day allocation for Tour 2.) The car ride through the park is in itself a worthwhile scenic experience. A drive through the Gates Pass is easy for even inexperienced mountain drivers. Two of Tucson's most popular attractions are located within the vast expanse of Tucson Mountain Park.

The first is **Old Tucson Studios**. The site was selected for the 1939 western motion picture epic *Arizona*. However, rather than tear down the extensive sets that were built, Columbia Pictures left them in place and later used them for many other motion pictures, television shows, and commercials. It is still used for actual production purposes, despite a major fire in April of 1995 which closed the attraction for more than a year. Besides the fun of walking around what looks like an authentic western town, you can watch daily gunfights and see old west-style entertainment as well as go on a stagecoach ride or venture underground into a mine. From time to time well-known national groups perform at Old Tucson Studios. *Located at the intersection of Gates Pass and Kinney Roads. Open daily from 10:00am until 6:00pm except for Thanksgiving and Christmas. The admission price is $15 for adults and $9.50 for children. There is reduced admission after 4:00pm. The only extra charge for attractions is for 30-minute long guided trail rides. Credit cards. Tel. 520/883-0100.*

A few miles north of the Studios on Kinney Road is the **Arizona-Sonora Desert Museum**. This facility is recognized as probably the finest of its type in the entire world. In my humble opinion it is also the most enjoyable – a place where nature comes to life and learning becomes fun for children and adults. Don't let the word "museum" fool you. It's a whole lot more than that, combining elements of a geology and natural history museum, zoological park and botanical gardens. In fact, you'll find more than 200 animals roaming natural habitats along with over 300 birds in walk-through aviaries and in excess of 1,200 different plants, all native to the fascinating Sonoran Desert environment. Reptiles, scorpions and tarantulas will be revolting to some, but it seems that little kids are especially fond of them. Sometimes you can even pet the tarantulas, under supervision of a museum staffer.

There is a beautiful overview of almost all of this huge complex from the ramada behind the natural history museum and entrance building. Some of the most interesting exhibits (listed in a counter-clockwise direction from the entrance) are the Cave and Earth History Room, made to resemble a real limestone cavern and showing the great variation in life resulting from the cooler underground temperatures; the Mountain Habitat; Desert Grasslands; Riparian Habitat containing animals that live by streams; the main Bird Aviary; underground Night Dwellers exhibit; and the Hummingbird Walk-Through. This last exhibit is one of my favorites. You can see dozens of these tiny and colorful birds, not much larger than some flying insects, furiously flapping their wings in a backwards motion to keep aloft while they feed on the nectar of equally colorful flowers. *The museum is open every day of the year. From March through September the hours are 7:30am to 6:00pm and from 8:30 to 5:00pm the remainder of the year. It is a good idea to visit before the heat of the day during the hottest months. The admission charge is $9 for adults but only $1.75 for children ages 6 through 12. Tel. 520/883-2702.*

After leaving the Desert Museum continue on Kinney Road. Adjacent to the border of the Tucson Mountain Park is the fascinating and beautiful **Saguaro National Park**. This park is divided into two sections, the Tucson Mountain District, which you'll visit on this tour, and the Rincon Mountain District to the east of Tucson and which is part of Tour 3. Let me say right off the bat that both sections are worth seeing because they are quite different. The largest specimens of the giant Saguaro Cactus are in the Rincon Mountain District. However, they are found in both parts of the park and the Tucson Mountain District has a much more diverse display of natural flora. Part of the diversity is created by the variation in altitudes, which can range up to as high as 6,500 feet in some portions of the park. Saguaro was until a few years ago a National Monument. It was upgraded to a National Park in 1995 with the addition of some land and new visitor facilities.

In the Tucson Mountain District be sure to visit the excellent new Red Hills Visitor Center which explains the Saguaro ecosystem. Kinney Road winds through the park and provides access to several dirt roads and hiking trails that lead the more adventurous to dozens of different types of cacti from small to huge. You'll frequently see birds and small animals, especially if you come in the morning or just before sunset. You may find that many Tucson area residents refer to the Tucson Mountain District as the West section or district, and the Rincon Mountain District as the East section or district. *The park is open from dawn to dusk but the visitor center hours are daily from 8:30am to 5:00pm. There is no admission charge for the Tucson Mountain Section of the park. Tel. 520/733-5153.*

To get back to downtown Phoenix simply reverse your route upon leaving the park and head east via Speedway Boulevard.

Tour 3: The Rest of Tucson and Nearby Sights

Approximate duration (including sightseeing) is a full day. Begin at Mission San Xavier del Bac.

Take the best route from your hotel to I-19 (beginning at Exit 260 of I-10) and get off at Exit 92. You'll see the colorful tower of the mission from the highway. The **Mission Sax Xavier del Bac**, located on the Tohono O'odham Indian Reservation about nine miles south of downtown Tucson, dates from 1700 when it was founded by Father Eusebio

Francisco Kino. It remains active to this very day, still serving the needs of the Tohono O'odham tribe. The current building was completed by Franciscan missionaries in 1797. The Mission church is considered to be perhaps the finest example of Spanish mission architecture ever built. Of greatest interest are the many domes, elaborate carvings and extensive use of flying buttresses. So beautiful is the building that is has become to be known as the "White Dove of the Desert." Recently, that beauty has been enhanced by careful cleaning of the interior. This lengthy process has restored the brilliant shades of red, blue, green, and yellow that the mission's builders so gloriously applied. *The Mission is open to visitors every day from 9:30am to 5:30pm, although access to the church may be restricted during services. There is no admission charge but donations are requested. Tel. 520/294-2624.*

Now head back north on I-19 to Valencia Road (Exit 95). About six miles east of the interchange is the **Pima Air and Space Museum**. The museum is adjacent to Davis-Monthan Air Force Base, a major employer in the Tucson area. The entire history of aviation in America can be traced through the museum's collection of over 200 vintage aircraft, which are located along pathways and in hangars. Among the most notable aircraft is a former Air Force One used by Presidents Kennedy and Johnson. There's a replica of the Wright Brothers 1903 Flyer. *6000 East Valencia Road. The museum is open daily except for Thanksgiving and Christmas from 9:00am to 5:00pm. The regular adult admission is $7.50 but seniors and military personnel with identification are admitted for $5.50. Children ages 10 through 17 pay $4. Tel. 520/574-9658.*

The next stop is a major part of Tucson's history. Continue on Valencia until you reach Kolb Road. Turn left and take that street north till its end. It will then curve along the river and run into East Grant Road. Make a right at Craycroft Road for the final leg to the **Fort Lowell Museum**, *open on Wednesday through Saturday from 10:00am until 4:00pm; no admission charge; Tel. 520/885-3832.* Set amid an attractive park, the museum contains the ruins of Fort Lowell, which was an important post during the time of the Indian Wars with the Apache. The quarters of the commanding officer have been reconstructed and there are displays that depict life at the fort during the frontier days.

Not far from the Fort is the interesting **DeGrazia Gallery in the Sun**. Take Fort Lowell Road to the intersection of Swan Road. Turn right and proceed about three miles. The DeGrazia Gallery is set amid the pretty Santa Catalina Mountains and provides a place to display the paintings and sculpture of artist Ted DeGrazia. Perhaps of greater interest is the adjacent beautiful open-air chapel that he built and decorated extensively with frescoes. *6300 N. Swan Road. The gallery and chapel are both open daily* *from 10:00am to 4:00pm except for Easter, Thanksgiving and Christmas. Admission is free. Tel. 520/299-9191.*

Go back on Swan Drive for about a mile to Sunrise Drive and make a left turn. About three miles up the road you'll come to Sabino Canyon Road. Make a left and you'll immediately be at the visitor center of **Sabino Canyon**. Here you'll find exhibits on the flora and fauna of this part of the higher Sonoran Desert. The canyon itself is closed to private vehicles but a shuttle service (admission charged) is offered that ventures some four miles into the narrow canyon and its pretty creek. Within the canyon are hiking trails both short and long, easy and difficult. Information on the various trails can be found at the visitor center. *Open daily during daylight hours. Visitor Center open from 8:00am until 4:30pm. The canyon is free but there is a $6 charge for the shuttle tour. Tel. 520/749-8700.*

Now it's time to visit the **Rincon Mountain District** of **Saguaro National Park**. To reach it from Sabino Canyon, take Sabino Canyon Road into Tanque Verde Road, continuing across the bridge to Kolb Road. Proceed south on Kolb for a short while to Broadway and turn left

THE STATELY SAGUARO

*One of the most amazing of all living things, the **Giant Saguaro** is probably what most people think of when they visualize a cactus. With a little bit of luck a Saguaro can live to be more than 200 years old. In the first 75 years of its life it can grow to a height of 20 feet and start to show off its first branch. Mature specimens can grow to more than 50 feet high but the majority top out somewhere between 30 and 40 feet and have many branches. Larger trees can weigh several tons!*

The Saguaro, like all cacti, is well-suited to the arid environment. The tree is a water reservoir, soaking up as much as it can get during wetter periods to use when it is dry. Depending upon how much of this reserve it uses, the Saguaro grows or shrinks in both girth and weight. The Saguaro blossom, which is the state flower, blooms brilliantly during May and into June. Indians have long used the Saguaro as an ingredient in food and beverages.

For all its mighty appearance, however, the Saguaro is quite delicate and severely threatened by encroaching civilization. As if pollution weren't enough of a problem, the popularity of cactus as a decorative item in southwestern homes made poaching of the Saguaro a big business. It is now illegal to remove the Saguaro. Actually, all of the trees in the national park have long been protected, but some people still want to take a souvenir. Don't – you're not only threatening the species, but if you get caught you will face a very severe fine.

to the park entrance. There is another visitor center in this section of the park but the main draw here is the paved one-way nine mile Cactus Forest Drive. This is the real heart of the Saguaro Forest, where hundreds of the tallest Saguaros can easily be seen from the road. Many long trails that rise to the higher elevations of Rincon Mountain are of interest to those who wish to extend their visits. *There is a $4 per vehicle charge unless you hold a Park Service passport.*

Upon exiting from Saguaro National Park, turn left onto the Old Spanish Trail and in ten miles you will come to fabulous **Colossal Cave.** Caverns are considered to be either wet or dry. Wet caverns, which are more common among major caves attracting visitors, are still active because the flow of water is still forming stalactites, stalagmites, and other formations. Colossal Cave is a dry cave and is considered to be one of the largest, if not the largest, such cave in the world. Much of it hasn't yet been explored. It contains many beautiful formations that can easily be seen on paved paths under illumination. The cave is actually the hollow interior of a mountain. The temperature is always a comfortable 70 degrees. *Admission to the cave is only via 45-minute long guided tours that leave frequently from 8:00am to 6:00pm daily (except till 7:00pm on Sunday and holidays). Admission is $7.50 for adults, $6 for ages 11 through 16 and $4 for ages 6 through 10. Tel. 520/647-7275.*

You've now completed this tour and it's time to return to Tucson. Head to the left upon leaving the parking area and in seven miles you'll reach I-10. Get on heading west and you'll be back in the city in almost no time at all.

NIGHTLIFE & ENTERTAINMENT
Out On The Town

As was the case in Phoenix, the fickle nature of the show going public can often change the status of a popular night spot almost overnight. Therefore, it is always a good idea to make inquiry about current policies before setting out to paint the town red.

Traditional nightlife is available in many parts of the city. The area around the University of Arizona has contemporary music and comedy clubs. Almost all of the resort hotels and many of the larger city hotels feature lounge entertainment. The following list is only a sampling of some of the more popular nightclubs in Tucson.

CACTUS MOON CAFE, *5470 E. Broadway Boulevard, Tel. 520/748-0049.*

Features both country and Top 40 music with continuous dancing.

CLUB CONGRESS, *311 East Congress Street, Tel. 520/622-8848.*

Tucson's premier rock club features name entertainment usually just below the level of the biggest names in the recording industry.

WILD WILD WEST, *4385 West Ina Road, Tel. 520/744-7744.*
Tucson's biggest and most popular country and western nightclub, Wild Wild West is in the northern part of the city but despite its distance from downtown attracts a huge following that fills up its two separate dance floors. They have live entertainment, video games, and a lot more.

Tucson also has several supper clubs offering entertainment. For something a little different try the **El Mariachi Restaurant**, *106 W. Drachman, Tel. 520/791-7793.* The Mexican cuisine is enhanced by the top-notch International Mariachi America group which performs Wednesday through Sunday.

Gentlemen looking for "sophisticated" strip clubs will find them at **Sunset Strip**, *3650 East Speedway Boulevard*, **TD's Showclubs**, *5822 East Speedway Boulevard*, and **Ten's Nightclub**, *5120 East Speedway Boulevard*. You can see from the addresses where this type of "action" is in Tucson.

Casinos
• **Casino of the Sun**, *7474 South Camino del Oeste. Tel. 520/883-1700*
• **Desert Diamond Casino**, *2731 East Elvira Road. Tel. 520/294-7777*

Performing Arts
Consult local newspapers and magazines or contact the venue directly to find out current productions.
• **The Act One Theatre Corporation**, *8842 E. 27th Street, Tel. 520/722-5652.* Offers a variety of plays.
• **Arizona Theater Company**, *330 S. Scott Avenue, Tel. 520/622-2823.* Another company offering Broadway style and other stage productions.
• **The Arizona Opera Company**, *3501 N. Mountain Avenue, Tel. 520/293-4336.* Has five productions annually from October through March. Performances are on Friday and Saturday evenings and matinee on Sundays.
• **The Tucson Symphony Orchestra**, *2175 N. 6th Avenue, Tel. 520/882-8585.* Performs a full schedule of concerts.

SPORTS & RECREATION
SPECTATOR SPORTS
Tucson doesn't have the same huge range of sports teams that Phoenix does. But if you like to get your exercise by shouting at athletes and hailing down the beer vendor, here's the rundown:

Baseball
The **Tucson Toros** of the high-minor Pacific Coast League play at Hi Corbett Field from April through August, *Tel. 520/325-2621.* The same

field is the host facility for the spring training season of the **Colorado Rockies** of the National League. Games are in March, *Tel. 800/388-ROCK.*

College Athletics

The **University of Arizona**, a member of the Pac-10 Conference, features a full program of men's and women's intercollegiate athletics. Men's basketball and football are the biggest attractions. For information, *call 520/621-5130.*

Racing

Tucson Raceway Park, *12500 S. Houghton Road, Tel. 520/762-9200*, holds stock-car racing on Saturday nights from March through October. For thoroughbred and quarter horse racing you can visit **Rillito Park Race Track**, *4502 N. First Avenue, Tel. 520/293-5011*. The ten week racing season begins in January. Greyhound racing takes place at **Tucson Greyhound Park**, *2601 S. Third Avenue, Tel. 520/884-7576*. Races are held daily, year-round.

PARTICIPANT SPORTS

Except for the fact that Tucson doesn't have any winter sports located nearby (there isn't anything that resembles "winter" because the mountains around Tucson aren't so high), Tucson can just about match the Phoenix area for every other type of participant recreation.

Amusement Parks

- **Funtasticks Family Fun Park**, *221 E. Wetmore Road, Tel. 520/682-2304*. Go-karts, bumper boats, min-golf, arcade, baseball/softball batting range and more.
- **Valley of the Moon**, *2544 E. Allen Road, Tel. 520/323-1331*

Ballooning

- **Balloon America**, *Tel. 520/299-7744*. Provides pick-up and return to most hotels. Flights available from October through June.
- **Fleur de Tucson Balloon Tours**, *4635 N. Caida Place, Tel. 520/529-1025*. Experienced service offering a variety of flight options.
- **Southern Arizona Balloon Excursions**, *Tel. 520/624-3599*. Seasonal champagne brunch flights.

Golf

All of the courses listed are open to the visiting public and have 18 holes:
- **El Conquistador Country Club**, *10555 N. La Ca Country Club, Tel. 520/791-4336*

- **Lodge at Ventana Canyon Course**, *6200 N. Clubhouse Lane, Tel. 520/577-4061*
- **Randolph Municipal North Course**, *602 S. Alvernon Way, Tel. 520/791-4336*
- **Raven Golf Club at Sabino Springs**, *9777 E. Sabino Greens Drive, Tel. 520/760-1253*
- **Silverbell Golf Course**, *3600 N. Silverbell Road, Tel. 520/791-4336*
- **Sun City Vistoso Golf Club**, *1455 E. Rancho Vitoso Boulevard, Tel. 520/825-0428*

Perhaps the easiest way to make arrangements for a golf outing is by contacting one of Tucson's golf reservation services. Among these are **Arizona Golf Outings**, *824 S. Saguraro Ridge Place, Tel. 520/206-0100* or **Tee Time Arrangers & Tours**, *6286 E. Grant Road, Tel. 800/742-9939.* These organizations will also be glad to arrange complete golf vacation packages.

Horseback Riding

Most dude ranches limit riding privileges to overnight guests. All of the following establishments will rent horses by the hour or day. All of the stables located on North Oracle Road utilize trails in the Santa Catalina Mountains. They provide a rural experience that's close to the city.
- **Desert High Country Stables**, *6501 W. Ina Road. Tel. 520/744-3789.* Features guided trail rides well suited to beginners.
- **El Conquistador Stables**, *10000 N. Oracle Road. Tel. 520/742-4200*
- **Pusch Ridge Stables**, *13700 N. Oracle Road. Tel. 520/825-1664*
- **Walking Winds Stables**, *11600 N. Oracle Road. Tel. 520/742-4422*

Tennis

Most of the major hotels in Tucson have courts. Many allow non-guests to play for a higher fee. However, if your hotel doesn't have a court, you can save money by playing at one of the following public courts. All have lighted courts for night play. Public play is also allowed at the University of Arizona and Pima Community College.
- **Fort Lowell Park**, *2900 M. Craycroft Road. Tel. 520/791-2584*
- **Himmel Park**, *Tucson Boulevard and Speedway. Tel. 520/791-3276*
- **Randolph Tennis Center**, *50 S. Alvernon Way. Tel. 520/791-4896*

SHOPPING

Tucson has almost as many opportunities to shop for southwestern and Native American items as does Phoenix. And, again, for those who just like to shop "period," there's a big assortment of malls and outlet centers. I'll detail the most important shopping areas for visitors and mention some of the special places that you might want to consider for getting that gift for someone special or something for your home as a trip remembrance.

For antiques you should immediately head to the **Antique Mall**, *3130 East Grant Road at Country Club Road*. More than a hundred different dealers sell their wares in the center of Tucson's antique district. Another good choice for antiques is the **Antiques Center**, *5000 E. Speedway Blvd.* They have only a few less dealers than the Antique Mall and the same general high quality merchandise.

The **downtown shopping district** is along Fourth Avenue between 4th and 7th Streets. **Del Sol**, *435 N. 4th Avenue*, is a great Indian and Southwestern store along 4th Avenue. Another downtown locale of special interest to tourists is the **El Mercado de Boutiques**, *Broadway and Wilmot*, which features Native American and Hispanic crafts. **Old Town Artisans**, *186 North Meyer Avenue*, in the El Presidio Historic Park area, may be the best place in town to get Native American items, including Kachina dolls and Navajo rugs.

Two other interesting places are the **Indian Village**, *72 E. Congress Street*, for a great selection of Native American craft items as well as southwestern goods; and the **Pottery Market**, *2925 N. Oracle Road*. The latter has one of the best selections of authentic Indian pottery that we've seen.

Tucson doesn't have a consolidated area for art galleries such as in Scottsdale, but good galleries are located throughout the city. Among the best places are **ART!!** in the El Mercado shops, **Above & Below the Equator Gallery**, *521 N. 4th Avenue*, the **Ironwood Gallery** at the Arizona-Sonora Desert Museum, and the aforementioned Old Town Artisans.

For malls, outlet centers, and specialty shops, the following list should provide you with a place to get what you want:

- **El Con Mall**, *3601 East Broadway Road*. 135 stores including four department stores
- **Factory Stores of America**, *440 N. Camino Mercado*
- **Foothills Mall**, *7401 N. La Cholla Boulevard*. Specialty shops for the fashion conscious.
- **Park Mall Shopping Center**, 5870 E. Broadway Boulevard. 120 stores, three department stores.
- **River Center**, *5605 E. River Road*. Boutiques and restaurants in a nice setting at the foot of the Santa Catalina Mountains.
- **Tucson Mall**, *4500 N. Oracle Road*. Tucson's largest mall with more than 200 stores and six department stores. Many stores feature southwestern clothing and gifts.

EXCURSIONS & DAY TRIPS

The three suggested excursions in this section require that you travel further than the outlying attractions in Tour 3. A car is almost essential but if you don't or won't drive then many of the attractions, especially in the first excursion, can be seen on tours offered by Grey Line and many other commercial tour operators.

To Nogales & Back

This adventure, which can even include a visit across the border into Mexico, covers about 200 miles, almost all of which is on I-19. Therefore, the driving is easy and the time spent behind the wheel will only be a little over three hours, allowing plenty of time to see the sights. You should allow a full day for this excursion, especially if you're going to spend time shopping while in Mexico.

Your first stop is located only about 30 miles south of Tucson. Take I-19 to Exit 69 in the town of Green Valley and follow Duval Mine Road for less than a mile to the **Titan Missile Museum**. This unique facility was once an actual ICBM launch site. There were once more than 50 of these scattered throughout the nation but all have been dismantled save for this one. It is has been left to look exactly as it did during its operational days including the missile in its silo. Of course, the warhead has been removed. Fascinating guided tours lead visitors through the launch control center, and a 200-foot long access way that connects the center to the 146-foot deep missile silo. The whole complex seems very solid but much of it is actually suspended 35-feet beneath the ground on heavy cables. This was to allow give in case of an earthquake or bomb. In fact, the place was designed to withstand all but a direct nuclear hit.

A launch sequence is simulated by your guide and leaves visitors with a very funny feeling in their throat. Fortunately, only exercises of this type took place – the real order to launch never came. The tour involves going up and down several flights of stairs. A small elevator is available for the disabled only if prior arrangements are made for its use. However, some of the surface level equipment and exhibits are accessible to all. Now I know that there are a lot of people who will say they do not want to see this museum because it glorifies the use or even the existence of nuclear weapons. To that, I say "rubbish." This is as much a part of our nation's (and our world's) history as a frontier outpost or Indian ruin. To miss it on such grounds would be a foolish mistake. *The museum is open daily from 9:00am to 5:00pm except during the months of May through October when it is closed on Monday and Tuesday. It is also closed on Christmas. Admission is $6 for adults, $5 for seniors and those on active military duty, and $4 for children ages 20 through 17. Tours are generally given on the hour and as space is limited, reservations are suggested. Call Tel. 520/625-7736.*

Two sites dealing with the region's earlier history are located just to the north and south of the small town of **Tubac**, which can be reached from Green Valley by continuing south on I-19 to Exit 34. Tubac dates back to prior to the arrival of the Spaniards. Today it is primarily an artist's community. You wouldn't know it today, but in the middle of the 19th century Tubac was the most populous town in Arizona. It had grown up in and around a presidio built in 1752.

The site is now encompassed by the **Tubac Presidio State Historic Park**, *open daily, except Christmas, from 8:00am to 5:00pm; admission is $2 for adults and $1 for children ages 12 through 17; Tel. 520/398-2252.* There is a visitor center which contains exhibits on both Native American and Spanish eras in Tubac. Adjacent to the park is an archaeological site containing the ruins of hundreds of dwellings. It's most interesting to visit on weekends when archaeological excavations are taking place. The public is invited to watch.

South of town is **Tumacacori National Historic Park**, a preservation of a huge Franciscan church that was started in 1800 but never finished due to shortages of both money and water as well as opposition from the Apache. Visitors can walk through the impressive structure as well as other buildings and areas of the mission. A museum built in the style of many Sonoran Desert missions documents both life in the mission as well as area history. *The museum is open only on Friday from 10:00am to 5:00pm, Saturday from 10:00am to 4:00pm and Sunday from 1:00pm to 4:00pm. The admission charge is $4 per person except for those who have a valid park service passport. Tel. 520/398-2341.*

Another 20 miles south on I-19 will bring you to the border town of **Nogales**, which is located directly across from it's Mexican sister city of the same name. The area was explored as early as the 1540's and is one of the most historic communities in Arizona. There are many old dwellings which can be located with a brochure available from the **Pimeria Alta Historical Society Museum**, *136 North Grand Avenue.* The museum is housed in a former city hall building and has nice displays on the history of both southern Arizona and the Sonoran Desert region dating back all the way to the ancient Hohokam Indians. *The museum is open Tuesday through Friday from 10:00am to 5:00pm and on Saturday from 10:00am until 4:00pm. It is closed on state holidays. There is no admission charge. Tel. 520/287-4621.*

A somewhat unexpected find in this desert region would be a winery, but there is one. The **Arizona Vineyards** are located two miles east of town on AZ 82. Tours explain the wine making process and tastings are offered in an historic 19th century structure. *The winery is open every day of the year except Christmas from 10:00am to 5:00pm. There is no charge for either the tour or wine tasting. Tel. 520/287-7972.*

A SHORT STAY IN MEXICO
- VISITING NOGALES

*While there isn't that much to see on the Mexican side of the border, many visitors to **Nogales** like to be able to say that they went into another country during their Arizona vacation. Probably the best thing to do in Nogales, Mexico is to take advantage of the very busy and colorful markets that can be found right across the border. You can get some excellent values on high quality native goods including clothing, pottery and jewelry.*

United States citizens need not have any special documentation to visit Nogales so long as you return within 72 hours and do not venture into the interior of Mexico. If you do either of those than it becomes necessary to get a Mexican tourist card. Regardless, it is a good idea to have some proof of your American citizenship with you. Things get more complicated if you intend to drive into Mexico because of insurance regulations. I suggest that you walk across the border. Customs offices on both sides are open 24 hours a day. If you have any questions about your visit it is advisable to inquire at customs on the American side before you venture across the border.

Oracle

The second suggested excursion covers only about 80 miles and can be done in about five to six hours. I don't consider the attractions on this itinerary to be as important as the first excursion or the in-city tours, so this one is only for those who have plenty of time or are especially intrigued by what is to be seen. Science buffs will, however, probably enjoy this trip as well as the third excursion.

AZ 77, known in Tucson as Oracle Road, will take you to all three attractions on this trip. Oracle Road can be reached by taking 6th Avenue North and following signs or by using Exit 255 on I-10 and then going east for one mile on Miracle Mile to AZ 77. At the intersection of Ina Road in the northern section of the city is **Tohono Chul Botanical Park**. Surrounded by the growing city landscape, the park is designed to preserve a desert environment and to provide education about that environment and how we interact with it. The 50-acre park does so through gardens and exhibits. The park has a lovely restaurant where you can get a great lunch (there can be a bit of a wait, so I suggest you inquire about lunch early if you know you want to eat here) and a small gift shop that sells high quality crafts. *7366 N. Paseo del Norte. The park is open daily from 7:00am to dusk with indoor exhibit hours being from 9:30am to 5:00pm (11:00am to 5:00pm on Sunday). The admission fee is $2 (no fee to browse the giftshop). Tel. 520/575-8468.*

A total of about 30 miles on AZ 77 will bring you to Biosphere 2 Road, which provides access to the now famous (or perhaps infamous) **Biosphere 2**. The Biosphere is an enclosed seven-acre ecosystem designed to test the recycling capabilities of air, water, and nutrients. You may recall that the first experiment was plagued with technical difficulties and many in the scientific community doubted whether the results had any significance. However, we won't concern ourselves with that. A visit to the Biosphere is an interesting experience. The white glass domes, pyramids, and other structures of the complex look like something from a science fiction movie.

Guided tours and exhibits take you through much of the complex and explain the work being done. (It is called Biosphere 2 because the developers consider the earth itself to be Biosphere 1.) The tour takes about two hours and covers over 2-1/2 miles so comfortable walking shoes are a must. There is a decent restaurant here if you want to have lunch. *The Biosphere is open every day of the year except Christmas from 8:00am to 6:00pm. The admission price is $13 for adults and $11 for seniors. Children ages 6 through 17 are admitted for $6. Credit cards. Tel. 520/896-6200.*

Return to Tucson by retracing your outbound route. If you're interested in getting a better view of the high desert scenery or wish to do a little bird watching or hiking, then you might want to make a stop at **Catalina State Park**, which is located about half-way between Tucson and the Biosphere. Equestrian activities are among the activities available in this lovely natural area that covers in excess of 5,000 acres. *There is a $3 vehicle admission charge to the park. Tel. 520/628-5798.*

Kitt Peak Observatory

The **Kitt Peak National Observatory** is located approximately 50 miles west of Tucson via AZ 86 and then via AZ 386 on 6,875-foot high Kitt Peak. To reach AZ 86 from Tucson, take I-19 to Exit 99 (Ajo Way) or any major north-south street to Ajo Way and then proceed west.

The three buildings in this complex run by the National Optical Astronomy Observatories comprise one of the best facilities of its type in the entire world. Among the more than 20 pieces of sophisticated equipment in use is a huge solar telescope. The observatory keeps a close watch on our sun as well as more distant stars and other things taking place in the Milky Way and other galaxies. The observatory encourages visitors and has exhibits which explain the work being done. Guided tours are the best way to see the facility.

Allow about 4-1/2 hours for this excursion. Call *Tel. 520/318-8726* to inquire about road conditions (the last nine miles of the trip can be difficult during or after rain). *There is no set admission fee but donations are requested. Guided tours are given daily at 10:00, 11:30am and 1:30pm. Reservation are required for telescope use.*

PRACTICAL INFORMATION
- **Airport**: *Tucson International Airport, Tel. 520/573-8100*
- **Airport Transportation**: *Arizona Stage Coach, Tel. 889-1000*
- **Bus Depot**: *2 South 4th Avenue, Tel. 520/792-3475*
- **Hospital**: *Tucson General, Tel. 520/327-5431; University Medical Center, Tel. 520/694-0111*
- **Hotel Hot Line**: *Tel. 800/266-7829*
- **Municipal Transit Information**: *Tel. 520/792-9222*
- **Police** (non-emergency): *Tel. (502) 791-4452*
- **Taxi**: *Checker Cab, Tel. 520/623-1133; Yellow Cab, Tel. 520/624-6611*
- **Tourist Office/Visitors Bureau**: *130 South Scott Avenue, Tel. 800/638-8350*
- **Train Station** *400 E. Toole Street, Tel. 520/623-4442*

14. FLAGSTAFF & SEDONA

Geographically speaking this is the smallest of the regional destinations in this guide. However, it certainly isn't lacking in beauty or diversity. The area surrounding both **Flagstaff** and **Sedona** is a combination of forested mountains, some of the state's largest natural lakes, deep valleys and a little bit of the unusual land formations associated with the Colorado Plateau. The area that I've chosen to call the Flagstaff/Sedona region is occupied primarily by portions of the Coconino, Kaibab and Prescott National Forests.

Both Flagstaff and Sedona themselves are completely surrounded by the national forests. While the single most famous attraction of this area is gorgeous Oak Creek Canyon, it is only one of many scenic places. The region is also home to a number of mysterious ancient Indian ruins and more recent historic sites.

Nature's bounty has made the Sedona area a major resort. Outdoor recreation runs the gamut from summertime hiking and swimming to skiing. Yes, skiing, as in real snow. Not far from Flagstaff is the highest point in Arizona and a major winter resort. Regardless of the season you can spend a lot of time in the Flagstaff/Sedona area. That's made even better by the fact that you don't have to travel very far to get where you're going.

ARRIVALS & DEPARTURES

You can easily reach Flagstaff from Phoenix via a number of methods. The Practical Information section at the end of this chapter has phone numbers for many of the services mentioned below.

Flagstaff is the largest gateway community to the canyon and you can make arrangements to see it by land, air or by raft. But more of that in the chapter on the Grand Canyon itself.

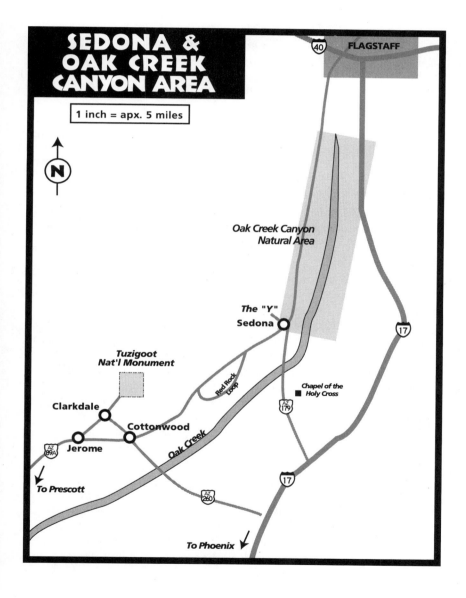

SEDONA &
OAK CREEK
CANYON AREA

1 inch = apx. 5 miles

N

FLAGSTAFF

40

Oak Creek Canyon
Natural Area

The "Y"
Sedona

17

Tuzigoot
Nat'l Monument

Chapel of the
Holy Cross

Clarkdale

Red Rock Loop

AZ
179

Cottonwood

Jerome

AZ
89A

Oak Creek

17

To Prescott

AZ
260

To Phoenix

By Air

Mesa Air flies into Flagstaff's Pullman Municipal Airport located a few miles south of the city off of I-17 and US 89A.

By Bus

Many companies, including Gray Line offer tours of area attractions. Besides Flagstaff, Oak Creek Canyon and Sedona, there are tours going to the Grand Canyon.
• **Greyhound bus station**, 399 South Malpais Lane, Flagstaff

By Car

To get to Flagstaff from Pheonix, take Interstate 17 north right into Flagstaff. Interstate 40 also goes right into Flagstaff from the east and west.

By Train

Amtrak's northern Arizona route also comes through town with its station located at 1 East Route 66.

ORIENTATION

Flagstaff and Sedona lie approximately 25 miles from one another along scenic highway AZ 89A. If you look at the regional map in the front of this book you can see that this region extends some miles in all directions from these two communities. Interstate highways 40 and 17, converging in Flagstaff, form a "T" through the region and make it highly accessible from anywhere in Arizona or the southwest.

A tour of this region can easily be combined with tours of several other regions as Flagstaff is only 140 miles from Phoenix and about 85 miles to the Grand Canyon. Besides the two Interstates the other major routes that you'll have to be familiar with are the aforementioned AZ 89A heading southwesterly and US 89, which heads north from Flagstaff. While the Interstates are excellent highways, many of the other routes in this region are mountain roads so you'll have to drive slower and be prepared for sharp turns and some steep grades.

Because this region covers a relatively small area it isn't necessary to do it as a loop, which is good news if you're going to be traveling through the region and just want to hit the highlights. You can select a base of either Flagstaff, Sedona or Cottonwood to name but a few places and fan out in different directions to cover all the area's attractions. However, I'll describe the sights in three primary sections. These are Flagstaff and the immediate area to the north; centrally located Sedona and Oak Creek Canyon, including Cottonwood and several other small towns; and the remainder of the region, including Williams, Prescott and the I-17 corridor.

Within Flagstaff itself the main streets are Milton Road (US 180 and AZ 89A) which runs north and south and old Route 66 which travels east to west. The latter roughly parallels I-40 and is also designated as Business I-40. It crosses Milton in the heart of downtown. Milton becomes Fort Valley Road as it leaves town on the north side. Aspen Avenue, a block north of Route 66 runs through the historic part of Flagstaff and is home to many stores, galleries, antique shops and restaurants.

GETTING AROUND FLAGSTAFF & SEDONA
By Car
It's easiest to get around by car. All of the major car rental companies, as well as a few local ones operate out of Flagstaff.

By Public Transportation
Local area transportation is by **Pine County Transit** buses, Tel. 520/ 779-6624 or by one of several taxi companies.

WHERE TO STAY
COTTONWOOD
Inexpensive
VIEW MOTEL, *818 South Main Street. Tel. 520/634-7581. 34 Rooms. Rates: $44-52, all year. MasterCard and VISA accepted. Located immediately to the west of the junction of AZ 89A and AZ 260 in the center of town.*

This is just a basic motel but it is one of the few decent inexpensive locations for those of you who are desperately seeking lower prices than can be found in nearby Sedona. It is a typical roadside motel, one story with parking right outside your door. Most of the rooms are a nice size and are comfortably furnished. Some rooms have efficiency kitchens. The best part about the View Motel is its hillside location that provides a splendid look at the verdant Verde Valley.

FLAGSTAFF
Moderate
THE INN AT 410 BED & BREAKFAST, *410 North Leroux Street. Tel. 520/774-0088, Fax 520/774-6354. Toll free reservations Tel. 800/774-2008. 9 Rooms. Rates: $125-175, all year, including full breakfast. MasterCard and VISA accepted. Located in the downtown area just north of Route 66 (Business I-40).*

A large two-story home built with loving care, the Inn at 410 is within a few short blocks of Flagstaff's historic downtown district. The 1907 structure is on a quiet street with nicely shaded grounds that include a small garden with a gazebo. Each room is decorated in a unique manner and features the southwestern decor of an earlier era including many antiques. Every room has a coffee maker and a refrigerator although only some are air conditioned. There are no in-room telephones or televisions which can be as much as an advantage as a shortcoming. A couple of units have a Jacuzzi.

The breakfast included each morning is abundant and wholesome and is served with the personal attention that makes the Inn at 410 so special. For other meals there are several restaurants located within walking distance.

REAL CITY SLICKERS

In the previous chapter you read about some of the many guest ranches which dot the Tucson area. But for a real cowboy experience nothing can quite match a stay on a working ranch where guests take part in working cattle and even get to sleep out under the stars. C & S City Slickers (both the name and the concept were inspired by the film of the same name) has been offering city folk the opportunity to become cowboys since 1992. Donna and Idy Bryson own a 550 acre ranch with 400 head of cattle in the beautiful Verde Valley. They offer several different types of stays depending upon how much experience you have riding a horse. For beginners there is a two to three day program that emphasizes basic riding and herding principles. Programs for experienced riders range up to two weeks in length. Prices start at around $500 and go all the way up to about $5,000 for an all-inclusive stay.

It's not possible to really become a cowboy in three days but it does give you a sense of what it would be like to actually be a cowboy. And it certainly will satisfy that desire to do something different that won't go away. If you're game then you can get additional information from C & S by writing them at C & S Cattle Company, 351 South El Rancho Bonito, Cornville AZ 86325 or by calling Tel. 520/634-1898. Goodbye, city slicker; hello cowboy and cowgirl!

See Chapter 19 for full details on Arizona's many guest ranches.

LITTLE AMERICA HOTEL, *2515 East Butler Avenue. Tel. 520/779-2741, Fax 520/779-7983. Toll free reservations Tel. 800/352-4386. 247 Rooms. Rates: High season (May 1st to October 31st): $99-109; Low season (January 1st to mid-March): $65-75. Major credit cards accepted. Located a little to the east of downtown at Exit 198 of I-40.*

Flagstaff's largest hotel is situated on a magnificent 500 acre ponderosa forest with views of the San Francisco Mountains to the north. It's a little like staying overnight in an arboretum because there are so many trees on the grounds – they surround all of the buildings and even the pool area. Guest accommodations are in several three-story lodge style buildings that go well with the natural surroundings. The rooms are unusually large and attractively decorated in a traditional way. Every room has a refrigerator and the TV features a built-in video game system which will most certainly please your little ones. The free form swimming pool is huge and is bordered by an equally big lounging area.

The Western Gold Dining Room is the best of the hotel's three restaurants and is described in the Where to Eat section. For more casual dining you can opt for another full service restaurant or the 24-hour coffee shop. Recreational facilities other than the pool include an exercise room, jogging and hiking trails, and a children's playground. The Little America offers free local transportation.

RADISSON WOODLANDS HOTEL, *1175 West US Route 66. Tel. 520/773-8888; Fax 520/773-0597. Toll free reservations 800/333-3333. 183 Rooms. Rates: High season (May through October): $109-129; Low season (January through mid-March): $79-89. Major credit cards accepted. Located 1-1/2 miles north of I-40, Exit 195B if traveling westbound. Eastbound, take Exit 191 and drive two miles on US 66.*

Excellent first-class hotel with beautiful decor in public areas and guest rooms. The style is a modern southwestern that is cheerful and eye-catching. Several suites with microwave and refrigerator also available. Facilities include a heated outdoor swimming pool, whirlpool and complete health and fitness center with spa, steam room and sauna. And when it comes time to eat you may not have to wander to other parts of town– the Woodlands Cafe features good American cuisine while Japanese food lovers will want to try the Sakura Restaurant & Sushi Bar.

Inexpensive

SAGA MOTEL, *820 West US Route 66. Tel. 520/779-3631. Toll free reservations 800/283-4678. 29 Rooms. Rates: $38-57, with upper end of scale during summer. Most major credit cards accepted. Located 1-1/2 miles north of I-40, Exit 195B if traveling westbound. Eastbound, take Exit 191 and drive two miles on US 66.*

Typical roadside one-story motel with basic comfortable accommodations. The rooms are clean and nicely kept but are a bit on the small side. Swimming pool is open during the summer only. Restaurants are located within a short drive.

PRESCOTT & PRESCOTT VALLEY
Expensive
HASSAYAMPA INN, *122 E. Gurley Street. Tel. 520/778-9434; Fax 520/ 445-8590. Toll free reservations 800/322-1927. 68 Rooms. Rates: Weekends, $110-185; weekdays, $99-160. All rates include full breakfast. American Express, Diners, Discover and MasterCard accepted. Located in the center of town, east of Court House Square.*

This historic property dates from 1927 and fits in just perfectly with the surroundings of Court House Square and its old shops and buildings. Exudes charm out every window and in every piece of furniture. Comfortable surroundings, although most of the rooms are kind of small. If you like big spaces then this might not be the best choice for you. There's a small restaurant on the premises, a great place for an evening nightcap even if you don't eat there. The ample breakfast is served in the attractive Peacock Room.

Moderate
FOREST VILLAS INN, *3645 Lee Circle. Tel. 520/717-1200, Fax 520/ 717-1400. Toll free reservations Tel. 800/223-3449. 63 Rooms. Rates: High season (mid-April to October 31st): $109-149 weekends and $89-149 weekdays; Low season (November 1st to mid-April): $79-119; all rates including continental breakfast. Major credit cards accepted. Located 2-1/2 miles east of AZ 89 on AZ 69.*

If there is a best buy in this region then the Forest Villas Inn may well be it. One of the newest hotels in the area, it offers a surprising amount of luxury for the price. Although its modern in every way the hotel tries to recreate the distinctive charm of a small European hotel. Indeed, the lobby with its provincial furniture, winding staircase, fireplace, and beautiful chandeliers is the epitome of that luxurious style. All of the rooms are spacious, nicely furnished, and well equipped with modern amenities. Private balconies are standard. There are several multi-room suites that have a fireplace, whirlpools and refrigerators.

Although there isn't any restaurant on the premises (several are within a five minute ride from the hotel), the continental breakfast will be enough for many guests. There is also an attractive bar located in the lobby. The beautiful pool area is built on a hillside and has dramatic views of the Prescott Valley. The Forest Villas has underground parking.

MOUNT VERNON INN, *204 North Mount Vernon Avenue. Tel. 520/ 778-0886, Fax 520/778-7301. 7 Rooms. Rates: $115-125, including full breakfast. Discover, MasterCard, and VISA accepted. Located to the east of downtown and south of AZ 89 off of Sheldon and Montezuma Streets.*

This is an historic B&B that was built in the early part of the century and has a main house plus a few separate cottages. A charming place on a tree shaded block that contains many Victorian style homes, the Mount Vernon is noted for several outstanding architectural features such as its unusual turret, stained glass windows, and many gables. The main house has a large and comfortable parlor where guests come to meet and mingle or just to relax. The bright and sunny dining room is the setting for outstanding breakfasts and afternoon refreshments.

All of the rooms are distinctively furnished. Main house rooms have bay windows that overlook the pretty residential street or have a view of a noted area natural landmark. Cottage facilities include kitchens and lots of space. Cottage guests do not receive breakfast as part of their stay.

Selected as one of my Best Places to Stay (see Chapter 11 for more details).

PRESCOTT RESORT AND CONFERENCE CENTER, *1500 Highway 69. Tel. 520/776-1666, Fax 520/776-8544. Toll free reservations Tel. 800/967-4637. 161 Rooms. Rates: High season (late April to late October): $129-149; Low season (late October to late April): $89-99. Most major credit cards accepted. Located east of the junction of Arizona highways 69 and 89.*

This is a beautiful mountainside resort with a great view of the historic center of Prescott in one direction and the valley in the other direction. The interior showpiece is the spacious atrium that is dramatically filled with paintings and sculptures by Arizonians, especially Native Americans. They give the Prescott Resort the atmosphere of a fine art gallery. The guest accommodations are first rate, about half of the units are one bedroom suites with separate living area. All rooms have coffee makers and mini-refrigerators.

There is a good full service restaurant on the premises as well as a cocktail lounge that offers live entertainment. In a separate building adjacent to the five-story hotel is Bucky's Casino, a limited casino where you can play either slot machines or video poker. Other forms of recreation are the heated indoor and outdoor swimming pools, exercise facility (professional massage available), whirlpool room, a racquetball court, and two lighted tennis courts. The Prescott Resort has a breakfast plan available for $5 per person per day. Beauty salon on premises.

HOTEL ST. MICHAEL, *205 West Gurley Street. Tel. 520/776-1999, Fax 520/776-7318. Toll free reservations Tel. 800/678-3757. 72 Rooms. Rates: $80, all year, including continental breakfast. American Express, Discover, MasterCard, and VISA accepted. Located downtown on "Whiskey Row" across from the Courthouse Plaza.*

Here's a moderately priced place that lets you experience some of Prescott's early history first-hand. Whiskey Row is the most historic section of town and the Hotel St. Michael is listed on the National Register of Historic Places. The rooms are on the small side but quite comfortable in an old-fashioned sort of way. A few suites are available if you want some more room to spread out. The St. Michael also has a small restaurant but many more are located within walking distance as is Prescott's shopping area.

SEDONA

Please note that virtually all bed and breakfast establishments in Sedona require a minimum two-night stay on weekends. If your plans call for being in Sedona on Friday or Saturday night be sure to check with the property in advance about these restrictions.

Very Expensive

ADOBE VILLAGE & THE GRAHAM INN, *150 Canyon Circle Drive. Tel. 520/284-1425, Fax 520/284-0767. Toll free reservations Tel. 800/228-1425. 10 Rooms. Rates: $119-329, all year, including full breakfast. Discover, MasterCard, and VISA accepted. Located six miles south of Sedona via AZ 179 and then west on Bell Rock Boulevard to Village of Oak Creek.*

The Graham is a bed and breakfast, something that usually conjures up a mental picture of a stately old house filled with antiques. While that's true in many instances, Sedona doesn't have a lot of old houses the Adobe Village & the Graham Inn is a large and contemporary southwestern style home with excellent views of towering red rocks. Each room, which includes the four large casitas, is uniquely furnished and has a private patio and balcony. The casitas are especially luxurious and features a beautiful fireplace and enclosed patio. A couple have their own Jacuzzi. All feature video cassette players which come in handy for reviewing all of the home videos you film each day. The Graham has an attractive heated pool and whirlpool. Your hosts will gladly loan you a bicycle to go exploring the nearby scenic attractions. A bike is also a good way to get around downtown Sedona and avoid some of the hassles of car traffic and on-street parking shortage in shopping areas.

ALMA DE SEDONA INN, *50 Hozoni Drive. Tel. 520/282-2737; Fax 520/774-2926. Toll free reservations 800/923-2282. 12 Rooms. Rates: $165-215, all year including full breakfast. American Express, MasterCard and VISA accepted. Located near the center of town off of State Highway 89A.*

One of the newest Bed & Breakfast establishments in the area (it opened at the end of 1998), the Alma is typical Sedona – elegant, warm and inviting, an interesting blend of modernity and traditional southwestern styling. Each of the spacious and cheerfully decorated rooms features a working fireplace and whirlpool tub. Almost every unit boasts an excellent view of the famous red rocks of Sedona. Breakfast is a delicious and ample affair served in lovely surroundings. The Alma also boasts a heated swimming pool. Restaurants are within a short distance.

ENCHANTMENT RESORT, *525 Boynton Canyon Road. Tel. 520/282-2900, Fax 520/282-9249. Toll free reservations Tel. 800/826-4180. 162 Rooms. Rates: High season (late August to early July): $260; Low season (early July to late August): $235. American Express, Discover, MasterCard, and VISA accepted. Located about eight miles north of Sedona via AZ 89A, Dry Creek Road, and then Forest Route 152C.*

One of Sedona's many full service resorts, Enchantment is beautifully situated away from the most crowded portion of town in a private area of a secluded canyon. The hotel is enveloped by and blends in with the natural red rock formations that have made Sedona famous. The resort is spread out in many different small buildings. All of the guestrooms are individual suites with one or two bedrooms or more elaborate casitas. The accommodations have many amenities, such as honor bars and private patios with outstanding views, and are beautifully furnished in a traditional southwestern manner.

The Enchantment Resort features two restaurants and a host of recreational facilities. Among them are five swimming pools, a putting green or pitch and putt golf course, croquet, and tennis courts. There is also an excellent fitness center with sauna and whirlpool facilities. Many guests like to explore the surrounding country by renting a bicycle from the hotel or taking part in one of their varied nature programs.

Selected as one of my Best Places to Stay (see Chapter 11 for more details).

L'AUBERGE DE SEDONA RESORT, *301 L'Auberge Lane. Tel. 520/282-1661, Fax 520/282-2885. Toll free reservations Tel. 800/272-6777. 57 Rooms. Rates: $190-395, all year except about $40 less from mid-November to mid-December. Major credit cards accepted. Located just north of the junction of AZ 89A and AZ 179, on the east side down the hill.*

Luxury and seclusion are the hallmarks of the L'Auberge de Sedona, a French country lodge and cabins located along the banks of Oak Creek in a setting of dramatic natural beauty. The rich stone and wood exterior front a red mountain backdrop. The pretty landscaped grounds are shaded by many mature ponderosa trees. L'Auberge caters to a select clientele who appreciate fine service and accommodations. All of the guestrooms are large and beautifully furnished. Most have a charming king-sized canopy bed that recalls the style of 18th and 19th century France. Cottage units have fireplaces. Every room has an honor bar and coffee maker.

Two restaurants both offer fine food and service. The more formal L'Auberge de Sedona Restaurant is described in the Where to Eat section. A heated swimming pool and whirlpool facility are great places to relax while looking at the red rocks.

Expensive

A TOUCH OF SEDONA BED & BREAKFAST, *595 Jordan Road. Tel. 520/282-6462, Fax 520/282-1534. Toll free reservations Tel. 800/600-6462. 5 Rooms. Rates: $119-159, all year, including full breakfast. American Express, Discover, MasterCard, and VISA accepted. Located north of the "Y" junction (AZ 89A/179) and west of AZ 89A.*

On a relatively quiet street in a residential neighborhood, A Touch of Sedona Bed and Breakfast is another modern home. The southwestern styled rooms are big, bright, and comfortable. Several have refrigerators and coffee makers. Perhaps the main pleasures of staying at this pretty establishment are the wonderful gourmet breakfasts and the refreshment service. Beverages and snacks are available any time of the day or night, great for those of you who frequently get the urge to raid the fridge at night and can't do so in many hotels.

CANYON VILLA BED & BREAKFAST INN, *125 Canyon Circle Drive. Tel. 520/282-2342, Fax 520/282-2399. Toll free reservations Tel. 800/453-1166. 11 Rooms. Rates: $145-199, all year, including full breakfast. MasterCard and VISA accepted. Located six miles south of Sedona via AZ 179 and then west on Bell Rock Boulevard to Village of Oak Creek.*

The Canyon Villa looks more like a small luxury hotel than a bed and breakfast. The contemporary one and two story adobe structure is built in the style of a turn of the century hacienda. Both the public areas and guestrooms are spacious. Luxury is the key word at Canyon Villa where the rooms each feature unique furnishings that run the gamut of Arizona history and style – Victorian, Territorial, and contemporary Southwestern are some of the decor motifs. Larger units may have whirlpool tubs, fireplaces, or full kitchens. All have a private patio or deck. There's also a heated swimming pool.

CASA SEDONA, *55 Horizon Drive. Tel. 520/282-2938, Fax 520/282-2259. Toll free reservations Tel. 800/525-3756. 15 Rooms. Rates: $125-205, all year, including full breakfast. MasterCard and VISA accepted. Located three miles southwest of town on AZ 89A and then northwest for three blocks on Tortilla Drive to Horizon Drive.*

Personalized service and luxurious extras are what makes Casa Sedona so special. A modern southwestern home, it's situated in a way that allows for great viewing of the red rocks. Innkeepers John and Nancy True will see to it that you start the day off with an excellent southwestern gourmet breakfast. They'll give you advice on seeing the sights, which include a pretty trail on their property. At days end you can settle into beautifully decorated rooms that have gas fireplaces, a refrigerator, and a jacuzzi. To make sure you're in the proper Sedona mood there is no television. Go outside and look up at the beautiful starlit sky or watch it from your room, comfy in the terry cloth robe that is provided to guests.

THE LODGE AT SEDONA, *125 Kallof Place. Tel. 520/204-1942, Fax 520/204-2128. Toll free reservations Tel. 800/619-4467. 13 Rooms. Rates: $145-195, all year, including full breakfast. MasterCard and VISA accepted. Located two miles southwest of center of town via AZ 89A and then south on Kallof Place.*

Located on 2-1/2 acres of grounds, the Lodge at Sedona is immediately different than most other B&B's because the architecture isn't southwestern. Owners Barb and Mark Dinunzio have chosen a charming European country decor for this ranch style home in a private and quiet area of Sedona. That peace and quiet extends to the guestrooms that don't have either telephones or televisions. They do have beautiful furnishings. About half the units have jacuzzis (one is located outside on a private deck) and fireplaces. Besides the full breakfast guests are treated to refreshments in the evening and in the afternoon if you aren't out shopping or seeing the sights. The homemade desserts in the evening are absolutely scrumptious. You should also try the excellent cappuccino.

SKY RANCH LODGE, *Airport Road. Tel. 520/282-6400; Fax 520/282-7682. Toll free reservations 888/708-6400. 94 Rooms. Rates: $85-175. American Express, MasterCard and VISA accepted. Located a mile southwest of the "Y" and then a mile south via Airport Road.*

This could be considered one of the better values in Sedona considering what you get for your money. The Lodge (although it's actually more motel style) is located away from the hustle and bustle of the main thoroughfares high atop a mesa, which affords spectacular views of the town and the surrounding red rocks. Brilliant by sun-filled day, the view takes on a special warmth in the evening as the lights of Sedona twinkle in the fading daylight. The spacious grounds feature beautiful gardens, a great place to take in the sights.

Rooms at the Sky Ranch are also worthy of note. All are spacious and well appointed with a southwestern motif. Several have fireplaces and there are two private cottages within the specified price range. The cottages have the best views of any guest unit. Some kitchenette facilities. The Lodge has a wonderful lounge area – a most comfortable place to admire the scenery through giant picture windows underneath a vaulted ceiling. Among the facilities are a swimming pool with whirlpool and an on-premise gift shop. Restaurants require about a five minute ride.

SOUTHWEST INN AT SEDONA, *3520 West Highway 89A. Tel. 520/ 282-3344, Fax 520/282-0267. Toll free reservations Tel. 800/483-7422. 28 Rooms. Rates: High season (February to October): $145-195; Low season (November to January): $99-175; all rates include Continental breakfast. American Express, Discover, MasterCard, and VISA accepted. Located about 3-1/2 miles west of downtown Sedona on the main highway (AZ 89A).*

This moderate sized inn (for Sedona) is among the prettiest in town.

The southwestern decor and architecture is, more specifically, Santa Fe style. All of the large rooms have a gas fireplace, private balcony or patio with excellent red rock views, and coffee makers. Some have refrigerators and jacuzzis. There is also an outdoor heated swimming pool and whirlpool. Although the breakfast is termed continental, it's quite abundant and will probably be sufficient for most guests.

Moderate

BELL ROCK INN, *6246 Highway 179. Tel. 520/282-4161, Fax 520/284-0192. Toll free reservations Tel. 800/881-7625. 96 Rooms. Rates: $89-150, all year, higher rates are on Friday and Saturday evenings. American Express, MasterCard, and VISA accepted. Located about 5-1/2 miles south of the "Y" junction (AZ 89A/179).*

As with Scottsdale, Tucson, and other popular areas in Arizona, coming across a good moderate priced hotel isn't the easiest of jobs. The Bell Rock Inn is, therefore, a welcome find and is a best value in Sedona. The one and two story buildings are an attractive adobe style with wood beams protruding out near the roof and a subdued color. It looks almost pink during the dimming hours of natural daylight. The location is away from the main traffic of Sedona although it's still fairly busy in this section which is known as the Village of Oak Creek. The hotel is within a few steps of some red rock formations – they almost look like they're touching the building as you gaze over the rooftops. The very name of the Inn comes from a nearby formation that is in the shape of an almost perfectly symmetrical bell.

A little more than half of the attractive southwestern styled rooms are mini-suites with fireplaces. Many rooms have refrigerators and personal safes while a smaller selection have in-room jacuzzis. All are spacious and comfortable. The grounds have two nice heated swimming pools and whirlpool. There is an on-premise restaurant that also has a full service cocktail lounge with live entertainment on weekends. The Inn is located close to many fine restaurants as well as upscale shopping.

DESERT QUAIL INN, *6626 Highway 179. Tel. 520/284-1433; Fax 520/284-0487. Toll free reservations 800/385-0927. 41 Rooms. Rates: High season (March through November): $79-150; Low season (December through February): $60-100. Major credit cards accepted. Located seven miles south of the "Y" via State Highway 179.*

Unusually attractive guestroom facilities about evenly divided between typical southwestern decor or more rustic lodgepole cabin style. Either way the rooms are a decent size, comfortable and with the warmth of home. Some units have gas fireplaces and a few have Jacuzzis. Although there isn't any restaurant or breakfast, guests are treated to complementary coffee or tea as well as fresh fruit.

Inexpensive

VILLAGE LODGE, *78 Bell Rock Boulevard. Tel. 520/284-3626; Fax 520/284-3629. Toll free reservations 800/890-0521. 17 Rooms. Rates: $49-65, all year. Major credit cards accepted. Located 6 miles south of Sedona via State Highway 179 and then west on Bell Rock to Village of Oak Creek.*

Clean and comfortable rooms at a most affordable price make this an ideal choice for the budget-conscious traveler spending overnight in Sedona. About a third of the units are one bedroom suites with full kitchen facilities and a cozy fireplace for atmosphere (just like the places that charge four times as much). For a few dollars more I suggest one of the suites. Restaurants and plentiful shopping are within walking distance in Oak Creek or you can make the short drive back into Sedona for an even wider choice.

WILLIAMS
Moderate

FRAY MARCOS HOTEL, *235 North Grand Canyon Boulevard. Tel. 520/635-4010, Fax 520/635-2180. Toll free reservations Tel. 800/843-8724. 89 Rooms. Rates: High season (April 1st to early September): $119; Low season (November to February): $69. American Express, Discover, MasterCard and VISA accepted. Located a half mile south of I-40, Exit 163, at the Williams Depot of the Grand Canyon Railway.*

Considering that Williams is a major gateway to the Grand Canyon, most of the available accommodations are rather undistinguished. The majority are chain properties, especially those in a mid-price range. So you have the choice of taking one of those or staying at the Fray Marcos, a new hotel that is one of the few in Williams that doesn't fit the cookie-cutter mold image. The attractive two-story motor inn has nice comfortable rooms and a great location if you plan on seeing the Grand Canyon by taking the Grand Canyon Railway trip. (Package plans are available.) There is a limited restaurant and cocktail lounge on the premises.

Inexpensive

NORRIS MOTEL, *1001 W. Bill Williams Avenue. Tel. 520/635-2202; Fax 520/635-9202. Toll free reservations 800/341-8000. 33 Rooms. Rates: High season (April through early September): $50-79; Low season (early September through March): $35-45. American Express, Discover, MasterCard and VISA accepted. Located on the I-40 business loop about one mile east of Exit 161.*

Decent rooms at an affordable price and little more. For large families or groups there are a couple of two and three bedroom units priced at $89-99 during the high season. Some units have refrigerators. Swimming pool. Restaurants within a short drive.

CAMPING & RV SITES

- **Bonito Campground**, *Junction of US 89 and FR 545, Sunset Crater area, Tel. 520/526-0866*
- **Circle Pines KOA**, *1000 Circle Pines Road, Williams, Tel. 520/635-4545*
- **Deadhorse Ranch State Park**, *north side of town, Cottonwood. Tel. 520/ 634-5283*
- **Flagstaff KOA**, *5803 N. Highway 89, Flagstaff, Tel. 520/526-9926*
- **Grand Canyon KOA**, *North Highway 64, Williams, Tel. 520/635-2307*
- **J & H RV Park**, *7901 N. Highway 89, Flagstaff, Tel. 520/526-1829*
- **Lo Lo Mai Springs Outdoor Resort**, *Page Springs Road, Sedona, Tel. 520/ 634-4700*
- **Point of Rocks RV Park**, *3025 N. Highway 89, Prescott, Tel. 520/445-7253*
- **Rio Verde RV Park**, *3420 Highway 89A, Cottonwood, Tel. 520/634-5990*
- **Sedona RV Resort**, *6701 W. Highway 89A, Sedona, Tel. 520/282-6640*
- **White Horse Campground**, *8 miles north on FR 109, Williams, Tel. 520/ 635-2633*
- **White Spar Campground**, *2-1/2 miles north of town on AZ 89, Prescott. Tel. 520/445-7253*
- **Willow Lake RV & Camping**, *Heritage Park Road, Prescott, Tel. 520/445-6311*
- **Woody Mountain Campground & RV Park**, *2727 W. Route 66, Flagstaff, Tel. 520/774-7727*

WHERE TO EAT
COTTONWOOD
Moderate

   CHANELLE'S, *2181 East Highway 89A. Tel. 520/634-0505. American Express, Discover, MasterCard, and VISA accepted. Lunch and dinner served daily. Reservations are suggested.*

   This small and warm restaurant features a nice selection of continental cuisine prepared to your order and served with friendly efficiency. The decor is that of a European country inn. Cocktails are served.

FLAGSTAFF
Expensive

   WESTERN GOLD DINING ROOM, *2515 East Butler Avenue, in the Little America Hotel. Tel. 520/779-2741. Major credit cards accepted. Lunch and dinner served Monday to Friday and dinner only on Saturday and Sunday. Reservations are suggested.*

   Several entrees are in the moderate price category. The atmosphere and decor of the dining room is in keeping with the name. It's elegant but retains a casual feel. The menu is mainly American with emphasis on beef and other western fare, though you can choose from several continental dishes such as chateaubriand. There is a buffet for lunch. Cocktails are served tableside or in the separate lounge that features live entertainment during the evening hours.

Moderate

BLACK BART'S STEAKHOUSE, *2760 E. Butler Avenue. Tel. 520/ 779-3142. Most major credit cards accepted. Lunch and dinner served daily.*

Real old west "cowboy" atmosphere that's a lot of fun for all ages. Singing waiters and a piano player provide additional good times. The menu includes well prepared steaks at surprisingly affordable prices along with a good selection of seafood and ribs. The sourdough biscuits are a special treat. Cocktails tableside or in separate lounge.

CHEZ MARC BISTRO, *503 Humphreys Street. Tel. 520/774-1343. Major credit cards accepted. Lunch and dinner served daily. Dress code. Reservations are suggested.*

This may well be the fanciest restaurant in town and the prices are surprisingly affordable although a few entrees do rise into the expensive category. Attentive service and expertly prepared French cuisine such as beef, pork, and veal are the hallmarks of Chez Marc. The atmosphere of the small dining room is enhanced by its location in a historic home near the downtown section. Cocktails are served. There is an elegant little lounge adjacent to the dining room. Good wine selection.

DOWN UNDER NEW ZEALAND RESTAURANT, *413 N. San Francisco Street. Tel. 520/774-6677. Major credit cards accepted. Dinner served nightly.*

Don't ask me how a Kiwi style restaurant wound up in Flagstaff but, however it did, the result is one of the better places to dine in town. The menu includes a good variety of fresh fish (including, of course, orange roughy), lamb and all the usual things associated with New Zealand cooking. Pleasant surroundings and service. Cocktails.

KELLEY'S CHRISTMAS TREE, *5200 East Cortland Boulevard. Tel. 520/526-0776. American Express, MasterCard, and VISA accepted. Lunch and dinner daily except Sunday when only dinner is served. Closed Monday during the winter. Reservations are suggested.*

A popular and attractive restaurant featuring a wide variety of entrees including prime rib, steak, and seafood. Kelley's is especially known for almost bringing chicken and dumplings into the gourmet class. All of the desserts are baked on the premises and are excellent. The dining room is decorated in a cheerful early American decor. The casual atmosphere of the busy 250-seat dining room and good food make this a wise choice for family dining. Cocktails are served.

Inexpensive
COUNTRY HOST, *2285 East Butler Avenue. Tel. 520/773-0248. Major credit cards accepted. Breakfast, lunch, and dinner served daily.*

Sometimes you don't want to spend a lot of money and are in the mood for some good home style cooking. When that's the kind of mood you're in head for the Country Host. Whatever the time of day you'll find friendly service and a wide selection of items to choose from. Full service bar.

PRESCOTT & PRESCOTT VALLEY
Expensive
MURPHY'S RESTAURANT, *201 North Cortez Street. Tel. 520/445-4044. American Express, Discover, MasterCard, and VISA accepted. Lunch and dinner served daily; Sunday brunch.*

First I should point out that Murphy's is only marginally in the expensive range. Many entrees qualify for the moderate category. Murphy's is in a refurbished commercial building dating from the 1890's in the heart of Prescott's historic downtown section. The decor is in keeping with that time period. The menu features fish and beef, mostly mesquite broiled, along with some pasta dishes. The fresh home baked bread is excellent. Murphy's offers full cocktail service but they are best known for their huge selection of domestic and imported beers.

Moderate
PEACOCK ROOM, *122 East Gurley Street, in the Hassayampa Inn. Tel. 520/778-9434. Major credit cards accepted. Breakfast, lunch, and dinner served daily. Reservations are suggested.*

The Hassayampa Inn is an historic hotel that was built in 1927. The decor of the Peacock Room is original. The service and food are both excellent. There's a good selection of beef, seafood, veal, and pasta entrees. A couple of surprise specials are usually featured so be sure to check them out. Save some room for one of the outstanding baked on the premises desserts. Cocktail service and separate lounge.

THE PORTERHOUSE RESTAURANT, *155 Plaza Drive. Tel. 520/445-1991. Most major credit cards accepted. Dinner is served nightly; Sunday brunch. Reservations are suggested.*

Occupying the site of a former restaurant, the Porterhouse opened in 1996 and has made quite an impression in a short time. The setting is absolutely beautiful – a spacious and rustic dining room with large windows overlooking the banks of the winding Granite Creek and the surrounding dense foliage of tall pine trees. The greenery extends indoors with numerous hanging plants. Seating on the outdoor patio is also available during the summer.

Co-owners Bill Kahl and Russ DuPlain have a simple formula for success. They serve prime certified Angus beef and prepare it in a simple fashion. This is, after all, primarily an all-American steakhouse where the beef speaks for itself. However, if you aren't in the mood for steak there's always a variety of beef, chicken, and seafood entrees available. A pasta special is also offered every night. If you like baby back ribs and barbecued dishes, Thursday night is the time to visit the Porterhouse. The service is first rate and there's full cocktail service. Definitely my choice in Prescott for great dining at reasonable prices.

ZUMA'S WOODFIRE CAFE, *124 N. Montezuma Street. Tel. 520/541-1400. American Express, MasterCard and VISA accepted. Lunch and dinner served daily.*

An attractive and cozy atmosphere prevail at Zuma's, located in the heart of Prescott's historic downtown shopping district. The menu features an excellent selection of American and southwestern entrees that are well prepared and nicely presented. Outdoor patio dining is available. Cocktail service. Children's menu.

SEDONA
Very Expensive

L'AUBERGE DE SEDONA RESTAURANT, *301 L'Auberge Lane, in the L'Auberge de Sedona Resort. Tel. 520/282-7131. Major credit cards accepted. Breakfast, lunch, and dinner served daily. Dress code. Reservations are suggested.*

For the fanciest and finest dining experience in Sedona there's no question that the L'Auberge de Sedona Restaurant best fits that description. An elegant atmosphere pervades the beautiful country French dining room. The formal service is impeccable but perhaps a bit heavy handed for some people. During the summer you can dine outside right by beautiful Oak Creek. The cuisine is strictly French with delicate sauces an integral part of the varied selections of beef, veal, and fish. L'Auberge also boasts an excellent wine list as well as a full service cocktail lounge. Not a good place to take the kids, but if you are looking for something special and you don't mind spending more than $50 per person, then look no further.

Expensive

FOURNOS RESTAURANT, *3000 West Highway 89A, Tel. 520/282-3331. Most major credit cards accepted. Two seatings for dinner Thursday through Saturday (6:00 and 8:00pm); Sunday brunch. Reservations required.*

For one of the most unique dining experiences anywhere, come to this small but charming restaurant lovingly operated by owner/chef Demetrios Fournos and his wife Shirley. Demetrious is a former New

Yorker and an attorney. Not that either is significant except to say that he gave up a lucrative career to pursue what he really wanted to do. I admire people like that. Anyhow, Fournos' tiny dining room is like going into a neighborhood cafe in Athens. The delicious and traditional Greek cuisine is superbly prepared and served with great care. The dessert selections are few in number but are excellent; the same can be said for the wine list.

SHUGRUE'S HILLSIDE GRILL, *671 Highway 179. Tel. 520/282-5300. American Express, MasterCard, and VISA accepted. Lunch and dinner served daily. Reservations are suggested.*

An excellent restaurant that specializes in fresh seafood but also has a decent selection of beef, chicken, and lamb dishes, Shugrue's is perched on a hillside and has huge picture windows that offer stunning views of the red rocks and mountains. During the summer you can even get closer to that view by dining on the outside deck. The service is quite good and the portions are ample. Cocktail service and separate lounge. Children's menu is available.

Shugrue's also has a more moderately priced restaurant (without the Hillside Grill suffix) at 2250 West Highway 89A. The menu is similar and the decor is modern southwest. I guess the price is a few dollars less because you don't have to pay for the view.

Moderate

COWBOY CLUB, *241 North Highway 89A. Tel. 520/282-4200. American Express, MasterCard, and VISA accepted. Lunch and dinner served daily.*

What would an Arizona town be without a good western style restaurant featuring a big selection of southwestern favorites? Nothing, of course. So the Cowboy Club comes along to save the day. The atmosphere is very casual, the service efficient, and the food excellent. It's a good choice for family dining (a children's menu is offered). Cocktail service and lounge. The Cowboy Club doesn't have a parking lot. Given its location on the main street it could mean you'll have to do a bit of hunting to find a place to leave your car. It's worth a little effort!

JUDI'S RESTAURANT, *40 Soldier's Pass Road. Tel. 520/282-4449. American Express, Diners Club, MasterCard, and VISA accepted. Lunch and dinner served Monday through Saturday; dinner only on Sunday.*

Judi's is a small restaurant with attractive but casual decor. It's definitely not fancy, which in the Sedona restaurant market is a welcome change of pace. The cooking isn't fancy either, just good steaks, seafood, chicken, and pasta. However, you would be making a mistake if you don't try Judi's famous (at least in Sedona) barbecued baby back ribs. They're meaty, lean, and juicy and served in a barbecue sauce that's just right. Cocktail service and separate lounge.

PIETRO'S, *2445 West Highway 89A. Tel. 520/282-2525. Major credit cards accepted. Dinner served nightly. Reservations are suggested.*

Considering how popular Italian food is in most places there aren't many restaurants in Sedona that feature it. Pietro's, however, is an exception. They serve a wide selection of chicken, veal, lamb, and seafood dishes in addition to great pasta selections. All are expertly prepared in classic Italian style. The dining room's decor is that of a casual bistro. Pietro's has a good selection of wines. Unfortunately, if you have small children this isn't the place to go to – children under six years of age are not admitted. Of course, if you don't like screaming little kids at the next table interfering with your meal than this is a big plus.

SASAKI JAPANESE RESTAURANT, *65 Bell Rock Boulevard. Tel. 520/284-1757. American Express, MasterCard and VISA accepted. Lunch and dinner served daily (except closed Tuesday afternoon).*

Husband and wife owner/chef team have created a delightful eatery with excellent Japanese cuisine in an atmosphere that combines typical Oriental features with some of the decor of the American southwest. Magnificent setting against a backdrop of red rocks. Diverse menu of well prepared entrees, some of which do nudge into the expensive category. Try the *shabu shabu* for two–thinly sliced beef with vegetables, noodles and a savory sauce prepared tableside. They also serve outstanding sushi.

SEDONA SWISS RESTAURANT, *350 Jordan Road. Tel. 520/282-7959. MasterCard and VISA accepted. Lunch and dinner served daily except Sunday. Reservations are suggested.*

The cosmopolitan nature of Sedona is reflected in the wide variety of cuisines available in its restaurants. This charming place serves both Swiss and French cuisine, including great fondues. There are indoor and outdoor dining areas. Desserts are among the best in town, coming from the adjacent bakery that specializes in pastries and candies. They have takeout so you can make your waiter think you're not ""pigging"" out and then go and get some to bring back to your hotel room! Devious, ain't I? Sedona's Swiss Restaurant has a children's menu and full cocktail service.

WILLIAMS
Moderate

MISS KITTY'S STEAKHOUSE, *642 East Bill Williams Avenue, in the Ramada Inn. Tel. 520/635-4431. Major credit cards accepted. Breakfast, lunch, and dinner served daily.*

Standard steakhouse fare in a nice looking dining room at decent prices is what you get at Miss Kitty's. Some chicken and seafood entrees are also on the menu. The adjacent cocktail lounge has entertainment in the evening.

SEEING THE SIGHTS
Flagstaff

With an altitude of over 6,900 feet, Flagstaff has four distinct seasons and is a year-round resort, but not in the same way as Phoenix. The neighboring San Francisco Mountains are home to Arizona's largest ski area, which is described in the accompanying sidebar. US 180, which leads northwest from Flagstaff towards the Grand Canyon, is especially scenic. You can make about a 50-mile loop through the best of the area's mountain scenery by taking US 180, the unpaved Schultz Pass Road and returning via US 89. Among the sights are the San Francisco Peaks, the Eden Mountains, and 12,663-foot Humphreys Peak, the state's highest.

Attractions are plentiful within the town of Flagstaff and you should allocate between three and four hours to do them all. First is the **Riordan Mansion State Historic Park**. This somber looking 40-room mansion was built in 1904 by a family who made their fortune in lumbering. Guided tours take you through many rooms which have original furnishings and artifacts. There's also a visitor center in the small park. *Located a half-mile north of the intersection of I-17 and I-40 at 1300 Riordan Ranch Street. Hours are from 8:00am daily (11:00am mid-September to mid-May); house tours conducted daily on the hour from 9:00-11:00am and 1:00 to 4:00pm except during winter months when it occurs from 1:00 to 4:00pm, closed on Christmas; admission is $4 for adults and $2.50 for children under 17; Tel. 520/779-4395.*

One of the most popular places for visitors to go in Flagstaff is the **Lowell Observatory**. Take Milton Road north from the State Park to Mars Hill Road and turn left. First stop is the visitor center where you can look at and touch exhibits and scientific equipment. Of special interest is the Pluto Walk – a sequential scale model of the planets in our solar system. Guided tours include a slide presentation about the facility. Nighttime viewing is available from February through November. *The observatory is open daily from 9:00am to 5:00pm April through October and from noon the remainder of the year. Admission is $3.50 for adults, $1.50 for children ages 5 to 17; $10 for the family. Tel. 520/774-2096.*

Return on Mars Hill to the intersection of Humphreys Street, which is also US 180. The name changes to Fort Valley Road. A couple of miles from downtown is the **Arizona Historical Society and Pioneer Museum**. Once the county hospital, the building now traces the Flagstaff area's history from pioneer days through the lumberjack era, building of the railroad and on to the present. *2340 N. Fort Valley Road; no admission charge but donations are appreciated; call for hours; Tel. 520/774-6272.*

A little further north, also on US 180, is the **Museum of Northern Arizona**, The facility explores the geology, biology, and culture of the Colorado Plateau region through a collection that numbers more than five million pieces, including a full-size model of a Dilophosaurus dinosaur. Local artists of the Hopi, Navajo and Zuni tribes display their works. On the grounds you'll find attractive nature trails and ponds. *Open daily except New Years, Thanksgiving and Christmas from 9:00am until 5:00pm; admission is $5 for adults, $4 for those over age 55, $3 for students with school identification, and $2 for children ages 7 through 17; Tel. 520/774-5213.*

Four miles further north on Fort Valley Road and then another seven on Snow Bowl Road will take you to **Flagstaff's Snow Bowl**. During the summer the ski-run's chair-lift is used to carry visitors on a journey of more than a mile to the 11,500 foot level from where there is a spectacular view of hundreds of square miles of northern Arizona. The panorama covers a distance of more than 70 miles. With a little hike you can even catch a glimpse of the Grand Canyon, about 40 miles distant as the crow flies. Give yourself about an hour for the basic trip, but more if you're going to be doing a lot of walking or hiking on the trails at the summit. *The summer chair-lift hours are daily from 10:00am until 4:00pm. The season is usually from the middle of June to the middle of September. However, if you're coming near to the start or end of the season it's a good idea to verify the dates. Tel. 520/779-1951 for information and prices.*

SKI ARIZONA!

*The Snow Bowl, sometimes referred to by its more formal name of **Fairfield Snow Bowl**, provides world-class skiing from approximately the middle of December through mid-April. The average annual snowfall is about 260 inches. There are 30 different ski runs of varying difficulty, reached by four chair lifts. The vertical drop is more than 2,300 feet. The skiing is on 12,356-foot high Agassiz Peak, once an active volcano. In addition to Nordic style skiing, snow lovers can opt to traverse one of the many cross-country ski trails.*

Two lodges at the summit offer great views, shopping and a place to eat. There's even a ski school providing lessons at the beginner and advanced levels. Daily lift tickets vary from $12 to $60 but there are also various packages that offer substantial savings. When heavy snow requires use of chains on Snow Bowl Road, the facility offers shuttle bus service from a parking area on US 180 (Fort Valley Road) at a round-trip cost of $4.

One last attraction is the **Arboretum at Flagstaff**, *located about seven miles south of Business I-40 (Old Highway 66) via Woody Mountain Road.* Consisting of gardens and solar greenhouses, the collection includes mainly rare and endangered plant species. Covering 200 acres of ponderosa pine forest at an altitude of 7,150 feet, the arboretum is both an educational and sensual experience. Shaded walks, birds, a tranquil brook, fragrant butterfly garden and fantastic views of the San Francisco Peaks along a mile long nature trail are the highlights of what will be a surprisingly rewarding visit. *The arboretum is open daily from 10:00am to 3:00pm May through September and the same hours on Monday through Friday from October through December 23rd and again from March 15th through April. It is closed from December 24th through March 14th. Admission is $3 for an individual age 18 or older. Tel. 520/774-1441.*

Monument Loop

Some of the most amazing attractions in the Flagstaff area aren't within the city but are on a loop route that covers a total of about 90 miles. You'll see three different national monuments on this tour that can, depending upon your level of interest and physical stamina, cover anywhere from a half to a full day.

Leave Flagstaff by taking US 89 north about 30 miles to just beyond the tiny town of Antelope Hills to the entrance of the **Wupatki National Monument**, the largest of the three monuments on the loop. The area now comprised by Wupatki was once home to the ancient native Anasazi and Sinagua civilizations. These people developed a highly complex society which is evidenced by the wide variety of architectural styles represented in the remaining ruins. These include some large pueblos and smaller field houses. After stopping at the visitor center to view the exhibits which explain the Hisatsinom (the collective name for both Anasazi and Sinagua as they are called by their Hopi descendants), you can take a walk on the easy trail that leads to five ruins.

The largest of the group is called Wupatki and had about 90 rooms. The other ruins have the names Citadel, Lomaki, Nalakihu, and Wukoki. The latter was three stories high. Also on the tour is an amphitheater used for ceremonial purposes as well as a ball court. The Wukoki ball court is unusual in ancient civilizations this far north of Mexico but is a definite sign that those cultures influenced developments in this region. Nearby are the "blow holes," where air streams in and out at a significant velocity. The natives believed that this was where the earth breathed. Scientists tell us that the phenomenon is caused by different air pressures in the crevices. Whatever the explanation, the sight of your companion's hair being tussled when someone right next to them remains perfectly coiffeured makes for an interesting photograph.

As you leave the 35,000 acre Wupatki at the opposite end of the Monument from which you entered, continue on the loop road. In about six miles there is an excellent vista of the **Painted Desert** and in another four miles you'll arrive at **Sunset Crater National Monument**.

A massive volcanic eruption and extensive lava flows occurred more than 900 years ago. Destructive as it was, the eruption had some good effects as well. One was a climatic change that resulted in increased rainfall. That water was the reason why many of the ancient people settled at Wupatki. On the self-guiding Bonito lava flow trail you can see some of the many different volcanic formations that remain a millennium after the 200-year long period of volcanic activity. The jagged black rock (which is sharp in places, so wear sturdy shoes) is partially covered with vegetation. A lookout provides a good glimpse of the lava flow if you don't want to take the trail. There is also a good view of the thousand foot high cinder cone. The red, yellow and orange shades of the cone offer a dramatic contrast to the dark, mostly black rock that surrounds it. The entire cone takes on a fiery tint near sunset, hence the name of the monument. It was named by the famous explorer John Wesley Powell, who was the first white man to notice the phenomenon. Although the trail isn't overly difficult you still have to be prepared for the rough surface.

Three miles beyond Sunset Crater you'll rejoin US 89. Take it south and just as you arrive back in Flagstaff look for the junction with I-40. Go east for three more miles to Exit 204 and follow the access road into **Walnut Canyon National Monument**. The canyon was the home of an Indian culture known as the Sinagua. Around 600A.D. they migrated from the southeastern portion of what is now Arizona to this area of deep canyons. They built impressive homes beneath the overhanging cliffs of the canyon's walls. What you see today are the remains of the community they developed between about 1125 and 1250. Like most of these civilizations, it disappeared mysteriously, probably because of the lack of water. It is interesting to note that the name given to this tribe means "without water."

Your trip to Walnut Canyon begins at the interesting visitor center where exhibits explain what archaeologists have learned about the Sinagua culture. From the balcony outside the center there is an excellent view of the steep cliffs and what remains of the Sinagua's dwellings. You can go past or into more than a hundred of the rooms by taking the paved trail. However, it is a little strenuous, including many steps on it's 185-foot descent and return. To make things even more difficult, the altitude of over 7,000 feet will make it seem double that amount.

All three monuments are open year-round, except for Christmas Day from 8:00am until 5:00pm. From Memorial Day to Labor Day the hours may be up to an hour earlier at opening and an hour later closing. Sunset Crater may sometimes be closed due to snow during the winter. The admission fee is $5 per vehicle or $2 per person to those visitors without a park service passport at Walnut Canyon and the same fee combined for both other monuments. Telephone numbers *are: Wupatki, 520/679-2365; Sunset Crater, 520/526-2502; and Walnut Canyon, 520/526-3367.* Return to Flagstaff by hopping back on I-40 west.

Another possible routing in the Flagstaff area which can be done by itself or in conjunction with the national monument loop takes you over the **Schultz Pass Road**. This unpaved route is passable to regular automobiles as long as the weather is dry. It runs from US 180 just north of the Museum of Northern Arizona and ends at US 89 south of the junction with the loop road to Sunset Crater and Wupatki. The road crosses mountainous terrain of an alpine nature. During the summer months the colorful wildflowers are spectacular.

Sedona & Oak Creek Canyon

Flagstaff and Sedona are separated by a distance of only 25 miles but it might as well be 2,500 because the differences between the two are so vast. Not that there's anything wrong with the way Flagstaff looks – but, it could be any number of towns in a number of different states (if you ignore the surrounding sights). Sedona, as you shall soon see, is a very unique community. But first you have to travel those 25 miles and what a trip it is! Some of the state's most beautiful scenery is contained within that short distance.

From Flagstaff head south on AZ 89A (which is known as Milton Road within the city). No sooner have you left town than the road will begin to climb through the thick greenery of the Coconino National Forest. What goes up must, as we all know, eventually come down. And does it come down! Soon you'll be twisting and turning your way along the two lane highway as it descends from the southern edge of the Colorado Plateau into the canyon. The road can be difficult to drive if you're pulling a trailer. As you reach the canyon the vivid red colored rock for which it is famous will soon become interspersed with the green trees.

Oak Creek Canyon stretches for about 16 miles in length and is generally less than a mile wide. In many places the sheer cliffs of the canyon will tower a thousand feet or more above you. It has been made world famous by the many movies and television commercials that have been filmed here. While the red rocks are the most prominent feature of the canyon, there are many other colors that add to the beauty of the picture before you. Some of the rocks are white and others are yellow. The entire canyon is also liberally filled with trees such as juniper and pine. Unusual rock formations and impressive deep gorges complete the scene.

Because of the narrow road and the often heavy traffic you shouldn't attempt to do your touring only by car. There are many pullouts where you can safely view the wonderful sights in the canyon. Among the best is the **Oak Creek Vista** near the northern edge of the canyon. A popular stopping place for families is the **Slide Rock State Park**, *$5 per vehicle* *admission charge, Tel. 520/282-3034.* Here you can go swimming in a natural water slide or pick apples in a pretty orchard. Many visitors spend a full day exploring the wonders of Oak Creek Canyon but even a cursory drive should be worth at least an hour of your time. *After Spring 2000, a fee will be charged for parking in Oak Creek Canyon.*

At the southern end of the canyon is the town of **Sedona**. This once sleepy little community is now abuzz with activity all year round. One of the attractions is the climate and topography – it is neither mountain nor desert, yet a little of both. It avoids some of the extremes of hot and cold that are found in many other parts of Arizona. In the 1950s and '60s Sedona was inhabited by a few hearty souls and a growing number of talented people who transformed the town into an artist's colony like many in New Mexico. But it has become more than that. \Thousands of vacationers crowd its streets, especially in summer and everywhere you look there are beautiful new residential communities. These range from retirement developments to luxury homes costing millions of dollars. In fact, many highly compensated corporate executives have discovered Sedona as a place to live. What's nice about all of this is how the architecture of the town blends in so nicely with the surroundings. Southwestern style buildings predominantly make use of the natural colors of the region and many homes have been designed to blend in with the terrain, often being built into hillsides.

Getting around Sedona is easy, as there are only two main roads that you have to concern yourself with in town. These are Arizona highways 89A and 179. The two converge in the heart of town and form the letter "Y," which is exactly the name that the intersection is known by. While AZ 89A is the main street, the other road is important because it provides a shortcut to I-17 if you're heading to Phoenix and other points south.

Besides shopping, which is popular in Sedona, the main attraction is located about three miles south via AZ 179 to Chapel Road. The famous **Chapel of the Holy Cross** is anything but a traditional church building. Built of the area's native red rock and approached by a gently sloping ramp, the structure is situated between two huge sandstone peaks. The interior of the chapel is strikingly unadorned; however, the 90-foot high cross is very imposing. It is fitting that the chapel blends in so well with the surrounding glory of nature because the panoramic view from this locale is splendid – the magnificent fiery red rocks can be seen in every direction. While it doesn't take long to see the chapel, many people will find themselves lingering in the area and finding it difficult to drag themselves away. *Chapel open daily from 9:00am until 5:00pm. There is no admission charge. Tel. 520/282-4069. Although the surroundings will make you feel like you're in a park, remember that this is an active church and proper behavior is requested.*

Much of the remaining natural wonders of the Sedona area are located to the west of town via AZ 89A to the **Upper and Lower Red Rock Loop Road**. The narrow road has a few steep hills and quite a few turns but is paved and not very difficult to drive. Along the loop is the **Red Rock State Park** which features, in addition to the colorful rocks that give it its name, quite a few different species of animals and plants that make their home along the banks of Oak Creek. There's a visitor center that explains the delicate ecosystem of the area as well as hiking trails.

Another famous scene, reputedly one of the most photographed spots in the United States, is also found along the Loop Road. This is the magnificent rock formations at Red Rock Crossing known as the **Cathedral Rocks**. Indeed, the many spire like projections do remind many of a cathedral but you're free to come up with your own interpretation. Give yourself about an hour to complete the loop but longer if you plan to hike some of the many trails or stop for a picnic in the park. *Park open daily from 8:00am until 6:00pm (to 5:00pm from October through April). There is a $5 vehicle use fee. Tel. 520/282-6907.*

I briefly mentioned that Sedona has become something of a shopper's Mecca. There are more than two dozen art galleries and even a greater number of chic specialty shops throughout town but especially along AZ 89A in vicinity of the "Y" intersection. Many are also concentrated in the **Tlaquepeque** shopping area located about a half mile south of the "Y" on AZ 179. For more traditional shopping you can sample the stores of the Oak Creek Factory Outlet about six miles beyond Tlaquepeque. Within the Factory Outlet Mall is the **Sedona SuperMax Theater**. It features films which highlight the natural beauty of the area. While it isn't a bad film I wouldn't use precious sightseeing time to view on screen what you can see in person. However, shows are given as late as 8:00pm, so you might want to end the day with this. *Call Tel. 520/284-3214 for information on films being shown, exact schedule and prices.*

Continuing on AZ 89A from Sedona, there are several interesting and often outstanding attractions within a 30-mile drive. Most are located either in Cottonwood (18 miles from Sedona) or neighboring Clarkdale. First up is the **Dead Horse Ranch State Park** in **Cottonwood** off of 10th Street. It's a nice place to relax and enjoy the surroundings. You can do that either in the picnic areas located by the Verde River, at the well stocked fishing pond or by taking a stroll through an orchard. There is a vehicle charge. *Park open daily from 8:00am until 6:00pm. Admission is by daily $4 vehicle use charge. Tel. 520/634-5283.*

From Cottonwood follow AZ 289 for about two miles. Just before you enter Clarkdale there will be signs pointing you toward a short side road that leads to the **Tuzigoot National Monument**. Meaning "crooked water" in the Apache language, Tuzigoot is what remains of a 12th century

SEDONA ON THE WILDER SIDE

If the sight seeing I've described sounds nice but not quite active enough for you, then how about sampling some of the most rugged countryside in the region by means other than a car or by foot. The Sedona area has lots of possibilities. The first is to get above it all and see the splendid red rocks and other sights by **hot-air balloon**. *These trips are generally given only in the morning, weather permitting. Reputable operators are:*

AeroZona Balloon Company, *Tel. 520/282-1499*
Inflated Ego Balloon Company, *Tel. 520/284-9483*
Northern Light Balloon Expeditions, *Tel. 800/230-6222*
Red Rock Balloon Adventures, *Tel. 800/258-3754*
Sky High Balloon Adventures, *Tel. 800/551-7597*

Don't you just love the catchy names? Numerous other operators offer helicopter and airplane tours (going as far as the Grand Canyon but also with local only options), or you might try out some **hang gliding** *off of those red rocks. The latter is at the* **AZ Hang Gliding Center**, *Tel. 800/757-2442. Another interesting option is to see the area via a real bi-plane.* **Red Rock Bi-Plane Tours**, *Tel. 888/866-7433, is the place to contact.*

Because of the many areas that require off-road vehicles to reach, jeep rentals are very popular and available at many different locations, including most car rental agencies in town. An alternative, in case you're afraid of getting lost or afraid of off-road driving, is to take one of the ever popular **jeep tours**. *Options vary greatly as to length and price but there's something for everyone. The scenery on all of them is nothing short of spectacular. Among the best are:*

Pink Jeep Tours, *Tel. 800/8-SEDONA*
Sedona Photo Tours, *Tel. 800/9-SEDONA*
Sedona Red Rock Jeep Tours, *Tel. 800/848-7728*

Sinaguan village constructed atop a ridge that rises above the Verde Valley. An easy trail leads from the visitor center and loops around the ruins which once contained more than a hundred rooms. Most of the structure was a single story but there is one area that had two. You can climb up to the top to get a good view of the entire ruins as well as the Verde Valley. A minimum of a half hour is necessary to visit Tuzigoot. *The Monument is open daily from 8:00am until 7:00pm, Memorial Day through Labor Day, and until 5:00pm the remainder of the year. The admission price is $2 per person over age 17 unless you possess a park service passport. Tel. 520/634-5564.*

Clarkdale, with a population of about 2,000 people, is also the starting point for a scenic ride on the **Verde River Canyon Excursion Train**. This is an exciting opportunity to traverse a portion of the **Sycamore Wilderness** that is not accessible by any road. The four hour long trip covers about forty miles before returning to Clarkdale and takes you over several trestles that cross deep canyons. You'll probably catch a glimpse of quite a bit of wildlife such as blue herons and deer. Even if you don't, you'll definitely see the remains of many cliff side **Sinaguan Indian villages**. The train features both open and enclosed cars and there is food service on board. *There is only one trip per day and it departs Wednesday through Sunday at 10:00am from June through August and at 11:00am the remainder of the year. Prices: $55 first class; regular fares are $37 for adults, $33 for seniors and $22 for children. Reservations are required. Call them at 800/ 293-7245 for reservations and to verify departure times. Credit cards.*

About five miles beyond Clarkdale you'll rejoin AZ 89A for he final mile or so into the town of **Jerome**. The town was once a city, boasting a population of more than 15,000 at the height of its copper mining days. With the closing of the last mine in the 1950's, Jerome almost became a ghost town. However, there are now about 500 residents and a number of art galleries and shops serving the growing visitor population. Jerome is quite a sight as its narrow streets wind up and down Cleopatra Hill, its houses seemingly precariously perched on the brink.

The town's mining days are chronicled at the **Mining Museum**, *200 Main Street; open daily from 9:00am to 4:30pm except for Thanksgiving and Christmas; nominal admission fee; Tel. 520/634-5477.* However, a much more comprehensive history is available heading back toward Sedona on AZ 89A at the **Jerome State Historic Park**. Occupying the mansion of a mining magnate, you'll learn about the Douglas family's involvement in the **United Verde Extension Mine** as well as about the community as a whole. Movies are shown. The mansion was built in 1916. One of the most interesting features is a large three dimensional model of the town as it appeared in its heyday, including a cutaway of the mines. *Open daily from 8:00am to 5:00pm except Christmas; admission is $2 for adults and $1 for children ages 12 through 17; Tel. 520/634-5381.*

AROUND THE REGION

All of the attractions in this section can be done in day trips from either Flagstaff or Sedona since the furthest distance is only 85 miles from Flagstaff or about 60 from Sedona. However, if you're not making a base in either of those locations, but traveling through, you'll find accommodations in, among other places, Williams and Prescott.

West of Flagstaff

The town of **Williams** is about 31 miles from Flagstaff via I-40. You can be there in about 25 minutes. Exits 161, 163 or 165 all serve the town. Williams has only about 2,500 people but is important because of its proximity to the Grand Canyon. It's only 56 miles from Williams to the South Rim via AZ 64, a drive of about an hour. For those coming into Arizona from California and Nevada, it is the most logical gateway. Besides being an important gateway to the Canyon (i.e., there are plenty of motels and restaurants), the town doesn't have a lot of attractions. One is the **Grand Canyon Deer Farm**. A variety of animals can be fed by hand. It's good for children but I think most adults might be a bit bored. *Located off of I-40 at Deer Farm Road. Open daily from 8:00am until 7:00pm during the summer and from 9:00am to 6:00pm at other times. Closed on Thanksgiving and Christmas. Admission is $5 for adults, $4 for seniors, and $2.75 for children. Tel. 800/926-3337.*

Williams is better known as the starting point of the **Grand Canyon Railway**, an unusual way to see one of the world's greatest natural wonders. The train offered a means to see the Grand Canyon before the construction of roads. Today, passengers pass through a log depot constructed in 1910 (and containing many exhibits and photographs about the train and area history) and board ornate coaches built in the 1920s. The locomotive depends upon the time of the year. During the summer turn-of-the-century steam locomotives are used while more modern diesel engines are put into service during other times of the year. The round-trip lasts approximately eight hours, including about 3-1/2 hours at the South Rim, either on your own or by bus tour at an additional fee.

There are actually three different bus tours offered which vary in length from about 1-1/2 to three hours. While it's not the fastest way to get to the Grand Canyon, and it provides a rather limited amount of sight seeing time, it is "different" and can be quite an enjoyable experience. Children will enjoy the ride, especially if your train happens to be held up by some nasty desperados – a very likely occurrence in summertime. There is food service on the train as well as entertainment provided by musicians who make their way from car to car. *The trip is offered every day at 9:30am except for December 24th and 25th. The round-trip fare is $49 for adults and $19 for ages 3 through 16. Credit cards. Passengers are urged to check in about an hour ahead of departure. The train returns to Williams at 5:30pm. Reservations are highly recommended. Call 800/THE-TRAIN.*

If you have time for about a 2-1/2 to three hour side excursion covering a total of about 50 miles, try heading into the beautiful **Sycamore wilderness area**. From Williams take 4th Street south which turns into Perkinsville Road. Eight miles ahead turn off on Forest Route 109. This road is unpaved but usually navigable to all cars. High clearance vehicles can do the trip much easier. Follow that road until it ends at the **Sycamore Canyon**. Sometimes known as Arizona's "Little Grand Canyon," this gorgeous chasm is a mile wide, 20 miles long and up to 3,400 feet deep. The walls of the canyon are brilliant shades of red, much like Oak Creek Canyon, and it is speckled with generous amounts of green trees and bushes. It's not one of Arizona's better known sights but certainly ranks among the most wonderful. Once the road ends the delights are just beginning for the hiker.

Along I-17

Between Flagstaff and the town of Cordes Junction there are three worthwhile attractions located right off of I-17. The first one is **Montezuma Castle National Monument**. Use Exit 289 from I-17 and follow signs. This is another example of the architecture of the Sinaguan culture, an impressive five-story dwelling with 20 rooms built in the early part of the 12th century. It was strategically placed in the hollow of a vertical cliff and was accessible only by ladders. Today you can reach this extremely well preserved dwelling by wheelchair accessible trails. However, to help maintain the state of preservation, visitors are not allowed inside the "castle."

The name was mistakenly given by early settlers who were so amazed by the structure that they assumed it must have been built by the Aztecs. Besides the main structure and a visitor center there are the badly deteriorated remains of a six story apartment building that had approximately 45 rooms.

A related sight is the so-called **Montezuma Well**, about 11 miles northeast of the main monument (use Exit 293). Here, a large sinkhole measuring almost 500 feet across was created by the collapse of a huge cavern fed by continuously flowing springs. This provided a good source of water for the native cultures. Even today it is a rather lush area amid the surrounding desert. You can see the remains of numerous pueblos and pit dwellings surrounding the sinkhole. You should allow at least 45 minutes to visit Montezuma Castle and another 30 minutes if you're going to the well. *The monument is open daily from 8:00am until 7:00pm during the months of September through May and until 5:00pm the remainder of the year. Admission is $4 for those not holding park service passports, but there is no charge if you're going only to Montezuma Well. Tel. 520/567-3322.*

A little to the south of Montezuma Castle at Camp Verde (two miles east of Exit 287) is **Fort Verde State Historic Park**. Back in 1866 the United States established a fort (then known as Camp Lincoln) to defend the local settlers against continual raiding by the Apache. The need for the post gradually faded away as the Apache were slowly vanquished. Four of the camp's original buildings have been restored and display artifacts of Indians, settlers and the American military during the 19th century. Many of the living quarters are furnished in period. A half hour is more than enough time to look around although it can take longer if you attend the living history programs that are offered on Saturday during the winter. *Open daily except Christmas Day from 8:00am until 4:30pm; admission fee is $2 for adults and $1 for children ages 12 through 17; Tel. 520/567-3275.*

Approximately 25 miles south of Camp Verde via Exit 262 of I-17 is the town of **Cordes Junction**. A signed dirt road (which is sometimes barely passable during or after severe weather) leads about three miles east to the very unusual **Arcosanti**. This is the vision of renowned architect Paolo Soleri – a complete urban community for 5,000 inhabitants that is in harmony with nature. Encompassing more than 4,000 acres of natural area, the 15-acre town-site is intended to be a working artist's community. It has been under construction for many years and may never be done, but it remains an interesting place to visit. *The visitor center is open daily from 9:00am to 5:00pm. The center as well as the grounds are free of charge. Guided one-hour tours are offered every half hour from 10:00am to 4:00pm every day of the year except Thanksgiving and Christmas. The fee for tours is $5 per person. Tel. 520/632-7135.*

Prescott Area

Prescott and the adjacent community of Prescott Valley can be reached from Sedona and Flagstaff via AZ 89A. It is about 35 miles past Jerome. The route continues to climb after Jerome, going by 7,743-foot Mingus Mountain before descending rapidly into the relatively flat valley between two sections of the Prescott National Forest. You can also get to Prescott from the I-17 corridor by taking AZ 69 which begins at Exit 262 in Cordes Junction. It's about 33 miles into Prescott from that point.

Prescott began as a mining town in the middle of the 19th century. These days, however, it is primarily a resort town because of the recreational opportunities in the surrounding mountains and the area's more moderate weather. It's not nearly as hot in the summer as southern Arizona and winters are not as cold as in the Flagstaff area. The city has grown to a population of almost 30,000 people. Many stately Victorian homes from Prescott's early days grace the city. Give yourself several hours to explore Prescott's sights.

If you're coming into town via AZ 89A, that road ends about seven miles north of Prescott at AZ 89. The second road has two attractions which you should see regardless of which way you're arriving. A mile to the north of the 89/89A junction is the **Phippen Museum**. This art museum has a sizable collection of works by famous Western artists. That is contrasted with works on the American west by contemporary artists. *open Wednesday through Monday from 10:00am to 4:00pm (from 1:00pm on Sunday) from March through December, at other times the days are the same but it opens at 1:00pm, closed New Years and Christmas; admission is $3 for adults and $2 for senior citizens and ages 7 through 21; Tel. 520/778-1385.*

Heading back south towards town now on AZ 89, you'll soon reach the gorgeous **Granite Dells**, sometimes known by the name Point of Rocks. Here you'll see large granite rocks on both sides of the highway for a distance of almost two miles. Pretty **Lake Watson** enhances the scene even further and is a good place to stop to get a better look at the Dells.

Within the town are a number of excellent cultural and historical attractions of which the most important (for those with limited time) is the **Sharlot Hall Museum**. The museum is named for a former state historian and comprises several different buildings on a three acre site. Among these are the 1864 **Governor's Mansion**, the home of famous explorer John Fremont (built in 1875) and the typically Victorian Bashford House. All three of these buildings can be visited and are furnished in a manner similar to when they were first built. The Governor's Mansion also has an excellent display of western transportation that includes a stagecoach and Conestoga wagon. Among the other structures at Sharlot Hall are a windmill, blacksmith shop and school as well as two small gardens. About an hour is required to see the museum properly. *415 W. Gurley Street, located on Prescott's primary east-west thoroughfare. The museum grounds and all buildings are open daily from 10:00am to 5:00pm (except from 1:00pm on Sunday) from April through October. During the rest of the year the hours are from 10:00am to 4:00pm Tuesday through Saturday and on Sunday from 1:00 to 5:00pm. It is closed on New Year's Day, Thanksgiving and Christmas. There is no set admission fee but donations are requested. Tel. 520/445-3122.*

The nearby **Smoki Museum**, *five blocks east on Gurley Street then just north on Arizona Avenue*, is a modern building that is designed in the traditional Pueblo style of architecture. This interesting facility has an extensive collection of artifacts that were found in several Indian ruins throughout northern Arizona, including some from the Tuzigoot site. In addition, a collection of excellent paintings bring various Indian tales and ceremonies to life. *The museum is open only during the months of May through September. The hours are from 10:00am to 4:00pm (Sunday from 1:00pm) every day except Wednesday. Donations are requested in lieu of an admission charge. Tel. 520/445-1230.*

A brief stop should also be made at Courthouse Plaza to see the impressive **Bucky O'Neill Monument**. Sculpted by **Solon H. Borglum** (a son of the creator of the Mount Rushmore Memorial), the monument is in honor of **William O'Neill**, the first volunteer in the Spanish-American

War and the man who founded the Rough Riders of Teddy Roosevelt fame.

Near the Courthouse and all along Gurley Street is the historic portion of town. Prescott has well over 500 buildings listed in the National Register of Historic Places, which is more than any other community in the state. Many of the historic buildings now serve as antique stores, specialty shops, galleries, and restaurants. The greatest concentration of shops, especially antique dealers, is located along a two block stretch of Cortez Street, north of the Courthouse Plaza.

One of Prescott's better known natural features is a rugged granite outcropping known as the **Thumb Butte**. It is located four miles west of town and is easily recognizable. (There's a $2 charge for parking.) A controversial plan to develop housing in the area has been criticized by those who feel it will detract from the view. The resolution is in doubt but even if it is built it shouldn't interfere with your view over the next couple of years.

NIGHTLIFE & ENTERTAINMENT

While the Flagstaff and Sedona area certainly isn't Phoenix or Tucson when it comes to nightlife, there is probably a lot more than you would expect in small towns. Undoubtedly it is because of the large number of visitors who come to this region.

Cultural events in Flagstaff are held in the 200-seat amphitheater of the **Coconino Center for the Arts**, *Tel. 520/779-6921*. The **Flagstaff Symphony Orchestra** puts on a series of eight different concerts each year during its season from October through May. Information is available by calling *Tel. 520/774-5107*.

There are some concerts, theater performances, and dance events held at **Northern Arizona University**. Information is available from the central ticket office, *Tel. 520/523-2000*. Nightlife in lounges and nightclubs is primarily in the major hotels, especially the lounge at the Little America where you'll find dancing to the top 40 tunes, and a few places in the historic downtown. You can contact the **Flagstaff Main Street Foundation**, *Tel. 520/774-1330*, for more information on what's going on in town during your visit. That also applies to Sedona. Various events also take place from time to time at the **Sedona Arts Center**, *Tel. 520/282-3809*.

Prescott has some nightlife as well. A number of pubs are located throughout the downtown area, concentrated in the vicinity of Gurley and Montezuma Streets, sometimes known as Whiskey Row. The **Prescott Fine Arts Association**, *Marina Street*, stages plays, music and dance at its theater and the **Elks Opera House**, built in 1904, also has shows. Summer evenings see performances held on the **Courthouse Plaza**. For current information you're best off checking with the local tourism office, *117 W. Goodwin between Montezuma and Cortez, just opposite the south side of the Courthouse.*

Casinos
- **Bucky's & Yavapai Gaming Center,** *Prescott. Tel. 520/776-1666*
- **Cliff Castle Casino,** *Camp Verde. Tel. 520/567-9674*

SPORTS & RECREATION

Bicycle Rentals
- **Absolute Bikes,** *18 San Francisco Street, Flagstaff, Tel. 520/779-5969*
- **Mountain Bike Heaven,** *Sedona, Tel. 520/282-1312*
- **Mountain Sports,** *1800 S. Milon Road, Flagstaff, Tel. 520/779-5156*
- **Sedona Sports,** *Sedona, Tel. 520/282-6956*

Fishing
- **Peaks Ranger District,** *Flagstaff, Tel. 520/527-3650*
- **Rainbow Trout Farm,** *Sedona, Tel. 520/282-3379*
- **Sedona Ranger District,** *Tel. 520/282-4119*

Golf
- **Beaver Creek Golf Resort,** *Sedona, Tel. 520/567-4487*
- **Eden Hills Golf Course,** *Oakmont Drive, Flagstaff, Tel. 520/527-7997*
- **Oak Creek Country Club,** *Sedona, Tel. 520/284-1660*
- **Sedona Golf Resort,** *Sedona, Tel. 520/284-9355*

Hang Gliding
- **AZ Hang Gliding Center,** *Tel. 800-757-2442*

Horseback Riding
- **Blazing Trails,** *Sedona, Tel. 520/567-6611*
- **Hitchin Post Stables,** *Flagstaff, Tel. 520/774-1719*
- **Kachina Stables,** *Sedona, Tel. 520/282-7252*

Hot Air Ballooning
- **AeroZona Balloon Company,** *Tel. 520/282-1499*
- **Inflated Ego Balloon Company,** *Tel. 520/284-9483*
- **Northern Light Balloon Expeditions,** *Tel. 800/230-6222*
- **Red Rock Balloon Adventures,** *Tel. 800/258-3754*
- **Sky High Balloon Adventures,** *Tel. 800/551-7597*

Jeep Tours
- **Pink Jeep Tours**, *Tel. 800/8-SEDONA*
- **Sedona Photo Tours**, *Tel. 800/9-SEDONA*
- **Sedona Red Rock Jeep Tours**, *Tel. 800/848-7728*

Rafting
The following operators are all Flagstaff based but offer rafting excursions on the Colorado River and through the Grand Canyon. Trips last a minimum of six days and it is advisable to make reservations at least a year in advance.
- **Arizona Raft Adventures**, *Flagstaff, Tel. 800/786-7238*
- **Canyoneers, Inc.**, *Flagstaff, Tel. 800/525-0924*
- **Canyon Explorations**, *Flagstaff, Tel. 800/654-0723*

Skiing
Fairfield Snow Bowl, *Snow Bowl Road, Flagstaff, Tel. 520/779-1951.* See the sidebar earlier in this chapter for more details on the Snow Bowl.

SHOPPING

Although **Flagstaff** is the largest community in this portion of the state, it certainly doesn't attract visitors for its shopping opportunities. However, of most interest is the **Downtown Flagstaff Historic Railroad District** centered along W. Aspen Avenue. A variety of shops occupy restored buildings. Antique hunters will enjoy **Black Bart's Antiques**, *2760 E. Butler Avenue.* This rather eclectic establishment has, among other things, a restaurant. More modern shoppers with a craving to buy can always run off to the **Flagstaff Mall**, *4650 North US Highway 89.*

Sedona, as was already alluded to, is a shopping town. In addition to the Outlet stores and other facilities in the Village at Oak Creek and near the "Y" you might also want to check out the so-called "Uptown" shopping district located on US Highway 89A on the north side of town. Native American arts and crafts as well as western wear are the featured attractions in many stores.

PRACTICAL INFORMATION

- **Airport**
    Flagstaff: *Pullman Airport, 6200 Pullman Drive (off of I-17, 2 miles south of town), Tel. 520/556-1234*

- **Bus Depot**
    Flagstaff, *399 S. Malpais Lane, Tel. 520/774-4573*
    Prescott, *820 E. Sheldon Street, Tel. 520/445-5470*

- **Hospital**
  Flagstaff: *Flagstaff Medical Center, 1200 N. Beaver Street, Tel. 520/779-3366*
  Cottonwood (22 miles west of Sedona): *Marcus J. Lawrence Medical Center, 269 S. Candy Lane, Tel. 520/639-6000*

- **Police** (non-emergency):
  Cottonwood, *Tel. 520/634-4246*
  Flagstaff, *Tel. 520/774-1414*
  Prescott, *Tel. 520/778-1444*
  Sedona, *Tel. 520/282-3100*

- **Public Transportation**
  Pine County Transit, *Tel. 520/779-6624*

- **Taxi**
  Flagstaff, A Friendly Cab, *Tel. 520/774-4444*; Flagstaff Taxi, *Tel. 520/526-4123*; Sun Taxi, *Tel. 520/774-7400*
  Sedona, Bob's Sedona Taxi, *Tel. 520/282-1234*

- **Tourist Office/Visitors Bureau**
  Cottonwood, *1010 South Main Street, Tel. 520/634-7593*
  Flagstaff, *1 East Route 66, Tel. 520/774-9541 or 800-842-7293*
  Sedona, *Tel. 520/282-7722 or 800-288-7336*

- **Train Station**
  Flagstaff, *Tel. 520/774-8679*

15. GRAND CANYON NATIONAL PARK

Any words used to describe the **Grand Canyon** are insufficient to do it proper justice. The same is even true for pictures or video because those mediums cannot capture the depth of the view that is held by an individual standing on the canyon's rim. As this chapter later takes you through a visit to the Grand Canyon, I'll try my best to convey at least part of the awesome feeling that can almost bring a first time visitor to tears and freezes you at the spot where you first look into the canyon.

But for now you'll have to settle for some statistics. The Canyon is 277 miles long, approximately 18 miles wide, and almost a mile in depth. So vast is the spectacle that the Colorado River, averaging about 400 feet in width, appears as a slender blue line to the visitor standing on the rim. In fact, the early explorers thought that the river was but a tiny creek which would be no problem to cross if only they could get into the canyon. Both were to present problems that would not be solved for a long time to come.

Besides the size, however, what is most awesome about the canyon is the wonderful array of colors in the rock. No two places are alike and even the same place can change radically from one part of the day to another depending upon how the sunlight plays on the rock face. If you're interested in the geologic and human history of the canyon there's a sidebar on each of them contained in this chapter.

Besides visiting both the South and North Rims of the Grand Canyon this chapter will let you discover a number of other natural wonders in this portion of the state. These are concentrated in the Glen Canyon National Recreation Area, located near the town of Page and straddling the border between Arizona and Utah. The journey by car from the Grand Canyon's South Rim to the North Rim is also filled with lots of scenery, especially in the area of Marble Canyon. And I'll conclude with some ways to visit the most remote western portions of the Grand Canyon.

THE GEOLOGY OF THE GRAND CANYON

One cannot fully appreciate their visit to the Grand Canyon without having at least some understanding of what you are seeing from a geologic perspective. For the walls of the Grand Canyon are a veritable museum of natural history which spans about one half of the earth's almost 5 billion year existence. The forces of erosion, primarily the cutting action of the **Colorado River** *but also wind and rain, have exposed many different layers of rock strata. The oldest of the twelve layers (about 1.7 billion years) is at the bottom and the youngest (only about 250 million years), buff-colored Kaibab Limestone, is at the top. These layers as well as each of the ten intervening layers have a different color and are composed of differing types of rock. You will be able during your visit to clearly see the distinctive separation of each layer.*

The area which is now called the **Colorado Plateau** *was once part of a vast plain that covered virtually all of the present day Southwest. A series of uplifting actions raised the plateau around the surrounding area. The Grand Canyon is today the lowest step in a long series of geologic formations known as the* **Grand Staircase.** *Because of the change in elevation the Colorado River started to flow more steeply on its southwesterly course, providing the impetus for the creation of the canyon. As a result of the mind boggling amount of time that the canyon has existed and the many changes in climate over the eons, the canyon has been home to a wide assortment of creatures, many of which are fossilized within the colorful walls of the canyon. There are countless books written on the canyon's natural history. One of the best, if you're really interested in this topic, is* **Introduction to Grand Canyon Geology** *by Michael Collier. (Grand Canyon Natural History Association, 1994).*

ARRIVALS & DEPARTURES

By car the South Rim is only 84 miles from Flagstaff and 223 miles from Phoenix. Travelers coming from the east should take I-40 to Exit 195 in Flagstaff and then US 180 to the Grand Canyon. If you're coming from the west, use Exit 165 in Williams and then go north on AZ 64 for about an hour to the canyon. Visitors from Phoenix will take I-17 north until it's end in Flagstaff and proceed as above via US 180. If you're going directly to the North Rim from points north, you'll need US 89A to get you to the town of Jacob Lake and then proceed south for just over 40 miles on AZ 67. I'll detail the route from the South Rim to the North later on.

There are a lot of alternative means to get to the Grand Canyon (at least the South Rim) if you don't want to drive there. I previously mentioned the Grand Canyon Railway from Williams. In addition to

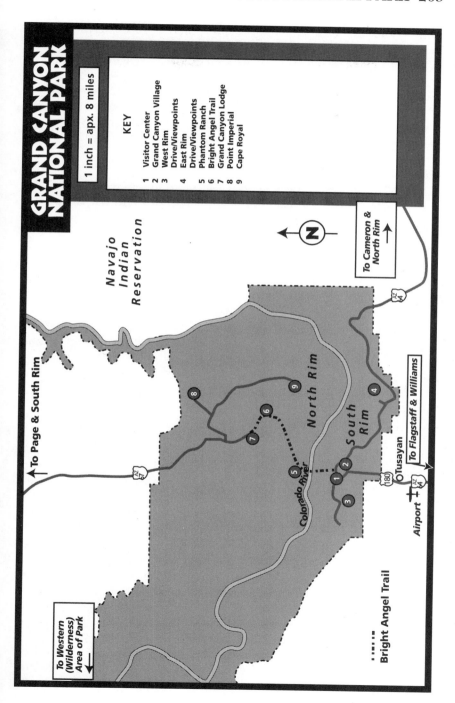

multi-day bus tours from the Phoenix area, there are also bus tours from Flagstaff and Williams provided by **Nava-Hopi Tours**, *Tel. 520/774-5003*. Nava-Hopi Tours also connect with Amtrak rail passengers at Flagstaff.

The Grand Canyon also has a small airport located to the south of the main entrance. Commuter flights operate from Phoenix, Las Vegas, Los Angeles, and several smaller Arizona localities. These are usual packaged as day trips and include a stop of several hours along the South Rim, usually via a guided bus tour.

ORIENTATION

The Grand Canyon National Park covers a tremendous area of 1,904 square miles, which is about half-way between the size of Rhode Island and Delaware! The Colorado River divides it into South and North Rim areas. Although it only averages around 15 miles across from one rim to the other, the canyon isn't traversed by any roads. So, if you don't hike into the canyon, cross it and then climb up on the other side, you have to travel by car from Grand Canyon Village on the South Rim to the North Rim village, a road distance of more than 210 miles. The South Rim is much more accessible from major population centers and is, therefore, more heavily visited. I'll first describe the South Rim, then the sights along the route to the North Rim, and then the North Rim itself. The final sight seeing sections involve areas to the east and west of the Grand Canyon National Park.

There is an extensive transportation system within the Grand Canyon National Park, especially on the South Rim. Besides the excellent roads, a shuttle service provides a free and frequent means of getting around. Two routes serve the South Rim, one within the so-called Village area where most of the lodging is located, and the other along the West Rim Drive. In the summer months you must use the West Rim Shuttle since that portion of the road is closed to private vehicles. In a way it's better because it eliminates some of the hassles of driving in traffic and finding a place to park. It also allows you to concentrate on the scenery. Disabled persons, however, can get a permit to operate their own cars year-round.

From May through November there is also a shuttle service that connects the South and North Rims. It operates once a day in each direction. Contact the Bright Angel Lodge transportation desk for the **Trans Canyon Shuttle** schedule and fares, *Tel. 520/638-2820*. There's even "transportation," of a sort, into the depths of the canyon itself for those who don't want to or can't hike in – a mule trip. This, too, isn't for everyone, so see the sidebar a little later on.

There is no set amount of time that I can suggest to devote to the Grand Canyon. You can see the highlights of the South Rim in a few hours but days could be spent there without seeing it all. To visit both rims requires a minimum of two days. While there are many similarities between the two rims, they are different enough to both have to be seen in order to say that you've really "seen" the Grand Canyon.

WHERE TO STAY
ON THE SOUTH RIM

First of all let me state that I wouldn't ordinarily recommend all of the lodging establishments listed here but make an exception because so many people want to stay within the Park. I will, however, make note of which ones aren't of the best quality. Even with more than a thousand hotel rooms within the park the demand is so great that reservations must be made well in advance. Never show up at the South Rim (especially during the summer months) and expect to find a room available. You'll be in for big trouble.

All of the hotels on the South Rim are run by a single operator authorized by the National Park Service. The Fred Harvey Company is the official concessionaire, as it has been for many years. Going under the name of Grand Canyon National Park Lodges, the Harvey Company is a subsidiary of Amfac, a big name in the resort hotel industry. All hotel reservations for the **National Park Lodges** are handled through a central office, *Tel. 303/297-2757*. Each of the six hotels on the **South Rim** has the same telephone number, which is *Tel. 520/638-2631 or 638-2401, Fax 520/638-9247*. However, you should use the other number for making reservations. Most major credit cards accepted at all properties.

Because of the great popularity of the Grand Canyon and the relatively small number of available hotel rooms, it isn't always possible to stay either on the South Rim or immediately outside the national park borders. The nearest large concentration of hotels is in Williams, which has to be considered as being within "commuting" distance of the Grand Canyon. See the listings for Williams in the previous chapter as well as the listing of chain properties in Chapter 6, *Planning Your Trip*.

Expensive

EL TOVAR HOTEL, *At Grand Canyon Village. 78 Rooms. Rates: $116-174, all year.*

The first hotel to be built at the Grand Canyon, this wonderful establishment was completed in 1905. The architectural style has become known as "rustic." It was the intention of the architect, who used native stone and massive pine logs, that the structure complement its surroundings. Today the same large fireplace in the lobby welcomes guests as it has been doing for more than 90 years. The spacious lobby has the appearance of a hunting lodge. El Tovar, named for a member of the original party of Spanish explorers who discovered the canyon, is still the grand dame of the South Rim's accommodations. While the famous Harvey Girls, attired in black dresses with white aprons, no longer cater to the needs of guests as in the old days, El Tovar is still known for its high level of stately service.

The guestrooms range from small to very large but are all nicely furnished, a combination of old world elegance and modern amenities. Some suites have brilliant views of the canyon. Be aware that the three-story hotel does not have an elevator, so you may want to request a ground floor room if you have difficulty negotiating steps. Among the facilities at the El Tovar is an excellent restaurant (see *Where to Eat*), a lounge with live piano entertainment in the evening, and possibly the park's best gift shop.

Moderate

BRIGHT ANGEL LODGE, *At Grand Canyon Village. 88 Rooms. Rates: $63-117, all year.*

Built in 1935, the Bright Angel is one of the park's more historic properties. The rustic style is simpler than that of the El Tovar. Like the former, however, it features an attractive and comfortable lobby with massive fireplace. Above it is a large mythical wooden thunderbird, known as the "bright angel of the sky" and, hence, the name of the hotel. The rooms are either in the main building or in small cabins. Eleven of the rooms do not have private bath which makes me unable to highly recommend staying here. The rooms vary greatly in size and quality. The better ones have fireplaces and canyon views. If you do opt to stay at the Bright Angel you should definitely go for the rooms in the higher price category. The hotel has a full service restaurant as well as a lounge with entertainment in the evening.

GRAND HOTEL, *On AZ 64 in Tusayan. Tel. 520/638-3333; Fax 520/ 638-3131. Toll free reservations 888/63-GRAND. 121 Rooms. Rates: High season (April through mid-October): $99-149; Low season (mid-October through March): $79-99. American Express, Diners Club, MasterCard and VISA accepted. Located approximately 9 miles south of the Grand Canyon Village.*

With a name like the Grand Hotel you might be expecting a stately old European-style inn. Far from it, this Grand is one of the newest establishments in Tusayan and a welcome addition. Spread out along the highway, this low-rise motor inn features nicely appointed rooms and attractive public areas. There's an indoor swimming pool and spa. The *Canyon Star* restaurant is a good place for steaks and barbecued fare. Cocktail lounge with live entertainment. The Grand also features authentic Native American dances.

KACHINA and THUNDERBIRD LODGES, *Adjacent to one another at Grand Canyon Village. 49 and 55 rooms, respectively. $112, all year.*

These sister properties, although slightly different in size, are nearly identical in appearance and facilities. The accommodations here are much more simple than in the El Tovar and are essentially modern style motor inns. Neither is anything to rave about but the location, within walking distance of all the facilities of the Village, is excellent. In addition, if you get a room that faces the canyon you'll be rewarded with one of the best views from any hotel in the park.

Neither facility has a restaurant but you can walk to neighboring lodges that do. Registration for the Kachina is done at the El Tovar while checking into the Thunderbird requires that you go to the Bright Angel Lodge.

MASWIK LODGE, *At Grand Canyon Village. 248 Rooms. Rates: $75-108, all year.*

Here's another hotel that wouldn't ordinarily make the grade for this book. Not that there's anything bad but there isn't a lot to say on the plus side either. The Lodge is modern and covers several acres. Rooms are either in the main two-story building or a number of cabins arranged in groups of four. The cabins are only available during the summer season. Rooms have showers but no tub. Facilities include a cafeteria which is great if you're on a tight budget and a lounge with entertainment.

YAVAPAI LODGE, *1 mile east of Grand Canyon Village. 358 Rooms. Rates: $88-103 from March 1st through mid-November. Closed remainder of year.*

Nestled amid a forest of piñon and juniper trees, Yavapai is the largest hotel in the park. It consists of a main building where all of the services are and guestrooms are spread out motel style in two branches, designated east and west. Paved walkways lead from the motel to the main building or you can drive. The rooms, like those in the Maswik Lodge, are quite basic but at least you have the convenience of staying in the park. There are no views of the canyon from any room in the Yavapai Lodge. There's a large cafeteria serving ho-hum but affordable food (beer and wine are available). Across the street are several shops including a large mini-market where you can pick up groceries and just about anything else.

PHANTOM RANCH, *on the canyon floor along the Bright Angel Trail. Tel. 303/297-2757 for reservations.*

For those of you who intend to spend the night at the bottom of the Grand Canyon, this is the only place that resembles a hotel. Located alongside Bright Angel Creek, Phantom Ranch was constructed in 1922 of uncut boulders taken from the Colorado River. To say the place is rustic is putting it mildly. It's accessible only to mule-back riders, river rafters, and those who take the strenuous hike from rim top to bottom. Individual cabins are available to guests taking the two-night mule trip, all other accommodations at the Ranch are dormitory style with no private facilities. Delicious breakfasts and dinners are included and the staff will even provide you with a box lunch if you're going on a day hike. There's also a canteen that sells a limited number of food items and supplies. Individual travelers (those not on a mule trip) should inquire at time of reservation as to the exact price. Accommodations are included in the rate for mule trippers.

NEAR THE SOUTH RIM – TUSAYAN
Expensive
GRAND CANYON SUITES, *On AZ 64, north of Tusayan. Tel. 520/638-3100, Fax 520/638-2747. 34 Rooms. Rates: High season (May 1st to October 31st): $148-168; Low season (November 1st to mid-March): $78-98. American Express, MasterCard, and VISA accepted. Located about two miles south of the entrance to the South Rim.*

This attractive all-suite facility is the newest lodging establishment in the vicinity of the South Rim. The combination living room/bedroom is spacious (there are also a few two bedroom units) and furnished in a contemporary manner. It's well suited to those staying in the area for a few days and who plan to do some housekeeping since all units have coffee makers, refrigerators, and microwave ovens. There are also room safes. Several restaurants are located in Tusayan or you can go back into the park to eat. The price can be considered to be in the moderate category if more than two people are going to stay in a single unit.

Moderate
MOQUI LODGE, *On AZ 64 about eight miles from the Village. Tel. 303/297-2757. 136 Rooms. Rates: $98. Both rates include full breakfast. Closed at other times of the year. Located just north of the town of Tusayan.*

Although not located within the park, the Moqui Lodge is still part of the Fred Harvey properties and reservations are made in the manner described at the beginning of this Where to Stay section. Consisting of several rustic buildings of ponderosa pine, the accommodations are quite decent. All rooms have full baths. Facilities include a restaurant described below, a cocktail lounge with entertainment, and a gift shop. Moqui Lodge also offers horseback riding in the Kaibab National Forest.

RED FEATHER LODGE, *On AZ 64 in Tusayan. Tel. 520/638-2414, Fax 520/638-9216. Toll free reservations Tel. 800/538-2345. 232 Rooms. Rates: High season (May 1st to October 31st): $98-128; Low season (November 1st to mid-March): $49-69. Major credit cards accepted. Located approximately nine miles south of the Grand Canyon Village area.*

The Red Feather is one of the biggest facilities near, but not in, the park. A little over half of the rooms were recently built. Not only are the rooms in the second building newer but they're bigger and decorated in a more attractive manner. The original wing, however, isn't bad either.

The Red Feather has a heated swimming pool and whirlpool and a fitness center. Children will enjoy using the video game room. A restaurant is located on the property and several others are nearby.

ON THE NORTH RIM

Because of limited availability of rooms on the North Rim it is essential that you make your reservations as early as possible.

Inexpensive/Moderate

GRAND CANYON LODGE, *Located at the end of the park road. Tel. 303/297-2757 for reservations, Fax 520/638-9247. Direct dial to hotel Tel. 520/638-2611. 201 Rooms. Rates: $89 for cabins; $55 for motel style accommodations. Closed October 16th through May 14th. Most major credit cards accepted.*

This is a wonderful place to stay because of the unparalleled natural setting and the charming accommodations. The latter consist of four guestrooms clustered together in a wooden cabin amid a forested area adjacent to the canyon rim. There are also many motel style rooms located further away from the rim. These are certainly adequate but for the best experience you should opt for the higher priced cabins. Those cabins facing the rim have partial canyon views. The setting is, in my opinion, even greater than that of the El Tovar Hotel on the South Rim.

The main building was constructed of limestone and massive timber beams back during the 1920s. A sunken lounge with large picture windows and two adjacent outside verandas have one of the most beautiful views of the canyon to be found anywhere in the Grand Canyon National Park. The adorable cabins are quite spacious and feature fireplaces and high timbered ceilings. The restaurant (see *Where to Eat*) is also excellent. Shops and other services are located in a village-like setting adjacent to the lodge's main building.

Selected as one of my Best Places to Stay (see Chapter 11 for more details).

PAGE
Expensive

WAHWEAP LODGE, *Lake Shore Drive. Tel. 520/645-2433, Fax 520/ 645-1031. Toll free reservations Tel. 800/528-6154. 350 Rooms. Rates: High season (May 1st to October 31st): $139-239; Low season (November 1st to April 30th): $69-159. American Express, Discover, MasterCard, and VISA accepted. Located 4 miles north of Page across the bridge from Glen Canyon Dam and off of US 89.*

Spread out on the shoreline of magnificent Lake Powell, the setting of Wahweap Lodge alone makes it a worthwhile place to stay. The two-story motor inn type buildings feature rooms that are attractive and comfortable. All have a patio or balcony but those that face the lake naturally have the best views. Some rooms have coffee makers, refrigerators, and microwave ovens. Lodge facilities include two heated swimming pools, whirlpool, and a well equipped exercise room. Wahweap Lodge is the focal point for recreational activities on the lake. There's a boat dock, marina, and launching ramp if you're bringing your own boat as well as boat and houseboat rentals (see the sidebar devoted to the latter activity). Guided boat tours of the lake and Rainbow Bridge National Monument depart from the Lodge. The Lodge also has a dining room and cocktail lounge. There's live entertainment most evenings.

Moderate

BEST WESTERN ARIZONAINN, *716 Rimview Drive. Tel. 520/645-2466, Fax 520/645-2053. Toll free reservations Tel. 800/528-1234. 103 Rooms. Rates: High season (April 1st to October 31st): $105; Low season (November 1st to March 31st): $49-56; all rates including continental breakfast. Most major credit cards accepted. Located about 3/4 of a mile east of US 89.*

Yes, the spelling is correct – no space between Arizona and inn. This is an attractive modified southwestern style motor inn located at the top of a hill that overlooks Lake Powell and the Glen Canyon Dam. If your room faces in that direction then you're in for a special treat. It's worth spending a few dollars more for the rooms that have the view. The location is convenient for activities both on the lake and in town, including dam tours. All of the rooms are spacious and nicely furnished in light shades. Many rooms have coffee makers. The inn has a convenient restaurant that serves cocktails as well as a heated swimming pool and whirlpool.

RAMADA INN PAGE/LAKE POWELL, *287 North Lake Powell Boulevard. Tel. 520/645-8851, Fax 520/645-2523. Toll free reservations Tel. 800/465-4329. 130 Rooms. Rates: High season (May 1st to September 30th): $105-125; Low season (November 1st to March 31st): $59-89. Major credit cards accepted. Located on US 89 (Lake Powell Boulevard) about a mile from the center of town.*

A typically modern motor inn facility with three stories, this former Holiday Inn is located adjacent to an 18-hole golf course (tee times can be arranged by hotel personnel). Many rooms have either a patio or balcony and overlook the beautifully manicured fairways. Some rooms on the upper floors also allow a glimpse of the lake. Televisions in all rooms are directly hooked into a video game system and some rooms have refrigerators. The Family Tree Restaurant & Lounge is a bright and airy dining room featuring good food at reasonable prices. You'll also find a heated outdoor swimming pool and an attractive gift shop on the premises.

CAMPING & RV SITES

For information on back country camping permits, regulations, and reservations it is best to secure a copy of the Back Country Trip Planner. Write to *Back Country Office, P.O. Box 129, Grand Canyon, AZ 86023*. For regular campgrounds within Grand Canyon National Park, central reservations are made through **Biospherics**, *Tel. 800/365-2267*, up to three months in advance.

South Rim

- **Desert View Campground**, *26 miles east of the Village. 50 sites.* First-come, first served.
- **Mather Campground**, *in the Village area. 320 sites.* No trailer hookups.
- **Trailer Village**, *adjacent to Mather Campground.* 84 RV sites with hookups.

Outside the Park Boundaries

- **Camper Village** *in Tusayan, Tel. 520/638-2887.* Privately owned.
- **Ten-X Campground**, *located three miles south of Tusayan, Tel. 520/638-2443.* Operated by the Forest Service, no hookups and is on a first come, first served basis.

North Rim

Within the park is the 86-site **North Rim Campground** with hookups. Contact Biospherics (above) for reservations.

Other Areas

- **Wahweap Campground**, *US 89 & Lake Shore Drive, Glen Canyon National Recreation Area, Tel. 520/645-1004*
- **Wahweap RV Park**, *US 89 & Lake Shore Drive, Glen Canyon National Recreation Area, Tel. 520/645-1004*
- **Jacob Lake Campground**, *Junction of US 89A & AZ 67, Jacob Lake, Tel. 520/643-7395*

WHERE TO EAT

ON THE SOUTH RIM
Expensive

EL TOVAR DINING ROOM, *in the El Tovar Hotel, Grand Canyon Village. Breakfast, lunch, and dinner served daily. Most major credit cards accepted. Reservations suggested.*

Considering the informality of the Grand Canyon you will be surprised at the formal nature of the dining experience at the El Tovar Dining Room. The room is spacious and attractive. Picture windows provide excellent views while you're waiting for your food. And the food is plentiful and delicious. A wide variety of selections is available to suit almost all tastes. Cocktails are available and there is an excellent wine list.

Moderate

ARIZONA STEAKHOUSE, *just east of the Bright Angel Lodge, Grand Canyon Village. Dinner served nightly. Most major credit cards accepted. Closed January and February. Reservations suggested.*

Tender, sizzling steaks are the main fare in this attractive Western style eatery. However, chicken and seafood dishes are also on the menu. There's an open kitchen where you can watch the chef prepare your meal. Cocktails and wine are served. Here, too, windows face the canyon.

BRIGHT ANGEL DINING ROOM, *in the Bright Angel Lodge, Grand Canyon Village. Breakfast, lunch, and dinner served daily. Most major credit cards accepted.*

A more casual experience than in the El Tovar Dining Room, this restaurant also features an ample selection of dishes including several vegetarian offerings. Service is friendly and efficient. Cocktails and wine are served.

NEAR THE SOUTH RIM – TUSAYAN
Moderate

MOQUI LODGE DINING ROOM, *located in the Moqui Lodge, on AZ 64 about eight miles from the Village. Breakfast and dinner served daily. Closed in December and January. Most major credit cards accepted.*

An attractive restaurant featuring both Mexican and American entrees, the Moqui Dining Room is a very casual place where good food and pleasant surroundings are in ample supply. A children's menu is available and cocktails and wine are served.

ON THE NORTH RIM
Moderate

GRAND CANYON LODGE DINING ROOM, *in the Grand Canyon Lodge, located at the end of the park road. Breakfast, lunch, and dinner served daily. Most major credit cards accepted. Reservations are required for dinner.*

Like the Lodge in which its located, the Dining Room is a spacious facility with high timbered ceiling beams and simply breathtaking views of the canyon from two different directions. The service is quick and efficient, the selection of food somewhat limited but nicely prepared. Cocktails are available. It is the only restaurant at the north rim. The only other choices are a couple of snack bars.

MARBLE CANYON
Moderate

MARBLE CANYON LODGE, *On US 89A, immediately north of the Navajo Bridge. Tel. 520/355-2225. Breakfast, lunch, and dinner served daily. Discover, MasterCard, and VISA accepted.*

The Marble Canyon Lodge has a coffee shop and dining room. It's kind of basic but more than adequate, especially when considering its location on the route between the two rims of the Grand Canyon. If you aren't going to Page it may be the only decent place to eat en route. You can choose from a wide selection of American, southwestern, and Mexican fare from sandwiches to full meals. Considering that you're literally in the middle of nowhere, it's quite good. Cocktails are served.

The motel doesn't meet the standards for this book but it also will do if you're in a desperate pinch.

PAGE
Moderate

BELLA NAPOLI, *810 North Navajo Drive. Tel. 520/645-2706. Dinner served nightly. Closed on Sunday from mid-November through February. American Express, Discover, MasterCard, and VISA accepted.*

An attractive dining room with a fair selection of Italian entrees, especially pasta dishes. Bella Napoli is best known and loved locally for their excellent pizza which comes in many different forms. An occasional fresh food or seafood entree will appear on the menu, especially on Friday evening. Beer and wine are served. There's a children's menu available and with pizza on the menu all the time you know this has to be a good place to bring the kids..

PEPPER'S, *600 Country Club Drive in the Courtyard by Marriott. Tel. 520/645-5000. Breakfast, Lunch, and dinner served daily. Major credit cards accepted.*

Both the decor and menu at Pepper's are distinctively southwestern but you can also select from a number of more traditional American dishes. The dining room isn't large but gives an open and airy appearance. The service is efficient and the food is prepared well – the seasoning is just right, not too hot but not so tame that you can't taste it. Full cocktail service either tableside or in the adjacent lounge.

SEEING THE SIGHTS
The South Rim

There are many guided tours of the **South Rim** offered by more operators than you can count. However, if you drove to the South Rim the best way to see it is with your own car, supplemented by the Park's shuttle

HUMANS & THE GRAND CANYON

*While mankind's association with the Grand Canyon has been short compared to the geologic history it is, nonetheless, another interesting topic that can enhance the enjoyment of your visit. Archaeologists have found evidence of humans in the canyon dating back as much as 11,000 years ago. They didn't live there but simply chased big-game. The **Anasazi** and other native groups settled in small communities in several places near the canyon rims. Many of these settlements are within today's park boundaries. Their descendants continued to flourish in the area for many more centuries and continue to do so.*

*The Spanish explorer **Francisco Coronado** led an expedition from Mexico City into the Southwest in search of the Seven Cities of Cibola in 1540. One of his officers, **Garcia Lopez de Cardenas** was detached from the main expedition and with the help of Hopi guides became the first European to gaze out upon the canyon. However, the Spaniards were only interested in finding tangible treasure. Not satisfied with the aesthetic value of their discovery, they returned in disappointment to Mexico. Later expeditions also came upon the canyon while searching for routes to California and each one was turned back by the seeming impossibility of crossing the void.*

*The first American to see the canyon was **Lieutenant Joseph Ives** during an 1857 exploration. He decided that the Grand Canyon was "altogether valueless." What an idiot! In 1869, however, **Major John Wesley Powell** and a small group journeyed a thousand miles on the Colorado River and through the entire Grand Canyon. Three men died during the expedition. Powell made another trip three years later and wrote extensively about what he saw. His appreciation of the beauty of nature helped to make the Grand Canyon a destination for travelers. With the failure of several mining attempts in the canyon (because of the difficulty of getting things out), things turned in other directions. **Fred Harvey** began transporting visitors to the canyon at the turn of the century and the first hotel opened up in 1905.*

*After visiting the canyon in 1903, **President Teddy Roosevelt**, so impressed by what he saw, decided that it must be protected. The Grand Canyon became a national monument in 1908 and a national park in 1910 when it more than doubled in size. Several smaller additions have been made over the years. The Grand Canyon National History Association puts out a great history called In the House of Stone and Light: A Human History of the Grand Canyon. It was written by Donald Hughes in 1978.*

service and, of course, by walking. Ranger guided walks, talks and other programs are listed in the free park newspaper that is distributed at many locations, including the entrance station. Be sure to pick one up. There's a separate edition for the North Rim.

The South Rim is the most heavily visited portion of the park and the crowds during the summer often times create traffic difficulties. To make things a little more confusing, the South Rim is further sub-divided into the West and East Rim Drives, with the Grand Canyon Village area separating the two. During the summer months, as I previously mentioned, the West Rim Drive is closed to private vehicles and you must either walk or take the free open-air tram shuttle, which operates at frequent intervals throughout the day. The East Rim is not nearly as busy as the West Rim, but receives more visitors than the North Rim.

While everyone usually thinks of the Grand Canyon only in terms of the majestic scenery, it is much more than that. A wide variety of wildlife and diverse vegetation inhabits the park, depending upon which of the three different life zones you're in. On the South Rim the animals that you're most likely to see are the large gray and white Abert squirrel, the long eared mule deer (usually seen at sunrise or sunset) and the silver-gray coyote. Bighorn sheep are often visible within the canyon. Many birds and reptiles also make the park their home. Please do not feed any of the animals and always keep your distance. Even the smallest squirrel will bite if it feels threatened.

Now to begin your tour of the South Rim of the unforgettable Grand Canyon National Park. From the entrance station on US 180/AZ 64 the road gently curves through a few miles of forest. You'll be saying to yourself "where's the canyon?" Actually, you won't see it until you're right upon it. Just after a junction in the road (where AZ 64 heads out along the East Rim), continue straight ahead to the first canyon viewing area at **Mather Point.**

While the view from here isn't the greatest one it has the advantage of being your first look into the canyon itself. For that reason alone it is simply unforgettable. Here, and at every other stop along the rim, you'll begin to understand that part of the wonderment that every visitor to the canyon feels is caused not by the majestic beauty of the scene, but by the sheer scale. The canyon simply dwarfs everything – people, cars, even the few buildings on the canyon's rim. It can make you feel very small and insignificant and does justice to the marvels of nature.

Back to the specifics of Mather Point. You won't see the Colorado River from here. In fact, there are only a few places where it's visible and I'll let you know where that is as we come upon it. A little further along the road is a short cutoff leading to a hauntingly beautiful view from **Yavapai Point.** The point area also contains the small **Yavapai Museum** which has some interesting information on the canyon's geology. Before proceeding any further you should be aware that the entire rim from Mather Point to Hermits Rest at the end of the West Rim Drive is accessible by a continuous trail. A portion of it (from Yavapai to Maricopa) is paved. It is the easiest trail in the park and the only one that doesn't require a descent into the canyon. So any time you don't want to ride between viewpoints or other points of interest you don't have to.

However, except for brief walks to "experience" the feel of strolling along the rim you should drive or take the shuttle unless you plan to spend many days within the park. All of the overlooks are adjacent to parking area/shuttle bus stops or are reached by short and easy walks. Do watch your footing at all overlooks since the rocky surface is often uneven.

Once you get past Yavapai Point you'll soon reach the **Grand Canyon Village** area, which is where the majority of services are located and is among the most crowded portions of the park at any time. It is also the location of the park's **Visitor Center**, a good place to see some more interesting exhibits on the park's natural and human history as well as to get information from the always helpful and friendly rangers. Several hotels are located right on the rim in this area and the walk behind them has some excellent canyon views. Finally, it is from the village area that both shuttle services begin. With that done, let's get on to the **West Rim Drive**.

THE GRAND CANYON BY AIR

Some people (even those who don't work for the companies offering air tours of the canyon) claim that the best way to see the Grand Canyon is by air. I don't think it's the best way to tour the canyon but it does have certain advantages for those with limited time. And, for those who have seen it from ground level, the perspective from on high will certainly add more beautiful memories.

*Because of safety concerns and noise pollution the Park Service has been steadily imposing restrictions on the routes that tour operators can fly and they want to limit the number of flights. Regardless of where this process winds up I'm sure that there will always be flights available for those who want them. In addition to flights originating from as far away as Phoenix, Los Angeles and Las Vegas, many operators offer trips from the Grand Canyon Airport. Among these are **Grand Canyon Airlines**, Tel. 800/528-2413 (airplanes) and **Papillon Grand Canyon Helicopters**, Tel. 800/528-2418. Half-day trips usually run around $75 per adult by airplane and from $125 for helicopter trips.*

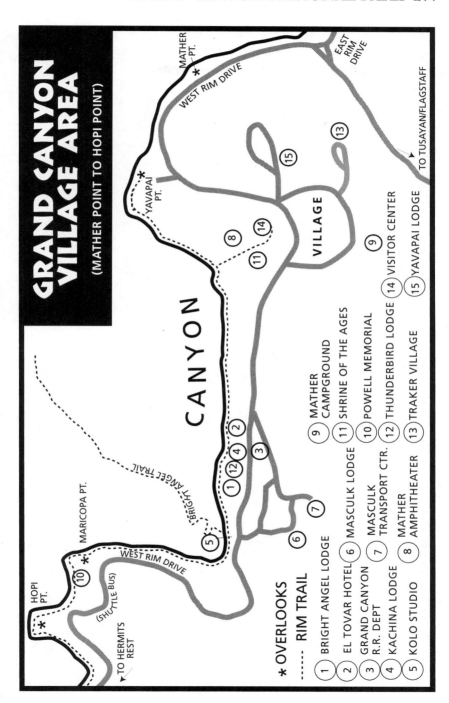

GRAND CANYON VILLAGE AREA
(MATHER POINT TO HOPI POINT)

* OVERLOOKS
----- RIM TRAIL

① BRIGHT ANGEL LODGE
② EL TOVAR HOTEL
③ GRAND CANYON R.R. DEPT
④ KACHINA LODGE
⑤ KOLO STUDIO
⑥ MASCULK LODGE
⑦ MASCULK TRANSPORT CTR.
⑧ MATHER AMPHITHEATER
⑨ MATHER CAMPGROUND
⑩ POWELL MEMORIAL
⑪ SHRINE OF THE AGES
⑫ THUNDERBIRD LODGE
⑬ TRAKER VILLAGE
⑭ VISITOR CENTER
⑮ YAVAPAI LODGE

THE WORLD FAMOUS MULE TRAIN

People have been riding mules to the bottom of the Grand Canyon just for the fun of it for more than a hundred years. Mules are preferable to horses because they are more sure-footed and have a better temperament for the task. In fact, there has never been a fatality on any of the tens of thousands of mule trips that have been made. Of course, the day after a mule trip can be a sore experience. Plan for a day where you don't have to sit a lot! In order to be allowed on the mule trip you must be in reasonably good shape and weigh no more than 200 pounds – after all, we have to think of the mule's welfare, too. Dress very casually. Water in a canteen is provided to all participants. Due to the popularity of the mule ride reservations are essential.

There are three different trips. One is an overnight trip to the Phantom Ranch while another is a three day journey. However, the one-day trip is the most popular. Departing daily all year at 8:00am (9:00am in winter) from both the South and North Rims, it descends over 3,000 feet to the canyon's Tonto Platform within 1,300 feet of the Colorado River from Plateau Point. The round-trip takes about seven hours. There is some additional time before departure for you to be acquainted with your mule.

Oh, yes, it's called a mule train because riders descend in large groups, one mule directly behind another. But don't embarrass yourself by asking a question that was once posed to a park ranger: Does the mule train have a dining car? I kid you not! For information and reservations contact the Grand Canyon National Park Lodges reservation department, Tel. 303/297-2757 for South Rim and 435/679-8665 for North Rim. The price for one day trips start at $108 and overnight trips (including all meals) run from around $300. There are half-day trips from the North Rim only.

The **Kolb Studio**, near the west end of the village area, was built early in the century literally at the edge of the canyon rim by two photographers. Today there are exhibits about these early canyon businessmen as well as some great views out of the studio window. Adjacent to this area is the trailhead for the most popular hike into the canyon – the **Bright Angel Trail**. It is the same trail that is used for the mule trips. By the way, mules always have the right of way should you encounter them on the trail. The trail descends to the Colorado River by a series of steep switchbacks. It is not for the faint of heart although inexperienced hikers often go a part of the way down just to get the feel of descending into the canyon.

Most hikers consider the river as their destination but the Bright Angel Trail actually crosses the river by a suspension bridge and then continues on the far side before finally making its way up to the North

Rim! A warning is in order here for all canyon trails: Never attempt to reach the Colorado River at the bottom of the canyon and try to get back in the same day. People have died from exhaustion trying to do so. Any hike to the river and back mandates an overnight stay at the **Phantom Ranch** or the adjacent campground along the river.

Among the viewpoints on the West Rim are **Hopi, Maricopa**, and **Pima Points**. Each affords a spectacular vista of massive walls and indescribable coloring but the West Rim's best spot is at **The Abyss**. Here the **Great Mojave Wall** of the canyon has an almost sheer vertical drop of 3,000 feet which provides visitors with a clear view of the **Tonto Platform** within the canyon and the **Colorado River**. The Abyss is the only place on the West Rim where the river itself can be seen. At **Powell Point**, besides another view, is a monument to explorer **John Wesley Powell**. The eight-mile long West Rim ends at **Hermits Rest**, so called because a French-Canadian named Louis Boucher lived a solitary life here in the 1890's.

Also at this point is the beginning of the 17-mile round-trip **Hermit Trail**. Like all trails into the canyon, the trip is a strenuous one. Always carry plenty of water even if you don't intend to go all the way. Park concessionaires offer eight different guided tours covering both the West and East Rims. Tours range from 90 minutes to about 11 hours. If this is the way you wish to see the South Rim then make inquiry at the tour desk located in each of the South Rim hotels.

The **East Rim Drive** covers a one-way distance of 23 miles. You can see the sights on the rim and return to the village area overnight or do the East Rim on the way out of the park on the way to the North Rim or other Arizona attractions. I'll follow the latter course in describing the sights of this region. Beyond Mather Point (but before you reach the park's entrance station) is the junction where AZ 64 heads east along the Rim. Follow that route. The less traveled East Rim has its overlooks spaced further apart than on the West Rim and most of them are reached by spur roads of about a mile in length. My own opinion is that many of the viewpoints on the East Rim afford more spectacular vistas than those on the west side.

Yaki Point has some of the best canyon views of any overlook and is also the beginning of the **South Kaibab Trail** which reaches Phantom Ranch and the river by a different route than the more popular Bright Angel Trail. Another trail begins at the next overlook, **Grandview Point**. The six-mile round trip **Grandview Trail** is good for a day hike as it doesn't go to the bottom of the canyon but to colorful **Horseshoe Mesa**. It is, however, very strenuous. The view from the overlook, while equal to many, doesn't match the inspirational name when compared to some of the other sights in the park.

SOUTH RIM CHANGES ARE COMING

Despite shuttle buses and other attempts to manage traffic on the South Rim (especially in the West Rim area), the presence of five million visitors a year has overwhelmed facilities. The constant battle for parking spaces at overlooks and long lines for everything from lunch to rest rooms can make visiting the Grand Canyon a stressful experience. In order to enable visitors to enjoy the awesome surroundings, the Park Service broke ground in April 1999 on its master plan for the future. It is hoped that this will not only increase visitor enjoyment but provide a model for traffic management at other heavily visited national parks.

The centerpiece of the plan is the construction of a light rail system with its hub near a new parking facility north of Tusayan. This system will handle far more people than the shuttle buses can and also control pollution by enabling park authorities to further restrict auto traffic. Plans also call for the demolition of several structures (including two older lodging establishments) to make room for new visitor facilities to educate visitors about the Grand Canyon. The current visitor centers are woefully inadequate.

*Lodging is another consideration. The Forest Service has approved the development of the **Canyon Forest Village**, to include 1,200 rooms, on forest land immediately outside the South Rim entrance. Scenic canyon flights are going to be limited to the number of flights made in 1998. There is opposition to these parts of the plan so delays in full implementation are probably inevitable. But, the rail system should be in operation by the end of 2002. Stay tuned.*

Moran Point, a couple of miles further along the East Rim Drive, is better. It, like **Lipan Point** which follows soon after, offer a different perspective than the West Rim overlooks. Here you'll be looking back into the canyon more than down upon it. I feel that it affords a greater appreciation of the vastness of the canyon because you can see the different layers within it. You can also see how the gorge which contains the Colorado River is actually in a canyon within the canyon. The river is also visible from more places on the East Rim than on the West.

Another sight that's different on the East Rim is the **Tusayan Ruin**, reached via a short spur from the rim road. This is a small but interesting remains of a prehistoric pueblo along with an interpretive museum. Soon after is **Desert View**. It is a fitting end to the East Rim because from this point is a truly spectacular panorama that includes, besides the canyon itself, the **Colorado River**, colorful **Vermilion Cliffs**, distant **San Francisco Peaks**, and a portion of the **Painted Desert**. A recreation of an ancient Anasazi tower, called **The Watchtower**, was built here early in the century. There's a gift shop in the base and you can climb the tower to get an even more glorious look at the scenery which surrounds you. The tower was built to look as if it were almost a ruin and many visitors don't realize that it isn't the "real thing." *The tower is open daily from 8:00am until 5:30pm and there is a nominal (25 cents) admission to climb to the top. Museum is open daily from 9:00am until 5:00pm and free of charge.*

Before exiting the park I want to make sure that you take advantage of either the beautiful canyon sunrise or sunsets. If you're staying in or near the park overnight it is something that shouldn't be missed. **Sunrises** are best at Lipan, Mather, Yaki, and Yavapai Points while the most spectacular **sunsets** are Desert View, Hopi, Lipan, Mojave and Pima Points.

The South Rim of the Grand Canyon National Park is always open. Admission is by seven-day pass costing $20 (for all vehicle occupants), by $40 annual permit, or through possession of any National Park Service Passport. The fee is only for entrance to the park and use of the shuttle system on the West Rim Drive and Village area. However, the entrance fee also covers the North Rim. All tours and activities run by park concessionaires are at additional cost. Tel. 520/ 638-7888.

The Overland Route to the North Rim

Continuing beyond Desert View you'll soon exit Grand Canyon National Park. However, the scenery won't end all of a sudden. The route to the North Rim passes through many beautiful areas although, I must admit, portions of the drive are rather mundane, too. It's approximately 30 miles from Desert View to the town of Cameron and the junction of US 89.

A good portion of the trip along AZ 64 parallels the **Little Colorado River Gorge**. This tributary of the Colorado joins the main river in an area of the National Park that cannot be reached by road. The Little Colorado is dry through much of the year. Along the road you'll pass several Indian trading posts. Be on the lookout for them even if you aren't in the market for shopping because it is near these posts that short spur roads lead to near the edge of the gorge. Brief walks will bring you to the precipice. Be extra careful because some of these "overlooks" are not fenced in – hold on to your children. The dark walls of this canyon drop some 800 feet to the bottom and are in sharp contrast to the bright colors of the Grand Canyon. Nevertheless, it is an interesting sight.

At Cameron you will head north on US 89 (unless you are not going to be doing the North Rim and wish to return to Flagstaff or Phoenix, in which case you'll take US 89 southbound). For the next 60 miles between Cameron and Bitter Springs the scenery isn't really remarkable except for scattered areas where colorful rock formations provide some visual delight. At Bitter Spring there is a split in the road between US 89 and US 89A. You'll keep to the left and US 89A for the North Rim. US 89 goes up to Page and the Glen Canyon National Recreation Area which is discussed separately later in this chapter.

The 14-mile drive from Bitter Spring to Marble Canyon is highly scenic with broad vistas of huge red sandstone cliffs surrounding an immense and equally colorful valley. At **Marble Canyon**, which is actually located in a narrow strip of the far eastern end of Grand Canyon National Park, is a scene of great beauty that you should definitely stop for. The 616-foot long and 467-foot high **Navajo Bridge** spans the Colorado River in a deep gorge that drops almost 800 feet to the water. Adjacent to the bridge is the original bridge built early in the century. Visitors can park at either end of the bridge and walk across the old structure to take in wonderful views of the gorge and river as well as the breathtaking backdrop of giant red sandstone cliffs. Marble Canyon is also a good place to stop for lunch if you're making the run between the two Grand Canyon rims.

Once you cross over the Colorado River you're in a part of the state known as the **Arizona Strip**. A large and roughly triangular shaped stretch of land that extends from the river north to the Utah border and west to Nevada, it is called the Strip because before the building of the bridge this portion of Arizona was physically cut off from the rest of the state. Even today the region shares more in common, both geologically and culturally, with southern Utah than with Arizona.

From Marble Canyon US 89A travels for 40 miles to Jacob Lake. During this time the road starts climbing, gently at first but much more steeply in parts, and the terrain changes from the monolithic red mountains to more forested areas. At Jacob Lake head south on AZ 67 for about another 40 miles through the thick greenery of the pretty Kaibab National Forest until you reach the entrance station of the North Rim.

The North Rim

About ten miles after passing through the North Rim gate of Grand Canyon National Park the main road ends at the center of all activities on this rim. It is sometimes called **Grand Canyon Lodge** or simply North Rim. It's not quite a village like on the South Rim but is the closest thing to "civilization" on the entire rim, which is much larger in size than the South Rim.

Until a few years ago the North Rim was so sparsely visited that it could almost be considered a wilderness area. Although it has become a much more popular tourist destination in recent years, the traffic levels are still only a small fraction of what the South Rim sees. In fact, only about

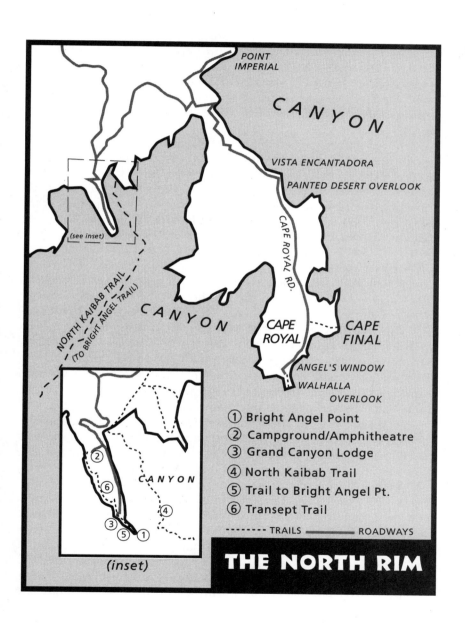

POINT IMPERIAL

CANYON

VISTA ENCANTADORA

PAINTED DESERT OVERLOOK

CAPE ROYAL RD.

NORTH KAIBAB TRAIL
(TO BRIGHT ANGEL TRAIL)

CANYON

(see inset)

CAPE ROYAL

CAPE FINAL

ANGEL'S WINDOW

WALHALLA OVERLOOK

① Bright Angel Point
② Campground/Amphitheatre
③ Grand Canyon Lodge
④ North Kaibab Trail
⑤ Trail to Bright Angel Pt.
⑥ Transept Trail

-------- TRAILS ——— ROADWAYS

THE NORTH RIM

CANYON

(inset)

ten percent of South Rim visitors make it to here. Most people coming to the North Rim come from vacations in southern Utah or in Las Vegas. However, it would be a shame if your Arizona vacation included a visit to the South Rim and not the North Rim.

Although there are many similarities between the two rims there are enough differences to make the experience here highly rewarding. Many people, including myself, actually feel that the vistas on the North Rim may be even more spectacular. Regardless of which way you wind up feeling the North Rim is truly one of the great sights to behold in all the world.

The North Rim is generally open from about the middle of May to the middle of October, depending upon weather conditions (i.e., the amount of snow). The amount of facilities and services is much more limited here than on the South Rim but you can find just about everything you need, including a small park ranger information station, in the vicinity of the Grand Canyon Lodge which serves as the hub for all activities. There are guided bus tours of the North Rim should you choose not to drive on your own.

Some of the best sights on the North Rim are located right by the Lodge, not the least of which is the spectacular panorama available from the Lodge itself either from the veranda or the enclosed sunroom. However, the probable highlight of a North Rim visit is to take the half-mile long **Bright Angel Point Trail** from directly behind the Lodge out to **Bright Angel Point**. The trail is easy but is entirely on an extremely narrow ridge that juts out into the canyon. There's a delightfully dizzying drop on either side. At an elevation of about 8,200 feet, you will immediately have the feeling of being "higher" than anywhere on the South Rim which averages about a thousand feet less in elevation.

The Bright Angel Point Trail provides views of the main and side canyons in three directions at one time and at the point itself you can hear and see the **Roaring Springs**, the only source of drinking water in the national park. Although the trail is quite easy you may not want to attempt it if you are fearful of narrow places and big drop-offs. The so-called **Transept Trail** stretches along the North Rim's edge for about three miles from the Lodge area to the campground. Most other trails in this part of the park are of a back country nature. The **North Kaibab Trail** descends into the canyon and reaches Phantom Ranch. It is an overnight trip if you're going all the way to the river.

Other areas of interest on the North Rim are reached by car. A couple of miles from the Lodge there is a split in the road. Turn right and proceed through the forest until you come to another fork. First go to the left for the short ride to **Point Imperial**. At 8,803 feet this is the highest point on either rim. The view is dramatic and beautiful. You gaze eastward into a

PRESERVATION VS. UTILIZATION: WHERE DO YOU STAND?

Since its inception the dual mission of the National Park Service has been to promote the enjoyment of our scenic and historic resources while, at the same time, protecting them from damage. This has become an increasingly complicated and, to some, a contradictory combination of objectives. Nowhere is this more evident than at the Grand Canyon. You'll be bombarded with literature and questionnaires as to where you stand on the issue.

In 1919 there were only 45,000 visitors to Grand Canyon National Park. Today the number is about five million each year and growing. Complaints range from too much people congestion on the rim ("you're blocking my right to a tranquil view of nature"), automobile exhausts and even distant sources of air pollution from cities that interfere with the park's historically clear skies, and even noise from overhead scenic air tours of the canyon.

*The question is do we limit visitation to protect the essential nature of the canyon environment or are we trampling on everyone's right to see this treasure in the way that each person deems appropriate for him or her. I certainly don't know the answer but I do encourage you to leave your opinion so that some sort of consensus can eventually be reached. If you wish to actively work for the benefit of the canyon you should contact the **Grand Canyon Association**, Tel. 800/290-9644.*

portion of the canyon that is not visible from anywhere on the South Rim's road system. It is wilder – the colorful rocks are more intertwined with vegetation. Clusters of huge ponderosa pines and other trees appear as tiny green specks in the distance. It is an unforgettable sight.

After tearing yourself away from Point Imperial return to the road junction and follow the sign in the direction of Cape Royal. There are a few places on Cape Royal Drive that you should stop for some more great sights. These include the **Vista Encantadora** (Enchanted View) and the **Walhalla Overlook**. Be sure to also take the short trail to the **Angel's Window**, a large rock formation where erosion has carved out a giant hole. You can see distant points through the window. Besides viewing the formation from a distance, a portion of the trail leads up on top of the window from which there is an even more spectacular canyon panorama.

Then you'll soon reach the end of the road at **Cape Royal** where one of the most colorful of all Grand Canyon vistas awaits you. To the south and west is the **Granite Gorge** portion of the canyon which is similar to the views from the East Rim Drive of the South Rim. However, only from

Cape Royal can you see **Wotan's Throne**, a giant rock formation rising proudly from a plateau within the depths of the canyon. There are many other beautiful and impressive rock formations visible from this point. To the east is a panorama of canyon, forest, and distant mountains. It's a spot that you will find it hard to drag yourself away from.

From Cape Royal, depending upon the time and your schedule, you'll either return to the Grand Canyon Lodge area or head north at the main road (AZ 67) to continue your journey.

Page & Lake Powell

The town of **Page** is the headquarters of the vast **Glen Canyon National Recreation Area**, a world class water playground that also contains magnificent scenery. From either rim of the Grand Canyon (and by extension from Phoenix and Flagstaff), you can easily reach Page via US 89. At the town of Bitter Springs where US 89 splits from US 89A be sure to follow "plain" 89. It is 23 miles from that point to Page. The town is an attractive looking community in an outstanding natural setting between the lake and the Colorado River. What will strike you most is how new it is – that's because it didn't exist until 1956 when construction of a great dam on the Colorado River began. The town was put up to house the workers and families of the dam builders. Since the 1964 completion of the dam Page has grown as a residential community and as a resort area.

The primary attraction of the town itself, besides being the gateway to the recreation area, is the breathtaking **Glen Canyon Dam** and its adjacent **Carl Hayden Visitor Center**. The center is nestled on the very edge of the canyon wall between the dam's front face and the bridge which spans the Colorado River. Far less known than another Colorado River dam, that being Hoover Dam, both the structure and the setting are equal if not better than its more famous brother (or is it sister – I can't tell with dams).

The view from the outdoor observation desk is magnificent. The river flows hundreds of feet beneath you, appearing somber in color because of that depth and the deep red color of the rocky canyon walls. You can frequently see people rafting on the river, the large rafts appearing to be so small because of the distance which separates you from them. The visitor center has interesting exhibits on the area and the construction of the dam and is also the place where you begin self-guided tours of the dam. The dam is 710 feet high and its crest is 1,560 feet long. It has eight massive generators in its power house at the base. You reach that point by descending an elevator and walking outside at the very base of the dam. Besides the wonder of how it was built you'll also have an extraordinary view of the canyon from the bottom. The edge of the visitor center, which juts out over the canyon, looks like a child's toy from this vantage point.

Give yourself a good hour to tour the visitor center and dam. *The visitor center and Glen Canyon dam can be toured daily between 7:00am and 7:00pm, Memorial Day through Labor Day, and from 8:00am to 5:00pm the rest of the year. There is no admission charge. Tel. 520/608-6404.*

Several miles north of Page off of US 89 is the resort and marina area known as **Wahweap**. It is the place to begin your visit to **Lake Powell**, the primary feature of the Glen Canyon National Recreation Area. Although all but a small percentage of the recreation area is within the borders of Utah, Page is the largest community on its shores and is thus where most visitor activities are concentrated. Besides, when you're out on the lake you won't know when you're in Arizona or when you're in Utah unless someone tells you.

Beautiful Lake Powell, shining a deep but bright blue in the almost certain brilliant sunshine, was created by the construction of the Glen Canyon Dam. It is 186 miles long and surrounded almost everywhere by towering red sandstone cliffs. Dozens of side canyons, some small and some quite large, add to its mystery for boaters. Because of all these indentations into side canyons the shore line covers many hundreds of miles. There are massive rock walls and oddly shaped formations includ-

HOUSEBOATING ON LAKE POWELL

If you do take a Lake Powell boat tour you'll see dozens of houseboats of varying sizes floating serenely on the lake or parked in side canyons. Del Webb Recreational Properties (see above for telephone numbers) has a fleet of about 300 houseboats in five different sizes for you to choose from. Rentals are for a minimum period of three days and two nights. I've always thought that this would be the most relaxing vacation possible – sailing the serene waters of the lake and taking in the beautiful scenery, exploring hidden side canyons while making believe that you're a John Wesley Powell type, and taking a dip or going fishing whenever the urge strikes. It's certainly a different type of vacation experience.

All boats, regardless of size, feature railed walkways, range, oven, refrigerator, ice chest, heater, shower, toilet, charcoal grill, and bunk-style beds. They are powered by two 70hp engines and have two pontoon floats for a stable ride. All necessary supplies, including a full tank of gas, are furnished to you except that you must provide your own bedding, linens, and towels. There are no electric outlets on board. You don't require any special skills or prior boating experience except for an understanding of basic boating rules and courtesy. Be sure to have a detailed map of the lake which is available at the time of rental.

Happy boating!

ing one that looks like a serpent. In the distance is 10,388-foot high **Navajo Mountain**, sacred to the Indians. While a small portion of the lake and the encompassing scenery is visible from the Wahweap Marina, the only good way to see the area is by boat since few roads penetrate any portion of the Glen Canyon Recreation Area.

A variety of boat tours are offered from Wahweap Marina. (Public boat ramps are available for those who arrive with their own vessel.) These are all operated by authorized National Park Service concessionaires, in this case the Del Webb organization which also operates lodging facilities at Wahweap. Boat trips vary from as short as an hour to all day. The two most popular tours are the half day (offered in the morning and afternoon) and the full day because they allow you to really experience the sights of the lake. In addition to passing by the scenery I mentioned above, these trips each make a stop at **Rainbow Bridge National Monument**.

This incredible sight (actually located in Utah but only reachable by land from Arizona via a difficult and long trail) is in a small side canyon. It is the largest known natural bridge in the world. With a height of 290 feet and a spread of about 270 feet, it's a sight that must be seen to be believed. Boat tours make a stop near the bridge and you can walk the short trail from there to the natural bridge. The greatest way to appreciate its size is to walk underneath the bridge and gaze up! Unless you have a lot of time to spend in the area I recommend the half-day tour over any shorter or longer trips.

General information on the Glen Canyon National Recreation Area is available from the superintendent, Tel. 520/608-6200. The admission fee to enter the recreation area is $5 for each vehicle without a national park service passport. Boat tour schedules, prices (credit cards accepted), and reservations can be obtained by calling Tel. 800/528-6154 or 602/278-8888. (Del Webb Recreational Properties is headquartered in Phoenix).

On the Fringes

The western reaches of Grand Canyon National Park contain the most undeveloped sections where you can see the canyon essentially as it was hundreds of years ago. It takes something of an adventure traveler, however, to get to these places either on the south or north side of the river. There is no direct access from within the park to these fringe areas. On the south you can get there by means of a long trip. Take I-40 west from Williams for 44 miles to Exit 121 and then west on AZ 66 for 34 miles to the junction of Indian Route 18. It is 62 miles on that road to a place known as **Hualapai Hilltop** on the **Havasupai Indian Reservation**. The route is all paved and not overly difficult.

But at that point you must leave your car and hike for eight miles to the town of **Supai**. Or you can go by horseback. The trail into **Havasu**

Canyon is precipitous and difficult and only for experienced hikers. There are fewer trails on the north side but the auto route is a problem. From Jacob Lake you have to proceed north on US 89A for 30 miles to the tiny town of Fredonia. From there a series of unpaved roads lead for almost 70 miles to the North Rim's **Tuweep** area. Outstanding views into the canyon's inner gorge as well as geologically recent lava flows and cinder cones are available. The scenery on both sides is marvelous but you have to decide whether the difficulty in getting there merits the rewards – the canyon without a lot of other visitors. Other somewhat easier ways to see the most westerly sections of the canyon are available from Kingman. See the Kingman touring section in Chapter 18, *The West: Water Playground in the Desert,* for further information.

While on the north side, or if you're coming into Arizona from southwestern Utah, you can also make a detour to **Pipe Spring National Monument**, located 14 miles west of Fredonia via paved AZ 369, the monument preserves an 1870 ranch. Several buildings can be toured. The ranch also served as a stopping point for travelers and is a memorial to all of the pioneers who settled the Southwest. Allow about 45 minutes. *Open daily from 8:00am to 4:30pm daily except New Year's, Thanksgiving, and Christmas; admission is $4 to those not holding a park service passport; Tel. 520/ 643-7105.*

NIGHTLIFE & ENTERTAINMENT
Grand Canyon

Watching the sunset or listening to the crickets isn't the only way to pass the time in the evening while at the Grand Canyon. There are, surprisingly, a number of other options. Most of the hotels at the South Rim have nightly entertainment in their lounges. "John Wesley Powell at the Grand Canyon" is an excellent one-man dramatization of the explorer's accomplishments and is held throughout the summer in the **Shrine of the Ages theater** located adjacent to the Visitor Center. During the month of September the **Grand Canyon Chamber Music Festival** is held at the same Shrine of the Ages.

For program information, call *520/638-9215*. Also be sure to consult the park's newspaper for other events that might be taking place during your visit. A final entertainment alternative is the **Grand Canyon Imax Theater**. The film traces the history of the canyon on a seven-story high screen. The theater is also open during the day but I can't see using precious daytime hours indoors when you can be out in the park. *The theater is located 8-1/2 miles south of the Village on AZ 64 in Tusayan; hourly showings with the last one at 8:30pm (6:30pm November through April); admission is $7.50 for adults and $4.5 for children; Tel. 520/638-2468.*

Page & Lake Powell

Since people come to this area for the water and the scenery, there isn't much in the way of nightlife. What is available is concentrated in the lounges of the Wahweap resorts and in the larger motor inns within Page.

SPORTS & RECREATION
GRAND CANYON
Bicycling

Bikes are allowed on all paved roads and others designated as such. There are, however, no rentals available so you'll have to bring your own bike if you intend to ride.

Fishing

The canyon is an excellent source of rainbow trout, especially during the fall months, but the problem is you have to reach the bottom of the canyon to go fishing. If you do, an Arizona fishing license is required.

Horseback Riding
• **Apache Stables**, *Moqui Lodge, Tel. 520/678-2891*

River Rafting

Both smooth and whitewater trips on the Colorado River are offered. **Smooth water trips** take approximately 12 hours and include round-trip bus transportation from the Grand Canyon Village. Trips are given daily from April through October. Make reservations through the Fred Harvey Company at any Grand Canyon hotel tour desk.

Whitewater rafting on the Colorado is one of the world's great experiences. Although a few operators offer trips as short as three days, the majority of Grand Canyon rafting adventures are between six and nine days. The season usually runs from April through October. You can contact the park office for a list of concessionaires, *Tel. 520/638-7843*. Many trips originate in Flagstaff and a number of operators are listed in that chapter.

Cross Country Skiing

There are no groomed trails but you are free to cross country ski as conditions permit. Ski rentals are available at **Babbitt's General Store** in the Village.

PAGE & LAKE POWELL
Golf
· **Glen Canyon Golf Course**, *Tel. 520/645-2715*

Water Sports
Recreational pursuits are almost entirely based on the presence of Lake Powell. Boating, swimming, fishing, and water skiing are the primary activities.

Almost any type of **boat**, power or sail, is allowed and available for rental. Be aware, however, that small boats can be dangerous during storms when Lake Powell can become rather turbulent.

Swimmers will find beaches in the Wahweap area and throughout the lake.

For those interested in **fishing**, bass, trout, and crappie are all popular catches in Lake Powell. Again, an Arizona fishing license is required. You may also be required to have a Utah permit if fishing from a boat. You can secure both locally.

Water skiing is done mainly on the wider channels and bays of the lake. Be alert for marked areas where water skiing is prohibited.

PRACTICAL INFORMATION
· **Hospital**

    Grand Canyon, *Tel. 520/638-2551* (Note: this is a medical clinic and not a hospital; there are no hospital facilities at the Grand Canyon.)
    Page, *Tel. 520/645-2424*

· **Police** (non-emergency)
    Page, *Tel. 520/645-2461*

· **Tourist Office/Visitors Bureau**
    Grand Canyon, Superintendent, Grand Canyon National Park, *Tel. 520/638-2901*
    Page/Lake Powell, *Tel. 520/645-2741*

16. THE NORTHEAST
- INDIAN RESERVATIONS & MORE -

If we played a word association game and said "Arizona places" I have a hunch that the three most common responses would be Phoenix, the Grand Canyon, and Tucson. Certainly they would be valid responses but the northeast region is, perhaps, even more representative of what Arizona really is all about. It has the greatest examples of the cultural legacy of Native Americans and a topography as diverse and beautiful as any part of the state.

A tour through this remarkable region will include natural sights ranging from the monolithic towers of **Monument Valley** to the amazing colors of the **Petrified Forest National Park** and the **Painted Desert**. But there's also some unexpected scenery in the southern portion of the region where the **Mogollon Rim** and the forested **White Mountains** offer scenery that is far different from what we usually associate with the desert-like Southwest.

History is plentiful here, too, especially that of Native Americans. Visit the ancient dwellings of **Canyon de Chelly** where the history is combined with outstanding scenery. You'll also have plenty of opportunity to see how contemporary Native Americans live while visiting some of the many towns located on Indian reservations. The large **Hopi Indian Reservation** and the even larger **Navajo Reservation** which completely surrounds it cover more than 20,000 square miles, an area that is bigger than the states of New Hampshire and Vermont combined. And that area doesn't even include the parts of the Navajo reservation that extend into neighboring Utah and New Mexico.

ARRIVALS & DEPARTURES

Interstate 40 passes through the entire east-to-west distance of the northeast touring region and provides easy access from Phoenix as well as other parts of the country. US 89 is another major point of entry. Your exact entry point will depend upon where you're coming from. I'll be following a more or less circular route so just pick up at the point that is closest to you.

As the biggest community in this area has less than 10,000 people, you won't find many ways to arrive by common carrier. Although either **bus**, **rail**, and **air service** is available to Winslow, Holbrook, Kayenta, and several other communities, getting around the vast expanse of the region by any method other than **car** is generally impractical unless, of course, you're taking a **guided tour** out of Phoenix. Should you have no choice but to get around by scheduled bus service the most efficient point-to-point system in the northeast is by the Navajo Bus System explained in Chapter 6, *Planning Your Trip.*

ORIENTATION

If you refer to the regional touring map at the beginning of the book you'll see that the northeast is a roughly rectangular block. The main east-west roads are I-40 in the south-central portion and US 180 in the north. AZ 264 cuts across the middle but most of the important attractions don't require using this road. The primary north-south route is US 191 located in the eastern section of the region. US 89, although not within the borders of this area, runs parallel to the western edge. Most of the other roads, both paved and unpaved, are designated as Indian Routes. While I'll try to provide you with as clear directions as possible (there aren't any complicated routings), it is best to have a decent Arizona road map. I've selected a clockwise method of presenting the route, beginning in the northwest corner of the area, but you can do it in any direction that's convenient based upon your arrival point.

Since the northeast is so big (extending more than 200 miles from north to south and an average of about 130 miles east to west), there's a good chance that you won't have the time or the inclination to tour the entire region. If so, portions of it can be done on their own with easy access from Phoenix, the Grand Canyon, or Page. While the area is loaded with attractions to be recommended, I would have to place Monument Valley, Canyon de Chelly, and the Petrified Forest in the category of "must see's."

WHERE TO STAY
CHINLE
Moderate

THUNDERBIRD LODGE, *In Canyon de Chelly National Park adjacent to the Visitor Center. Tel. 520/674-5841, Fax 520/674-5844. 72 Rooms. Rates: $89-95, all year. Major credit cards accepted. Located 3-1/2 miles east of the junction of US 191 in Chinle.*

Not only does the Thunderbird Lodge provide the convenience of staying right in Canyon de Chelly National Park but it's a most attractive and pleasant facility to boot. It's not within sight of the canyon (even though it's only several hundred yards away from the beginning of it). However, that is made up for by the fact that it is surrounded by a large grove of pretty cottonwood trees.

The lodge consists of a small original stone building and a more modern motel like facility adjacent to it. The rooms in the older structure are rather small but they have a charm which the newer and larger rooms lack. The latter are also nice because of their southwestern and authentic Native American decor. It should be authentic since the Thunderbird is operated by the Navajo people. There aren't any recreational activities at the Lodge since most visitors spend all of their time touring the park. See the *Where to Eat* section for a description of their restaurant.

HOLBROOK
Inexpensive
RAINBOW INN, *2211 East Navajo Boulevard. Tel. 520/524-2654, Fax 520/524-2654. Toll free reservations Tel. 800/551-1923. 40 Rooms. Rates: High season (June 1st to September 30th): $47-51; Low season (October 1st to April 30th): $41-43. Major credit cards accepted. Located a mile west of I-40, Exit 289.*

The rooms at the Rainbow Inn aren't big but they are nice and comfortable, all with queen size beds and refrigerators. The level of cleanliness is excellent and the front desk staff is friendly. No swimming pool or other amenities to speak of but it is a convenient location for hopping on the Interstate and getting to the Petrified Forest. And at the prices they charge, it's a great value.

KAYENTA
Expensive
HOLIDAY INN MONUMENT VALLEY, *Center of Town. Tel. 520/697-3221, Fax 520/697-3349. Toll free reservations Tel. 800/465-4329. 164 Rooms. Rates: High season (May 1st to October 31st): $99-150; Low season (November 1st to April 30th): $69-89. Major credit cards accepted. Located at the junction of US Highways 160 and 163.*

On the Navajo Indian Reservation, this is kind of a basic Holiday Inn but, then again, there aren't many hotels in the vicinity and there really isn't anything wrong with it. The rooms are average size and probably overpriced but the two-bedroom units are a better buy if you're traveling with several people. The on-premise restaurant is one of the few places to eat in town and isn't bad. Try the authentic Navajo dishes – they're different and better than the more traditional menu items.

Trinket hunters will be delighted by the excellent gift shop which features authentic Navajo jewelry and arts and crafts. Navajo country tours, including Monument Valley, can be arranged at the hotel. There's a swimming pool as well as a small wading pool.

Moderate

WETHERILL INN MOTEL, *On US 163. Tel. 520/697-3231, Fax 520/697-3233, Toll free reservations 800/528-1234. 54 Rooms. Rates: High season (April 15th-October 15th): $98; Low season (mid-November to January 31st): $50. Major credit cards accepted. Located a mile north of the junction of US 160.*

This motel is one of several in northeastern Arizona that are owned and operated by members of the Navajo Nation, although it is now affiliated with the Best Western chain. It isn't anything special, just a standard two story roadside motel with outside corridors and decent rooms. On the other hand, it's clean and comfortable and a little less costly than the Holiday Inn. All rooms have coffee makers. There isn't any restaurant on the premises but one is nearby (you guessed it – the one at the Holiday Inn!).

PAYSON
Moderate

INN OF PAYSON, *801 N. Beeline Highway. Tel. 520/474-3241; Fax 520/472-6564, Toll free reservations 800/247-9477. 99 Rooms. Rates: $89-149, all year including Continental breakfast. Most major credit cards accepted. Located on State Highway 87, 3 miles north of the junction with State Highway 260.*

Attractive mountain lodge architecture amid the greenery of the Mogollon Rim. Rooms surround a spacious courtyard filled with mature trees. The lobby and lounge are warm and inviting. Guest units are a nice size and comfortably furnished. Most have refrigerators. During the summer there is a heated outdoor swimming pool and spa. Restaurant on premises.

KOHL'S RANCH LODGE, *East Highway 260. Tel. 520/478-4211, Fax 520/478-0353. Toll free reservations 800/408-2442. 49 Rooms. Rates: High season (May 1st to September 30th): $100-110; Low season (October 1st to April 30th): $80-90. American Express, Discover, MasterCard, and VISA accepted. Located about 15 miles east of Payson on the south side of AZ 260.*

This is a delightful forest surrounded lodge that almost qualifies as a guest ranch. The variety of accommodations is varied and includes motel type bedrooms, multi-bedroom units, and several large cabins. Some of the cabins have a deck with a private whirlpool (at a higher price). Many rooms have coffee makers and refrigerators. A dozen include full kitchens. All of the units have recently undergone major renovations which have brought the attractive furnishings up to date. The Lodge has a decent on-premises restaurant.

The recreational facilities are extensive and impressive. Starting with the usual heated swimming pool, sauna, and whirlpool, they go on to include an exercise room, sports court with facilities for horseshoes, volleyball, and bocciball. You can putt around on the golf course or putting green or wander through the thick green trees on a number of hiking and jogging trails. For an additional fee you can rent a bicycle or go horseback riding.

Inexpensive
   PAYSON PUEBLO INN, *On East Highway 260. Tel. 520/474-5241, Fax 520/472-6919. Toll free reservations Tel. 800/888-9828. 39 Rooms. Rates: High season (May 1st to September 30th): $54-69; Low season (October 1st to April 30th): $49-59. Major credit cards accepted. Located about a mile east of the junction of AZ 87.*

Not that Kohl's (previous listing) is expensive for all the facilities that they have, but if you want to spend less and aren't in the market for a major recreational outing, than you certainly can't go wrong with the Payson Pueblo Inn. It's a most attractive motel featuring authentic pueblo style construction and nice size comfortable rooms. The larger units at the upper end of the price scale have their own Jacuzzi and some have a cozy gas fireplace. A few also have microwave ovens. All rooms have coffee makers and refrigerators. There isn't any swimming pool or restaurant. However, there's a coffee shop located close by and several restaurants are within a mile or two either way along the main highway.

PINETOP-LAKESIDE
Expensive
   THE MEADOWS INN, *453 North Woodland Road. Tel. 520/367-8200, Fax 520/367-0334. 7 Rooms. Rates: High season (July 1st to September 30th): $120-145; Low season (October 1st to June 30th): $95-130; all rates including full breakfast. American Express, Discover, MasterCard, and VISA accepted. Located 1/4 mile south of AZ 260 on Woodland Road. Follow entrance road to the inn.*

This small and attractive country style inn's name comes from its location in a pretty wildflower meadow on the edge of a thick forest. The rooms are pleasantly furnished on the old fashioned side (no telephones and no air conditioning although it's not likely that you'll need the latter). The small dining room serves excellent food for lunch and dinner as well as the included hearty breakfast. The Inn usually requires a two day minimum stay. This is the type of place you go to in order to get away from the hectic modern world. If that is your travel intention then you'll be very happy at the Meadows Inn.

Moderate

BARTRAM'S WHITE MOUNTAIN BED & BREAKFAST, *Woodland Lake Road. Tel. 520/367-1408. 5 Rooms. Rates: $85 all year including full breakfast. No credit cards accepted. Located two miles south of AZ 260 via Woodland Road to Woodland Lake Road.*

Bartram's is in many respects a less expensive version of the Meadows Inn, only its even smaller and besides not having telephones or air conditioning it also excludes television from its list of amenities. What you will get is peace and quiet in charmingly decorated rooms. The entire property fits that description as it is a carefully restored ranch home dating from the 1940's. The proprietors serve a bountiful and delicious breakfast in a large traditional family dining room. For other meals you'll have to make your way a couple of miles out to the state highway.

NORTHWOODS RESORT, *165 East White Mountain Boulevard. Tel. 520/367-2966, Fax 520/367-2969. 12 Rooms. Rates: $115-145, all year. MasterCard and VISA accepted. Located on AZ 260.*

Consisting of individual cottages ranging from one to three bedrooms and full kitchen (except for one unit), the Northwoods is a pretty property set on several acres of heavily wooded grounds. Accommodations feature nice furniture and home-like decorating touches. Most have fireplaces, either wood burning or gas lit. Trails on the property lead to picturesque Woodland Lake. An outdoor area has a playground for children, horseshoe pit, and barbecue area. There aren't any telephones in rooms or air conditioning. The Northwoods is ideal for people who plan to set up housekeeping in the White Mountains for a couple of days. In fact, minimum day restrictions may apply during the peak months of July and August, so inquire at the time you're ready to book. You have to travel by car to get to the nearest restaurant.

SHOW LOW
Inexpensive

KC MOTEL, *60 West Deuce of Clubs Avenue. Tel. 520/537-4542, Fax 520/537-0106. 36 Rooms. Rates: $48-85 all year. Most major credit cards accepted. Located about a mile west of the center of town on US 60 and AZ 260.*

All of the accommodations in Show Low seem to be pretty much alike – basic motels, some independent and some part of major chains. Since we all know what to expect from the chains I'll concentrate on two acceptable private establishments. This one has nicely furnished units with refrigerator and morning coffee in the lobby. An indoor whirlpool facility is a good place to unwind at the end of the day. Restaurants are located within close proximity.

KIVA MOTEL, *261 East Deuce of Clubs Avenue. Tel. 520/537-4542, Fax 520/537-1024. 20 Rooms. Rates: $48 all year. Major credit cards accepted. Located a half mile west of town on US 60 and AZ 260.*

The Kiva is quite similar to the KC in both accommodations and facilities, although there is a greater variation in the rooms at the Kiva. Some are on the smallish side while others are big but all have been attractively decorated and feature in-room coffee makers and refrigerators. There is also an indoor whirlpool, sauna room, and exercise equipment available to guests. Again, several eating places are just a short ride away.

WINDOW ROCK
Inexpensive
NAVAJO NATION INN, *48 West Highway 264. Tel. 520/871-4108, Fax 520/871-5466. Toll free reservations Tel. 800/662-6189. 56 Rooms. Rates: $67-77 all year. American Express, Diners Club, MasterCard, and VISA accepted. Located on AZ 264 in the center of town.*

Another Navajo Nation property, this inn is located in the Navajo "capital." The motel is standard in every way but is nonetheless a welcome sight in the sparsely populated region where towns with places to stay are few and far between. It can be used as a base for Canyon de Chelly, Monument Valley, and other area attractions so I decided to include it in these listings for your convenience. Tours can be arranged at the motel. The restaurant is kind of average but there aren't too many alternatives so you'll probably wind up using that as well.

WINSLOW
Inexpensive
BEST WESTERN ADOBE INN, *1701 North Park Drive. Tel. 520/289-4638, Fax 520/289-5514. Toll free reservations Tel. 800/528-1234. 72 Rooms. Rates: High season (June 1st to September 30th): $59-69; Low season (October 1st to April 30th): $50-60. Major credit cards accepted. Located just off of Exit 253 of I-40.*

The Adobe Inn is one of the more attractive motor inns along the I-40 corridor and represents a real lodging value. The spacious grounds house a thoroughly modern building that is softened with hints of southwestern style and colors. There's a beautiful atrium that contains a huge heated swimming pool, whirlpool, and a generous amount of green foliage. All of the rooms are large and furnished in a modern southwestern decor. Some feature refrigerators and microwave ovens. The full service restaurant is also a little better than average.

Moderate

LA POSADA HOTEL, *303 E. 2nd Street. Tel. 520/289-4366; Fax 520/ 289-3873. 23 Rooms. Rates: $75-95, all year including Continental breakfast. Major credit cards accepted. Located at the intersection of Historic Route 66, a half mile south of I-40, Exit 252.*

If you're looking for a taste of the old west then this small historic property will be just what the doctor ordered. It's been around for many years but, until completion of major renovations last year, was not up to the standards required for inclusion in this book. Now it is a charming inn with attractively decorated rooms and expansive grounds. It's purposely not too modern (for example, no in-room telephones) but that is part of the atmosphere the owners are attempting to create. There are a couple of decent restaurants within a short drive.

CAMPING & RV SITES

- **Casa Malpais Campground & RV Park**, *On US 60 & 191, Springerville, Tel. 520/333-4632*
- **Cottonwood Campground**, *Canyon de Chelly National Monument, Tel. 520/674-5500*
- **Fools Hollow Recreation Area**, *Fool Hollow Road off of AZ 260, Show Low, Tel. 520/537-3680*
- **Holbrook KOA**, *102 Hermosa Drive, Holbrook, Tel. 520/524-6689*
- **Meteor Crater RV Park**, *Exit 233 of I-40, adjacent to Meteor Crater, Tel. 520/289-4002*
- **Payson Campground**, *808 East Highway 260, Payson, Tel. 520/472-6954*
- **Rainbow Forest RV Park**, *Rainbow Lake Drive, Pinetop-Lakeside, Tel. 520/ 368-5286*
- **Rimcrest RV Resort**, *Southwest of AZ 260 via signs, Pinetop-Lakeside, Tel. 520/537-4660*

WHERE TO EAT

CHINLE

Inexpensive

THUNDERBIRD LODGE, *In the Thunderbird Lodge hotel at Canyon de Chelly National Monument. Tel. 520/674-5841. No credit cards (unless you're a guest and putting it on your room bill). Breakfast, lunch, and dinner served daily.*

This multi-room dining facility serves a good variety of American, southwestern, and Native American food cafeteria style. Don't let that put you off – cafeteria has the connotation of lesser quality in some cases but definitely not here. You can choose from sandwiches, salad platters, or hot entrees. The dining rooms are modestly attractive. For lunch, especially, when most visitors are anxious to resume touring Canyon de

Chelly the quick cafeteria format is a plus. Should you want a sit-down dinner you won't find it within the park. Your best bet then is probably to go to the restaurant in the Holiday Inn just west of the park entrance.

HOLBROOK
Inexpensive
MESA ITALIANO RESTAURANT, *2318 East Navajo Boulevard. Tel. 520/524-6696. MasterCard and VISA accepted. Lunch and dinner served daily except Mondays when only dinner is served.*

Nothing fancy at Mesa Italiano. Despite the name it's not a combination of southwestern and Italian fare. You'll find a menu filled with all of the traditional Italian favorites including many types of pasta, veal, and fish. The atmosphere is small town casual and friendly and the service is laid back but efficient. There's cocktail service as well as a separate lounge. The prices are almost unbelievably low.

KAYENTA
Moderate
AMIGO CAFE, *On US 163 north of the intersection of US 160. Tel. 520/697-8448. MasterCard and VISA accepted. Breakfast, lunch, and dinner served daily.*

Unless you want to eat in the higher priced restaurant in the Holiday Inn this is the logical choice in town. The cafe serves excellent Mexican dishes in a casual and friendly atmosphere. Several entrees are in the inexpensive price category.

PAYSON
Moderate
COUNTRY KITCHEN RESTAURANT, *210 East Highway 260. Tel. 520/474-1332. Most major credit cards accepted. Breakfast, lunch, and dinner served daily.*

The name says it all in this case of this good family restaurant. It's just the type of place you're often looking for when you don't want something fancy (which is a little difficult to find in Payson) and junk food won't do. The feature is home style cooking of traditional American favorites like turkey and burgers and excellent country fried steak. The atmosphere is about as informal as you can get. Children's menu.

THE OAKS RESTAURANT, *302 West Main Street. Tel. 520/474-1929. Major credit cards accepted. Lunch and dinner served daily; Sunday brunch. Reservations are suggested during the summer season.*

The prettiest looking restaurant in town and excellent food to go along with it. The atmosphere is warm and friendly, something like being in the home of a friend. During the summer months you can dine outside on the patio amid the scent of the forest. Prime rib, steaks, and seafood are the specialties of the house and they're all expertly prepared to your order. There's also a good selection of other entrees including chicken and veal. You know that the Sunday brunch is outstanding because it always draws the local folks. Cocktail lounge on the premises.

PINETOP-LAKESIDE
Moderate
    CHARLIE CLARK'S STEAK HOUSE, *AZ 260 at east end of town. Tel. 520/367-4900. Most major credit cards accepted. Dinner is served nightly. Lunch is available only in the separate lounge. Reservations are suggested.*

Serving a big number of both locals and visitors for sixty years, this is a fun and casual place to have a real western dinner. The building is reminiscent of a frontier cabin and is distinctive for the large brick fireplace on the exterior. The woods form a nice backdrop. Western decor and atmosphere continue once inside where you can select from a host of hearty fare that includes delicious slow cooked prime rib, rotisserie prepared chicken, succulent baby back pork ribs, and mesquite steaks grilled to perfection. It doesn't get much better than this. Cocktails are served either tableside or in the lounge. A children's menu is available. I might add that the atmosphere and food at Charlie Clark's is one that will appeal to both grownups and your kids.

    THE CHRISTMAS TREE RESTAURANT, *455 N. Woodland Road, Lakeside. Tel. 520/367-3107. Discover, MasterCard, and VISA accepted. Dinner served nightly except Tuesday. Reservations are suggested.*

No matter what time of the year you dine at the Christmas Tree Restaurant there's a little of December in the air. The holiday decor provides a cheerful note at any time. Some people think that they're a little slow in taking down the decorations. Well, the proprietors of the Christmas Tree go one better – they never have to bother putting them up!

After filling yourself up on the freshly baked cinnamon rolls you'll have a big menu of chicken, beef, and fish entrees to choose from. The chicken and dumplings is considered to be the specialty of the house. There's a full service cocktail lounge and children can select dishes from their own menu.

    HON-DAH INDIAN PINE RESTAURANT, *Junction of AZ 260 and AZ 73 in the Hon-Dah Casino. Tel. 520/369-0299. Most major credit cards accepted. Lunch and dinner served daily; Sunday brunch.*

This restaurant features a big variety of entrees that will make it easy for just about everyone to find something they like and all at reasonable prices. The prime rib in a red wine au jus and served with tangy horseradish sauce is an excellent choice as are the pork spare ribs.

Combination plates of beef and chicken are good for those who can't make up their minds. Thursday is "barbecue night" and Wednesday is "prime rib night." These things are always on the menu but on those nights you can get them for inexpensive category prices. The Sunday brunch is an extensive feast served in the adjacent Timbers Lounge and Showroom. Cocktails.

SHOW LOW
Moderate
   AUNT NANCY'S FAMILY RESTAURANT, *21 North 9th Street. Tel. 520/537-4839. MasterCard and VISA accepted. Breakfast, lunch, and dinner served Monday through Saturday. On Sunday only breakfast and lunch are served.*
   With a name like this could you possibly go wrong? Well, not here at least. This warm and friendly restaurant is located in a converted large house and features nicely prepared American home style cooking. A number of Mexican dishes also appear on the menu. In fact, the chimichangas and fajitas are among the best choices at Aunt Nancy's. Beer is available.

WINSLOW
Inexpensive
   FALCON RESTAURANT, *1113 East 3rd Street. Tel. 520/289-2342. MasterCard and VISA accepted. Breakfast, lunch, and dinner served daily.*
   The Falcon features a good selection of American fare (some in the moderate category) including beef, pork, and fish. The semi-old west decor is attractive and casual. Cocktails are served and there is a separate bar. Children's menu.

SEEING THE SIGHTS
The Navajo Nation & Monument Valley
   I'll begin my tour of the northeast at the point where US 160 originates. This is 16 miles north of the town of Cameron on US 89, which is near to both the east entrance of Grand Canyon and to Flagstaff. You will have entered the Navajo Reservation a little while before. While most maps label the area as the "Navajo Indian Reservation" the proper name is actually the **Navajo Nation**. Be aware that gasoline and other services are not frequently available on the Reservation. The best places to secure services are in Kayenta and Chinle. Always start out in the morning with a full tank of gas.

VISITING THE INDIAN RESERVATIONS

The Navajo and Hopi welcome visitors. However, Indian reservations are sovereign political entities with their own laws. Visitors are expected to comply with the rules and regulations concerning visitation. In general, you should never photograph, sketch or record Native Americans without their permission and certainly never enter a home uninvited. When you are given permission it is customary to give a small gratuity for the privilege. It is illegal to carry alcoholic beverages in your vehicle while on any reservation.

What may appear as ordinary or unimportant to us could very well be sacred to the Native Americans. Therefore, never remove any rock or artifact that you may come across, no matter how innocent it may seem. Don't climb on rock formations unless you have been told that it is all right to do so. Many tribal ceremonies are open to visitors but don't walk into a ceremonial dance unless you have confirmed that visitors are welcome. Again, photography at such events may or may not be restricted. Always be sure before you act.

The rules are few and simple to obey. Please show your respect for the culture and privacy of others. It will result in a more enjoyable visit for you.

Along US 160 are a number of small Native American towns, each of which has plenty of places to buy authentic Navajo goods. If you're coming from Page, take AZ 89 until it reaches US 160 and then turn left. It is 82 miles from US 89 (98 miles from Page) to the town of Kayenta, one of the larger reservation communities with about 4,500 people. Nearby is the impressive and stunningly beautiful **Navajo National Monument**. Accessible by AZ 564 (southwest of Kayenta off of US 160) and a series of rough and unpaved roads, three separate pueblo ruins dating from the 13th century are preserved beneath enormous cliffs. Two of the ruins, **Betatakin** and **Keet Seel** can be visited by ranger conducted tours. Both involve strenuous walks of, respectively five and 16 miles, although the longer Keet Seel trail can be done on horseback.

The five mile trail also drops the equivalent of a 70-story building. If that isn't enough to deter you keep in mind that you have to return the opposite way. There is, however, a way to see the Betatakin Ruin without being an experienced hiker in excellent physical condition. There is a paved pathway leading from the Navajo monument's visitor center that crosses nine bridges and descends only about 150 feet that leads to an overlook from which there is an excellent view of the ruin. The cave in the side of the cliff containing the Betatakin Ruin is vast. It almost appears as if a huge futuristic dome has been built over a strange city. Betatakin means House on the Ledge. The round trip covers about one mile. *Tel.*

520/672-2366 for schedules and tour information. Allow at least a half day, unless you're only going to the Betatakin overlook. The latter trip requires only about 45 minutes to an hour.

While the Navajo National Monument is for the more adventurous, the next attraction is one that can and should be done by all. **Monument Valley Navajo Tribal Park** is located 22 miles northeast of Kayenta via US 163. Although almost all of Monument Valley is located within Arizona, the entrance is about a mile north of the Utah state line. An area of gorgeous orange-to-red colored rock formations dating back about 160 million years, Monument Valley has been made famous throughout the world because many movies, television programs, and commercials have been filmed here.

Large buttes, mesas, and canyons alternate for your attention along with unusual free-standing rock formations. Some of them can best be described by simply stating their names – The Mittens, Elephant Butte, the Three Sisters, Totem Pole, and the Thumb, for example. Some of the sandstone monoliths rise to heights of a thousand feet above the valley.

DO YOU KNOW WHAT TIME IT IS?

A good question when traveling through the Indian country. You see, although the state of Arizona doesn't observe daylight savings time, the Navajo Nation does. So, it's easy to get real confused as to what time it is. Here's how I try to keep track: Arizona is on Mountain Time but is the equivalent of Pacific Time during DST. If that's the case, then the Navajo Reservation remains on Mountain Time all year. Don't be embarrassed to ask what the correct time is – people in the tourist industry are used to having visitors who can't tell the time of day! It doesn't matter so much if you're out in the wild, but if you have to be at a certain place at a certain time (a canyon tour, for example) you could wind up being in trouble if you aren't on the correct clock.

A few miles into the valley is a visitor center where you can obtain information and arrange for guided tours on four wheel drive vehicles that penetrate less frequently visited areas. Many people like to drive their own cars on the 17-mile long **Valley Drive**, which passes most of the major formations at 11 marked stops. The road is not paved but isn't that difficult unless it has been raining recently. In that case, four-wheel drive is recommended.

No matter how you see it, Monument Valley is one of the most awe inspiring sights in the world. *The tribal park is open daily from 7:00am until 7:00pm from May through September and from 8:00am to 5:00pm the remainder* *of the year. Closed only on New Year's and Christmas. Admission is $2.50 for ages 8 and above and $1 for age 60 and above. Additional charges for guided tours. Tel. 435/727-3353.*

Canyon de Chelly & the Reservation Continued...

After visiting Monument Valley you will return on US 163 to the junction of US 180 and then continue east on the latter for about 40 miles to US 191 at Mexican Water. The route then continues south on US 191, however, there is a detour available at this point. About 35 miles further east on US 163 is the **Four Corners Monument**. This is the only place in the United States where four states come together – Arizona, Utah, New Mexico, and Colorado. The symbol of each state is on the ground at that point and people just love to get down on all fours and have their picture taken so they can show their friends that they were in four states at one time. Thrilling. There's also an Indian market surrounding the monument. It is interesting and somewhat unique but whether it's worth a 70-mile round trip is highly debatable. *Four Corners is open 7:00am until 7:00pm from May through August and 8:00am until 5:00pm the remainder of the year. There is a $1.50 admission charge.*

About 63 miles south of Mexican Water on US 191 is the town of **Chinle**. By the way, you haven't left the Navajo Reservation all this time and you're still going to be on it for quite a while to come. Chinle is a small town with nothing special to see but it is the service headquarters for the memorable **Canyon de Chelly National Monument** which is located about two miles east of town following signs. The monument covers almost 84,000 acres and is of interest for both scenic and historic reasons. The canyon, though not nearly as deep or dramatic as the Grand Canyon, is beautiful because of the deep color of the rocky walls which are smooth and sheer. Within the canyon are the remains of various Anasazi and later cultures that span the period from about 350 to 1300 AD. A small number of Navajo still reside within the canyon.

Visiting Canyon de Chelly, a sure highlight of any Arizona journey, is actually like going to two completely different attractions – namely the scenery from on the canyon rim and then the historic interior of the canyon. The former is done by car via two separate drives and the latter can only be done with an authorized Navajo guide. Let's take it one step at a time. You can visualize the layout of Canyon de Chelly by turning the letter V on its side. Where the sides meet is the visitor center as well as the beginning of the drives that extend along each rim. This is also the point where you enter the canyon.

There is a **North Rim Drive** and a **South Rim Drive** (hmm, sounds a bit like the Grand Canyon). Each rim drive is about 25 miles long, one way. If you have time for only one, then take the South Rim because that has the best sights. The North Rim Drive extends along the **Canyon del Muerto** (Canyon of Death) and there are four overlooks. The South Rim Drive is near the edge of the actual **Canyon de Chelly** and has six overlooks. At the **White House Overlook** you can see the remains of a large cliff dwelling on the opposite side of the canyon. There's also a trail that descends 600 feet to the ruin. It's a strenuous trip and not for the novice hiker. Another ruin can be seen from the **Sliding House Overlook**.

At the very end of the south rim road is the **Spider Rock Overlook**. This, from a scenic standpoint, is the most beautiful part of the Monument. You will see a split in the canyon and the tall Spider Rock standing at the junction. It looks narrow but isn't really so. It just seems that way because it stands more than 830 feet above the canyon floor. At this point the colors of the canyon walls are remarkable and so is the distant view of the mountains which form a backdrop to the canyon. In many places the canyon's walls are streaked with dark lines. These are evident from some of the overlooks but are even more clearly seen from within the canyon.

Now for going into the **canyon** itself. You can drive your own vehicle into the canyon as long as you have a Navajo guide with you. Four wheel drive is a necessity since there are no roads in the canyon. I think it's far more fun to take either the half-day or full-day guided tour. You sit with other visitors on the back of an old eight-wheel drive truck that somehow manages to keep on going through the rough terrain. A real Navajo is your guide and frequent stops are made to see some of the historic points of interest within both Canyon de Chelly and Canyon del Muerto. He'll tell you a lot of tales about both the ancient and not so long-ago inhabitants of the canyon. You'll have ample time to visit the Antelope House and White House ruin areas.

Probably the best way to see Canyon de Chelly is to allow almost a full day – this way you can take the half-day guided tour and do the rim drives on your own. *All canyon tours depart from the Thunderbird Lodge located just past the visitor center. Visitor center open daily from 8:00am to 6:00pm (till 5:00 from October through April). There is no admission fee for the canyon rim drives. The half day (3-1/2-4 hours) tour departs at 9:00am and 2:00pm and costs $35 ($25 for under age 12) while the full-day tour leaves at 9:00am and is $55 including lunch. Credit cards. It returns at 5:30pm. From fall through spring the afternoon half day tour starts at 1:00pm and there is no full day tour. If you are going to use your own vehicle the cost of a Navajo guide is $10 per hour with a minimum of three hours. Tel. 520/674-5501 for Monument headquarters. Reservations for tours can be made by calling 800/679-2473.*

Upon completion of your fascinating visit to Canyon de Chelly return to US 191 and continue south for 37 miles to Ganado and the **Hubbell Trading Post National Historic Site**. The post was established by John Hubbell in 1878 and he soon became one of the foremost Indian traders in the American Southwest. There is a visitor center and you can visit the Hubbell home which looks much as it did at the time it was acquired by the Hubbell family. Native Americans display and sell their crafts and demonstrations are given. It is interesting to note that the Trading Post still serves the same purpose today as it did in the last century. You can see the site in under an hour but give yourself more time if you plan to shop for Native crafts. *Site open daily from 8:00am until 6:00pm from April to September and to 5:00pm the rest of the year. Closed Christmas and New Year's Day. Admission is free. Tel. 520/755-3475.*

A VISIT TO THE HOPI RESERVATION

*The **Hopi Reservation**, surrounded by the Navajo Nation and off of the main roads, is less visited. However, there is quite a bit to see, especially if you're interested in learning more about Native American cultures. This side trip from Ganado covers about 120 miles and can be done in about four or five hours. From the junction of US 191 and AZ 264 (just west of Ganado), take AZ 264 west. You'll reach the Hopi Reservation in about 30 miles. Most of the attractions are located a little past the reservation border along a 20-mile stretch between the towns of Keams Canyon and Second Mesa. No photography is allowed on the Hopi Reservation.*

*Besides presenting an opportunity to shop for Hopi crafts, there's an excellent museum at Second Mesa. The **Hopi Cultural Center Museum**, Tel. 520/734-6650, has an outstanding collection of all kinds of Hopi crafts including the famous Kachina dolls. You'll also learn about the ancestral spirits that play such an important role in Hopi life. The museum is open weekdays from 8:00am to 5:00pm and on weekends from 9:00am to 3:00pm. It is closed on major holidays. Admission is $3 for adults and $1 for children under age 13.*

The capital of the Navajo Nation is located in **Window Rock**, about 30 miles east of Ganado via AZ 264. If you're interested in the Navajo culture then the side trip is probably worth a couple of hours due to the presence of the **Navajo Tribal Museum**. The museum offers a complete history of the Navajo people as well as the natural history of the Four Corners region. There's a recreation of a trading post and exhibits of Navajo artists. *Located right on AZ 264, open every day except Sunday from 8:00am to 6:00pm (from 9:00am November through March), closed New Year's, Thanksgiving, and Christmas; donations are requested, Tel. 520/871-6673.*

Also of interest is the **St. Michaels Historical Museum**. Dating from 1898 and restored to its appearance at that time, this museum not only provides further background on Navajo culture but it tells the interesting story of the work of the Franciscan Friars within the Navajo Nation. *Located off of AZ 264 in the St. Michaels Mission.Open daily from 9:00am to 5:00pm (except 10:00am to 6:00pm on Sunday) from Memorial Day through Labor Day. Donations are requested. Tel. 520/871-4171.*

From Ganado you'll be continuing south on US 191 for about 35 miles to the town of **Chambers** where you'll finally leave he Navajo Reservation. Chambers is the junction for I-40 and is a good place to fill up the car's gas tank as well as yours.

Petrified Forest National Park

Get on the Interstate at Chambers in a westbound direction and take it for 22 miles to Exit 311. As soon as you leave the highway you'll enter one of Arizona's greatest attractions – the **Petrified Forest National Park**. Once part of a gigantic flood plain, tall trees in this area fell and were covered by silt and mud. Eventually they were buried by volcanic ash which slowed the decay of the logs. Silica in the ground water seeped into the logs and crystallized, turning the trees into petrified wood. That occurred about 225 million years ago. Uplifting from various natural processes eventually exposed the logs. The same minerals that were responsible for the petrification process also resulted in the incredible colors of the **Painted Desert** which encompass a large section of the park's north. That quickly tells the geologic story. But seeing is believing. The landscape of the Petrified Forest National Park is one of the most colorful and unusual to be found anywhere.

Seeing the park couldn't be much easier. After boning up on your natural science at the **Visitor Center**, *about a half mile from the Interstate*, you'll embark on the paved 29-mile long road which traverses the park from north to south and comes close to just about all the major points of interest. The road is essentially straight and pretty flat except for the first couple of miles which have some sharp turns as the road descends from a ridge. The first section has several excellent overlooks. These are **Tiponi Point**, **Tawa Point**, **Kachina Point**, **Chinde Point**, **Pintazo Point**, **Nizhoni Point**, **Whipple Point**, and **Lacey Point**. These eight stops along the rim top (the overlooks are all just steps from the parking area) provide a sweeping and ever changing panorama of the fantastic Painted Desert.

About seven miles further down the road are the **Puerco Indian Ruins** dating from around 1400. Some of the ruins have been partially restored. Nearby is an overlook which provides a good view of **Newspaper Rock**. It is so called because of the petroglyphs inscribed on the huge sandstone rock. You used to be able to go down to the rock but it is no longer allowed in order to preserve the inscriptions.

Soon after this area you'll reach one of the most unusual sights in the park – **The Tepees**. These badlands type formations are, indeed, shaped much like the well known plains Indian dwelling and are striated into layers of differing colors by the presence of iron, manganese, and various other assorted minerals. Some of the tepees are hundreds of feet high. South of The Tepees is a three-mile long spur road that leads to the **Blue Mesa**. This is the first great concentration of petrified wood. Other big areas of petrified logs will come up shortly at **Agate Bridge**, the **Jasper Forest** and the **Crystal Forest**. The first two are overlooks but there is a short and easy trail at the Crystal Forest.

The points of interest in the southern section of the park are more spread out. These are the **Flattops**, large remains of a huge layer of sandstone, the **Long Logs** and **Agate House Trails** which lead to hundreds of petrified logs in an area known as the Rainbow Forest. Finally, there is a trail to the **Giant Logs** located a couple of miles north of the park's southern entrance station at the **Rainbow Forest Museum**. It will require a minimum of two hours to see the Petrified Forest, but it's possible to spend a half day or more. While it is tempting to take a sample of petrified wood with you – don't. It is against the law and can result in heavy fines. Besides, think about future generations. We want to leave the park as it is so that everyone else will have the same opportunity to see these wonders as you have. *The park is open every day of the year from 8:00am to 5:00pm with hours sometimes extended during the summer. Admission is $10 per private vehicle for those not holding a national park service passport. Tel. 520/524-6228.*

Upon exiting the park you'll be at US 180. Our route continues to the east. However, if you are only interested in the northeast for the Indian reservations and related scenery you can go west on 180 to Holbrook and continue on I-40 to make connections to other parts of the state. You might also want to go to Holbrook if the end of the day is near as there's a better choice of lodging in that town than in nearby communities to the east. If you go to Holbrook you can spend a few minutes checking out its historic downtown, including the 1898 Courthouse, the Bucket of Blood Saloon, and the Blevins House (sight of an 1888 shoot-out between the sheriff and a gang of cattle rustlers).

Arizona's White Mountains

It's about 40 miles from the south entrance of the Petrified Forest to the town of St. Johns, located at the junction of US 180 and US 191. The **Apache County Historical Society Museum** contains exhibits on ancient inhabitants and the pioneer days. *180 West Cleveland Street, Tel. 520/337-4737, open Monday to Friday from 9:00am to 5:00pm; no admission charge but donations are accepted.*

Ten miles south of town on US 191 is the **Lyman Lake State Park and Petroglyph Trail**. The park has a 1,500 acre lake with boating facilities as well as a trail that leads past a number of petroglyphs. The trail is of moderate difficulty and takes between one and 1-1/2 hours. There is also a small herd of buffalo located near the park entrance. *The park is open daily from 8:00am to 6:00pm (till 5:00pm October through April) and there is a $4 per vehicle admission charge. Guided tours of the petroglyph trail are offered at 10:00am and 2:00pm on weekends for $1. Tel. 520/337-4441.*

Four miles further south is the **White Mountain Archaeological Center** (known locally as the Raven Sight). Use the Tucson Electric Power Road and a half-mile gravel road for access off of US 191. The hillside site overlooks the Little Colorado River and contains the remains of a pueblo that was occupied as early as 100 A.D. There are two ceremonial chambers, called kivas, and two massive dwellings containing as many as 800 rooms. There are also many exhibits about the site and visitors can often watch archaeological excavations or reconstructions taking place. *Open daily from 10:00am to 5:00pm, May 1st through the end of October; guided tours (fee $3.50 for adults and $2.50 for children 12 to 17 and for senior citizens) are offered on the hour from 10:00am to 4:00pm except noon; full day and multi day archaeological expeditions on foot or by horseback are available by prior reservation; Tel. 520/333-5857.*

Once you return to US 191 and continue south you'll soon reach the **White Mountains**, generally contiguous with the **Apache-Sitgreaves National Forest**. There are several things that make the White Mountains unusual. First of all, the general appearance of the area is not what you would expect to find in Arizona. These are heavily forested mountains that look more like the mountains of the east than the usually arid looking western peaks. Then there is the large number of natural lakes. The reasons for this are that the mountains are located in what is known as the high country. With elevations generally in the five to six-thousand foot level, the weather is cooler and there is more rainfall. The result is a vast oasis that has become a popular playground for the residents of the Phoenix area. Outside of Arizona the area isn't that well known.

While recreational opportunities of every kind are the major draw for Arizonians, visitors can also take advantage of the many historic and scenic points of interest. Another feature of the White Mountain region is the **Mogollon Rim**, a huge plateau that stretches for more than 200 miles through central Arizona. Much of the suggested tour through the White Mountains parallels the rim.

Springerville and Round Valley are the first two communities you'll reach in the White Mountains and the area contains two places worth visiting. First is the **Casa Malpais Pueblo**. There is a museum about the Mogollon Indian culture and you'll also view an orientation film before being taken on a guided tour to the 15-acre ruin site which is located two miles from town. The pueblo, built around 1250, contains the main pueblo with more than a hundred rooms, the Great Kiva, and an enclosing wall among other structures. Allow about 90 minutes if you take the guided tour. *318 Main Street, Springerville. The museum is open daily from 9:00am to 5:00pm and guided tours are given at 9:00am, 11:00am and 2:30pm, weather permitting. Reservations are suggested. The admission fee is $3 for adults and $2 for those over age 55 or ages 12 through 18. Tel. 520/333-5375.*

Also on Main Street, across from the Post Office in the center of town, is the **Madonna of the Trail**, one of twelve statues built in the 1930s in various parts of the country ranging from Maryland to California to honor the spirit of America's pioneer women. The statue is ten feet high and clothed in frontier dress and a large sunbonnet. She is holding a rifle and an infant while a small child is by her side.

Immediately to the south of Springerville is the town of **Eagar**. The first point of interest in Eagar is the **26 Bar Ranch** on AZ 260 about a mile west of town. Once part of a much larger ranch, it is best known because John Wayne was at one time a part owner. No tours are given but the attractive barn buildings usually attract the attention of visitors. Another three miles west on AZ 260 and then south on Southfork Road is **The Little House Museum**. Situated within the canyon walls of the Little Colorado River, the museum presents a vision of the west through stories about visitors and residents. Give yourself at least a half hour to visit the museum. *Open daily except Wednesday from 10:00am to 4:00pm, mid-May to Labor Day and by appointment the rest of the year; guided tours are offered; admission price is $4; Tel. 520/333-2286.*

You'll now continue west on AZ 260 as you enter the heart of the White Mountains. Many side roads lead to recreational facilities (see the Sports and Recreation section for further information). In about 25 miles is the small town of **Hon-dah**. From there a side road (AZ 73) leads 19 miles into the **Fort Apache Indian Reservation** and to **Whitewater**. The town of Whitewater is the administrative center of the Reservation. Many of the Apache, especially women, still wear their traditional colorful dress. Visitors can purchase crafts at several trading posts. Four miles south of town is the **Fort Apache Historic Park**. Established in 1870, it was the home of the famous First Cavalry and a base of operations against Geronimo and other noted Apache leaders. More than 20 buildings still stand from the end of the post's active days in 1922. Take about 45 minutes to explore the park. *The site is open on weekdays from 7:30am to 4:30pm and on weekends from 9:00am to 4:00pm. Admission is $2 for adults and $1 for senior citizens. Children under 13 pay only 50 cents. Tel. 520/338-4625.*

If you have a little more adventure in you try the **Kinishba Ruins** located seven miles west of town via a dirt road. Check on the reservation concerning road conditions. A four-wheel drive, high clearance vehicle is recommended. The ruins are more than a thousand years old and contain over 200 rooms. It is believed that the site was visited by the Coronado expedition during their search for the Seven Cities of Cibola. The interior may be dangerous so only view the ruins from the outside. There are no services at the site.

Upon your return to the junction of AZ 260 turn left and continue west. In a few miles you will reach **Pinetop-Lakeside**, the recreational center of the White Mountains. It is an area of beautiful lakes and outdoor enthusiasts will love the extensive system of trails that dots the region. If you have a vehicle that can handle rough roads you may want to stop at the **Lakeside Ranger Station**, *Tel. 520/368-5111*, and pick up a cassette tape (loaned free of charge with player) and map that will give you two tour options into the backcountry. A highlight of this area that can be done by all is the **Mogollon Rim Overlook**, two miles northwest of Pinetop-Lakeside and reached by a short spur road off of AZ 260. An easy nature trail is marked with signs pointing out the abundant natural resources found in this area that attracted Indian settlement. The trail ends at the top of a sandstone rock outcrop and affords an outstanding view of the valley beneath the rim.

The Mogollon Rim to Payson

About ten miles past Pinetop-Lakeside AZ 260 reaches Show Low, one of the bigger towns in the White Mountains and a good place to stop for food or lodging. You can cut short the northeast excursion here by taking US 60 back to Phoenix, a scenic route through the Salt River Valley. Those wishing to continue will stay on AZ 260 to Payson, a distance of approximately 110 miles. The entire drive is scenic and parallels the **Mogollon Rim**.

The adventurous traveler can have access to more beautiful scenery by taking the Old Rim Road which runs from AZ 260 near **Woods Canyon Lake** and ends at AZ 287 north of Payson. This route bypasses Payson so you'll have to back track if you need the services offered there. The road has some of the most wonderful scenery in all of Arizona, especially the rim top view offered from **Hi-View Point**. The road is unpaved but not that difficult except that under no circumstances should you attempt it during or after a rainfall. Four-wheel drive is a better means of seeing the Old Rim Road, especially if you want to do some of the detours off of that road.

The main route passes through a number of towns and recreational areas. The final stretch into Payson is the best – a series of rather steep switchbacks brings you from the top of the rim on into Payson which sits pretty as a picture at the very base of the Mogollon Rim. Like Pinetop-Lakeside, Payson is a center for services related to the many recreational pursuits found in the White Mountains and all along the Mogollon Rim.

One attraction in town is the **Payson Zoo,** *open every day from 10:00am to 3:30pm unless closed by bad weather; admission price is $4 for everyone over 12 and $1 for under 12; Tel. 520/474-5435.* The small facility has only about 50 animals but many of them have been trained for use in the entertainment industry and make an hour or so spent here a most pleasant and enjoyable time. You may also be interested in paying a brief visit to the **Museum of the Forest,** *Old Main Street.*

You can also make your way back to Phoenix from Payson by taking AZ 87 south from the center of town. But lets continue onward. Go north on AZ 87 for ten miles and then via a three mile newly paved road to the **Tonto Natural Bridge State Park.** Composed of travertine, the bridge is 183 feet high while the space beneath it measures about 150 feet in height and almost 400 feet across. It is one of the largest natural structures of its type in the entire world and is visible from several viewpoints. There is also a trail that leads from the top of the bridge into the canyon beneath it but it is quite steep. Anyone with a physical disability should not attempt it. *Open daily from 8:00am until 6:00pm, April through September and from 9:00am to 5:00pm the remainder of the year, closed only on Christmas; admission is $5 per vehicle (for up to six persons); Tel. 520/476-4202.*

On the Way Back

From Tonto Bridge AZ 87 continues north for about 75 miles to the town of Winslow at the intersection of I-40. Within town is the **Old Trails Museum,** where various exhibits trace the history of Winslow. *212 Kinsley Avenue (one block west of AZ 87), open 9:30am to 5:00pm (closed from noon to 1:00pm for lunch), Tuesday through Saturday from March to October (call for winter hours); donations accepted; Tel. 520/289-2435.*

Three miles east of town via I-40 (Exit 257) and then a mile north on AZ 87 is the **Homolovi Ruins State Park.** A major archaeological site dating from the 14th century, these pueblos were occupied by the ancestors of the modern day Hopi. The 300 sites include small campsites, the larger pueblo and many petroglyphs. There is also a visitor center which documents the life of the Homolovi people. Allow a minimum of about an hour to visit the site. *The park is open daily from 8:00am until 5:00pm all year except Christmas Day. Admission is $4 per vehicle (for up to six people). Tel. 520/289-4106.*

Return to I-40 and now head west for the final leg of your Northeastern journey. Get off at Exit 233 and follow the road south for about six miles to one of the most unusual sights you're likely to encounter in Arizona or anywhere else. **Meteor Crater** is the most well preserved meteor impact site on the face of the earth. Scientists tell us that about 50,000 years ago a giant meteor weighing millions of tons hurtled towards the earth at a speed of 45,000 miles per hour! When it hit the earth it did so with the force of 15 million tons of dynamite and displaced some 300 million tons of rock. All of this occurred within the space of about 10 seconds. It's not so difficult to imagine all of this when you stand on the overlook (which juts out over the crater) and you can see this giant hole in the ground – it measures almost a mile across and is about 570 feet deep. It would take a walk of about three miles to circle it. The bottom of the crater could easily accommodate 20 football fields!

The terrain is so similar to that of the moon that Apollo astronauts used it to train. There is an excellent exhibit area that explains the process which created Meteor Crater and how it aids in the study of both earth and space science. On display is a 1,400-pound meteor fragment. Allow at least a half hour. Guided tours around the rim are offered at various intervals. No one is allowed to climb into the crater. The site is open every day of the year. *Hours are 6:00am to 6:00pm from May 15th to September 15th and 8:00am to 5:00pm the rest of the year. The adult admission price is $8, seniors pay $7 and children ages 6 through 17 are charged $2. Tel. 520/289-2362.*

Once you return to the Interstate it's less than 35 miles to Flagstaff and the junctions of I-17 and US 89. From there you can return to Phoenix or tour the Flagstaff/Sedona or Grand Canyon regions as well as having easy access to all other parts of the state.

NIGHTLIFE & ENTERTAINMENT

Of all the areas in Arizona, the northeast probably has the least in the way of nightlife. Composed of mainly small towns and Indian reservations (where the residents prefer to entertain tourists during the day except for occasional evening ceremonies), you're most likely to find something to do in the lounges of hotels and larger motor inns.

Seasonal entertainment can be found in a couple of locales. First is the **Round Valley Auditorium** in the town of the same name. Presented by the Round Valley Fine Arts Association, you can get information from the Chamber of Commerce, *Tel. 520/333-2123*. Near Show Low is **Theater Mountain** which offers a variety of shows on Friday and Saturday evenings from April through October and also during Thanksgiving and Christmas. Again, the local chamber of commerce is your best source for specific show information and ticket prices.

You can also find a few nightspots with live music in Payson. Try the 600 block of West Main Street.

Casinos
• **Apache Gold Casino**, *San Carlos. Tel. 800/272-2438*
• **Mazatzal Casino**, *Payson. Tel. 800/777-7529*
• **Hon Dah Casino**, *McNary. Tel. 800/929-8744*

SPORTS & RECREATION

Boating
- **Lyman Lake**, *AZ 180, south of St. Johns*

Fishing
Numerous lakes within the White Mountains. These include:
- **Fred's Lake**, *1/4 mile south of AZ 260 between Hon-Dah and Pinetop-Lakeside*
- **Rainbow Lake**, *off of AZ 260 in Lakeside*
- **Scott's Reservoir**, *north of Pinetop-Lakeside via Porter Mountain Road off of AZ 260*
- **Woodland Lake**, *in Pinetop-Lakeside, south of AZ 260 in Woodland Lake Park*

Golf
- **Alpine Country Club**, *three miles east of Alpine off US 666, Tel. 520/339-4944*
- **Payson Golf Course**, *Payson, Tel. 520/474-2273*
- **Pine Meadows Country Club**, *Overgaard, off of AZ 260, Tel. 520/535-4713*
- **Pinetop Lakes Golf and Country Club**, *South of Pinetop on AZ 260, Tel. 520/369-4351*
- **Show Low Country Club**, *2 miles west of Show Low on AZ 260, Tel. 520/537-4564*
- **Snowflake Municipal Golf Course**, *on AZ 277 west of Snowflake, Tel. 520/536-7233*

Hiking
The extensive **White Mountain** trail system covers more than 180 miles. Contact the Lakeside Ranger Station for detailed information, *Tel. 520/368-5111.*

Horseback Riding
If you want to take a ride through the back country but on a llama instead of a horse, then contact **Llama Pack Trips**, *Troutback, Tel. 520/333-2371.* Otherwise, try:
- **Pinetop Lakes Stables**, *Pinetop, Tel. 520/369-1000*
- **Lee Valley Outfitters**, *Greer, Tel. 520/735-7454*
- **Thunderhorse Ranch**, *Pinetop-Lakeside, Tel. 520/368-5593*

Skiing
Cross-country skiing is available throughout the **White Mountain trail system**. Downhill skiing is at the **Sunrise Ski Area**, *AZ 273 about halfway between Springerville and Pinetop-Lakeside, Tel. 520/735-7669.*

Swimming
- **Lyman Lake**, *AZ 180, south of St. Johns*
- **Snowflake Swimming Pool**, *AZ 77, north of Show Low, Tel.* 520/536-2160
- **Show Low Aquatic Family Fitness Center**, *Tel.* 520/537-2800

Tennis
- **Woodland Lake Park**, *Pinetop-Lakeside*

Water skiing
- **Lyman Lake**, *AZ 180, south of St. Johns*

PRACTICAL INFORMATION

- **Bus Depot**
  Holbrook, *Tel.* 520/524-3832
  Show Low, *Tel.* 520/537-4539
  Winslow, *Tel.* 520/289-2171

- **Hospitals**
  Show Low, *Tel.* 520/537-4375
  Springerville, *Tel.* 520/333-4368
  Winslow, *Tel.* 520/289-4691

- **Police** (non-emergency):
  Navajo Reservation (Navajo Tribal Police), *Chinle area, Tel.* 520/674-5291, or *Western part of Reservation, Tel.* 520/283-5242
  Hopi Reservation, *Tel.* 520/738-2233
  Springerville, *Tel.* 520/333-4240

- **Tourist Office/Visitors Bureau**
  Holbrook, *Tel.* 800/524-2459
  Navajo Nation, *Window Rock, Tel.* 520/871-6436
  Payson, *Tel.* 800/6-PAYSON
  Pinetop-Lakeside, *Tel.* 520/367-4290
  Round Valley, *Springerville/Eagar, Tel.* 520/333-2123

- **Train Station**
  Winslow Station, has no ticket office. Contact Amtrak, *Tel.* 800/USA-RAIL

17. THE SOUTHEAST
- UNEXPECTED DISCOVERIES -

Arizona's southeastern corner is, to most visitors, the land of the old west – cowboys and Indians, and boisterous boom towns from the mining days of the late 19th century. Certainly that is true and some of the region's famous attractions are based on that perception. But like all of Arizona it is wrong to try to fit a particular region into a single category. While my borders for the southeast take up a much smaller area than in the previous chapter, it is, nonetheless, an area of wonderful variety.

Tombstone is the best known of the frontier towns but such places as **Bisbee** and **Douglas** got their start in much the same way. The economies of some communities still rely heavily on the mining of precious minerals. The "glory" days of the U.S. Cavalry can be relived at places like Fort Huachuca. Straddling the Mexican border, the southeast is an area where the Mexican influence is still strong. So is that of Native Americans. Although there aren't any large Indian reservations, the remote canyons of the southeast provided great hiding places for the Apache and other tribes in their struggles against the inevitable tide of white settlers. Those same canyons today, besides being of historical interest, offer an opportunity to experience the southeast's other attraction – nature. Places like **Cave Creek Canyon** and the **Chiricahua National Monument**, largely unknown outside of Arizona, will delight you with their beauty as well as some unusual geologic formations.

Outdoor recreation and just finding a place in the sun also bring people to the southeast. Consisting mostly of high desert, the southeast offers warm summers (not nearly as hot as in, say, Phoenix) and comfortable winters. There's abundant sunshine throughout the year. There are also patches of higher elevations with forested mountains where winter can even bring some significant snowfalls and the summers can almost be classified as cool. So let's get started.

ARRIVALS & DEPARTURES

By Car

The southeast region is located within a short drive east of Tucson via I-10. That highway runs through the entire region to the New Mexico border, so you can get there directly from other states along the country's southern edge. Besides I-10 from Tucson and, hence, Phoenix and other points north and west, you can reach this corner of the state from the northeast region by taking US 191 south from the Springerville-Eagar area of the White Mountains. US 191 runs close to the state's eastern border and traverses some very nice scenery between the towns of Alpine and Clifton. This stretch is known as the Coronado Trail. US 191 then continues on through Safford, which is part of my southeastern itinerary, and on to I-40 so it provides good access to the entire region.

By Public Transportation

Public transportation into the area is kind of limited. You can easily get from Tucson to Tombstone but beyond that you'll have to rely on bus service to the larger towns. Many of the best sights aren't located that close to those towns so you still need a car unless you're taking guided tours. Amtrak does serve Benson.

ORIENTATION

The southeast region is only about 80 miles wide and a hundred miles from north to south (not counting a side excursion on the Coronado Trail), so it isn't too difficult to cover the entire region in a relatively modest amount of time. The major routes within the region are the same as the access roads – I-40 for east-to-west travel and US 191 for north-to-south travel. The only other significant road is AZ 80 which runs from Benson near the region's western edge, southeast through Tombstone and on to Douglas at the Mexican border. We'll be following a loop route that can be joined from either the west or east edges along I-10. There are also a couple of side trips for those who really want to explore in depth.

WHERE TO STAY

BENSON

Inexpensive

BEST WESTERN QUAIL HOLLOW INN, *699 North Ocotillo Street. Tel. 520/586-3646, Fax 520/586-7035. Toll free reservations Tel. 800/528-1234. 89 Rooms. Rates: $48-60 all year. Major credit cards accepted. Located at Exit 304 of I-10.*

Benson doesn't have too many motels considering that it's located on the Interstate. This is the best of the lot. Combining aspects of southwestern and ranch style architecture, the Quail Hollow features good sized rooms that are pleasingly decorated and comfortable. All rooms have coffee makers and most have refrigerators. The motel has a heated swimming pool and whirlpool. There isn't any restaurant on the premises but several are located within a short distance.

BISBEE
Moderate
COPPER QUEEN HOTEL, *11 Howell Street. Tel. 520/432-2216, Fax 520/432-4208. Toll free reservations Tel. 800/247-5829. 47 Rooms. Rates: $70-135 all year. Most major credit cards accepted. Located in the historic center of town just west of Brewery Gulch and a block north of Main Street.*

The Copper Queen is a small (some would say intimate) and charming historic hotel dating from the wildest days of Bisbee's boomtown era. The Mining Museum is practically in it's back yard. Each room is uniquely furnished in period and has been faithfully restored to its original appearance. A stay at the Copper Queen will be an experience from another era. The amenities and facilities aren't modern or even first class but it's quite comfortable and can be a lot of fun. Dining at the Copper Queen, however, is first-rate – see the description of their dining room in the *Where to Eat* section.

Inexpensive
BISBEE GRAND HOTEL, *61 Main Street. Tel. 520/432-5900. Toll free reservations Tel. 800/421-1909. 11 Rooms. Rates: $55-78 all year including full breakfast; suites are $95-200. American Express, Discover, MasterCard and VISA accepted. Located in the heart of downtown.*

Another charming historic property in the old part of town, the Bisbee Grand is actually a bed and breakfast facility consisting of eight nice sized antique filled rooms and three larger suites. Personalized service is the hallmark of this property. An old-time saloon is adjacent. Several restaurants are located within a short walk.

THE INN AT CASTLE ROCK, *112 Tombstone Canyon. Tel. 520/432-4449. Toll free reservations Tel. 800/566-4449. 16 Rooms. Rates: $55-90 all year including full breakfast. MasterCard and VISA accepted. Located on the route into town from AZ 80 just before the name changes to Main Street.*

We might as well make it three-for-three in Bisbee. By that I mean that the Inn at Castle Rock is another historic treasure. Situated on the edge of town, the three-story building (no elevator) is about as eclectic as you can get. The rooms (standard rooms in the lower price range and suites in the upper) are generally furnished with antiques and have such wonderful features as authentic wood burning fireplaces and separate seating areas. Public areas are equally marvelous and are highlighted by two large parlors where guests can shoot the breeze about the days' events or you can simply sit back in a plush leather chair and let your mind drift back a hundred years.

The Inn has a number of other nice touches both inside and out. There's a gallery of western art, a colorful garden covering almost an acre and a picturesque fish pond. A restaurant is on the premises.

SAFFORD
Inexpensive
BEST WESTERN DESERT INN, *1391 Thatcher Boulevard, Tel. 520/ 428-0521, Fax 520/428-7653. Toll free reservations Tel. 800/528-1234. 70 Rooms. Rates: $65-71 all year. Most major credit cards accepted. Located on US 70 a mile west of downtown and the junction with US 191.*

A typical modern two-story motor inn facility with clean and comfortable rooms. The decor features the light and natural shades of the southwest that are soft on the eyes. Accommodations are varied and include two bedroom units and suites (priced up to $80). All rooms have coffee makers and many have refrigerators. The motel has a heated swimming pool in season. There's a coffee shop located in a separate building on the same property.

SIERRA VISTA
Moderate
WINDMERE HOTEL AND CONFERENCE CENTER, *2047 South Highway 92. Tel. 520/459-5900, Fax 520/458-1347. Toll free reservations Tel. 800/825-4656. 149 Rooms. Rates: $76-96 all year including full breakfast. Major credit cards accepted. Located on AZ 92 about 1-1/2 miles south of the junction with AZ 90.*

The largest and most attractive lodging establishment in town, the Windmere is also the only one that provides many of the facilities and services that travelers often look for. The public areas are spacious and attractively decorated. Complimentary beverages are served to guests every evening. Guestrooms are oversized and decorated in a modern southwest motif that is quite pleasing. In-room amenities include coffee makers (all rooms), microwave ovens, and refrigerators. The included breakfast is buffet style and boasts a quite nice selection. There's a heated swimming pool and whirlpool facility.

Although the hotel doesn't have a health club or golf course, free privileges are extended to guests at facilities located only minutes away. Nickels' Restaurant is one of the best in Sierra Vista and is described in the *Where to Eat* section below.

Inexpensive

SIERRA SUITES, *391 East Fry Boulevard. Tel. 520/459-4221, Fax 520/459-8449. 100 Rooms. Rates; $61-77 all year including continental breakfast. Most major credit cards accepted. Located 2-1/2 miles west of the junction of Arizona highways 90 and 92.*

A modern southwestern style inn, the two story structure features rooms grouped around several small but pretty courtyards. The rooms are spacious and well decorated and all feature microwave and refrigerator. Considering all of that, and what hotels are charging these days, the price that Sierra Suites is asking practically has to be considered a steal. The inn has a heated swimming pool and whirlpool. Several restaurants are located close by.

THUNDER MOUNTAIN INN, *1631 South Highway 92. Tel. 520/458-7900, Fax 520/458-7900. Toll free reservations Tel. 800/222-5811. 102 Rooms. Rates: High season (mid-January to October 31st): $75; Low season (November 1st to mid-January): $60. Major credit cards accepted. Located on AZ 92 about one mile south of the junction with AZ 90.*

Here's another excellent value. Although Sierra Vista is almost an hour south of Tucson you could consider staying in this town if you want to save some bucks and don't mind extra driving. Getting back to Thunder Mountain, this is a nice and recently remodeled facility that offers good mountain views from some rooms. Those rooms are large and well furnished. Refrigerators are standard.

Many people visiting Sierra Vista go birding in adjacent riparian lands and often stay at Thunder Mountain. The inn offers birding packages and the knowledgeable staff provides weekly Audubon Society reports on bird sightings. They have a heated swimming pool and whirlpool. For dining you can select from an informal coffee shop or step up a notch to Baxter's, an attractive dining room featuring American cuisine.

TOMBSTONE

Accommodations are extremely limited. See also Sierra Vista.

Moderate

BEST WESTERN LOOKOUT LODGE, *AZ 80. Tel. 520/457-2223, Fax 520/457-3870. Toll free reservations Tel. 800/OK-CORRAL (direct to hotel) or Tel. 800/528-1234 (Best Western central reservations). 40 Rooms. Rates: High season (late December to late May): $66-85; Low season (late May to late December): $55-80, all rates including continental breakfast. Major credit cards accepted. Located on the main road into Tombstone about one mile north of the historic area.*

One of the newer lodging establishment in Tombstone (not that many have been built since the days of Wyatt Earp), this is an attractive property situated amid a desert landscape and located far enough away from the historic area to be private and quiet but close enough to be convenient to everything.

Boot Hill graveyard is, in fact, less than a quarter mile away. Some rooms provide good views of the nearby Dragoon Mountains. The accommodations are standard motel fare but that is about as good as you can get within Tombstone. The Lodge has a small heated swimming pool. Many restaurants are located within a short ride.

WILLCOX
Inexpensive

BEST WESTERN PLAZA INN, *1100 Rex Allen Drive. Tel. 520/384-3556, Fax 520/384-2679. Toll free reservations Tel. 800/528-1234. 92 Rooms. Rates: $69-79 all year including full breakfast. Major credit cards accepted. Located immediately south of I-10, Exit 340.*

The Plaza Inn is Willcox's fanciest lodging facility. That doesn't mean that it's a luxurious place. It is an attractive and modern motor inn with landscaped grounds around the large outdoor swimming pool. The guestrooms are spacious. Although they aren't anything special when it comes to decor they do have a number of amenities including coffee makers and refrigerators. Some of the higher priced rooms have Jacuzzi. One of the Plaza's best features is its fine restaurant, The Solarium, which is listed separately in the *Where to Eat* section.

DESERT BREEZE MOTEL, *556 North Haskell Avenue. Tel. 520/384-4636. 29 Rooms. Rates: $25-45 all year. Major credit cards accepted. Located in the center of town. From the interstate highway follow Business Loop I-10.*

The Desert Breeze is a decent place that doesn't do anything for me but, at these prices, is almost impossible to ignore. Also, the pickings get quite slim after The Plaza Inn. There are no recreational facilities here but the rooms have just about everything you expect from a motel. Considering the number of rooms the accommodations are quite varied. There are rooms with king or queen beds, some have refrigerators, even several with kitchenettes.

Being on one of the two main streets in town makes it convenient to several restaurants.

CAMPING & RV SITES
- **Chief Four Feathers KOA**, *Ocotillo Road, 1 mile north of I-10 Exit 304, Benson, Tel. 520/586-3977*
- **Chiricahua National Monument Campground**, *On Highway 181, Tel. 520/824-3560*
- **Lifestyle RV Resort**, *622 N. Haskell Avenue, Willcox, Tel. 520/384-3303*
- **Roper Lake State Park**, *US 191, Safford, Tel. 520/428-6760*

- **Queen Mine RV Park,** *Highway 80, Bisbee. Tel. 520/432-5006*
- **Tombstone KOA,** *1 mile north on AZ 80, Tombstone, Tel. 520/457-3829*

WHERE TO EAT
BISBEE
Moderate

CAFE ROKA, *35 Main Street. Tel. 520/432-5153. MasterCard and VISA accepted. Dinner served nightly. Open only on Friday and Saturday evenings from June through August. Reservations are suggested.*

It seems that almost everything in Bisbee is located in an historic building and the Cafe Roka is no exception. Next door to the Historical Society Museum, the Cafe occupies the first floor of a three-story 1907 commercial building. All of the varied entrees are expertly prepared, often using only natural seasonings found in Arizona. The cuisine ranges from southwestern to Italian and even includes several vegetarian dishes. Cocktails are served. The Cafe Roka doesn't have a parking lot but it usually isn't too difficult to find an on-street spot within close proximity.

COPPER QUEEN DINING ROOM, *11 Howell Street, in the Copper Queen Hotel. Tel. 520/432-2216. Most major credit cards accepted. Breakfast, lunch, and dinner served daily.*

The old-time flavor of the Copper Queen Hotel continues with the Victorian decor of this wonderful little restaurant. During warmer weather the patio dining area is open and that has as much atmosphere as the interior. Entrees are strictly American with an emphasis on western beef and steak dishes. Warm and efficient service. Cocktails are served and there is a children's menu.

EL COBRE RESTAURANT AND LOUNGE, *1002 Naco Highway, in the San Jose Lodge just off of AZ 92. Tel. 520/432-7703. Major credit cards accepted. Breakfast, lunch, and dinner served daily.*

This is technically in San Jose and not in Bisbee but it's only a couple of miles west of the Lowell Circle at the end of Bisbee. El Cobre features outstanding Mexican entrees, all prepared in an authentic manner (no Tex-Mex type influence). Some American cuisine is also available if someone in your party isn't into Mexican. Cocktails are served.

SAFFORD
Moderate

CASA MANANA, *502 1st Avenue. Tel. 520/428-3170. American Express, Discover, MasterCard, and VISA accepted. Lunch and dinner served Monday through Saturday, lunch only on Sunday.*

This is an excellent authentic Mexican restaurant that has been in business for more than 45 years so they must be doing something right.

The atmosphere is casual and the service friendly and efficient. The food isn't overly spicy nor are the prices. Cocktail service.

SIERRA VISTA
Moderate
THE MESQUITE TREE RESTAURANT, *6398 South Highway 92. Tel. 520/378-2758. American Express, Discover, MasterCard, and VISA accepted. Dinner only served nightly. Reservations are suggested.*

This is a popular restaurant even though it's located a few miles south of the main part of town. An efficient and friendly staff serves up sizable portions of delicious western oriented entrees such as barbecued fish and chicken, mesquite grilled steaks, and prime rib. A few pasta dishes round out the menu. Guests can dine either in the attractive indoor room or, during warmer weather, on the outdoor patio. The Mesquite Tree features full cocktail service and a separate lounge.

NICKELS' RESTAURANT, *2047 South Highway 92, in the Windmere Hotel. Tel. 520/459-6870. Major credit cards accepted. Breakfast, lunch, and dinner served daily.*

The decor at Nickels' is an interesting and colorful mix of southwestern and contemporary styles that is both bright and cheerful enough to get your day off to a sunshine start or to ensure a casual but enjoyable dinner. The menu is American and diverse enough to include something for just about everyone – beef, fish, chicken, and salads. Nickels' has a children's menu, cocktail service, and lounge.

TOMBSTONE
Moderate
LONGHORN RESTAURANT, *Southeast corner of 5th and Allen Streets. Tel. 520/457-3405. Most major credit cards accepted. Breakfast, lunch, and dinner served daily.*

Housed in a nineteenth century building in the heart of historic Tombstone, the Longhorn fits perfectly into its surroundings. Actually, with its western themed decor it would be as appropriate for Texas as it is for Arizona. They serve a wide selection of American, Mexican, and Italian dishes although it's best known for the excellent pork ribs. The Longhorn is super casual and well suited for family dining. Alcoholic beverages are served.

NELLIE CASHMAN'S RESTAURANT, *Northwest corner of 5th and Toughnut Streets. Tel. 520/457-2212. American Express, MasterCard, and VISA accepted. Lunch and dinner served nightly.*

Most of the many restaurants in Tombstone feature both western food and atmosphere. Nellie Cashman's has some of that but also includes elements of a finer dining experience without the stiff service or prices so often associated with better restaurants. This is a large restaurant that occupies a building dating back to 1879 and it has plenty of authentic period pieces. The food is what I would term "family American," nothing fancy but lot's of well prepared favorites. Cocktail service.

Inexpensive
MS. CLANTON COFFEE AND NATURAL JUICE COMPANY, *Southwest corner of 2nd and Allen Streets. No credit cards. Breakfast and lunch served daily.*

This is a great place to stop for a lunch break during a busy afternoon of sight seeing in Tombstone. It's located on the western edge of the historic area (where you'll likely be parked), and serves a large variety of sandwiches and hot soups. During breakfast they feature the best muffins in town and plenty of other fresh baked goodies as well as great coffee. Ms. Clanton remains open into the evening but the menu remains lunch oriented so it's only good for dinner if you're looking for something light.

WILLCOX
Moderate
SAXON HOUSE, *308 South Haskell Avenue. Tel. 520/384-4478. MasterCard and VISA accepted. Dinner only served Wednesday through Sunday. Reservations are suggested.*

The Saxon House occupies an 1916 Willcox home that has been extensively restored. The small dining rooms are intimate and attractive, the service attentive and friendly. The menu isn't large but features a good selection of American and continental cuisine with prime rib being the specialty of the house. The chef also prepares a daily special that your server will be happy to tell you about. Cocktail service and bar.

SOLARIUM DINING ROOM, *1100 Rex Allen Drive, in the Best Western Plaza Inn. Major credit cards accepted. Breakfast, lunch, and dinner served daily. Buffet on Sunday.*

A modern looking facility with one side a big glass wall that looks out on the nicely landscaped courtyard, the Solarium is filled with potted and hanging plants. The atmosphere is bright and cheerful. The menu features American and southwestern cuisine, with steaks and seafood being the staples. They also have a good salad bar. Full cocktail service.

Inexpensive
CACTUS KITCHEN RESTAURANT, *706 South Haskell Avenue. Tel. 520/384-3857. Most major credit cards accepted. Breakfast, lunch, and dinner served daily except on Sunday when only breakfast and lunch are served.*

This is a decent family style restaurant that features better than average food in a comfortable dining room. You can't go wrong for the money even with some of the selections going into the moderate price range. The menu features both southwestern and Mexican entrees. The Cactus Kitchen has an excellent salad bar.

SEEING THE SIGHTS

Sierra Vista & Tombstone

Our trip through the southeast begins at Exit 302 of I-10 at the town of **Benson**. (This is a distance of only 45 miles from central Tucson.) The town has long been an important transportation hub for the region. The remains of the impressive adobe **Butterfield Stage Depot** are still visible. A pleasant ride awaits those who book passage on the four-hour **San Pedro & Southwestern Railroad**. This excursion will take you alongside the San Pedro River through a diverse area that features unspoiled riparian lands, old ghost and mining towns, the scenic **Charleston Narrows Canyon**, as well as views of mountains near and afar. A western style barbecue lunch is available at additional cost. On some holidays and special events the regularly scheduled departures are replaced by special holiday and theme trains, usually at a higher price. *The depot is at 796 East Country Club Drive. Adult fare is $28, seniors pay $25, and children get on for $19. A family plan for two adults and up to four children is priced at $88. Credit cards. Departures are as follows: October through April – Thursday through Sunday at 11:00am; May through September – Friday at 4:00pm and Saturday at 10:00am and 4:00pm. Tel. 800/269-6314. Reservations are recommended. Always call to confirm departure time.*

Leave Benson via AZ 90 (reached via Exit 302 of I-10) and head south. Nine miles later you'll reach the newest member of the Arizona State Park system–**Kartchner Caverns State Park**. This large system of beautiful limestone caves was first discovered at the end of 1974 but was kept secret for 14 years. It first opened to the public in November 1999. All of this time was used to prepare the caverns for visitors in such a way as to minimize the impact of man on the delicate and pristine environment. In fact, in no other cave in the world have such extraordinary measures been taken. This not only took a long time but also explains why the admission price to tour the caverns is so high – perhaps too high for many family budgets.

The park's **Discovery Center** explains the geology of the cave, its bat residents as well as the development of visitor facilities. Hour-long guided tours of the cave are the only way to gain access and begin from the center (no flash photography or video recording allowed inside the cave.) Hiking trails on the surface provide good views of the San Pedro River Valley. Within the caves are more than two miles of passages. Highlights include two rooms that are more than a hundred feet high and longer than a football field. **Kubla Kahn** is one of the most notable formations and has the distinction of being the tallest cave column in Arizona. All of the cave walks are well lighted, paved and not overly strenuous. *The park is open year round and cave tours are offered from 8:00am until 6:00pm except Christmas. Reservations are strongly suggested and can be made up to one year in advance. There is a $10 daily use fee per vehicle to enter the park. Cave tours cost an additional $14 for everyone age 14 and up and $6 for ages 7 through 13. Tel. 520/586-CAVE.*

Upon leaving the cave, continue south on AZ 90 as it passes through a verdant valley and the **Fort Huachuca** military reservation on a 20-mile journey to the town of **Sierra Vista**.

The town of Sierra Vista's pretty setting is one of it's prime attractions. It sits on the lower slopes of the Huachuca Mountains and overlooks the San Pedro River Valley. However, the activity that brings the greatest number of visitors is Sierra Vista's status as one of the best bird watching areas in the entire nation. More than 400 different species of birds have been documented and although many of them are seasonal, you'll easily find over a hundred types at any particular time of the year.

Surprising to many visitors to this part of Arizona are the large number of natural areas with diverse bird life. Both first-timers and experienced bird watchers can do no better than by visiting the **San Pedro Riparian Conservation Area**, which extends some 30 miles parallel to AZ 80. It is crossed by AZ 82 in the north and AZ 90 in the south. The latter passes through Sierra Vista and links up with AZ 82 so you can drive around the area in sort of a loop. It has been designated by the respected Nature Conservancy as one of the "last great places" to view many species of birds. There's a visitor center that provides information on trails that cross the area and provide excellent viewing places. Depending upon your level of interest in birds, a visit can be completed in under an hour or can take all day. *Open daily during daylight hours; visitor center open from 8:00am until 5:00pm. Admission is free. Tel. 520/458-6940.*

Located within the Conservation Area (about three miles off of AZ 82 following signs) is the **Santa Cruz de Terrenate Presidio National Historic Site**. Quite a mouthful, but also quite interesting, the fort was built to protect settlers from Apache raids. It was never fully completed and the site is in a mostly ruined state. Perhaps that makes it even more interesting. A dirt trail about 1-1/4 miles in length takes visitors through the area. Because of the fragile condition of the presidio, visitors are asked to refrain from touching anything. There are no facilities at the site. *Open daylight hours; no admission charge.*

About three miles west of Sierra Vista is the headquarters area for the 73,000 acre **Fort Huachuca**. The fort is the oldest active cavalry post in the nation and many of the buildings date from the 19th century. Today the fort serves, among other things, as the headquarters for the U.S. Army

Intelligence Center, and is the biggest single employer in southern Arizona. Of special interest to visitors is the **Fort Huachuca Museum**, *open weekdays from 9:00am to 4:00pm and on weekends from 1:00 to 4:00pm, closed on all national holidays; admission is free; Tel. 520/533-5736*, which traces the history of the U.S. Army throughout the southwest. Allow about a half hour for your visit. Proceed 3-1/2 miles northwest of the Main Gate to Boyd and Garrison Avenues. You must obtain a pass at the gate. In order to obtain a pass you have to present your driver's license, vehicle registration, and proof of insurance coverage.

The major attraction south of Sierra Vista is the **Coronado National Memorial** which can be reached by taking AZ 92 for about 17 miles and then following a signed road for an additional five miles. The Memorial is located on the United States-Mexican border and was created to commemorate the 1540 expedition of **Francisco Vasquez de Coronado**.

As I have mentioned on several previous occasions, the 1,400-man expedition failed in its five month attempt to find the Seven Cities of Cibola. However, they did discover many Pueblos as well as the Grand Canyon and helped pave the way for further exploration and, ultimately, colonization. The Memorial is one of the region's excellent bird watching locales as well as a home for many types of wildlife such as bobcats. Covered with yucca and several types of cactus, the Memorial has an outstanding view of the region from a parking area at the Montezuma Pass. The pass is located about three miles from the visitor center, which contains exhibits on the Coronado expedition as well as the area's flora and fauna. Wildlife can also be viewed from the visitor center.

The Memorial contains good hiking trails for those who don't wish to ride. **Coronado Cave** has two chambers connected by a narrow passageway. It is reached by a steep three-quarter mile trail from the visitor center. The cave is in its natural state and is not recommended for those who haven't done at least some real spelunking. *The memorial's visitor center is open daily from 8:00am to 5:00pm except for Thanksgiving and Christmas. There is no admission charge. Tel. 520/366-5515.*

The next important destination is **Tombstone**. The best way to reach it from Sierra Vista is to return north on AZ 90 for approximately ten miles to the junction of AZ 82. Take that road west for 16 miles to AZ 80. About four miles southeast on that road will bring you into Tombstone. The town of Tombstone is one of Arizona's most popular tourist destinations. It is filled with history and is fun for all ages. It appears much the same as it did in the 1880's when it was one of the most famous (infamous would be more correct) of the wild west's mining communities. Today the entire town has been designated as a National Historic Landmark.

Almost every building has an interesting history associated with it and, because the town is only a few blocks long and wide, can easily be seen on a half to full day walking tour. Almost all of the attractions (as well as services) are located within an eight-square block area from 3rd to 6th Streets and bounded by Fremont Street on the north, and Toughnut Street on the south. Many of the historic buildings within this area have been converted into shops and restaurants.

As you drive into town on AZ 80 you'll first encounter **Boot Hill**, the final resting place of more than 250 Tombstone residents, many of them notorious criminals that include those killed in the shoot-out at the O.K. Corral. Most of the graves have been authenticated and date from 1879 through 1884. Some of the headstones have humorous sayings on them, making this one of the few graveyards you'll likely be laughing in as you walk through. While many old west towns have their own Boot Hill, this was the first one to be so named. Adjacent to the entrance is a large gift shop. *The site is open every day of the year from 7:30am to 6:00pm. There is no entrance fee but donations are appreciated. Tel. 520/457-9344.*

THE TOWN TOO TOUGH TO DIE

Tombstone's official slogan is more truth than advertising. It has had a difficult history but has managed to outlast most other towns with similar origins. The name of the town comes from the tale told by the prospector and town founder, **Ed Schieffelin.** *It seems that soldiers from nearby Fort Huachuca told him that he was more likely to find his own tombstone than silver. But he did find a rich vein of silver in 1877 that turned a small camp into a major boomtown almost overnight. The settlers who followed decided that Tombstone would be an appropriate name.*

Unfortunately, the silver mines brought with it an era of lawlessness and violence that took the lives of many people, both innocent and otherwise. The famous shoot-out at the **O.K. Corral** *marked the beginning of the end for that era. Gunmen weren't the only perils which faced the good town folk of Tombstone. Rising waters in the mines caused cessation of operations on several different occasions. Fire almost completely destroyed the town on another occasion. Despite these hardships the people of Tombstone refused to give up. Each time they rebuilt their town, reopened the mine and continued to earn their livelihood from the riches of nature.*

Ultimately it was water in the mine that would end the search for silver for good. However, even that failed to destroy Tombstone. Many other mining communities throughout Arizona and the southwest were to become ghost towns. Tombstone didn't. It picked up on its already widespread reputation and turned the entire community into a historic attraction. You'll be glad they did because Tombstone is a fascinating place to visit.

AZ 80 runs into Fremont Street where you should find the most convenient place to park your car. Now let's begin our walking tour of historic Tombstone. While I'm only going to describe Tombstone's major sights, keep in mind that every building within the historic area is vintage old west and worth taking a brief look at, even if it's only from the outside.

Most of the streets remain unpaved and the "sidewalks" are an old western style boardwalk. Hitching posts also remain in place. Proceed one block south of Fremont to Allen Street. Two attractions are located adjacent to one another between 3rd and 4th Streets. The first one is the **O.K. Corral**, the location of America's most famous western gunfight. The town's livery stable had a large open area out back where, on October 26, 1881, **Wyatt Earp** and his brother deputies shot it out with members of the Clanton gang. Life size figures show where each participant stood during the well documented encounter. (Live recreations of the fight also take place – see the information at the end of the walking tour description.)

Also at the Corral is the **Camillus Fly Studio** which recreates the frontier studio of a major western photographer. Many photographs of early Tombstone are on display. Next door to the Corral and Studio is the **Historama**. Actor Vincent Price provides a taped narration of Tombstone's colorful history while visitors watch that history being recreated before them on a large revolving animated diorama. *The combined admission for the Corral, Fly Studio, and Historama is $5 for adults, $2.50 for children. The Historama alone is $2 as is the Corral/Studio. Hours of operation of the Corral are daily from 8:30am to 5:00pm. Historama shows are given on the hour, every day of the year from 9:00am until 4:00pm. The telephone number for all these attractions is Tel. 520/457-3456.*

At the corner of 4th Street turn left and return to Fremont Street, then turn right. Across the street is **Schieffelin Hall**, named for **Ed Schieffelin**, the prospector who founded Tombstone. It is one of the biggest adobe structures in the state and is the site for community meetings and other events. Continue on Fremont to 5th Street and turn right. Off the corner are the offices of the *Tombstone Epitaph*. The newspaper is the oldest continually published paper in Arizona. You can view some interesting free exhibits on the paper and town in the office lobby during regular business hours.

Next door to the Epitaph offices is one of Tombstone's most famous saloons – the **Crystal Palace**, *Tel. 520/457-3611.* Meticulously restored to its 1880 appearance, the Crystal Palace was the place to be if you were anyone in Tombstone. It was one of the most elaborate and luxurious saloons in all of the west, a sure indication of the wealth that flowed through the town's streets during its heyday. The Palace is still a saloon.

At the corner of Allen Street turn to the left and proceed not quite to 6th Street. The **Bird Cage Theater** is, except for the O.K. Corral, Tombstone's best known structure. It was built in 1881 and almost everything inside is original. More than a theater, the Bird Cage was also another of Tombstone's many saloons as well as a dance hall where lonely miners and others could find comfort in the arms of ladies of the night. It had a reputation for being one of the wildest establishments in all of the west, with some of its patrons winding up on Boot Hill.

The name comes from the 14 compartments suspended from the ceiling above the gambling hall. It was from these cages that the ladies plied their trade. It was from this spot that the words to the refrain of "Only a Bird in A Gilded Cage" come from. The quality of the entertainment was high because the owners could afford to bring in famous acts from all over the world. French Can Can dancers were a popular attraction. If you do only one thing in Tombstone, do enter the Bird Cage Theater and take a tour. *The theater is open every day from 8:00am until 6:00pm. Admission is $4.50 for adults, $3.50 for senior citizens, and $2.25 for children under 18, family rate of $11. Tel. 520/457-3421.*

Now you can walk back on Allen Street to the intersection of 4th Street and turn right. Near the end of the block by Toughnut Street is the **Rose Tree Inn**. This is a historical museum but the main feature is the world's largest rosebush. It covers more than 8,000 square feet and is listed in the Guiness Book. It was planted from a Scottish seedling in 1885 and has been doing nicely ever since. You can even purchase rose slips – perhaps you'll soon have a record setter, too. *Open daily from 9:00am until 5:00pm except for Christmas Day; admission is $2 for ages 14 and older, children under 14 are admitted for free; Tel. 520/457-3326.*

Take a left onto Toughnut Street and go past 3rd Street to our final stop, the **Tombstone Courthouse State Historic Park**. Constructed in 1882, the brick building has exhibits on both Tombstone and surrounding Cochise County. Many visitors are more impressed with the yard that contains the frequently used gallows. *Open daily from 8:00am to 5:00pm except for Christmas; admission is $2 for adults and $1 for children ages 12 through 17; Tel. 520/457-3311.*

Reenactments are a part of Tombstone. The most popular, of course, is the **shoot-out at the O.K. Corral**. It takes place at 2:00pm on the first and third Sundays of each month. The **Tombstone Vigilantes** put on their show at the **Helldorado Amphitheater**, *4th and Toughnut Streets*, on the Sundays when the O.K. Corral doesn't have it's fight. An 1880s fashion show is included in the latter. The Amphitheater is the place for the **Boothill Gunslingers** to stage their show, every Monday through Saturday at 2:00pm. Another popular diversion is to take a horse drawn tour of Old Tombstone by **stage coach**. Tours leave frequently from along Allen Street. For information, call *Tel. 520/457-3018.*

More Mining Towns & The Chiricahua National Monument

Leave Tombstone by continuing on AZ 80 for 24 miles to **Bisbee**. With the discovery of the **Copper Queen Lode** during the 1880's, Bisbee became one of the largest towns between St. Louis and San Francisco. Today there are about 6,500 residents. Although most mining operations have ceased, the miners of the Bisbee area brought out more than two billion dollars worth of copper and silver, as well as gold, zinc, and lead from the **Mule Mountains** which surround the town. In fact, you'll travel through the Mule Pass Tunnel on AZ 80 just before reaching town.

From there, Tombstone Canyon Road leads directly onto Main Street. All of the attractions of Bisbee are located within a limited area on or just off of Main. The Main Street area is also the place to go shopping for antiques, souvenirs, and gifts as well as to find a place to eat. While Tombstone is almost entirely an historic tourist site, Bisbee combines a visit to the past with a thriving modern community. It is picturesquely located in the mountain shadows. Like Tombstone, it's best to see most of Bisbee on foot. A tour of about two to three hours will enable you to take in most of the in-town sights but not the mines.

Upon passing through the tunnel get onto Tombstone Canyon Road. Take a brief look at the **Historic Courthouse**. Public parking in Bisbee is available in several lots located at each end of Main Street and off of Shearer Street in the center of town. A good place to start your walking tour is at the **Historical Society Museum**, *37 Main Street*, where many exhibits trace the history of Bisbee. Hours vary and admission is free.

Of greater interest and significance is the **Bisbee Mining and Historical Museum**, located just a few blocks further down Main Street at the intersection of Brewery Gulch. The displays here also document the entire history of the town, with an emphasis on mining. One exhibit will enable you to see what it was like to work in the mines during the old days. *The museum is open daily from 10:00am to 4:00pm except for New Year's and Christmas. Admission is $3 for adults, $2.50 for senior citizens, and free for those 18 and under. Tel. 520/432-7071.*

Now walk up the street called **Brewery Gulch**. The name, of course, comes from the fact that there was a brewery built there to supply the drinking needs of the local populace. It still stands, along with a number of other shops and restaurants. At the end of Brewery Gulch on the other side of the intersection of Youngblood Street is the **Muheim Heritage House**. Another of Bisbee's historical museums, this one is housed in the 1898 home of Joseph and Carmelia Muheim, a Swiss immigrant who made his fortune in Bisbee by establishing the brewery, taking part in mining and real estate investments. The house, which was enlarged several times, served as the family residence until as recently as 1975. It was restored several years later and now offers guided tours of the interior which is decorated in period furniture. The house itself is situated on a hill that overlooks Bisbee. In fact, it's probably the best place to get a good view of Bisbee and the surrounding area. *Open only from Friday through Monday; hours are 10:00am to 4:00pm; $2 donation is suggested.*

The remaining sights of Bisbee are best reached by car. Along AZ 80 at the south end of town is the well known **Queen Mine**. Former miners conduct 1-1/4 hour tours on an old mine car into an underground copper mine. Old mining techniques are demonstrated on this interesting adventure. Temperatures in the mine are cool so a sweater or light jacket is advisable at any time of the year. *Tours leave daily (except for Thanksgiving and Christmas) at 9:00am, 10:30am, noon, 2:00pm, and 3:30pm. Admission is $10 for adults, $3.50 for children 7 through 11, and $2 for ages 3 through 6. Credit cards. Reservations are suggested. Tel. 520/432-2071.*

For a different perspective on copper mining you might want to take the **Surface Mine and Historic District Van Tour**. The highlight of the tour is a view of a former copper mining pit that measured more than a mile in length and width and was about 950 feet deep. In all more than 40 million tons of copper worth in excess of $25 million was recovered from this site. Despite the fact that such a big chunk of the earth has been removed, there's something beautiful about what remains. Even if you don't particularly find that beauty, it's still an impressive sight. The 1-1/4 hour tour covers 11 miles. Tour times are the same as for the Queen Mine. You can also view the surface mine without taking the surface tour. An overlook from AZ 80 crosses a corner of the vast pit. *$7 per person; reservations are also suggested; Tel. 520/432-2071.*

Before leaving the Bisbee area you might want to take a six mile detour south of Bisbee (via Arizona Street just past the Lowell traffic circle at the intersection of AZ 80 and AZ 92) to the **Arizona Cactus Botanical Garden**. You can stroll around the attractive garden or take a guided tour and learn about the many different types of cactus that are found throughout Arizona. *Open daily from sunrise to sunset; admission is free.*

Continue on AZ 80 after Bisbee for about 25 miles to the border community of **Douglas**. Another historic mining town, Douglas also is known as a center for ranching. Of interest is the interior of the **1906 Gadsden Hotel**, *1046 G Avenue*. The lobby has a beautiful stained glass mural and a gracefully curving staircase. If you have a couple of hours you might consider taking a 16-mile long side trip (one way) via 15th Street (which becomes the **Geronimo Trail**) to the **Slaughter Ranch Museum**. Purchased in 1884 by a former Texas Ranger who became sheriff of Cochise County, the ranch is preserved as it was at the turn of the century.

The richness of the house is of primary interest although many other ranch buildings can also be explored. *Open from Wednesday through Sunday from 10:00am until 3:00pm. Admission is $3 for adults. The road to the ranch is not passable during or after heavy rain. Tel. 520/558-2474.*

From Douglas travel north on US 191 for about 40 miles to AZ 181. Turn right and follow that road for 22 miles to one of Arizona's most beautiful but relatively unknown natural wonders – the **Chiricahua National Monument**. Situated in the Chiricahua Mountains, the area is known as the "Wonderland of Rocks." The mountains rise sharply from the surrounding arid lowlands and provide a haven for many types of wildlife. It was also a haven for man – the Chiricahua Apache used it as a place to hide from the U.S. Cavalry and launch attacks on nearby white settlements (see the sidebar below).

Besides beautiful mountain scenery, Chiricahua's gray rocks often take unusual shapes and form ranging from the sublime to almost grotesque. Many of the park's best features can be seen from the **Scenic**

LEGENDARY INDIANS: COCHISE & GERONIMO

The area around Chiricahua was a hiding place for these two famous Indian chiefs. Many of us have, unfortunately, grown up with the idea of the good cowboys being harassed by the bad Indians. That, however, is strictly history by the victor. While Americans deplore the aggressive acts of other nations both now and in the past, what we did to the Native Americans was as close to genocide as you can get. Cochise, Geronimo and others like them weren't villains – they were heroes trying only to protect their own people against a foreign invader.

__Cochise__ (around 1815-74) was a Chiricahua Apache chief. Originally friendly to the white settlers he turned against them in 1862 after the massacre of innocent tribe members. He led a brilliant series of attacks against the settlers for a period of almost ten years. After the Civil War, when the cavalry was able to devote more strength to the Indian wars, he was finally forced to surrender in 1871. However, he escaped when he learned that his people were to be moved to a distant reservation. He surrendered again about a year later.

__Geronimo__ (1829-1909), another Chiricahua Apache, saw his family killed by Mexicans in 1858 and then undertook a series of raids against both Mexicans and Americans. His career closely resembles that of Cochise – fighting for many years and finally surrendering but then renewing the fight upon learning of the unacceptable terms to be imposed by the Americans. Geronimo, in his retirement years, did slowly became a hero to many people. He even visited Washington.

Drive, a good eight mile long one-way trip to the crest of the mountain. The rise in elevation from the entrance is almost 2,000 feet but the road shouldn't present any problem even for relatively inexperienced mountain drivers. Stop at the visitor center near the monument entrance for information on ranger talks and other activities. There are quite a few pullouts along the road where you can pause to get a better look at some of the more unusual formations. These include the **Organ Pipe Rocks**, **Sea Captain**, and **China Boy**. Once you see them it won't take much imagination to see why they have those names. At the end of the road is **Massai Point** from which there is a fabulous panorama of tree covered mountains and huge rock formations.

Also in the monument is the **Faraway Ranch**, a little more than a mile past the visitor center. The Ranch is a restored homestead originally built in 1888. It was both a cattle ranch as well as a guest ranch for early visitors to the area. Guided tours are given.

Those with the time or inclination for further exploration can set out on the monument's more than 20 miles of improved trails. A series of trails from Massai Point will take you to a wild area of formations that includes the **Punch and Judy, Duck on a Rock, Pinnacle Balanced Rock,** and **Big Balanced Rock**. A shorter trail is the **Echo Canyon Loop Trail** that descends into a narrow canyon. You can get a brochure at the visitor center that details each off the trails. They range in length from about a quarter of a mile to more than nine miles.

If you're only going to be traveling Scenic Drive and take in the overlooks and maybe some short trails, you can see Chiricahua in about two to three hours. However, you can spend a full day or even more if you are going to challenge some of the longer trails. *The monument is open at all times, although the visitor center is only open from 8:00am to 5:00pm (except Christmas). Admission is $6 per car for those not holding a park service passport. Tel. 520/824-3560.*

If you're an experienced mountain driver you might be interested in taking the unpaved road from near the monument entrance to **Cave Creek Canyon**, a one-way distance of about 15 miles. En route is some spectacular mountain scenery and Cave Creek is a lush oasis with colorful red rock walls. Allow at least 2-1/2 hours for this side trip. Four-wheel drive and a high clearance vehicle are helpful but not mandatory. Don't attempt the road in bad weather or after heavy rain.

After visiting Chiricahua take AZ 181 back eight miles to he intersection of AZ 186. That road leads to the town of Willcox, a distance of about 35 miles.

Near the I-10 Corridor

Willcox began as a commercial center for the many surrounding ranching operations. It still retains that function and now has about 3,500 residents. The town's cowboy past has not been forgotten. Nor has its long-standing history of struggle with the Native Americans. Two interesting attractions in those categories are located a distance from town and one is somewhat difficult to reach. However, they are easier to do so if you are arriving in town by my suggested route on AZ 186.

The first one would be the **Fort Bowie National Historic Site**, which was established in 1862 to protect the **Butterfield Stage route** from attacks by the Apache in the vicinity of the **Apache Pass**. The pass was known as the "Puerto del Dado" or Pass of Chance by the Spaniards.

A visit to the site will reveal the uncomfortable reality faced by the soldiers in this isolated and dangerous outpost. To reach Fort Bowie take the graded road off of AZ 186 (25 miles southeast of Willcox or 9 miles northwest of the junction of AZ 181 if coming from the Chiricahua National Monument). The final mile to the fort is by a foot trail. Including the walk to and from the parking area, you should plan on spending at least 90 minutes visiting Fort Bowie. *The site is open daily from 8:00am to 5:00pm except Christmas. There is no admission charge. Tel. 520/847-2500.*

The second attraction is located right on AZ 186 about 15 miles from Willcox. The **Dos Cabezas Ghost Town** has only a few buildings remaining from the frontier days. If you stop to explore some of the structures more closely exercise caution as they aren't in the best of condition.

Within Willcox are two fine historical museums. The **Cochise Visitor Center and Museum** was formerly known as the Museum of the Southwest. On display are excellent examples of Indian pottery and tools, an exhibit showing what life was like in an Apache village, and a beautiful bust of Cochise with some of his sayings. The sayings are interesting because they reflect some of the differences in thinking between the Apaches and the white settlers. Other exhibits pertain to the history of the Butterfield Stage Line and the U.S. Cavalry's role in the area's development. There's a good gift shop located on the premises. Give yourself at least 30 minutes to visit the museum. *1500 Circle I Road, just off of the intersection of AZ 186 and I-10, open daily from 9:00am to 5:00pm except on Sunday when it closes at 1:00pm; no admission charge; Tel. 520/384-2272.*

The other good museum is the **Rex Allen Arizona Cowboy Museum**. Take Haskell Avenue, which is Business I-10, from either Exit 336 or 344 of I-10 to Maley Street. Go one block south to Railroad Avenue and turn left to the museum. Mr. Allen was born in Willcox in 1920 and starred in 19 movies during the early 1950s as well as in television shows. (His son is a country-western singer who appears in Las Vegas and other Western cities.) *155 Railroad Avenue, open daily from 10:00am to 4:00pm except for*

New Year's Day, Thanksgiving, and Christmas; admission is $2 per person or $3 for a couple, a family rate of $5 is also available; Tel. 520/384-4583.

The museum is housed in an adobe building dating from the early 1890s and, among other things, once served as a saloon. Outside is a larger than life bronze statue of Rex, reached by a walkway imprinted with the brands of several local ranches. The museum's first gallery documents the life and career of Rex Allen while the other gallery features exhibits on the pioneers that paved the way out west. Emphasis is on local ranching history. Also within the museum is the **Willcox Cowboy Hall of Fame.** The thrust of the exhibit is to contrast the real life of frontier cowboys and ranchers with how they have been depicted in the movies. You should plan on spending about 45 minutes here.

A different type of diversion available in Willcox is to pick apples, peppers, melons, corn, and other fruits or vegetables from area farms located off of Fort Grant Road. Check with the visitor center adjacent to Exit 340 of I-10 for what's in season, which farms allow harvesting, and any restrictions. Fort Grant Road begins to the west of the interstate right by the visitor center.

From Willcox we'll be taking a slight detour to the north. However, if you are short of time you can skip this section without missing anything of super importance. Take I-10 east to Exit 352 and then follow US 191 north for about 35 miles to the town of Safford and its neighboring community of Thatcher. **Safford** is another agricultural and ranching town. It is also known for the presence of several hot springs that supposedly have beneficial effects. If you're interested in bathing at one of the area's spas, contact the local Chamber of Commerce, *Tel. 520/428-2511.*

Another activity popular with some is **rockhounding.** Surrounding areas have several types of semi-precious stones. The roads into these areas are often difficult. Four-wheel drive is highly advisable. For information on rockhounding and how to reach the best spots you should contact the local office of the Bureau of Land Management, *Tel. 520/428-4040* or visit them at their office at *711 14th Avenue, Safford.* **Roper Lake State Park,** six miles south of town on US 191, has a host of outdoor recreational facilities. *There is a $4 vehicle admission charge; Tel. 520/428-6760.*

A relatively new addition to the Safford touring scene is the outstanding **Discovery Park,** a multi-discipline science center and park that deals with a variety of physical and natural sciences that looks as if it's going to only get even better. A project of the Mount Graham International Science and Culture Foundation, at the present time only the astronomy section (which opened in the fall of 1995) has been completed. Its exhibits showcase the origins of the universe and methods used to produce telescopes but the highlight is a "ride" through outer space on a 12-

passenger motion simulator that is both educational and fun. Visitors are encouraged to use a 20-inch telescope. Future sections will deal with agriculture and mining. *1651 Discovery Park Boulevard; from US 191 take Discovery Park Boulevard to 20th Avenue; from US 70 head south on 20th Avenue, which runs into the park. The park is open daily except Tuesday and major holidays from noon until 9:00pm. Call Tel. 520/428-6260 for the latest information on prices and progress on other exhibits and facilities.*

Thatcher is located a couple of miles west of Safford on US 70. The main attraction is the **Museum of Anthropology at Eastern Arizona College**. The museum has a collection of artifacts taken from excavations throughout the southwest, but primarily in this area of Arizona. The artifacts date back to pre-Columbian times. Interactive exhibits geared towards children are a good way of arousing the young one's interest in ancient cultures. *College Avenue and Thatcher Boulevard, 1/4 mile south of US 70. The museum is open weekdays from 9:00am to 4:00pm except that it closes for lunch for an hour at noon. It is also closed from the middle of December to the middle of January and from the middle of May to the latter part of August. Call for exact dates. Admission is free. Tel. 520/428-8310.*

If you have time for a 90-mile round-trip extension, then a trip to the town of **Morenci** is in order. This is especially warranted if you're interested in mine tours. While I've already described a few of these places, the tour in Morenci is absolutely the best of its kind and is worth going out of the way for. Take US 70 east and US 191 north from Safford or Thatcher to reach Morenci. The **Morenci Open Pit Copper Mine** is one of the largest of its kind and is operated by the Phelps Dodge Corporation. The pit is absolutely tremendous – huge trucks and mechanized shovels weighing as much as 240 tons look like little toys riding on narrow ledges from up on top.

In most open pit mines all you do is get to look in. Well, here you can enter the pit. Three-hour long tours are conducted by retired Phelps Dodge employees. The van trips cover 81 square miles and, besides going down into the pit for a better look, take you to the crushing operation, concentrators, and other mine functions. A most fascinating experience. *Morenci Open Pit mine tours leave from the company office at 4521 US Highway 191. Tours are offered on weekdays at 8:30am and 1:15pm only. Because of limited space reservations are strongly suggested. The tours leave from the Morenci Hotel along US 191 in town and are given free of charge. Tel. 520/865-4521.*

Now we'll pick up the main route from Willcox. Take I-10 westbound to Exit 318 and then go a mile southeast to the tiny town of **Dragoon**. One of the country's best archaeological museums is located in this unlikely place. The **Amerind Foundation Museum** has exhibits and artifacts on almost all of the major native cultures of North America west of the Mississippi as well as South America. *Open daily from 10:00am to 4:00pm*

THE CORONADO TRAIL

Although not on the route of this region or any other, the **Coronado Trail Scenic Byway** *has some beautiful scenery to offer as it winds its way through a large portion of the Apache-Sitgreaves National Forest. It starts at the town of Clifton, 45 miles northeast of Safford via US 191 (and only five miles past Morenci if you're already planning to go that far) and extends for approximately 120 miles north to the town of Eagar at the edge of the White Mountains in the northeast touring region.*

Portions of the route were traversed by the Coronado Expedition and much of the surrounding area looks just as it did almost five centuries ago. Among the highlights are the thrilling corkscrew climb to 8,550 foot high Rose Peak from which there is a tower that has a magnificent view of the mountains and forests. The highest portion of the trail reaches an altitude of about 9,200 feet. The northernmost section of the trail is best during the autumn months when the changing colors of the forest are simply spectacular. Although the entire road is paved it is quite narrow and has steep grades. You don't have to be driving any special type of vehicle but experience on mountain roads is advisable. Trailers in excess of 20 feet in length should not be taken on the Coronado Trail.

While a round-trip on the Coronado Trail will cover a large amount of mileage which may or may not be worth it depending upon your appreciation of scenery, it makes a great shortcut for connecting the northeast and southeast touring regions.

from September through May, during the rest of the year it is open for those same hours on Wednesday through Sunday, closed on state holidays; admission price is $3 for adults and $2 for seniors age 60 and over as well as children ages 12 through 18; Tel. 520/586-3666.

William Fulton of Connecticut did archaeological research in Texas Canyon (a beautiful and rugged looking wilderness which is now the home to the town of Dragoon) during the 1930s and established the Amerind Foundation to promote archaeological research. The extensive collection covers ten millennia of native history and has more than 25,000 different artifacts. There is also an excellent art gallery featuring works by Native Americans and famous western artists. Some of the best examples of Hopi kachinas are on display. Finally, the museum store sells authentic native crafts of the highest quality. Even the dramatic setting of the museum building amid the massive rocks of Texas Canyon is worth the visit. Allow a minimum of one hour for a visit here.

Returning to I-10 and continuing west, it is only 20 miles to Benson and the completion of the southeast regional loop. You can be back in Tucson in under an hour.

NIGHTLIFE & ENTERTAINMENT

Given the size of the towns in the southeast it isn't surprising that this region doesn't have too much opportunity to paint the town red during the evening hours. That isn't to say, however, that there's nothing to do.

In Bisbee the **Bisbee Grand Theater**, *Tel. 520/432-5900*, offers old fashioned melodramas on weekends. The **Brewery Gulch** area of downtown Bisbee also has numerous night spots offering live entertainment, usually either country or rock. Many of the old west saloons in historic Tombstone also feature entertainment.

SPORTS & RECREATION

Much of the outdoor activity in this region of deserts and mountains consists of **hiking** or exploring the back country in such places as the Chiricahua National Monument or the **bird watching** activities in the San Pedro Valley mentioned in the touring section.

Fishing
- **Roper Lake State Park**, *six miles south of Safford on US 191, Tel. 520/428-6760*

Golf
- **Coyote Hills Golf Course**, *Benson, Tel. 520/586-2585*
- **Mount Graham Golf Course**, *Safford, Tel. 520/348-3140*
- **Pueblo del Sol Golf Club**, *Sierra Vista, Tel. 520/378-6444*
- **Turquoise Valley Golf Course**, *Naco Highway, Bisbee, Tel. 520/432-3091*
- **Twin Lakes Golf Course**, *Willcox, Tel. 520/384-2720*

Swimming
- **Roper Lake State Park**, *six miles south of Safford on US 191, Tel. 520/428-6760*

SHOPPING

The shopping situation, although not top notch compared with many other parts of the state, is better than the nightlife. This is especially true in Bisbee where many interesting shops can be found in the historic buildings along Main Street. Native American crafts, southwestern goods and antiques are all well represented. Of special note is the **Pentimento**, *29 Main Street*. Occupying the old Woolworth Building, it contains some 20 different shops.

Tombstone has a large number of gift and souvenir shops. Although much of the merchandise is on the tacky side, careful shopping will reveal a number of establishments with quality southwestern goods as well. Sierra Vista and Willcox are the two other towns in this region that have what can be termed shopping districts. However, both of these are primarily stores serving the needs of local residents. But you can find a number of southwestern and craft shops among them.

PRACTICAL INFORMATION

· **Airport**
   Sierra Vista Municipal Airport, *1224 North Avenue, Tel. 520/452-7091*

· **Bus Station**
   Benson, *Tel. 520/586-3141*
   Bisbee, *Tel. 520/432-5359*
   Safford, *Tel. 520/428-2150*
   Willcox, *Tel. 520/384-2183*

· **Hospital**
   Benson, *Tel. 520/586-2261*
   Bisbee, *Tel. 520/432-3091*
   Safford, *Tel. 520/348-8000*
   Sierra Vista Regional Health Center, *Tel. 520/458-4641*
   Willcox, *Tel. 520/384-3541*

· **Police** (non-emergency)
   Benson, *Tel. 520/586-2211*
   Safford, *Tel. 520/384-4673*
   Sierra Vista, *Tel. 520/458-3311*
   Willcox, *Tel. 520/384-4673*

· **Tourist Office/Visitors Bureau**
   Benson, *Tel. 520/586-2842*
   Bisbee, *Tel. 520/432-5421*
   Safford, *Tel. 520/428-2511*
   Tombstone, *Tel. 520/457-9317*
   Sierra Vista, *Tel. 800/288-3861*
   Willcox, *Tel. 800/200-2272*

18. THE WEST
- WATER PLAYGROUND IN THE DESERT -

Stretching for more than 300 miles from north to south and covering a considerable distance from west to east as well, the western region of Arizona is a land of wide open spaces dotted by widely spaced towns. **Yuma**, with close to 60,000 people, is more than two times the size of the next largest community. If you think of deserts when you hear "Arizona," you won't be off the mark when it comes to the state's western frontier. Almost all of the land in this region is high desert. There are mountains, but they aren't as high as in most other parts of the state, and there are some small forested areas. But none of those features define the true nature of the area. That can only be conveyed by describing the importance of the region's most dominant natural feature – the **Colorado River**.

Continuing from the western end of the Grand Canyon National Park, the river turns sharply south at Hoover Dam in the Lake Mead National Recreation area, and flows into Mexico at the town of San Luis, some 340 miles from the dam. The river is more than a natural border between Arizona and its neighbor states of Nevada and California. It is the lifeblood of millions of people who live both near and far from the river. That's because it provides the water for drinking, for agriculture, and for industry for a large portion of the American southwest.

The wild nature of the river has been tamed by dams beginning well out of the region (Glen Canyon) as well as several more along the portion of the river that traverses western Arizona. The river and its dams are the basis for numerous communities that have sprung up along both banks of the Colorado. These towns have their share of history, too, but their major importance today is in the wealth of recreational services that they offer. The Colorado River in Arizona is, indeed, an unusual dichotomy – a water playground for millions within yards of a great desert. It's yours to enjoy, so let's take a closer look.

TOURING WESTERN ARIZONA

Because of the immense area covered by the western region of Arizona it would be very difficult to design a loop unless you had lots of time available. In addition, although there are many wonderful things to see and do, the attractions are generally more scattered than in other parts of Arizona. Consequently, I'll depart from the format of all the previous touring chapters and separate western Arizona into five distinct areas, namely: Wickenburg, Kingman, Lake Havasu City, Yuma and Gila Bend. For each area that you decide to visit it would be best to use a "base" approach to seeing the surrounding area of each city. Wickenburg, however, can be seen from Phoenix should you not want to change hotels and won't be going on to one or more of the other areas. The same can also be said for Gila Bend, although some portions of the excursions from that town are too far for a day trip from Phoenix or Tucson.

WICKENBURG

This town traces its origins to prospector **Henry Wickenburg**, a German immigrant who discovered gold in 1863. The **Vulture Gold Mine** sustained development for many years. It grew so rapidly that it missed being named the Arizona territorial capital by the slimmest of margins. Since the closing of the mine, Wickenburg has continued to prosper because of its great weather and the presence of a number of dude ranches.

In fact, dude ranch stays were popular in the Wickenburg area long before it became an "in" thing to do. It still bills itself as the dude ranch capital of the world. Although the Tucson area probably has more ranches catering to guests these days, on a per capita basis Wickenburg can surely still claim its share of that title.

ARRIVALS & DEPARTURES

By Bus

You can reach Wickenburg by Greyhound bus from Phoenix.

By Car

From Phoenix take US 60 into Wickenburg. Travelers from the north can reach it by taking I-17 to Exit 223 and then following AZ 74 into US 60 and on into town. From southern California I-10 will bring you into Arizona. Then get off the Interstate at Exit 31 and take US 60 east into Wickenburg. From the northwest US 93 brings you directly into the center of town.

ORIENTATION

Wickenburg is less than an hour northwest of Phoenix. Getting about in the Wickenburg area is easy – US 60 is the main thoroughfare. The main intersection of town is where US 93 terminates at US 60.

WHERE TO STAY

Very Expensive

MERV GRIFFIN'S WICKENBURG INN, *34801 North Highway 89. Tel. 520/684-7811, Fax 520/684-2981. Toll free reservations Tel. 800/942-5362. 73 Rooms. Rates: High season (February 1st to April 30th): $345; Low season (May 1st to July 31st and September): $240, rates include all meals. Closed for the month of August. Major credit cards accepted. Located six miles north of town on US 89.*

This "inn" is better described by its full name, which adds Dude Ranch and Tennis Resort as a suffix. Secluded on a hillside in a fabulous desert setting that is part of an Arizona nature preserve, the Inn opened for business in 1996. It combines some of the features of a guest ranch with the more upscale qualities of a luxury resort. The excellent accommodations consist of both lodge rooms and 43 casitas. The casitas boast separate living rooms, fireplace, coffee maker, refrigerator and such nice little amenities as hair dryers. Some of the casitas are even more deluxe – they have a rooftop terrace area with its own fireplace. What better place than to watch the brilliant star filled evening sky of the Arizona desert?

Activities at the Wickenburg Inn are extensive. There are three heated swimming pools, whirlpool, volleyball, nine tennis courts, horseback riding, nature trails, and a fully equipped exercise facility. More relaxing pursuits are also available such as a native arts and crafts program or nature program. At the other extreme you can take part in cattle drives or other ranch programs. Unlike traditional guest ranches these are not offered all the time so be sure to inquire in advance if you want to include those type activities as part of your stay. Additional services are professional massage and a well supervised children's program.

The resort has two restaurants. One is casual and is open 24 hours a day. The other, called Griff's is featured in the *Where to Eat* section. There is also a cocktail lounge with entertainment on some evenings.

Moderate

SOMBRERO RANCH BED AND BREAKFAST, *31910 West Bralliar Road. Tel. 520/684-0222, Fax 520/684-0222. 3 Rooms. Rates: $75 including full breakfast. MasterCard and VISA accepted. Located 3/4 mile past the center of town via US 93. Turn left on Bralliar Road to the top of the hill.*

This B&B is an excellent price value. Covering 49 acres, the Sombrero isn't a guest ranch in the usual sense of the term so we're including it here with the regular lodging. With only three rooms and plenty of space, guests don't come here for the working ranch atmosphere but rather for the privacy and serene pace that takes you about as far away from the hectic real world as you can get.

Set on a scenic hilltop location, the Sombrero features uniquely furnished accommodations in an attractive ranch style house that dates back to 1937. There's a small swimming pool and a pretty screened in ramada overlooking the desert surroundings. Host Peter Nufer gives his guests plenty of things to do, including hiking, tennis, and horseback riding. Individualized or group desert tours through the desert are also popular.

Inexpensive

WESTERNER MOTEL, *680 West Wickenburg Way. Tel. 520/684-2493. 12 units. Rates: $60 all year. Discover, MasterCard, and VISA accepted. Located in the center of town.*

Not everyone passing through Wickenburg will want to stay at a guest ranch or luxury resort. That's where the Westerner Motel comes in. One of only a handful of traditional style motels, this small facility features comfortable modern rooms with refrigerators and coffee makers. There's a restaurant and full service cocktail lounge on the premises that offers decent food and service at reasonable prices.

CAMPING & RV SITES

For additional sites in the greater Phoenix area that aren't too far from Wickenburg, see Chapter 12, *Phoenix.*
• **Desert Cypress Trailer Ranch,** *Jack Burden Road, Tel. 520/684-2153*

WHERE TO EAT

Expensive

GRIFF'S, *34801 North Highway 89 in the Merv Griffin Resort and Dude Ranch. Tel. 520/684-7811. Major credit cards accepted. Breakfast, lunch, and dinner served daily. Reservations are suggested.*

Although Wickenburg may be a small and casual western town the style of dining at Griff's is first class big city elegance but in a casual sort of way. The staff is personable and friendly but professional. The attractive dining room features prime Angus certified beef steaks, fresh grilled fish, and rotisserie style chicken. Now, as far as casual is concerned, try coming on either Tuesday or Saturday when Griff's goes outdoors for a real cowboy cookout. Full cocktail service and children's menu available.

Moderate

THE GOLD NUGGET RESTAURANT, *222 East Wickenburg Way, in the Rancho Grande Motel. Tel. 520/684-2858. Most major credit cards accepted. Breakfast, lunch, and dinner served daily.*

A large and friendly place consisting of separate full service restaurant and coffee shop. Both are decorated in a Victorian era style and serve a good variety of American entrees including beef and seafood. The menu also includes a limited number of Italian dishes. Cocktails are served and there is a separate lounge with live entertainment from 6:00 to 10:00pm nightly except Monday and Tuesday. Children's menu. The Gold Nugget fits the bill nicely for both family and grown-up dining.

RANCHO BAR 7 RESTAURANT, *111 East Wickenburg Way. Tel. 520/684-2492. American Express, MasterCard, and VISA accepted. Lunch and dinner served daily.*

This is real home style cooking in a relaxed western atmosphere that resembles an old west saloon (cocktails, beer, and wine are served). Mexican selections include great chimichangas (filled either with chili, beef, chicken or beans), enchiladas, tostados, and burritos. On the American side are baby back ribs, several types of steak, barbecue beef ribs, chicken fried steak, and several types of fresh fish including cod and rainbow trout. Everything is prepared quite well and is tasty without being fancy. There's a daily special for lunch and dinner which can be a lower priced version of regular menu items or something different like filet mignon or pot roast. Rancho Bar 7 also has an excellent salad bar. For dessert you simply have to have the Mud Pie, a delicious combination of butter pecan ice cream with chocolate cookie crust, and topped with fudge and whipped cream.

The sandwiches selection for lunch is a sizable list of American and Mexican favorites. Or you might want to opt for the salad bar and soup, which can be a meal in itself. Before or after lunch you might want to try your hand at a game of shuffleboard or pool. If I'm in Wickenburg, I head for this place.

SEEING THE SIGHTS

If you're coming from Phoenix the first attraction you'll reach is the **Hassayampa River Preserve** located on US 60 about three miles southeast of town. The Preserve was once part of a large ranch. The visitor center was one of the original adobe buildings and was constructed in the 1860s. The working ranch became one of Arizona's first guest ranches in 1913. In 1986 the ranch came into the hands of the Nature Conservancy. Numerous trails wind their way through this riparian ecosystem which is known for the large number of birds that make it their home. Guided walks are conducted at various intervals – check at the visitor center for times. *The preserve is open Wednesday through Sunday from 8:00am to 5:00pm, mid-September to early May, and from 6:00am through noon during the remainder of the year. The suggested donation is $5.*

The best attraction in town is the **Desert Caballeros Western Museum** which, although not the biggest museum of its genre in Arizona, manages to pack a lot of interesting things into a small place. In addition to rotating special exhibits, the permanent collection includes a fine Western art exhibit featuring such famous American artists as **Frederick Remington**, a street scene depicting Wickenburg at the turn of the century, several furnished period rooms, an excellent Native American gallery with emphasis on the Navajo and Hopi, and various video presentations. Authentic western and native items are on sale at the museum's store. You should give yourself at least 45 minutes to see the museum. The name desert caballeros (or gentlemen of the desert) applies to a group of civic minded individuals interested in preserving Wickenburg's heritage. Every year as many as a hundred people suit up in old-time western gear and set out on horseback for a hundred mile ride into the desert. The ride, which takes place every April, is a colorful event that's popular with locals and visitors alike. *21 North Frontier Street. The museum is open daily from 10:00am to 5:00pm (except noon to 4:00pm on Sunday). The admission fee is $4 for adults, $3.50 for seniors age 55 and up, and $1 for children ages 6 through 16. Tel. 520/684-2272.*

The **Wickenburg Chamber of Commerce**, *corner of Frontier and Yavapai Streets in the historic Santa Fe Depot*, can provide you with a map for a walking tour of historic buildings. Besides the depot, the tour passes several 19th century houses, stable, general store, hotel, and the old town hall and jail. Interestingly, the jail cells were removed several years ago and placed in a new jail facility. Before the construction of the old jail in 1909, Wickenburg's citizens were too busy to bother having a real jail. They just tied prisoners to the **Jail Tree**, *Tegner Street and Wickenburg Way*, a large 200-year old mesquite tree!

NIGHTLIFE & ENTERTAINMENT

Wickenburg certainly doesn't qualify as a hot spot during the evening. Some live music can be found in lounges of the larger motels. Wickenburg's guest ranches, especially the Merv Griffin Resort, are also places where you can spend some time being entertained. **The Gold Nugget Restaurant**, *222 E. Wickenburg Way*, features live entertainment Wednesday through Sunday evenings.

SPORTS & RECREATION
Golf
• **Los Caballeros Golf Club**, *South Vulture Mine Road, Tel. 520/684-2704 or 520/684-5484*

Horseback Riding
In addition to the numerous dude ranches which offer horseback riding to their guests, day visitors can rent horses for periods of an hour to a full day at the following:
• **The Big Corral**, *520 North Tegner, Tel. 520/684-2317*

Jeep Tours
• **Wickenburg Jeep Tours**, *295 East Wickenburg Way, Tel. 520/684-0438.* Four wheel adventures in the surrounding Sonoran desert.

PRACTICAL INFORMATION
• **Bus Depot**, *Tel. 520/684-2601*
• **Hospital**, *Tel. 520/684-5421*
• **Police** (non-emergency), *Tel. 520/684-5411*
• **Tourist Office/Visitors Bureau**, *Tel. 520/684-5479*

KINGMAN

Tracing its beginnings to the coming of the railroad in 1880, Kingman is sustained by its important location on the interstate highway. It serves as a gateway to the Colorado River region, Grand Canyon, and even to Las Vegas to the northwest. Among the attractions that visitors to Kingman want to see, besides some outstanding scenery located nearby, are historic sites connected with Kingman's role as a stop on the old Route 66, the first paved transcontinental road in the country and, perhaps, the most famous road in America.

ARRIVALS & DEPARTURES
By Bus & Train
Kingman is served by daily bus service to Phoenix. Amtrak has a Kingman station on its northern Arizona route which stops three times a week.

By Car
If you're coming from the eastern part of the state, take I-40 due west into town. The same is true if you're coming from California – I-40 eastbound is the main approach. I-40 has three exits for Kingman, one each on the east and west sides of town and one in the middle (Stockton

Hill Road). From Phoenix US 93 reaches I-40 about 20 miles east of Kingman. From the northwest US 93 leads directly into the heart of town and crosses I-40.

ORIENTATION

Kingman's location on I-40 makes it an important hub that can be reached easily from anywhere in Arizona. The main thoroughfare through town is Andy Devine Avenue. This street forms part of historic Route 66, today designated as AZ 66. A few miles north of town via US 93, AZ 68 leads to Bullhead City and the recreation areas of the Colorado River.

WHERE TO STAY

KINGMAN

Inexpensive

BEST WESTERN A WAYFARERS INN, *2815 East Andy Devine Boulevard. Tel. 520/753-6271, Fax 520/753-9608. Toll free reservations Tel. 800/528-1234. 100 Rooms. Rates: High season (May 1st to September 30th): $68-71; Low season (October 1st to April 30th): $55-57. Major credit cards accepted. Located a half mile south of I-40, Exit 53, on the I-40 business loop.*

This inn has unusually large rooms decorated in the light shades of the southwest that are so popular in Arizona. The furnishings are modern and among the amenities in all rooms are mini-refrigerators and microwave ovens. The inn has a heated swimming pool open seasonally and an indoor whirlpool facility. Several restaurants are located within a block or two of the property.

KINGMAN TRAVEL INN, *3241 East Andy Devine Boulevard. Tel. 520/ 757-7878, Fax 520/692-8366. 28 Rooms. Rates: $40-49, all year. Major credit cards accepted. Located approximately a quarter of a mile north of I-40, Exit 53, on AZ 66.*

A small and basic motel that offers clean and comfortable accommodations at a price that's almost ridiculously low for these days. The rooms are really just as good as you'll find at any of the lower priced chain establishments. Some of them even have Jacuzzi tubs. However, there is no swimming pool. Restaurants are located within a short distance.

BULLHEAD CITY

Inexpensive

SUNRIDGE HOTEL, *839 Landon Drive. Tel. 520/754-4700, Fax 520/ 754-1225. Toll free reservations 800/977-4242. 155 Rooms. Rates: $49 weekdays; $79 on Friday and Saturday nights, all year. Major credit cards accepted. All rates include Continental breakfast. Located about 1-1/4 miles east of AZ 68, which is reached by taking AZ 95 about three miles north of the center of town.*

A modern four story motor inn on a hillside location that overlooks

HISTORIC ROUTE 66

*This important piece of Americana had its origins in a series of roads built starting as a result of the California gold rush in the mid-19th century. It was officially designated as **U.S. Highway 66** in 1926 but at that time only about a third of its 2,200 mile length was paved. The Great Depression and the Dust Bowl renewed the westward trek of the gold rush era in even greater numbers and spurred improvements in the road as well as development along its route. The continuing increase in traffic was one of the reasons that prompted the building of the Interstate Highway System beginning in the 1950s. I-40 paralleled Route 66 and eventually was responsible for its demise as one of America's most important roads. However, the mystique of the westward expansion has helped to keep Route 66 alive in the minds of many people.*

*The **Historic Route 66 Association of Arizona** was formed in 1987 and is among several such groups that promote visiting the old route. Route 66 has gone by any number of names, including The Main Street of America, the Will Rogers Highway, and the Mother Road. In the Kingman area, which is in many ways the heart of historic Route 66, you'll have the opportunity to discover many aspects of this fascinating road that has been an integral part of the lives of so many people.*

the river gorge. The rooms aren't special but they're nice and clean. Some have refrigerators. The hotel has a heated swimming pool, whirlpool, sauna, and exercise room. A restaurant and cocktail lounge are on the premises. For a better selection of restaurants you can hop across the river to Laughlin, Nevada and the bargain prices of the casino eateries. Actually, hotel prices are also lower across the river but I'm sticking to the Arizona side of the border.

CAMPING & RV SITES
- **Hualapai Mountain Park Campground**, *Hualapai Mt. Road, Kingman, Tel. 520/757-3859*
- **Kingman KOA**, *3820 N. Roosevelt Avenue, Kingman, Tel. 520/757-4397*
- **Mirage RV Resort**, *2196 Merrill Avenue, Bullhead City, Tel. 520/754-1177*
- **Ridgeview RV Resort**, *775 Bullhead Parkway, Bullhead City, Tel. 520/754-2595*
- **Quality Stars RV Park**, *3131 McDonald, Kingman, Tel. 520/753-2277*
- **Silver Creek RV Camp**, *1515 Gold Rush Drive, Bullhead City, Tel. 520/763-2244*
- **Snowbird RV Resort**, *1600 Joy Lane, Bullhead City, Tel. 520/768-7141*

WHERE TO EAT
KINGMAN
Moderate

DAMBAR STEAKHOUSE, *1960 E. Andy Devine Blvd. Tel. 520/753-3253. American Express, Discover, MasterCard and VISA accepted. Lunch and dinner served daily.*

Although thick and juicy steaks are the main attraction at Dambar, the menu has a wide variety of items that includes everything from salads to sandwiches to complete meals. Friendly and efficient service. Cocktails served tableside or in the separate lounge. Children's menu. Popular with the locals so you might expect to wait a bit, especially on weekends.

JR's, *1410 East Andy Devine Avenue. Tel. 520/753-1066. Most major credit cards accepted. Breakfast, lunch, and dinner served daily.*

Good food and efficient service in an attractive atmosphere are in abundant supply at this popular family style restaurant. The menu has a diverse selection of Italian and Mexican selections as well as many American favorites. Children's menu available. Cocktail service.

BULLHEAD CITY
Inexpensive

EL ENCANTO, *125 Long Avenue. Tel. 520/754-5100. MasterCard and VISA accepted. Lunch and Dinner served daily.*

With so many places to eat at reasonable prices across the river in Laughlin there isn't much incentive for visitors to stay on the Arizona side when it comes time to dine. El Encanto, however, is definitely an exception. This attractive restaurant has lovely and authentic Mexican decor and delicious food to match. Dining outside on the patio makes it even better. The prices are low enough to make it the best value in town. El Encanto has a full service bar. Children's menu available.

SEEING THE SIGHTS
Around Town

The old downtown area is centered around Beale Street (at the junction of US 93 and I-40, Exit 48 on the west side of town) and contains more than 60 structures listed on the National Register of Historic Buildings. Two attractions on this street are the **Mohave Museum of History and Art,** *open Monday through Friday from 9:00am to 5:00pm and on weekends from 1:00pm to 5:00pm; admission is $2 for adults and 50 cents for children,* Tel. 520/753-3195, and the **Bonelli House,** *generally open Thursday through Monday from 1:00pm to 4:00pm but make inquiry at the Museum.*

The museum contains historical displays and several dioramas that trace area history including that of the Mohave and Hualapai Indian tribes. One section houses a tribute to the most famous person to come out of Kingman – television and movie star Andy Devine. There is also a portrait gallery of American presidents and first ladies. The Bonnelli House is considered to be one of the best examples of the so-called Anglo-territorial architectural style. It contains many original and period pieces and is typical of a prosperous Kingman family at the turn of the century.

Also of interest in this same vicinity are an old steam engine sitting in downtown's **Locomotive Park** and two turn of the century hotels – the **Hotel Brunswick** and **Hotel Beale**. They are still operating as lodging establishments but you might want to take a peak at them regardless of where you're staying. You should be able to see all of downtown Kingman's attractions within one to two hours.

NIGHTLIFE & ENTERTAINMENT

Kingman

Like most small Arizona towns, Kingman's nightlife is comprised principally of lounges in the larger motels.

Bullhead City

Although a town of this size has its own assortment of bars and lounges, most residents will tell you to head across the river to Laughlin. The casino hotels all have lounge shows providing a wide assortment of entertainment. Nationally recognized name entertainment is also featured at prices far below what they would be in most other locations, including even Las Vegas. Contact the Laughlin Visitors Bureau for information, *Tel. 702/298-3321.*

SPORTS & RECREATION

Fishing
- **Chets Fishing Guide Service**, *1775 Riverside Drive, Bullhead City, Tel. 520/758-6232*

Golf
- **Chaparral Country Club**, *1260 E. Mohave Drive, Bullhead City, Tel. 520/758-3939*
- **Desert Lake Golf Course**, *5835 Desert Lakes Drive, Bullhead City, Tel. 520/768-1000*

Watersports
- **All Wet Sports**, *1734 Highway 95, Bullhead City, Tel. 520/763-4938*
- **Lake Mohave Resort**, *Katherine's Landing, Bullhead City, Tel. 520/754-3245*
- **Water Craft Beach**, *1643 Highway 95, Bullhead City, Tel. 520/763-8789*

EXCURSIONS & DAY TRIPS

Several trips ranging from a couple of hours to a full day can be taken in just about any direction from Kingman.

North of Kingman/Hoover Dam

We'll start with a trip to the north which, depending upon how much you do can be done as a single trip or a couple of different ones. Leave Kingman by US 93 for about 17 miles and turn right. This signed side road will take you four miles and bring you to the old mining town of **Chloride**. At one time more than 75 separate silver mines supported a population of over 2,000 people. Now there are only about 300, mostly artists and craftsmen who have set up shop in some of the town's historic buildings. It's a great place to go if you're looking for antiques. The old jail can still be visited.

Return to US 93 and head north for 60 miles through desert terrain in view of distant mountains. Eventually you'll enter those mountains which have a dark and rather forbidding appearance. The last few miles of the trip are in the **Lake Mead National Recreation Area**. Stop at the overlook past the **Willow Beach** cutoff for a beautiful view. The last couple of miles zig-zag through the mountains and drop precipitously to the Nevada-Arizona border, located in the middle of Hoover Dam.

One of the great engineering wonders of the world (and certainly one of the most famous), **Hoover Dam** sits majestically in a narrow canyon. Several parking areas on the Arizona side provide a panoramic view of the top of the dam, with the brilliant azure blue of **Lake Mead** behind it and the dark **Colorado River** below it. Most of the recreational activities associated with 115-mile long Lake Mead are located a few miles into Nevada. The main parking area for visiting the dam is located on the Nevada side of the border as is the visitor center where films on the dam's construction can be viewed and dam tours originate. US 93 crosses the crest of the dam. There is also a sidewalk on either side of the dam that allows for better views of both the lake and the river. The new visitor center is housed in a gleaming gold colored glass building that adds to the imposing scene.

Hoover Dam is 726 feet high and was completed in 1935. Forty minute long guided tours begin from the visitor center as passengers swiftly descend in an elevator to the bottom of the dam, walk through a long tunnel, and finally reach the powerhouse. Competent guides explain the construction process as well as the function of the dam. *The visitor center (located on Nevada side of the dam) is open daily from 8:00am until 5:45pm. Tours are given at frequent intervals from 8:35am until 5:15pm. There is a $4 charge ($2 for children) for viewing the exhibits at the Visitor Center. Dam tours cost $8 for adults, $7 for seniors and $2 for children ages 6 through 16. Hard* *hat tours cost $25. Free parking is limited and is on the Arizona side. A large covered pay garage is on the Nevada side nearest to the visitor center. It is best to arrive early in the day since throngs of visitors coming from nearby Las Vegas can result in considerable lines. Tel. 702/293-8321.*

An additional sight seeing option is available on your return trip to Kingman. About half way between Hoover Dam and Kingman is a side road leading to the town of **Dolan Springs**. Beyond that town, a total distance of almost 50 miles from US 93, is an area that is known as **Grand Canyon West** on the **Hualapai Indian Reservation**. The remote western end of the Grand Canyon is without crowds, commercial development, or even guard rails. What it does have, however, is an awesome view of the canyon. You can take a five mile long bus tour given by the Hualapai that tells you about Indian legends as well as the canyon. *Call 520/699-0269 for tour information and schedules.* (Grand Canyon West can also be reached from AZ 66 on our next excursion but the road is much more difficult.)

East of Kingman

An excursion to the east of Kingman covers the heart of Route 66. Take I-40 east from Kingman to Exit 53 and then onto AZ 66 passing through such towns as Hackberry, Truxton, and Peach Springs. All of these towns began as rest stops for weary travelers on Route 66. **Truxton** is especially attractive as it is surrounded by colorful hills and valleys. About 60 miles from Kingman right on AZ 66 are the **Grand Canyon Caverns**. This large cavern is filled with colorful formations and marine fossils dating back more than three million years when this area was covered by a great inland sea. The cave contains the mummified remains of some animals and evidence of visitation by Native Americans.

Guided tours begin with a 21-story elevator descent into the cool 56 degree cavern. Well-lit paved trails make the tour easy to do for just about anyone. Tours last approximately 45 minutes. *Open daily except for Christmas from 9:00am to 6:00pm, mid-June through Labor Day, and from 10:00am to 5:00pm the rest of the year. Admission is $10 for adults, $8 for senior citizens, and $7 for children ages 4 to 12. Credit cards. Tel. 520/422-3223.*

From the caverns you can continue east on AZ 66 to Seligman and return via I-40 to Kingman, or just retrace your route on AZ 66. The latter will save you about 50 miles.

West of Kingman

An excursion to the west from Kingman can provide an interesting and fun day that combines scenery and history. You can even throw in some gambling. This is a loop route that covers under a hundred miles. Begin by heading north from Kingman on US 93 for four miles to the intersection of AZ 68. Take that road west for 27 miles into the southern portion of the Lake Mead National Recreation Area and the **Davis Dam** across the Colorado River. The dam is certainly not as big or as impressive as either Hoover or Glen Canyon Dams. By comparison it's a "low rise" style spreading across the Colorado. *Self guided tours of the dam can be taken daily from 7:30am to 4:00pm. Admission is free. Tel. 702/293-8907.*

South of the dam is the town of **Bullhead City**. It is one of the fastest growing communities in a fast growing state. Its population depends upon who you ask and on what day of the week. A good estimate is around 28,000. Besides being a popular resort destination it is gaining increasing favor with retirees and others looking for a relaxing way of life. The biggest lures for visitors are the casinos on the other side of the river (see the sidebar) and the outdoor recreation (see the Sports & Recreation section for more details). The recreation is provided by Lake Mojave which extends north from Davis Dam for about 70 miles. One in-town attraction is the **Colorado River Museum**. This is a small museum that occupies a 1947 church built for Davis Dam construction workers and their families. It documents several hundred years of area history. *The museum is on AZ 95 about a half mile north of the bridge connecting Bullhead City with Laughlin, open Tuesday through Saturday from 10:00am to 3:00pm; admission is $1; Tel. 520/754-3399.*

River tours are a popular diversion as the mountains on either side of the Colorado provide some pleasant scenery. These tours are available from the Laughlin side of the river. Contact **Laughlin River Tours**, *Tel. 702/298-1047.*

Head south from Bullhead City on AZ 95 for about ten miles to Boundary Cone Road and turn left. This will eventually link up with the Oatman Highway, a portion of the old Route 66, and bring you into historic **Oatman**. This town is part ghost-town, part living old west history, and part out of this world. For 36 years beginning in 1906 Oatman was one of the most prosperous gold mining sites in the state of Arizona, yielding almost $40 million worth of the precious ore. Its 10,000 residents have dwindled to less than 200 today. Perhaps the only reason it survived at all is because of its Historic 66 location.

You can spend an interesting hour or so in Oatman by visiting some of the historic buildings that include a jail and a hotel. The latter is famous because Clark Gable and Carole Lombard stayed there on their wedding night. You're also sure to encounter some wild burros roaming the town's streets. These animals are the descendants of burros used by miners but who were let free when mining operations ceased in 1942. They're the unofficial mascots of Oatman. Reenactments of gunfights are staged on weekends.

After Oatman AZ 66 climbs and twists through the Sitgreaves Pass before reaching I-40 about five miles southwest of Kingman. The road

GAMES ACROSS THE COLORADO

*The town of **Laughlin, Nevada** is a modern day boomtown created not by mining but by gambling. It's not like Las Vegas or Atlantic City but has a little bit of both in them. Despite its rather isolated location, Laughlin receives several million visitors a year, mostly residents of California or Arizona who just want the opportunity to gamble and figure they can save the time of driving an extra hour or two to get to Las Vegas. Laughlin sits across the Colorado River from Bullhead City (you can get there by driving across the bridge or by taking frequent water taxi service). All of the hotel-casinos are lined up along the river and it makes for a pretty picture. A waterfront promenade connects most of the hotels.*

The hotels are generally on the glitzy side but not nearly to the extent found in Las Vegas. They're also smaller than their brethren to the north but aren't tiny by any means. Most of the hotels have around a thousand rooms and the casinos are spacious. All of the usual casino games found in Las Vegas are available in Laughlin. In fact, most of the casinos here are "branches" of some of the major hotel-casino operators in Las Vegas. Room rates, should you decide to spend the night, are ridiculously low, and you can also eat at buffets or regular restaurants for far less than you could just about anywhere in the world. So, if you have some itchy fingers that want to part with some bucks, give gaming in Laughlin a try.

isn't the easiest in the world to drive but there are fabulous views of Arizona, Nevada, and California from the top. You'll also pass a couple of true ghost towns. If you do stop to explore them exercise caution as the buildings are not in good repair and aren't maintained by anyone. If the prospect of driving through this mountainous terrain doesn't appeal to you, you can return to Kingman by taking AZ 66 west to I-40 at Topock and then east on that road to Kingman.

South of Kingman

A final and shorter excursion available from Kingman goes to the **Hualapai Mountain Park**. From I-40's Exit 51, take Stockton Hill Road south. It changes name to Hualapai Mountain Road and after 14 miles of pretty scenery you'll reach the park. With an elevation of 8,400 feet the park provides relief from the hot summer of the surrounding lower terrain. The mountain is even forested and is home to deer, elk, mountain lion, and several other species. There are extensive hiking trails.

ARIZONA'S WEST COAST

Conventional wisdom states that the West Coast of the United States is the Pacific Ocean. Hence, California, Oregon, and Washington are considered to be the west coast states. But don't try telling that to an Arizonian. You see, the entire 340-mile long western border of Arizona is formed by the mighty Colorado River and the beautiful blue lakes created by several dam impoundments. As one of the most popular areas in the country for water sports, Arizona proudly proclaims this area to be the "West Coast." The state's tourism office and locals alike emblazon Arizona's West Coast on travel brochures. I'm not sure what they call the California coast – maybe the West West Coast!

PRACTICAL INFORMATION

Airport
> **Laughlin/Bullhead City International Airport,** *north of town and east of Colorado River. Tel. 520/754-2134*

· Bus Depot
> **Kingman,** *Tel. 520/753-2522*
> **Bullhead City,** *Tel. 520/754-4625*

· Hospital
> **Kingman,** *Tel. 520/757-2101*
> **Bullhead City,** *Tel. 520/763-2773*

· Police (non-emergency)
> **Kingman,** *Tel. 520/753-2191*
> **Bullhead City,** *Tel. 520/763-1999*

· Taxi
> **Bullhead City,** *Tel. 520/754-7433 or 520/758-1024*

· Tourism Office/Visitors Bureau
> **Kingman,** *333 West Andy Devine Avenue, Tel. 520/753-6106*
> **Bullhead City,** *1251 Highway 95, Tel. 520/754-4121*

· Train Station
> **Kingman,** *Tel. 520/753-6886*

LAKE HAVASU CITY

Another of Arizona's popular "west coast" resort destination, Lake Havasu City sits on a the east side of a lake of the same name. The lake, which measures 45 miles from north to south and about three miles across, appears more like a big bulge in the Colorado River than like a lake. It was created by the impoundment of the river at Parker Dam to the south of Lake Havasu City. Somewhat smaller than Bullhead City and growing not quite at Bullhead's frenetic pace, Lake Havasu City is a beautiful and tranquil resort destination, highlighted by the famous London Bridge.

ARRIVALS & DEPARTURES

By Air

There is regular air service from Phoenix and Las Vegas.

By Bus

Public transportation is available to Lake Havasu City by daily bus service from either Phoenix or Las Vegas.

By Car

Lake Havasu City is located 23 miles south of I-40 (Exit 9) or 80 miles north of I-10 (Exit 1), both via AZ 95. Either one of those interstate highways and those that connect with it will provide easy access. It is about 220 miles from Phoenix by way of I-10 westbound and AZ 95.

ORIENTATION

Lake Havasu City is about 220 miles west of Phoenix. Getting around town couldn't be more of a snap – the most important road that visitors have to be acquainted with is AZ 95. That runs alongside the river and will bring you to most of the places you want to be either in town or to the north or south. McCulloch Boulevard is the primary east-to-west street.

WHERE TO STAY

Expensive

LONDON BRIDGE RESORT, *1477 Queen's Bay Road. Tel. 520/855-0888, Fax 520/855-9209. Toll free reservations Tel. 800/624-7939. 150 Rooms. Rates: rooms $75-150; suites $179-249, all year. Highest rates are generally on weekends. Most major credit cards accepted. Located just west of AZ 95 in the center of town on Thompson Bay.*

A most attractive 110-acre waterfront resort, the London Bridge is part of a complex that is Lake Havasu's main attraction: the relocated London Bridge and the shopping village that has grown up around it.

Many rooms have excellent views of the lake. Both rooms and the large suites are attractively decorated in a modern style. All suites have an in-room Jacuzzi.

The Resort has extensive recreational facilities that include three swimming pools, spa, tennis, and golf. Just about any type of water sport as well as cruises on the Colorado River can be arranged. Area tours depart from the Lodge. They also have a private sandy beach. For dining there are two restaurants and a cocktail lounge. One of them, the Bridgewater Cafe, is listed in the *Where to Eat* section.

Moderate

INN AT TAMARISK, *3101 London Bridge Road. Tel. 520/764-3033, Fax 520/764-3046. Toll free reservations Tel. 800/226-1869. 17 Rooms. Rates: $43-115, all year. Major credit cards accepted. Located about 4 miles north of the center of town via London Bridge Road that hugs the lake shore.*

This small and intimate property consists of multi-bedroom suites, many with a pleasant lake view. All are nicely furnished and feature such amenities as coffee makers, refrigerators, and microwave ovens. Over half have full kitchen facilities. If you don't plan on cooking in your room, however, restaurants all require a short car ride, the only real drawback to the Inn at Tamarisk. For recreation you can jump in the attractive swimming pool or play in the horseshoe pit or shuffleboard court. There's also a putting green.

ISLAND INN HOTEL, *1300 West McCulloch Boulevard. Tel. 520/680-0606, Fax 520/680-4218. Toll free reservations Tel. 800/243-9955. 116 Rooms. Rates: High season (March through October): $70-90; Low season (December through February): $59-69. Major credit cards accepted. Located on the small island reached by crossing over the London Bridge.*

The Island Inn has a great location on the narrow neck of the island that separates the main body of Lake Havasu from Thompson Bay, within walking distance to the shopping and restaurants of the London Bridge village. Many of the modern four-story motor inn's guest rooms feature balconies that provide excellent vistas. The accommodations are among the nicest in Lake Havasu and represent perhaps the best value in town. Some rooms have microwaves and refrigerators.

Facilities at the Island Inn include a restaurant with adjacent cocktail lounge, heated swimming pool, and a whirlpool.

SANDS VACATION RESORT, *2040 Mesquite Avenue. Tel. 520/855-1388, Fax 520/453-1802. Toll free reservations Tel. 800/521-0360. 42 Rooms. Rates: $110-130, all year. Major credit cards accepted. Located north of the junction with London Bridge and then one mile east of AZ 95.*

Another all-suite facility featuring either one or two bedrooms, so the prices are also quite good. The furnishings and decor are pleasant and comfortable. All rooms have coffee makers and kitchenette with refrigerator and microwave. There's a separate living area in these spacious accommodations. The recreational facilities are a heated pool, lighted tennis court, and play courts for horseshoes, shuffleboard, volleyball and bocce. Restaurants are located within a short ride.

CAMPING & RV SITES
• **Cattail Cove State Park Campground,** *North on AZ 95, Lake Havasu City, Tel. 520/855-1223*
• **Emerald Cove Campground,** *Parker Dam Road, Parker-California side, Tel. 760-663-3737*
• **Havasu Springs Resort,** *North on AZ 95, Parker, Tel. 520/667-3361*
• **Sandpoint Marina & RV Park,** *North on AZ 95, Lake Havasu City, Tel. 520/855-0549*

WHERE TO EAT
Expensive
VERSAILLES RISTORANTE, *357 South Lake Havasu Avenue. Tel. 520/855-4800. American Express, MasterCard, and VISA accepted. Dinner served nightly except Monday. Reservations are suggested.*

For a bit of elegance in a relaxed setting the Versailles is first rate. The prices aren't bad at all. In fact, although I've listed it as expensive you'll be able to find several entrees that are in the moderate category. The dining room is attractive and casual, overlooking the lake. At night with the lights sparkling it's almost like a fairy tale setting. The staff is efficient and knowledgeable.

The menu is, as you would expect from the name, mainly French. However, "ristorante" is definitely not French, so you'll also be able to select from several delicious Italian entrees as well. Appetizers at the Versailles are a special experience. Escargot and frog's legs highlight the list. Cocktails are served tableside or in the lounge. The wine list isn't big for a French restaurant but it's adequate.

Moderate
CITY OF LONDON ARMS PUB, RESTAURANT & BREWERY, *422 English Village. Tel. 520/855-8782. American Express, Discover, MasterCard, and VISA accepted. Breakfast, lunch, and dinner served daily.*

With its location in the village that abuts London Bridge, it isn't surprising to find a restaurant in the style of an old English pub. You could well be in London not only for the atmosphere but for the menu which has a lengthy list of English entrees. There's also a good variety of American fare. The beverage service is certainly unique in Lake Havasu – besides the usual cocktails (there is also a separate lounge), London

Arms has an excellent selection of real English ales. To add even more Mother Country realism, a formal tea is served daily in the afternoon. London Arms has a children's menu, too. Do I have any complaints? Only a small one – they charge for parking!

BRIDGEWATER CAFE, *1477 Queens Quay Road, in the London Bridge Resort. Tel. 520/855-0888. Major credit cards accepted. Breakfast, lunch, and dinner served daily.*

The Bridgewater serves well prepared American and western dishes in an attractive dining room. During warm weather you can eat outside on the patio which overlooks the famous London Bridge. The service is efficient and friendly. Cocktails and lounge.

KRYSTAL'S FINE DINING, *460 El Camino Way. Tel. 520/453-2999. MasterCard and VISA accepted. Dinner served nightly.*

I guess one naturally has high expectations when the name of a restaurant includes the words fine dining. Well, first of all, Krystal's is quite casual so you don't have to worry about a stuffy atmosphere. The food is simply excellent. There are a few meat dishes on the menu (including delicious ribs) but their bread and butter is the fresh fish and seafood. Speaking of bread, it's homemade and served piping hot from the oven. Krystal's also has a reputation for their fabulous desserts. Cocktail service and lounge on the premises.

SHUGRUE'S, *1425 McCulloch Boulevard, in the Island Fashion Mall. Tel. 520/453-1400. Lunch and dinner served daily.*

Located in a pretty setting that overlooks the narrow channel connecting Lake Havasu and the London Bridge, Shugrue's has a rather eclectic menu. You can have fresh fish, including sushi, pasta, American favorites like steak and prime rib, and even several wok-prepared dishes. A variety of pastries and breads are fresh baked on the premises. But the best news is that whatever you select should prove to be enjoyable as the chef certainly seems to know his way around a kitchen. Shugrue's has cocktail service, lounge, and children's menu.

Inexpensive

CHILI CHARLIE'S, *790 North Lake Havasu Avenue. Tel. 520/453-5055. Most major credit cards accepted. Lunch and dinner served daily.*

Lake Havasu is most definitely a tourist oriented community but the locals have to eat somewhere too. They often come to Chili Charlie's for value oriented Mexican fare. It's lively and the drinks always seem to be flowing around the video games and pool tables. A fun place to eat although not the best place to go if your little ones are coming along.

SEEING THE SIGHTS

Around Town

By a huge margin the main attraction in Lake Havasu City is **London Bridge** and the resort that has grown up around it. It was transported from its original Thames River location, brick by brick, and rebuilt across a small man-made channel of the Colorado River. It has, by all accounts, literally put Lake Havasu City on the map. First let me tell you that it might not be the bridge you expect to see. Many Americans, when they think of London Bridge, think of the tall structure with striking high brick towers. That, my friends, is Tower Bridge and still proudly spans the Thames in London. London Bridge is a far older low bridge with several graceful arches. The bridge is open at all times and is illuminated at night. The surrounding resort area covers 110 acres and features all sorts of recreation, lake cruises and a marina. Day visitors are most interested in, besides the bridge itself, the more than 50 specialty shops. Allow a minimum of an hour to visit the bridge and adjoining village.

The lake and river can be seen best by one of several available boat tours. The types of boats, length of excursion and prices vary a great deal so it is best to call the operators for information. Among these are:
- **Blue Water Charters**, *Tel. 888/855-7171*
- **Lake Havasu Boat Tours**, *Tel. 520/855-7979*
- **London Bridge Watercraft**, *Tel. 800/732-3665*

NIGHTLIFE & ENTERTAINMENT

Most of the nightlife in Lake Havasu is in the lounges and bars of the resort hotels both in the London Bridge area and all along the waterfront. Among the most popular are:
- **Chili Charlie's**, *790 North Lake Havasu Avenue, Tel. 520/453-5055*
- **Club Nautical Captain's Table Lounge**, *1000 McCulloch Boulevard, Tel. 520/855-2141*
- **Gallagher's**, *3524 McCulloch Boulevard, Tel. 520/855-5944*
- **Kokomo's**, *1477 Queen's Bay Road, Tel. 520/855-8782*
- **Shakespeare Lounge**, *2190 McCulloch Boulevard, Tel. 520/855-1261*
- **Sunset Lounge**, *271 Lake Havasu Avenue, Tel. 520/855-1111*

SPORTS & RECREATION

All locations are in Lake Havasu City.

Beaches
- **London Bridge Beach**, *on the island across London Bridge*
- **Rotary Park Beach**, *south of the bridge*
- **Lake Havasu State Park**, *north of the bridge*

Boat Rentals
- **Funtime Boat Rentals**, *Tel. 520/680-1003*, pontoon boats
- **River Rat Rentals**, *Tel. 520/855-4600*, jet boats and pontoons
- **Palm Oasis Rentals**, *Tel. 520/680-1131*, jet boats and pontoons
- **Sandpoint Marina**, *Tel. 520/855-0549*, pontoons and houseboats

Fishing
- **Lee Regnier Fishing**, *Tel. 520/505-HOOK*

Golf
- **Havasu Island Golf Course**, *1000 McCulloch Boulevard, Tel. 520/855-2131*
- **London Bridge Golf Club**, *2400 Clubhouse Drive, Tel. 520/855-2719*
- **Queen's Bay Golf Course**, *1477 Queen's Bay Road, Tel. 520/855-4777*

Hiking
- **Lake Havasu State Park**, *south of the bridge*

EXCURSIONS & DAY TRIPS

A couple of excellent wildlife refuges are located within twenty or so miles of Lake Havasu City. These are the **Havasu National Wildlife Refuge** to the north and the **Bill Williams River National Wildlife Refuge** to the south. The Havasu refuge's biggest section is located in scenic Topock Gorge, just south of the junction of I-40 at the Colorado River. It can be seen by either boat or by foot trail. The Bill Williams refuge is located at the confluence of the Bill Williams and Colorado Rivers. It, too, is accessible only by boat or foot. *Both refuges are open daily from 8:00am to 4:00pm and have free admission. The number for the Havasu Refuge is 619/326-3853 and for the Williams Refuge is 520/667-4144.*

Portions of the Bill Williams Refuge can be seen on a four hour jeep tour provided by **Outback Off-Road Adventures**, *1350 McCulloch Boulevard, Lake Havasu City. Tours daily at 8:00am and 1:00pm. The fare is $65. An all day trip for $130 is also offered. Tel. 520/680-6151.* The Topock Gorge section of the Havasu Refuge can be seen via London Bridge **Watercraft Tours**, *1519 Queen's Bay Road, Tel. 800/SEA-DOO5 for information and rates.*

An excellent half-day excursion via AZ 95 travels about 35 miles one-way to **Parker**. The first stop on this trip would be about half-way at the **Parker Dam**, the southernmost of the many Colorado River dams. This is considered to be the world's deepest dam but you wouldn't know it to look at it from the outside. That's because about two-thirds of its height is beneath the riverbed. On the self-guided tour you'll descend to the bottom in an elevator and visit the power plant as well as several exhibit areas. You can also drive across the dam above the water or detour along scenic roads on either side of the river. *Tours are available Monday to Friday from 8:00am to 5:00pm and are free of charge. Tel. 619/663-3715 or 520/669-2174.*

The town of Parker is the commercial center for the Colorado River Indian Reservation as well as for the dam. Of interest in town is the **Colorado River Indian Tribes Museum**. Exhibits explain the history and culture of the Mojave, Chemehuevi, Navajo, and Hopi tribes as well as some of the prehistoric cultures. An excellent collection of Indian baskets found nearby is a highlight. There is also a library for those interested in doing research on Native Americans and an excellent gift shop selling authentic Indian crafts. *Open Monday to Friday from 8:00am to 5:00pm and on Saturday from 10:00am to 3:00pm, closed on major holidays; admission is free but donations are appreciated; Tel. 520/669-9211.*

PRACTICAL INFORMATION
• **Bus Depot**, *Tel. 520/855-1039*
• **Hospital**, *Tel. 520/855-8185*
• **Police** (non-emergency), *Tel. 520/885-4884*
• **Tourist Office/Visitors Bureau**, *Tel. 800/242-8278*

YUMA
Despite being one of the hottest locations in the United States (during the summer, of course), it is Yuma's weather which attracts so many visitors. Comfortable winters, low humidity, and sunshine a staggering 93 percent of the time (so says the weather bureau), Yuma is ideal for every sun worshipper. It has become big enough in recent years to provide all of the services that people want and expect while maintaining a distinctively western atmosphere. Named for the Yuma Indian tribe, the city and surrounding area have many interesting attractions of historic significance. Opportunities for recreation are also abundant.

ARRIVALS & DEPARTURES
By Air
America West, United, and Delta all have commuter service to Yuma from Phoenix and Tucson operating under the name's America West Express, United Express, and Skywest Airlines.

By Car
I-8 runs through the city and provides access from San Diego and other points within Southern California. To the east I-8 runs into I-10 and then goes on to Tucson, a total distance of about 220 miles. US 95 runs

to the north up to I-40 where it becomes AZ 95 and connects with other locations on Arizona's West Coast.

By Public Transportation
The Greyhound bus station is located at *170 East 17th Place* (daily service to Tucson, Phoenix, and San Diego). The Amtrak **train** station (service to Los Angeles and Tucson) is at *670 East 32nd Street.*

ORIENTATION
Yuma is located on the Colorado River directly across from the Californian and Mexican border to the west. It is within 15 miles of Mexico to the south.

I-8 runs along the north and east side of the city. Business I-8 is called 4th Avenue and is the primary north-south street. The main east-to-west thoroughfare is 16th Street (which is also US 95). Both streets have exits on I-8. Numbered streets always run east to west (beginning at the Colorado River) while Avenues run north-south. Avenues with letters of the alphabet also run north to south on the city's west side. There aren't that many named streets so the numbered grid format is a breeze to negotiate.

WHERE TO STAY
Moderate
LA FUENTE INN, *1513 East 16th Street. Tel. 520/329-1814, Fax 520/343-2671. Toll free reservations Tel. 800/841-1814. 96 Rooms. Rates: High season (January 1st to April 30th): $79-96; Low season (May 1st to December 31st): $70-79; all rates including continental breakfast. Most major credit cards accepted. Located on US 95 just to the east of I-8.*

My view is that this is the nicest hotel in town and one of the better values. The grounds are spacious and attractive. The building's architecture is southwestern style and the front entrance features a large fountain whose waters tumble down a series of boulders. The inner courtyard has well manicured lawns bordered by trees and shrubs that enclose the swimming pool and a pretty gazebo. Regular rooms and suites are thoughtfully furnished and feature coffee makers and refrigerators. Some have microwave ovens and hair dryers.

Facilities include a heated pool, whirlpool, and nicely equipped exercise room. Restaurants are plentiful within a short distance. Although they don't have an on-premise restaurant the continental breakfast is adequate and during the evening complimentary beverages are served. Hors d'oeuvres accompany the drinks two nights each week.

RADISSON SUITES INN YUMA, *2600 South Fourth Avenue. Tel. 520/726-4830, Fax 520/341-1152. Toll free reservations Tel. 800/333-3333. 164 Rooms. Rates: High season (January 1st to April 30th): $109-122; Low season (May 1st to December 31st): $82-109; all rates including continental breakfast. Major credit cards accepted. Located about a mile south of US 95 on the I-8 business loop.*

The Radisson is, like La Fuente Inn, an all-suite facility that is well above average in appearance and quality. I rank it below the former only because you're paying about ten dollars more and not getting much more for it. However, for the well respected Radisson name, it is also a good value. The single bedroom suites all have a wet bar, microwave, coffee maker, refrigerator and hair dryer. The rooms in this three story southwestern mission style building are beautifully decorated and large. Each also has two telephone and two televisions. The grounds feature many stately palm trees.

The Radisson has a heated swimming pool and whirlpool. Guests receive free privileges at a nearby health club. Breakfast consists of a nice buffet spread which goes somewhat beyond the continental name given to it. Other restaurants and ample shopping are located within a few minutes of the property. Complimentary evening beverages are served and they have an hors d'oeuvres night on Wednesdays.

Inexpensive

YUMA CABANA HOTEL, *2151 South Fourth Avenue. Tel. 520/783-8311, Fax 520/783-1126. Toll free reservations Tel. 800/874-0811. 63 Rooms. Rates: High season (January 1st through February): $65-88; Low season (April 1st to November 30th): $42-60; all rates including continental breakfast. Major credit cards accepted. Located a half mile south of US 95 on the I-8 business loop.*

An attractive motel featuring regular rooms and multi-bedroom facilities, including some with kitchens or efficiencies. All have coffee makers and some have microwaves or refrigerators. The rooms have recently been redecorated and are comfortable. The level of cleanliness and maintenance is well above that of most facilities at a comparable price for this area. The rooms are also a good size and many have patios or balcony. There is a heated swimming pool and shuffleboard court on the premises but no restaurant. However, you are within walking distance of several places to eat. Another good value for the money.

CAMPING & RV SITES

The Bureau of Land Management operates a number of camping sites in the vicinity of Imperial Dam and Martinez Lake, about 20 miles northeast of downtown Yuma. Contact the BLM's Yuma office for details, *Tel. 520/726-6300.*

- **Azure Sky RV Park**, *5510 East Highway 80, Tel. 520/726-0160*
- **Headquarters Campground**, *Organ Pipe Cactus National Monument, Tel. 520/387-6849*
- **Hitchin Post Trailer Park**, *2837 West 1st Street, Tel. 520/783-8063*
- **Shangri-La RV Park**, *10498 N. Frontage Road (I-8), Tel. 520/342-9123*
- **Spring Garden RV Park**, *3550 West 8th Street, Tel. 520/783-1526*
- **Yuma Mesa RV Park**, *5990 East Highway 80, Tel. 520/344-3369*

WHERE TO EAT

Moderate

HUNTER STEAKHOUSE, *2355 South 4th Avenue. Tel. 520/782-3637. Most major credit cards accepted. Lunch and dinner served nightly.*

A good family style place featuring mainly prime rib and steaks all well prepared to your specifications. The service is quick and efficient and the surroundings pleasant enough. Cocktail service.

MANDARIN PALACE, *350 East 32nd Street. Tel. 520/344-2805. American Express, Diners Club, MasterCard, and VISA accepted. Dinner served nightly, lunch on Monday through Friday.*

Perhaps Yuma isn't the place where you would expect to find great Chinese food. Well, think again. The Mandarin Palace serves an excellent selection of Mandarin and Szechuan style cuisine. The latter is spiced just right – hot enough without chasing you out of your seat. If one or more people in your party aren't in the mood for Chinese, the Palace has a small selection of decent American dishes that certainly aren't anything special. For lunch there is a plentiful buffet that is colorful as well as delicious. The Mandarin Palace has full cocktail service and a lounge.

Inexpensive

THE GARDEN CAFE, *250 Madison Avenue. Tel. 520/783-1491. American Express, MasterCard, and VISA accepted. Breakfast and lunch served daily except Monday. Closed July through September.*

A charming little place that serves a nice selection of sandwiches and salads as well as soup and a variety of quiches. The desserts are top notch. It's too bad they aren't open for dinner. The atmosphere is wonderful – a restored 1887 building surrounds an outdoor patio that is nicely shaded by trees and beautifully landscaped. Sunday brunch is a Yuma favorite and will be for you too!

SEEING THE SIGHTS

Our tour of the city begins at the **Yuma Territorial Prison State Park**, located adjacent to the 4th Street exit of I-8 (Giss Parkway and Prison Hill Road) and situated on a high bluff overlooking the Colorado River. The most hardened of Arizona's criminals were incarcerated in this maximum security prison from 1876 through 1909. Many of them earned their stays during what was then still the wild west we think of from movies and television.

Although the thick adobe walls that once surrounded the prison are gone, visitors can take self or guided tours and see actual cells, the main gate, and guard tower. A solitary confinement area known as "the hole" is of unusual interest. A small museum has exhibits which tell the story of the prison's history. Give yourself at least a half hour to visit the park. *Open daily from 8:00am through 5:00pm (guided tours at 11:00, 2:00, and 3:30). Closed on Christmas Day. Admission is $3 per person. Tel. 520/783-4771.*

Nearby on 2nd Avenue on a site by the Colorado River that also faces Yuma's city hall is the **Yuma Crossing State Historic Park**. During the middle of the 19th century there were many military posts scattered throughout the Arizona Territory. The Quartermaster Depot was established in 1865 to serve as a major storage and distribution point for supplies. A total of 12 buildings are located on the ten acre site, half of which are original. The others have been built to the original specifications. Guides costumed in period clothing are on hand to relate tales and history of the site. Also located here is a **Southern Pacific steam locomotive** built in 1907. The 194,000-pound engine saw service in the Yuma area. By the time it was retired in 1957 it had seen an estimated 2-1/2 million miles of work. You should be able to complete your visit within 45 minutes to an hour. *Open daily from 10:00am until 5:00pm except for Christmas; admission price is $4 for adults, $2.50 for age 55 and older, and $2 for children, also a combined family rate of $8 available; Tel. 520/343-2500.*

A final downtown stop is the **Century House Museum**. The former home of a wealthy Yuma merchant, the house now exhibits furnishings and artifacts representative of Yuma's frontier period. The original owner of the house had a colorful garden with bird aviaries and these are also maintained as they were in the past. The talking birds are sure to delight children. *240 Madison Avenue, open 10:00am to 4:00pm, Tuesday through Saturday, closed on state holidays; no admission charge; Tel. 520/782-1841.*

Several other fine attractions are located in close proximity to the city center. The first is the **Fort Yuma Quechan Museum**, which occupys a former officer's mess hall built in 1851. The museum was established by the Quechan tribe to depict their early history as well as the Spanish explorers and American military and settlers. Two missions, including the attractive Spanish colonial style **St. Thomas Mission** are located nearby. *Located on Indian Hill in Fort Yuma Indian Reservation on the California side of the border, open weekdays from 8:00am to 5:00pm and on Saturday from 10:00am to 4:00pm, November through April; during the remainder of the year* *the hours are 7:00am to 4:00pm, Monday through Friday, closed on major holidays; admission is $1 for those over age 12; Tel. 619/572-0661 .*

The **Saihati Camel Farm** is reached by taking Avenue 3E south from town for five miles, then west on County Route 16 to Avenue 1E. The farm is dedicated to the preservation of the wildlife of the Arabian desert. Besides the distinctive humped camels, Saihati is home to the oryx, pygmy goats, water buffalos and other unusual animals. Camels were originally brought to the American southwest because it was believed that they would be well suited to working in the dry heat.

However, unlike their native habitat, the land in most parts of the southwestern desert is hard rather than sandy. Consequently, it was damaging to the camel's soft hooves. The camels here are kept in an area that is more to their liking. *The farm can only be seen by guided tour's lasting approximately one hour. They are offered Monday through Saturday at 10:00am and again at 2:00pm. On Sunday it is only given at 2:00pm. It is closed June through September except by appointment and on Thanksgiving and Christmas. Admission is $3 for ages 3 and up. Tel. 520/627-2553.*

NIGHTLIFE & ENTERTAINMENT

Besides the usual assortment of bars and cocktail lounges in hotels, Yuma has quite a few spots where the locals can enjoy their evenings. Popular lounges with entertainment are as follows:

- **California Bakery**, *284 S. Main Street, Tel. 520/782-735*. An unusual name for a bar and lounge with live bands showcasing Arizona home-grown entertainers.
- **Jimmie Dee's**, *38 W. 2nd Street, Tel. 520/783-5647.* Currently the hot spot of the local entertainment scene, there are live bands several nights each week.
- **Martinez Lake Cantina**, *west end of Martinez Lake Road, Tel. 520/783-0253.* Features dancing in addition to live music. Country western and rock nights.

Yuma's nightlife has also developed a cultural side in recent years. The **Yuma Ballet Theatre**, *Tel. 520/341-1925*, is part of a regional ballet association and gives performances during April and December. The **Yuma Chamber Orchestra**, *Tel. 520/344-7574*, has been performing since 1976 and gives six performances each year. Finally, the **Yuma Community Theater**, *Tel. 520/783-1780*, utilizes local residents to perform major Broadway shows.

Casinos

- **Blue Water Casino**, *119-B W. Riverside Drive, Parker. Tel. 800/747-8777*
- **Cocopah Casino**, *Yuma. Tel. 800/237-5687*

• **Golden Ha'san Casino**, *Ajo. Tel. 520/362-2746; Paradise Casino, Yuma. Tel. 888/777-4946*

SPORTS & RECREATION

Auto Racing
• **The Yuma Speedway**, *US 95, five miles south of Yuma, Tel. 520/726-9483,* holds about two dozen events each year. Prices vary depending upon the event.

Boating & Water Sports
   The Imperial Dam area (Martinez Lake and Ferguson Lake) offers every type of water recreation. Facilities include beaches and boat ramps. All of these sites are on lands owned by the Bureau of Land Management. Their office is the best source of information. *Tel. 520/726-6300.*

Golf
   All courses listed are 18 holes and open to the visiting public.
• **Arroyo Dunes**, *32nd Street and Avenue A, Tel. 520/726-8350*
• **Desert Hills Municipal Golf Course**, *1245 West Desert Hills Drive, Tel. 520/341-0644*
• **Mesa del Sol Public Golf Course**, *10583 Camino del Sol, Tel. 520/342-1283*

EXCURSIONS & DAY TRIPS

   There are some other worthwhile things to see and do within a relatively short drive of Yuma. A popular activity is to take a boat ride on the **Colorado River**. Two companies offering trips are the Colorado King I Paddle Boat and Yuma River Tours. Both leave from Martinez Lake which can be reached by taking US 95 northeast to Martinez Lake Road and then north ten miles to Fisher's Landing. The **Colorado King**, *Tel. 520/782-2412*, is the shorter of the two rides. **Yuma River Tours**, *Tel. 520/783-4400*, last from 9:30am to 2:30pm and make several stops that give you the opportunity to see, among other things, Indian petroglyphs.
   Back on US 95 you can continue north for several more miles to the fascinating **McPhaul Swinging Bridge to Nowhere**. It once crossed the Gila River but the river is now an area of desert. It was quite an engineering feat when completed in 1929. In fact, the famous Golden Gate Bridge was built in its style.
   The **Yuma Valley Railway** consists of a 1953 45-ton diesel engine pulling historic 1922 Pullman coaches along the banks of the Colorado River for 17 miles through picturesque countryside and farmlands. Mexico is visible from most of the route. *8th Street and Levee Road.*

Generally operates on weekends from October through May but it is best to call for schedules and fares and reservations. Tel. 520/783-3456.

To the east of Yuma via I-8 to **Dome Valley** and then on Old Highway 80 (a total distance of about 35 miles) is the **McElhaney Cattle Company and Museum.** This isn't a ranch but a large collection of buggies, carriages, wagons and antique cars. Some have been restored to their original appearance while others are in the process of being restored. While you may not be interested in driving about 70 miles round trip to see this, it's a good stop if you happen to be heading back to Tucson or other points via I-8. *Open Monday through Friday from 9:00am to 4:00pm and admission is free; Tel. 520/785-3384.*

PRACTICAL INFORMATION

- **Airport**, *Tel. 520/726-5882*
- **Bus Station**, *Tel. 520/783-4403*
- **Hospital**, *Tel. 520/344-2000*
- **Police** (non-emergency), *Tel. 520/782-3236*
- **Taxi**
    Yellow Taxi, *Tel 520/782-4444*
    Yuma City Cab, *Tel. 520/782-0111*
- **Tourism Office/Visitors Bureau**, *377 South Main Street, Tel. 520/783-0071*
- **Train Station**, *Tel. 520/344-0300*

GILA BEND & AJO

The origins of European settlement in the Gila Bend area go back to before 1700. It is now primarily an area for ranching and farming that is supported by the water of the Gila River Valley. A small town of less than 2,000 people, Gila Bend is a gateway community to some interesting sights to the south, an area of desert and mountains as well as a large Indian reservation.

Even though Ajo is larger and has more to see and do than Gila Bend, I gave Gila Bend "co-headliner" status for this section because of it's proximity to Phoenix and its location on the main interstate highway.

ARRIVALS & DEPARTURES

GILA BEND

By Bus

Regular bus service is available from Phoenix.

By Car

Gila Bend is located about 65 miles from Phoenix via I-10 to Exit 112 and then south on AZ 85. AZ 85 continues south from Gila Bend and provides the major means of getting to most of the area's attractions. From Tucson it is a distance of approximately 120 miles via I-10 to I-8. Exits 115, 116, and 119 of I-8 serve Gila Bend. I-8 also provides access from Yuma and points further west in southern California.

AJO
By Car

The town of Ajo, 42 miles south of Gila Bend on AZ 85 can also be used as the base of operations for this area, especially if you're coming from Tucson. The quickest way to Ajo from Tucson is to take AZ 86, a ride of about 130 miles.

WHERE TO STAY
GILA BEND
Moderate

BEST WESTERN SPACE AGE LODGE, *401 East Pima Street. Tel. 520/683-2273, Fax 520/683-2273. Toll free reservations Tel. 800/528-1234. 41 Rooms. Rates: High season (February 1st to March 31st): $64-78; Low season (April 1st to mid-December): $46-59. Major credit cards accepted. Located in the center of town on the I-8 business loop.*

The pickings are slim in Gila Bend but you can't go wrong with this place. The design is well beyond "contemporary" – a portion of the building looks like a space ship. Why they have that design in this traditional Native American and Hispanic area is beyond me. The rooms are clean and comfortable and feature coffee makers; some have refrigerators. The motel has a swimming pool and whirlpool. The on-premise restaurant features American and Mexican entrees and although just average may well be the best place in town to eat.

AJO
Moderate

MINE MANAGER'S HOUSE INN, *1 Greenway Drive. Tel. 520/387-6505, Fax 520/387-6508. 5 Rooms. Rates: $89-105; all year including full breakfast. MasterCard and VISA accepted. Located about 3/4 mile south of AZ 85. Go south on La Mina Avenue and then Hospital Drive to Greenway.*

Accommodations in tiny Ajo consist of a few below standard motels and a couple of bed and breakfasts. The Mine Manager's House is the better of the latter category. In fact, it's quite good. The historic house was built in 1919 on the side of a hill overlooking the town and desert. Each comfortable room is individually decorated in styles representing a range of Arizona's history. The one-story house has a whirlpool out back. The home cooked breakfast is excellent. Most of the satisfactory eating places in Ajo are located a short ride away in the town's plaza area.

CAMPING & RV SITES
- **Ajo RV Park**, *Highway 85, Ajo, Tel. 520/387-6796*
- **Organ Pipe Cactus National Monument Campground**, *Tel. 520/387-6849*

WHERE TO EAT
AJO
Inexpensive

   COPPER KETTLE, *On the Plaza. Tel. 520/387-7000. Most major credit cards accepted. Breakfast, lunch, and dinner served daily.*

   Don't expect to find any great dining in this remote portion of the state. On the positive side, though, is that you aren't going to encounter any stuffy overpriced dining rooms either. In Ajo most of the places to eat are in the Plaza vicinity. The Copper Kettle is a typical family style restaurant serving a good variety of American entrees, dominated by southwestern fare. The service is friendly and the pace relaxed.

SEEING THE SIGHTS
   Pima Street (AZ 85) is the main street through **Gila Bend**. The town's visitor center is located here and has a small free museum that documents area history. About three miles north of the east end of Pima Street on Stout Road is the **Gatlin Archaeological Park**. Within the park are the remains of an Hohokam ceremonial platform from around the year 800, a sports arena, several dwellings, and an irrigation canal. Excavations of the area began only in 1958 and although the park opened to the public in 1993 it is still being developed.

   Proceed from Gila Bend to **Ajo** by driving south on AZ 85. The road passes through a series of low mountain ranges, much of it on restricted land that is part of the **Luke Air Force Base Gunnery Range**. Volcanic rock formations are frequently seen in the **Crater Range**.

   The origin of the town's name is a matter of dispute. It could be from a Papago Indian word meaning "paint" or the Spanish word for "garlic." The center of town is the location of **Plazatown Square**, a surprisingly attractive spot containing mission style churches and other Spanish style structures. The buildings, however, date from no earlier than 1917, the founding date of Ajo. Also in town is the **Ajo Historical Museum**, which has artifacts and photographs tracing the history of Ajo. *Indian School Road, open from October 1st to April 15th, Tuesday through Saturday from 10:00am to 4:00pm; admission is free; Tel. 520/387-7868.*

Nearby on Indian School Road is the **Mine Lookout**, an open pit copper mine that is 1-1/2 miles across. The adjacent visitor center describes the various stages of the copper mining process. *The lookout is open during daylight hours all year but the visitor center operates October 1st to April 15th only. Hours are 10:00am to 4:00pm, Tuesday through Saturday.*

The vast **Tohono O'odham Indian Reservation** begins a scant ten miles south of Ajo at the town of **Why** (no question mark required, ha ha – this is one of my favorite place names in all the world). AZ 86 runs through the reservation and contains many trading posts, good places to find jewelry, baskets, blankets, and other Native American products.

The **Caberza Prieta National Wildlife Refuge** covers more than 860,000 acres of the Sonoran Desert and is home to bighorn sheep, jackrabbits, lizards, bats, and many other forms of desert wildlife. A four-wheel drive vehicle is required to negotiate the refuge's non-roads. You must also obtain an entry permit from the refuge headquarters located in Ajo (1611 North Second Avenue). *Access is allowed between 7:30am and 4:30pm, Monday to Friday. Tel. 520/387-6483.*

The Ajo area's biggest attraction is located on AZ 85 a few miles south of Why. The huge **Organ Pipe Cactus National Monument** borders on the Mexican state of Sonora. This is one of the most pristine areas of true Sonoran Desert in the United States. Wonderful specimens of the organ pipe cactus can be found throughout the 516 square mile monument. Other types of vegetation include saguaro cactus and the palo verde tree. The monument has a visitor center located 17 miles south of the entrance station. Exhibits describe the area's natural history as well as cultural development. Near the visitor center is the beginning of the park's two self guiding driving tours. One is the 21-mile long Ajo Mountain Drive and the other is the 53-mile Puerto Blanco Drive. Neither road is paved but the graded way is well maintained and easily passable for any car so long as it hasn't rained. If it has rained recently you should make inquiry at the visitor center before setting out on either drive. Trailers and RVs over 25 feet in length are not recommended.

Either drive will provide plenty of opportunity to view the monument's diverse flora. The shorter route takes about 90 minutes while at least 2-1/2 to three hours is required for the longer road. *The monument is open at all times but the visitor center operates daily from 8:00am to 5:00pm. Admission is $5 per vehicle for those not holding a park service passport. Summer visitors are advised to carry adequate drinking water. Tel. 520/387-6849.*

Finally, some odds and ends on the Ajo and Gila Bend area. There isn't any nightlife to speak of. In fact, even the chamber of commerce suggests watching the beautiful desert sunsets as an evening activity. Recreational facilities are similarly limited. Those who like to explore the outdoors on their own can certainly wander around the desert near either town. However, there are no state parks in the immediate vicinity.

PRACTICAL INFORMATION

• **Police** (non emergency for both Ajo and Gila Bend), *Tel. 520/387-7621*
• **Tourist Office/Visitors Bureau**
    Ajo, *Tel. 520/387-7742*
    Gila Bend, *Tel. 520/683-2002*

COVER ALL OF WESTERN ARIZONA

A last note before closing this chapter. At the outset I mentioned that given the number of widely scattered attractions the west region might well be too large for most visitors to handle in one trip. However, I'm sure that there are going to be some readers who opt to do so. For you, then, I include a routing that covers all five areas. It departs from Phoenix and can be done in either direction.

Take US 60 west to **Wickenburg**. *After touring that town travel north on US 93 to I-40 and then west to* **Kingman**. *You can take as many of the Kingman area excursions as you like but save the loop to Bullhead City for last. This way you don't have to return to Kingman but can continue south on AZ 95 to* **Lake Havasu City**. *Upon completion of that section routes AZ 95 and US 95 south will take you into* **Yuma**. *The final western touring area,* **Gila Bend & Ajo**, *can be reached by taking I-8 east to AZ 85. Return to Phoenix by taking AZ 85 back north past Gila Bend to I-10. A few miles east on the interstate returns you to Phoenix. Alternatively, you could end up in Tucson. Just take AZ 86 east from just above the entrance to the Organ Pipe Cactus National Monument. The total mileage for this routing (Phoenix to Phoenix) is approximately 650 miles, exclusive of side excursions.*

19. ARIZONA FOR COWBOYS & COWGIRLS

The fascination that the historic American west holds for millions of people continues unabated. That, combined with the increase in adventure travel and a desire to relive a more simple time, has resulted in tremendous growth for dude ranches, more commonly known today as **guest ranches**.

While these facilities can be found throughout the American west, and particular in the southwest, it is Arizona that has a special connection to them. In fact, while other states may have surpassed Arizona in the total number of their ranches, Arizona was the first to popularize the genre. To this day, many of the nation's premier guest ranches are still found in the Grand Canyon State.

It is possible to find guest ranches in almost every part of Arizona although they are concentrated mostly in two areas. These are in and around **Wickenburg** (located only about 50 miles northwest of Phoenix) and the greater **Tucson** area. The list of guest ranches in this chapter will, however, cover the entire state.

Different people have far ranging ideas of exactly what a guest ranch vacation entails. And that's fine because, indeed, there is a great variety to be found among Arizona's ranches. They range from simple to luxurious and from carefully controlled experiences to working ranches. So let's take a closer look at the features of these venerable institutions.

The basic distinction in guest ranches is whether or not they are a working ranch. Those that are will often have less variety of recreational opportunities because you will be spending much of your time taking part in such activities as cattle roping lessons, herding and so forth. The ultimate experience at a working ranch is to take part in a real cattle drive. These are seasonal by nature so if you do select to visit a working ranch with the intention of participating in a drive, be sure to find out the dates when the drives will be taking place.

SO YOU WANNABE A COWBOY...

*The listings in this chapter will show you how to spend a few days or maybe a couple of weeks on a ranch herding cattle a la Billy Crystal in the movies. Well, pardner, you can try your hand at this even if you only have a day to spare. The **Rocky Mountain Cattle Moo-vers** of Tucson conduct one-day cattle drives in the Tortolita Mountains to the north of Tucson. If you even have rudimentary horseback riding skills you can sign up for this adventure which includes a steer roping lesson, lunch and dinner, and entertainment around a sunset campfire. The cowardly cowboys among us can opt to go along for the ride by haywagon or by jeep. The excursions are offered from the middle of October to mid-May and, depending upon the method of transportation, cost anywhere from $80 to $190.*

For further information you can write to the Rocky Mountain Cattle Moo-vers, 7501 North Wade Road, Tucson, AZ, 85743, Tel. 800/826-9666. Credit cards accepted.

Non-working ranches were frequently, in the past, "real" and have subsequently been turned into a vacation destination. Some were specifically established to be guest ranches. Although they won't have any cattle drives, horseback riding is still a principal activity. All levels of riding experience are accommodated at every ranch. Formal lessons are generally available and there are horses to fit the particular needs of individual riders. Among the other many activities to partake in at a guest ranch are various sports such as horseshoes, volleyball, swimming (usually in a river or lake rather than at a pool), nature walks, four-wheel drives into isolated scenic spots, and fishing. The latter is probably the second most popular activity for many guest ranch visitors after horseback riding. Ranches are usually located close to one or more scenic or historic attractions and ranch personnel will often conduct tours to these sites.

Some of the things you will generally not find at a ranch are in-room telephones and televisions (although they are often available in the main ranch building) and the nice amenities found in luxury hotels. Ranches located in hotter climates will, however, have air conditioning. While the level of accommodations will range from spartan (bunk houses without private facilities) all the way to large private cabins, the nature of the living can best be described as simple. A big plus for many visitors, however, is the private nature of a ranch experience. The number of guests present at any ranch at a particular time is rarely more than a hundred and many of those listed here keep their guest counts under 50. So you can expect individual attention from a large and friendly staff that will almost always include a ranching husband/wife combination and members of their family.

Most ranches quote their rates on a weekly per person basis. Be sure to carefully read the rate basis in the listings – generally for two persons. The minimum stay is indicated. Keep in mind that rates for longer stays (especially by the week) usually offer a discount from the daily rate. Children are generally charged at a lower price. All of the ranches welcome children but only a few have special programs for youngsters. If you're traveling with children it is best to make direct inquiry with the ranch of your choice to find out exactly what their facilities for children are.

Rates generally include three meals a day but there is sometimes an extra charge for meals served while on trail rides or on overnight camping expeditions. Ranch food can be characterized as plentiful and wholesome family style cooking. Don't expect the flair and style of a fancy big city restaurant. Exactly what else is included in the rate quoted to you depends upon the specific ranch. It is customary for the rate to cover all activities but many, unfortunately, charge additional for one of the main reasons to come to a ranch in the first place – horseback riding. When such fees are imposed they can often run up to an additional $100 a day per person. Again, get as much information on these extra charges before you actually confirm a reservation. Deposit and payment policies will be told to you at the time of booking. It is not uncommon for ranches not to accept credit cards.

The 16 guest ranches listed here are all members of one or more reputable dude ranch associations, including the **Arizona Dude Ranch Association**. If you are looking for a ranch vacation I would avoid any establishment that doesn't belong to such an organization. While such places may be beautiful, relaxing and more, you can't be sure that they'll provide an authentic ranch experience. The preceding general information and what follows on each ranch can only provide some of the answers to your questions. So, especially if you're a first time dude rancher, don't hesitate to ask as many questions of the ranch operator before making a decision.

GUEST RANCHES

BAR BK MULESHOE, *Bagdad Route, 37 miles southwest of Prescott. Tel. 520/442-3244. Toll free reservations 800/830-MULE. Rates: $270-575 per day. 3-day, 4-day and weekly packages available.*

This is a working cattle ranch. However, it has a large variety of recreational facilities. Accommodations range from a no-frills (no private bathroom) bunk house that houses 7 people to nice units in the main ranch house, and all the way up to spacious cabins for one to four persons.

CIRCLE Z RANCH, *Patagonia. 65 miles from Tucson via I-10 east, AZ 83 south and then AZ 82 to the ranch, 4 miles southwest of Patagonia. Tel. 520/394-2525. Toll free reservations 888/854-2525. Rates: $750-945 per week with a three night minimum stay (at higher per day rate).*

Set amid the lovely scenery of the Santa Rita mountains on 5,000 acres not far from the Mexican border, the Circle Z consists of seven Spanish adobe style cottages that can accommodate up to ten people. Depending upon the size of the cottage and the number in your party, you may be sharing a cottage with other folks.

ELKHORN RANCH, *north of Sasabe (50 miles southwest of Tucson). Take AZ 86 (Ajo Highway) west from Tucson to AZ 286 and proceed 20 miles south to Elkhorn Ranch sign. Proceed on dirt road for 7 miles. Tel. 520/822-1040. Rates: Call for information.*

A nice small ranch (limited to 32 guests), visitors are housed in attractive cabins surrounded by mesquite trees. Situated in pretty Sabino Canyon and established in 1945, the ranch has been in the same family for three generations. It was formerly a working cattle ranch. Among the amenities are a heated swimming pool and a tennis court. The Longhouse serves as a lounge and area for guest interaction.

FLYING E RANCH, *2801 Wickenburg Way, Wickenburg; 4 miles southwest of town off of AZ 60. Tel. 520/684-2690. Toll free reservations 888/684-2650. Rates: $225-$350 per night.*

With only 16 rooms, the Flying E offers personalized vacations on a 20,000 acre working ranch. Situated on the outskirts of Wickenburg in the shadow of Vulture Peak, the ranch traverses picturesque desert scenery. It is one of the few ranches with a heated swimming pool. There are also complete exercise facilities and a sauna.

GRAPEVINE CANYON GUEST RANCH, *Pearce. Take I-10 east from Tucson to Exit 318 (Dragoon) and follow Dragoon Road to US 191. Turn south and go past Sunsites to Treasure Road and the ranch. Tel. 888/BE-A-DUDE for information; toll free reservations 800/245-9202. Rates: $300-340 per night. 3 night minimum stay; lower weekly rates are available.*

With the rugged Dragoon Mountains as a setting, the Grapevine Canyon covers a vast 64,000 acres. That's plenty of room for the maximum 30 guest policy. Accommodations are quite nice whether you take the lower priced cabins or the slightly more expensive casitas.

KAY EL BAR GUEST RANCH, *Wickenburg. From the center of town (at the traffic light), drive west for two miles and then make a right on Rincon Road. Follow signs to ranch. Tel. 520/684-7593; toll free reservations 800/684-7583. Rates: $275-300 per night.*

Built in 1926, the Kay El Bar features authentic adobe style buildings that house only 24 guests at one time. There are 8 rooms in the main Lodge building (lower price). The remainder of the accommodations are in individual buildings. These include the Homestead House (two bedrooms with fireplace) and the Casas de la Rosita, Grande and Monterey.

LA TIERRA LINDA GUEST RANCH, *Tucson. Take I-10 north to Exit 248 and proceed west on Ina Road to Wade Road. Turn right on Wade (a dirt road) to the ranch. Tel. 888/872-6241. Rates: $165-335 per night depending upon season and size of accommodation.*

Nicely situated not far from downtown Tucson in the Tucson Mountains (within view of Sombrero Peak), this small ranch of only 30 acres started way back in the 1930's. It was completely remodeled in 1997 and offers accommodations that are better than in most guest ranches. They even offer in-room cable TV. All of the lodging is in individual casitas of one bedroom or two to three room suites. Located on the edge of Saguaro National Park, the property is home to many stately saguaro cacti. Because the ranch is so small, most of the riding takes place off-ranch. Not that it really matters.

LAZY K BAR GUEST RANCH, *8401 N. Scenic Drive, Tucson. Use Exit 248 from I-10 and follow Ina Road west for 1-1/2 miles to Silverbell Road. Then go 2 miles north and make a left on Pima Farms Road. Tel. 520/744-3050. Toll free reservations 800/321-7018. Rates: $300-375 per night. 3 night minimum stay.*

Located only 16 miles north of Tucson and overlooking the Santa Cruz Valley, the Lazy K offers an all-inclusive price which makes it more affordable than the prices would otherwise indicate. There are 23 guest rooms ranging from standard to deluxe and also some suites. Despite the difference in categorization by the owners, there isn't that much difference. The higher rates are for the larger suites. One nice feature of the Lazy K is that they have an excellent Children's Summer Camp program which makes this place very suitable for families. Call for dates as the camp doesn't run the entire summer.

PRICE CANYON RANCH, *near Douglas. From that town take AZ 80 north to mile marker 400. Then go west for 7-1/4 miles to the ranch. Tel. 520/ 558-2383. Rates: From $250 per night.*

Another working cattle ranch, Price Canyon is one of the more isolated of all the ranches in this list. Sitting at the 5,600 foot level of the beautiful Chiricahua Mountains, the 120-year old ranch provides a cool and relaxing environment whether or not you wish to partake in the hard work of the ranch. Accommodations and everything else about the Price Canyon Ranch are plain and simple. This is definitely a real ranch experience and many of the little niceties of civilization are out of sight and mind. There are a few cabins of one or more rooms with private facilities or you can opt to stay in the 12-person bunkhouse and live like the cowboys on the ranch did a hundred years ago.

RANCHO DE LA OSA, *in Sasabe (on the Mexican border) 55 miles southwest of Tucson. Take AZ 86 west to AZ 286 and then south on the latter to the signed cutoff road for the ranch just north of the town of Sasabe. Tel. 520/823-4257. Toll free reservations 800/872-6240. Rates: $250-375.*

Not that any of these ranches aren't a great experience, but the Rancho de la Osa is definitely one of the most lovely. Once a part of a vast Spanish hacienda, today's ranch is smaller but still retains the atmosphere of a time long since past. The 1880's hacienda (or main house) is the center of all social activities at the ranch. There are only 16 guest rooms and these simple but attractive units are located in a Territorial style building. Also on the ranch site is a 17th century Franciscan mission outpost. It is reputedly the second oldest building still standing in Arizona.

RANCHO DE LOS CABALLEROS, *1551 S. Vulture Mine Road, Wickenburg. Take Wickenburg Way 5 miles west of town to Vulture Mine Road and turn right. Tel. 520/684-5484. Toll free reservations 800/684-5030. Rates: $289-500.*

With 77 rooms, this is one of the largest guest ranches in Arizona. It certainly ranks as one of the more luxurious, although you wouldn't confuse it with a Scottsdale resort. Of course, visitors to Rancho de los Caballeros aren't looking for that kind of luxury. An historic property covering some 20,000 acres of mountain and desert scenery, the ranch has a golf club and swimming pool among its many amenities. There is also a good children's program. The Grant family has been lovingly in charge for more than 50 years.

Basic accommodations are in Ranch Rooms, the original units of the ranch. More upscale lodging is (in increasing level of luxury) Hermosa and Sunset Rooms, the Bradshaw Mountain Rooms (excellent views) and the Maricopa Suites. Kiva-style fireplaces, refrigerators or kitchenettes, and attractive Mexican or southwestern decor are among the things you'll find in the upgraded lodging.

SPIRIT HORSE GUEST RANCH, *Pearce. 75 miles from Tucson. Take I-10 east to Exit 318. Follow Dragoon Road to US 191 and then turn south to 10 miles past Pearce. Turn left onto State Route 181 and drive 13 miles to mile marker 51. Turn right on Sunrise Drive and then left on Quail Hollow Drive to the ranch. Tel. 520/824-3667. Rates: $320. 3 night minimum stay.*

The tiny ranch has a maximum of ten guests that are housed in rather simple but pleasant bunkhouses plus one room called the Cowboy Room. The rate is all-inclusive. Isolated amid the scenery of the Chiricahua Mountains, Spirit Horse is definitely for the person who is really trying to get away from it all. The service is personalized and friendly. If those are the things you're looking for, then Spirit Horse is a wise choice. ·

SPRUCEDALE GUEST RANCH, *Alpine. Take US Highway 60 to Eagar and then travel south on US 191 to 14 miles past Alpine. Then follow signs to ranch. Tel. 520/333-4984. Rates: $770 for six days.*

Located in the cool and rarified air of Arizona's White Mountains and surrounded by the Apache National Forest, Sprucedale is a small ranch consisting of 14 cabins. Each cabin can accommodate from three to seven people but there is a maximum of 50 guests at any one time. The cabins have a special charm as they have working wood-burning stove, home-made quilts and many other old time touches.

SUNGLOW GUEST RANCH, *Turkey Creek Road, Pearce. Use the Willcox exit of I-10 (following signs for Chiricahua National Monument) and then follow US 181 south to Turkey Creek Road. Take this dirt road for four miles to the ranch entrance. Tel. 520/824-3334. Rates: $89-149.*

Probably about the lowest priced guest ranch you'll find in Arizona, Sunglow is situated in the high terrain of the Coronado National Forest. Established in 1879, the original house now serves as the kitchen and dining room. Accommodations are quite nice. The nine individual casitas each feature a fireplace, private courtyard entrance, kitchenette and great views. You can also rent out a real tepee! The Padre Kino Hall is the center of social activities.

TANQUE VERDE RANCH, *14301 E. Speedway Boulevard, Tucson. Follow Speedway (from north of downtown) east directly to the ranch entrance. Tel. 520/296-6275. Toll free reservations 800/234-DUDE. Rates: $300-460 per day.*

One of the most luxurious of Arizona ranches, Tanque Verde is an historic working cattle ranch with all of the activities you would expect. Situated on 640 acres in the Rincon Mountains near the Saguaro National Park, the ranch boasts a stable of 130 horses. Tennis courts and a complete health spa are among the many amenities. There is an excellent children's program as well as tours to nearby points of interest. The 71 guest units range from standard rooms to deluxe rooms to suites. Most have a fireplace and patio. The accommodations are more on a par with a fine hotel than in many other ranches. Likewise for the food. Breakfast can be ordered from a menu or taken from the buffet. Lunch is buffet-style. Other than special cookouts, dinners are closer to gourmet than to home-style country cooking.

WHITE STALLION RANCH, *9251 W. Twin Peaks Road, Tucson. Take I-10 north to the Cortaro Road exit. Drive west to Silverbell then make a right and proceed to Twin Peaks Road. Tel. 520/297-0252. Toll free reservations 888/WS-RANCH. Rates: $225-350 per day.*

The 3,000-acre ranch opened its doors to guests back in 1965 in its attractive Tucson Mountain setting adjacent to Saguaro National Park. It has 32 rooms that are quite nice. Deluxe suites feature fireplaces and whirlpool tubs. The rate is all-inclusive. White Stallion features one of the better children's programs.

RODEO ARIZONA

Rodeo is as much a part of the Arizona scene as chili peppers and adobe construction. There is, of course, some opposition to this sport on the grounds that it is cruel to animals. I won't take sides in this dispute. However, because of its historical association with the west, and because many people love rodeo and even many non-rodeo enthusiasts will want to see what it is like when they do visit the southwest, it is appropriate to offer some basic information here.

Rodeo (pronounced either roh-dio or row-day-oh) comes from the Spanish verb rodear which means to surround. Such was the connotation of the word when it was first applied to the round-up. Cowboys would celebrate the conclusion of the roundup by putting on demonstrations that showed off the skills they used. The practice became more formalized over time and the first modern rodeo was held in 1872.

*Today rodeo is guided by the **Professional Rodeo Cowboys Association** (PRCA). A rodeo can consist of many different events but five are basic to all contests. These are saddle bronco riding, bareback bronco riding, bull riding, steer wrestling, and calf roping. In the riding events the objective is to remain mounted for a prescribed amount of time while the roping and wrestling competitions are awarded to the best time achieved. There are large prizes awarded in PRCA sanctioned championship events but it is the smaller local event that is the heart of rodeo.*

Rodeos occur throughout the year in dozens of Arizona communities large and small. Here's a selective listing:

Alpine (June)	*Parker (October)*
Buckeye (February)	*Payson (May)*
Bullhead City (Jan.)	*Phoenix (October)*
Flagstaff (June)	*Prescott (July)*
Globe (March)	*Scottsdale (February)*
Goodyear (Feb.)	*Williams (September)*
Holbrook (April)	*Winslow (September)*
Kingman (October)	*Yuma (February)*

INDEX

Accommodations 61-65; see also regional destination chapters
Adventure Travel 67-68
Airfares 51-52
Airlines Serving Arizona 53-54
Airports
Phoenix 112
Tucson 183-184
Regional, see regional destination chapters
Ajo 371-373
Alternative Travel 68
Apache Junction 177
Apache Sitgreaves National Forest 310
Arcosanti 248
Arizona, State of
Road and Travel conditions 56
Tourism information 46-48
Arizona State Parks 85-86
Catalina State Park 222
Dead Horse Ranch State Park 252
Fort Verde State Historic Park 254-255
Jerome State Historic Park 252
Kartchner Caverns State Park 326-327
Lost Dutchman State Park 177
Lyman Lake State Park 309-310
McFarland Historical State Park 179-180
Red Rock State Park 250
Riordan State Park 244
Roper Lake State Park 337
Slide Rock State Park 249
Tombstone Courthouse State Park 331
Tonto Natural Bridge State Park 313
Tubac Presidio State Historic Park 220
Yuma Territorial Prison State Historic Park 367-368
Arizona Strip 282

Benson 318-319, 326
Best Places to Stay 97-109
Bicycling 80; see also regional destination chapters
Bisbee 319-320, 323, 332-333
Boating 80-81; see also regional destination chapters
Booking Your Vacation 48
Bullhead City 349, 350, 351, 355
Buses 54; see also regional destination chapters

Camping 65-66; see also regional destination chapters
Camp Verde 254
Canyon de Chelly National Monument 305-306
Car Rentals 57, 59
Casa Grande 179
Casa Grande Ruins National Monument 180
Catalina State Park 222
Cave Creek 335
Chambers 308
Chinle 293-294, 299-300, 305
Children, traveling with 69-70
Chiricahua National Monument 334-335
Chloride 353
Clarkdale 252
Coconino National Forest 248

Cordes Junction 255
Coronado National Memorial 328
Cottonwood 227, 238
Cuisine, Arizona and Southwestern 94-96
Customs regulations for foreign visitors 46

Davis Dam 355
Dead Horse Ranch State Park 250
Desert Driving 55
Dining 94-96; see also regional destination chapters
Disabled travelers 79
Douglas 333-334
Dragoon 338-339
Dude Ranches, see Guest Ranches

Eagar 311
Emergencies, see Health and Safety
Events, Major Annual 88-93

Fishing 81; see also regional destination chapters
Flagstaff 224-229, 238-240, 244-246
Florence 179
Fort Apache 311
Fort Bowie National Historic Site 336
Fort Huachuca 327-328
Fort Verde State Historic Park 254-255
Fountain Hills 164
Four Corners 305
Fredonia 289

Gambling 72-73; see also regional destination chapters
Geography of Arizona 34-36
Gila Bend 371-372
Glen Canyon Dam 286
Glen Canyon National Recreation Area 286-288
Globe 178
Golf 81-82; see also regional destination chapters
Grand Canyon Caverns 354
Grand Canyon National Park 261-286
    North Rim 281-286
    South Rim 273-281

Green Valley 219
Guest Ranches 82, 376-383

Health 70-72
Highways and Roads 54-56
History of Arizona 39-42
Holbrook 294, 300
Hoover Dam 353-354
Hopi Indian Reservation 307
Horseback Riding 82; see also regional destination chapters
Hot Air Ballooning 80; see also regional destination chapters
Hotels, see Accommodations
Hubbell Trading Post National Historic Site 306-307
Hunting 82

Indian Gaming 72-73
Indian Reservations 37
    Etiquette when visiting 37
    Fort Apache 311
    Havasupai 288
    Hopi 307
    Navajo 302
    Tohono O'odham 212
Itineraries, suggested 20-33

Jacob Lake 282
Jerome 252
Jerome State Historic Park 252

Kaibab National Forest 282
Kartchner Caverns state Park 326-327
Kayenta 284-285, 300
Keams Canyon 307
Kingman 348-352
Kitt Peak National Observatory 222-223

Lake Havasu 362
Lake Havasu City 358-363
Lake Mead National Recreation Area 353
Lake Powell 287-288
Lost Dutchman State Park 177
Lyman State Park 309-310

Magazines 73
Marble Canyon 282
Maricopa 180
McFarland Historical State Park 179-180
Mesa 136-137, 150, 151, 165-166
Meteor Crater 313-314
Mission San Xavier del Bac 211-212
Montezuma Castle National Monument 254
Monument Valley Navajo Tribal Park 304-305
Morenci 338

National Park Service areas 83-84
Canyon de Chelly National Monument 305-306
Casa Grande Ruins National Monument 180
Chiricahua National Monument 334-335
Coronado National Memorial 328
Fort Bowie National Historic Site 336
Glen Canyon National Recreation Area 286-288
Grand Canyon National Park 261-286
    North Rim 281-286
    South Rim 273-281
Hubbell Trading Post National Historic Site 306-307
Lake Mead National Recreation Area 353
Montezuma Castle National Monument 254
Navajo National Monument 303-304
Organ Pipe Cactus National Monument 374
Petrified Forest National Park 308-309
Saguaro National Park 211, 213-214
    Rincon Mountain District 211
    Tucson Mountain District 213-214
Sunset Crater National Monument 246-247
Tonto National Monument 178

Tumacacori National Historic Park 220
Tuzigoot National Monument 250-251
Walnut Canyon National Monument 247-248
Wupatki National Monument 246
National Park Service Passports 85
Navajo Indian Reservation 302
Navajo Nation 302
Navajo National Monument 303-304
Newspapers 73
Nightlife 74; see also regional destination chapters
Nogales 220-221

Oak Creek Canyon 248-249
Oatman 355
Off-roading 82; see also regional destination chapters
Oracle 221-222
Organ Pipe Cactus National Monument 374

Page 286
Parker 363-364
Parker Dam 363-364
Payson 295-296, 300-301, 312-313
People of Arizona 36-38
Petrified Forest National Park 308-309
Phoenix 110-181
    Seeing the Sights 152-166
    Where to Eat 141-151
    Where to Stay 116-140
Pinetop-Lakeside 296-297, 301-302, 312
Pipe Spring National Monument 289
Planning Your Trip 43-66
Police; see regional destination chapters
Prescott 230-232, 240-241, 255-257
Prescott National Forest 255

Rafting 86-87; see also regional destination chapters
Railroads
    Amtrak 60; see also regional destination chapters

Scenic and historic 60-61
Red Rock State Park 250
Riordan State Historic Park 244
Rodeo 383
Roper Lake State Park 337

Sacaton 179
Safety 74
Safford 320, 323-324, 337-338
Saguaro National Park 211, 213-214
   Rincon Mountain District 211
   Tucson Mountain District 213-214
San Pedro Riparian National
   Conservation Area 327
Scottsdale 126-135, 137-138, 148-151,
   160-164
Second Mesa 307
Sedona 224-226, 232-237, 241-243, 249-
   250
Shopping 74-78; see also regional
   destination chapters
Show Low 297-298, 302
Sierra Vista 320-321, 324, 327
Skiing 83; see also regional destination
   chapters
Slide Rock State Park 249
Spectator Sports 170-171, 215-216
Springerville 310-311
Sunset Crater National Monument 246-
   247
Supai 288
Superior 178
Swimming 87

Taxes on sales 78
Telephones 78

Tempe 127, 137-139, 165
Tennis 87
Thatcher 338
Time Zones 78-79
Tipping 79
Tombstone 321-322, 324-325, 328-332
Tombstone Courthouse State Historic
   Park 331
Tonto National Monument 178
Tonto Natural Bridge State Park 313
Tourism offices 46-48; see also regional
   destination chapters
Tour Operators 50-51
Trains, see Railroads
Travel Agents 49
Tubac 220
Tucson 182-223
   Seeing the Sights 204-214
   Where to Eat 195-204
   Where to Stay 186-195
Tumacacori National Historic Park 220
Tusayan 268-269, 272
Tuzigoot National Monument 250-251

Walnut Canyon National Monument
   247-248
Weather 43-44
Wickenburg 343-347
Willcox 322, 325-326, 336-337
Window Rock 298, 307-308
Winslow 298-299, 302, 313
Wupatki National Monument 246

Yuma 364-370
Yuma Territorial Prison State Historic
   Park 367-368

THINGS CHANGE!

Phone numbers, prices, addresses, quality of food, etc, all change. If you come across any new information, we'd appreciate hearing from you. No item is too small! Drop us an e-mail note at: Jopenroad@aol.com, or write us at:

Arizona Guide
Open Road Publishing, P.O. Box 284
Cold Spring Harbor, NY 11724

TRAVEL NOTES

TRAVEL NOTES

OPEN ROAD PUBLISHING

U.S.A.

America's Cheap Sleeps, $16.95
America's Grand Hotels, $14.95
America's Most Charming Towns & Villages, $16.95
Arizona Guide, $16.95
Boston Guide, $13.95
California Wine Country Guide, $12.95
Colorado Guide, $16.95
Disneyworld With Kids, $14.95
Florida Golf Guide, $16.95
Golf Courses of the Southwest, $14.95
Hawaii Guide, $18.95
Las Vegas Guide, $13.95
National Parks With Kids, $14.95
New Mexico Guide, $16.95
San Francisco Guide, $16.95
Southern California Guide, $18.95
Texas Guide, $16.95
Utah Guide, $16.95

MIDDLE EAST/AFRICA

Egypt Guide, $17.95
Israel Guide, $17.95
Jerusalem Guide, $13.95
Kenya Guide, $18.95

UNIQUE TRAVEL

CDC's Complete Guide to Healthy Travel, $14.95
Celebrity Weddings & Honeymoon Getaways, $16.95
The World's Most Intimate Cruises, $16.95

SMART HANDBOOKS

The Smart Home Buyer's Handbook, $16.95
The Smart Runner's Handbook, $9.95

CENTRAL AMERICA & CARIBBEAN

Bahamas Guide, $13.95
Belize Guide, $16.95
Bermuda Guide, $14.95
Caribbean Guide, $19.95
Caribbean With Kids, $14.95
Central America Guide, $17.95
Chile Guide, $18.95
Costa Rica Guide, $17.95
Guatemala Guide, $17.95
Honduras & Bay Islands Guide, $16.95

EUROPE

Austria Guide, $15.95
Czech & Slovak Republics Guide, $18.95
France Guide, $16.95
Greek Islands Guide, $16.95
Holland Guide, $16.95
Ireland Guide, $17.95
Italy Guide, $19.95
London Guide, $14.95
Moscow Guide, $15.95
Paris Guide, $13.95
Portugal Guide, $16.95
Prague Guide, $14.95
Rome & Southern Italy Guide, $14.95
Spain Guide, $18.95
Turkey Guide, $18.95

ASIA

China Guide, $21.95
Japan Guide, $19.95
Philippines Guide, $17.95
Tahiti & French Polynesia Guide, $18.95
Tokyo Guide, $13.95
Thailand Guide, $18.95
Vietnam Guide, $14.95

To order any Open Road book, send us a check or money order for the price of the book(s) plus $3.00 shipping and handling for domestic orders, to: Open Road Publishing, PO Box 284, Cold Spring Harbor, NY 11724